THE POPULAR
JEWISH
ENCYCLOPEDIA

by

RABBI BEN ISAACSON
DEBORAH WIGODER

VALLENTINE, MITCHELL—LONDON

FIRST PUBLISHED IN GREAT BRITAIN IN 1973
BY VALLENTINE, MITCHELL & CO. LTD.
67 GREAT RUSSELL STREET, LONDON WC1B 3BT

ALL RIGHTS RESERVED. NO PART OF THIS PUBLICATION MAY BE
REPRODUCED, STORED IN A RETRIEVAL SYSTEM, OR TRANSMITTED, IN
ANY FORM OR BY MEANS, ELECTRONIC, MECHANICAL, PHOTOCOPYING
OR OTHERWISE, WITHOUT THE PRIOR PERMISSION IN WRITING OF
VALLENTINE, MITCHELL & CO. LTD.

ISBN : 0 853 03122 3

© 1973 BY MASSADA PRESS LTD.

© 1973 BY VALLENTINE, MITCHELL & CO. LTD.

PRINTED IN ISRAEL BY PELI PRINTING WORKS LTD.

The authors and publisher gratefully acknowledge the cooperation of the Israel Museum of Jerusalem for permission to reproduce the color plates facing pages 32, 168, 192, 208, 304 and the Shrine of the Book, Israel Museum, for those on the jacket and facing pages 40 and 56. Color photographs by David Harris. Frontispiece by Werner Braun.

HEBREW ALPHABET
AND SYSTEM OF TRANSLITERATION

First row (right to left), names: aleph, bet, vet, gimel, dalet, heh, vav, zayin, het, tet, yod, kaph, khaph, khaph sophit, lamed, mem, mem sophit

א ב ב ג ד ה ו ז ח ט י כ כ ך ל מ ם — **printed**

(written forms) — **written**

Second row (right to left), names: nun, nun sophit, samekh, ayin, peh, pheh, pheh sophit, tzadeh, tzadeh sophit, koph, resh, shin, sin, tav, tav

נ ן ס ע פ פ ף צ ץ ק ר שׁ שׂ ת ת — **printed**

(written forms) — **written**

א is not transliterated	ו = v (where not a vowel)	ל = l	פ = ph
ב = b	ז = z	מ = m	צ = tz
ב = v	ח = ḥ	נ = n	ק = k
ג, ג = g	ט = t	ס = s	ר = r
ד, ד = d	י = y	ע is not transliterated	שׁ = sh
ה = h	כ = k	פ = p	שׂ = s
	כ = kh		ת, ת = t

◌ָ = a	◌ֱ = e
◌ַ = a	◌ִ = i
◌ֹ, וֹ = o	◌ֵ = e
◌ֻ, וּ = u	◌ְ = e
short ◌ָ = o	◌ֳ = o
י◌ֵ = ei	◌ֲ = a

vocal *sheva* = e
silent *sheva* is not transliterated

AARON: The first High Priest. Aaron was the brother of Moses, and, as his spokesman before Pharaoh, one of the leading figures in the events leading up to the Exodus from Egypt. He and his descendants were consecrated to serve as priests in the tabernacle. He assisted Moses in molding the people of Israel into a nation, and, except for the incident of the golden calf which he made either out of fear or because of his desire for peace, he pursued his task with loyalty and dedication. Aaron officiated as High Priest until his death at the age of 123.

He was buried on Mt. Hor on the border of Edom. In rabbinical literature, Aaron is regarded as the symbol of those who love and pursue peace (Avot 1:12).

ABRAVANEL *(also written Abrabanel),* ISAAC BEN YEHUDA (1437–1508): Philosopher, statesman, and Biblical commentator. One of the darkest periods of Jewish history — the expulsion of the Jews from Spain — occurred in his lifetime. Born in Portugal, the son of an influential merchant and financier, young Abravanel studied Jewish history and literature, as well as Greek, Roman, and Christian literature, and philosophy. His talents were recognized, and he became Minister of Finance at the Portuguese court, but in 1483 he was falsely accused of plotting against the King and was forced to flee to Spain.

During his first years in Spain, Abravanel devoted himself to writing commentaries on the Bible and philosophical works which stressed the importance of Divine Revelation and the coming of the Messiah. He became tax collector for King Ferdinand and Queen Isabella and was a private agent for members of the royal family. He lent the court huge sums of money, and personally financed the war with Granada, the last Arab stronghold in Spain. Granada fell to the Christian Spaniards in 1492, but Abravanel's reward was a bitter one: like all the other Jews in Spain, he was forced to leave the country. In vain did he plead with the monarchs to let the Jews remain. It was the end of Jewish history in Spain.

In exchange for his many services and help to the Spanish Court, all that Abravanel received was permission to take a small sum of money with him when he fled to Naples in Italy. In Naples, he again held a high post in the government, but after the French invasion of that city he had to flee. In 1503, Abravanel arrived in Venice, and here, too, he was called to serve the government.

There he died, a man who had suffered much as a Jew, but who never gave up his belief in the Messiah or his strong love for the land of Israel.

ABSALOM: Third son of King David. He killed his half-brother Amnon in order to avenge the rape of his sister Tamar. Absalom was the cause of much heartbreak to David. He succeeded in raising a revolt against his father, who was compelled to flee beyond the Jordan. In the ensuing battle, Absalom was defeated, and, while he was fleeing, his long hair became entangled in a tree, thus enabling Joab, David's general, to kill him. David deeply mourned the loss of his son. A monument in the valley of Kidron outside Jerusalem, traditionally referred to as Absalom's tomb,

Absalom's Tomb in Jerusalem's Kidron Valley

is in fact a Graeco-Roman monument of the 1st century B.C.E. or C.E.

ACADEMIES OF BABYLONIA: The academies were the ancient Jewish schools of higher learning in Palestine and Babylonia. After the destruction of the Second Temple, Babylonia developed as a vital center of Jewish learning. Its two famous academies, Sura and Pumbeditha, produced a rich legacy of legal research and folklore.

Babylonia's first academy, apparently a small one, was at Nehardea, an active center of Jewish life. The great teacher there was Samuel, and, under his supervision, the academy grew. Early in the third century, Rav, who had studied in Palestine under Judah Ha-Nasi, founded a new school at Sura, and for eight centuries this was one of the major seats of scholarship in Babylonia and in the Jewish world as a whole. After Nehardea was destroyed in 259 C.E., the academy was transferred to Pumbeditha under the direction of Judah ben Ezekiel, a pupil of both Rav and Samuel. Pumbeditha competed with Sura for eight centuries.

The basic study material for pupils at the academies was the Mishnah. Their analyses of the Mishnah, their teachers' explanations, the laws they deduced from its material, and the legends and parables they recounted during their years of study, later took form in the Talmud. Rav Ashi, who started the massive task of editing the Babylonian Talmud in the early 5th century, headed the Sura academy for fifty-six years.

The great scholars at the Babylonian academies did not limit their teaching to regular pupils. They also guided large numbers of the lay population in religious studies. They stressed the importance of ritual observances to those who were not strict enough, and they founded a new institution for laymen known as the *Kallah* study program. Twice each year, in the months of *Adar* and *Elul,* the program taught a different section of the Talmud and expounded the laws of the festivals. Rav's *Kallah* lectures are said to have regularly drawn 12,000 laymen.

The rabbis who discussed the Mishnah at the academies and whose views are incorporated in the Talmud are known as the *Amoraim.*

From the end of the 6th to the end of the 12th centuries, the heads of the two academies were called *Geonim,* and their influence extended throughout the Jewish world. Wherever Jews lived, they used to send their queries and problems to the Babylonian academies.

The importance of these academies began to decline from the middle of the 10th century, and the center of gravity of Jewish religious life passed first to North Africa, then to western Europe. The Sura and Pumbeditha academies finally closed in the 13th century.

ACCENTS: Signs employed in the Biblical text to mark sentence structure and the manner of cantillation. In the Hebrew Bible, the accent signs *(te'amim)* serve both as punctuation marks for the division of sentences and phrases, and as musical guides for the chanting of the text. These signs, along with the vowel-signs which guide pronunciation of Hebrew words, were introduced in the 8th–9th centuries C.E.

Originally, three different accent systems were developed, but the one that was eventually universally adopted was developed by the Academy of Tiberias in Palestine, under the supervision of the great Hebrew grammarian Aaron ben Asher. In this Tiberian system, the accents are separated into dividing accents, which indicate various kinds of pauses in the reading, and connecting accents, which show where there should be no pauses. There are two separate sets of accent signs: one for the books of Psalms, Proverbs, and Job, and the other for the rest of the Bible. These accents are very important for a proper understanding of Biblical sentences, as they are the commas and periods of biblical Hebrew.

As musical guides, each accent sign refers to a special grouping of musical notes, and the chant which accompanies these notes is known as cantillation. The accents indicate when to raise, lower, or sustain the voice. But how long to hold certain notes and how much emphasis to give them are left open to varying interpretations. As a result, oral training is essential in order to know how to use the accents as guides for cantillation.

Because different patterns of cantillation can result from the same accent signs, the various Jewish communities throughout the world developed their own styles of cantillating Scripture. Each community absorbed, to some extent, the musical culture of its surroundings. Thus there are German-Ashkenazi and Slavic-Ashkenazi, Sephardi, Persian, Baghdadi, Arabian, Egyptian, and Yemenite, and each shows unmistakable signs of the locality from which it comes. The impact of the Hebrew accent system has extended far beyond the music of the synagogue.

Because the first Christians were originally Jews, they carried with them into the Christian tradition their Jewish training in how to read Scripture. The Gregorian chants, and even the musical liturgy of the contemporary Catholic Church, owe a clear debt to the Hebrew cantillation system.

ACRE (Hebrew, **Akko**): Today a modern industrial town and center for steel and glass manufacture in Israel, Acre is one of the most ancient cities of Eretz Israel. Built on a peninsula overlooking the harbor of Haifa Bay in northern Israel and protected by a fortified wall and strong citadels, the city has been an important center of trade and a scene of battle since very early times. When the Israelites settled in the land of Israel, Acre was included in the territory assigned to the tribe of Asher. But, in fact, it was inhabited by the Canaanites, and was consequently regarded as being outside the boundaries of the land of Israel. Eventually the town was captured by the tribe of Asher, but still its ground was not considered sanctified and Jews did not bury their dead within its boundaries.

As was true of most eastern Mediterranean port cities, the Greeks settled in Acre in the 3rd or 2nd century B.C.E. They believed that the town's Hebrew name *Akko* was derived from the Greek word *Aka,* meaning "cure." This belief arose from a tale that when the Greek hero Hercules was seriously injured, herbs were found in Acre which miraculously cured his wounds. Romans followed the Greeks in settling Acre, and both peoples called the city Ptolemais, after Ptolemy II, King of Egypt, who ruled Palestine and fortified Acre in the year 261 B.C.E. Julius Caesar visited the city during his rule, and Herod the Great constructed many buildings there. Throughout the Greek and Roman occupations of Acre the city had a large Jewish population, and at the time of the Jewish war against Rome in 66 C.E. some 2,000 Jews were massacred.

In 638 Acre passed under Moslem rule and declined in importance, but revived

The ancient walls of Acre

with the Crusader invasion in 1104. Under the Crusaders it was renamed St. Jean d'Acre, as it was the headquarters for the Order of the Knights of St. John (Jean). The great Arab warrior Saladin took the city from the Crusaders in 1187, but England's Richard the Lion-Hearted recaptured it four years later, and it remained the Crusader capital of Palestine for a century until the final Moslem conquest in 1291. With Crusader power vanquished, the conquering Arabs also completely destroyed the Christian and Jewish settlements of the city.

For centuries after the Crusader defeat, Acre was nothing but a forsaken village. In 1750, a Bedouin sheikh restored the city and made it his capital, and the invading Turks preserved its importance. The Turkish Pasha Ahmed el-Jazzar (Ahmad the Cut-Throat, 1775–1804) surrounded the city with a strong wall and rebuilt a large fortress on the old Crusader foundation. He also erected many public buildings. In 1799, when Napoleon Bonaparte wanted to penetrate the Middle East, he landed in Egypt and moved up the coast, but he was stopped at Acre, as he could not get beyond Jazzar's strong fortifications. Jazzar, with the help of the British Navy, defeated Napoleon so decisively that his whole Middle Eastern expedition collapsed. During the British Mandate in Palestine (1917–1948), Acre was a center of Arab hostility against the aspirations of the Jews, and its large fortress was used by the British as a central prison where members of the Jewish underground were executed. The city was captured by the Israel Army in the 1948 War of Independence and became a part of the State of Israel, with a mixed Jewish and Arab population.

Since the 1948 War, a new city has grown up outside the walls of Acre's Old City, mostly inhabited by new immigrants. Acre's 33,000 inhabitants have developed the city into a thriving industrial center. Many parts of Acre's Old City are still in good repair, and the city's narrow, cobbled streets and dark, covered markets, as well as the old Crusader ruins, which have been extensively excavated, are a popular tourist attraction. The fortress is now a museum in memory of the members of the Jewish underground who were imprisoned and executed there.

AGGADAH (probably from a Hebrew word meaning "narrative"): Those portions of the Talmudic literature which use stories, fables, legends, or historical anecdotes to teach moral, and sometimes legal, lessons. The *Aggadah* developed through a tradition of explanations and stories meant to supplement and elaborate the legal and religious regulations known as *Halakhah*.

While *Halakhah* concentrates on the Five Books of Moses, *Aggadah* draws from all parts of the Bible for its arguments and illustrations. It can be found in the Talmud and in the many collections of books of *Aggadah* called *Midrash*. It developed in the early synagogues as sermons given after the reading of the Torah and is still often quoted by rabbis. Because its purpose was to help people understand the importance and beauty of Judaism while teaching them moral lessons, the *Aggadah* often presented stories and legends in popular language, using parables, stories, and sayings to communicate its message. While it was originally an oral tradition, it was eventually written down.

Aggadah includes many themes. There is ethics, taught through fables and sayings, and history related through legends. Theology and philosophy are important subjects in *Aggadah,* and there are extensive sermons interpreting the Bible. In addition, thought is given to such sciences as astronomy and medicine. There are sections which consist of mystic and messianic speculation, and there are even long passages which discuss the interpretation of dreams.

Many non-Jewish influences can be found in *Aggadah*. Because it developed from generation to generation, it reflects Judaism's reaction to whatever outside ideas were important in various periods. For example, some passages mirror the streams of Greek thought and other ancient philosophies current between the 2nd and 10th centuries C.E. Because of this awareness of outside thought, *Aggadah* was often used as a source of arguments with which to defend Judaism against attacks by Christians and the followers of other faiths.

The most important modern collection of *Aggadah* in English is Louis Ginzberg's *Legends of the Jews* which describes all the legends about Biblical characters and forms a fascinating companion to the Bible.

AGNON, S.Y. (1888–1970): Hebrew writer. Born in Galicia, Agnon moved in 1909 to Israel where he lived for the rest of his life, with the exception of the years 1912–23 when he was in Germany. His first story written in Israel, *Agunot* (Deserted Wives), achieved immediate success, and it was from the title of this work that he took his Hebrew name (his name had been Czaczkes). Most of the themes and motifs of Agnon's stories are related to the inner life of Galician Jewry which he wished to depict. Even when the setting is in the land of Israel, most of his heroes are Galician. In reality, however, the picture Agnon paints of Galician Jewry as he knew it in his youth could well be applied to all the East European Jewries of that period. This world, as it emerges from Agnon's writings,

S.Y. Agnon at the Nobel Prize ceremony

was based on four pillars: God, the Torah, love of the people of Israel, and love of the land of Israel. The last is not nationalistic love, but rather the spiritual love of a land saturated with holiness. Agnon made eloquent use of legends, folk-stories, and popular tales, using these as his means of expression. He had an original Hebrew style in which he skillfully blended Biblical and Talmudical elements. The best known of his Galician works is *Hakhnasat Kallah,* translated into English as *The Bridal Canopy.* Agnon also wrote love stories such as *Bidmei Yomehah* (In the Noon of Her Life), and even tales of fantasy and horror.

Agnon, who is regarded as the great epic writer of modern Hebrew literature, received the Nobel Prize for literature in 1966, together with the German-Jewish poetess, Nelly Sachs (1891–1970).

AGRICULTURAL SETTLEMENTS: The attachment of the people of Israel to the soil of their land dates back to the very beginnings of Jewish history and, specifically, to the conquest of the land of Israel in the days of Joshua. The economy of ancient Israel was agricultural, and this is reflected by the laws of the Bible. Thus, the land was divided according to tribal areas, and within these areas each family received its portion. The law of *Shemittah,* the seventh (Sabbatical) year in which all debts were cancelled, and the law of the fiftieth (jubilee) year when all land was returned to its original owners, reflect the agricultural nature of the economy. In later years, as economic conditions changed, the rabbis were compelled to amend these laws somewhat. Most of the festivals enumerated in the five books of Moses, in addition to their religious significance, have an agricultural basis. They occur at specific times in the agricultural year, and their common denominator is the duty incumbent upon all to give thanks to God for His bounty. In Jewish thought, the soil of the land of Israel is sacred, and therefore,

in the opinion of the rabbis, most of the agricultural laws have Biblical authority only in that land, and some of them apply only to the period of the Temple. Even after the destruction of the Second Temple in 70 C.E., Jews continued to practice farming in the various lands in which they lived. With the rise of Christianity, however, restrictions were imposed on the purchase and possession of land by Jews, and this led to a drastic decrease in the number of Jewish farmers. In the 16th century, Joseph Nasi, with the encouragement of the Turkish Sultan, made an attempt to promote the settlement of the land in the Tiberias area, but his effort was premature.

Cotton combine in Israel

The first modern Jewish agricultural settlements were established in Russia in the 19th century. Extensive stretches of fertile land were made available to Jews in the southern and western provinces. Jews who took up agriculture were exempted from military service, and, in the harsh conditions of military service in Czarist Russia, this was an inducement to many Jews to leave the provinces of the northwest and southwest in order to devote themselves to the cultivation of the land. By the outbreak of World War I, one hundred thousand

Russian Jews were occupied in farming. After the Bolshevik revolution, the Soviet government permitted resumption of Jewish colonizing activities, so that by the end of the 1920s the Jewish farming population had grown to 250,000. Increasing indust-rialization led to a decline, and, during the course of World War II, the Jewish farms were all destroyed, although many farmers returned to their land after the war. Today, there are no figures available as to the numbers of Jewish farmers in the Soviet Union, and it is unlikely that their numbers are significant.

In the U.S.A., a number of Jewish com-munal settlements were established in the late 19th century but these did not last very long. Jews also settled on the land in Canada, but their numbers have gradually diminished over the past half-century.

In the Argentine, Jewish settlement was patronized from the year 1891 by the European Jewish philanthropist, Baron Maurice de Hirsch. He was motivated by the rising anti-Semitism in Russia, and under his scheme five thousand Jewish families were to have been transferred annually from Russia to the Argentine. This figure was never reached. Here, too, the number declined, and in 1968 the settlements had a total population of 3,200 families. These families are well-established economically, and the total area of Jewish-owned land in Argentina is 750,000 acres, of which two-thirds are cultivated by Jews.

The history of Jewish agricultural settle-ment in the land of Israel in modern times runs almost parallel to the history of Zionism. In 1855, Jerusalem Jews pur-chased a plot of land at Motza but made no use of it. Sir Moses Montefiore pur-chased land near Jaffa and financed the planting of citrons, which proved unsuc-cessful. In 1870, the agricultural school of Mikveh Yisrael was established near Jaffa. Added impetus to agriculture was given by the First Aliyah (from 1882), when the first wave of settlers known as the *Biluim* arrived

in the country and established Rishon Le Zion, Nes Tziyyona, and Zikhron Yaakov. These first settlers suffered from lack of knowledge and experience, to which was added disease and lack of funds, so that the settlements were on the verge of col-lapse. The French philanthropist, Baron Edmond de Rothschild, came to their assistance, and, for the remainder of his lifetime, made the development of Jewish agricultural settlement in the land of Israel one of his principal cares.

The Second Aliyah, which began early in the 20th century, represented a turning point in the struggle to reclaim the desolate land. It brought with it ideological beliefs which led to the establishment of the first

Tending vines at Moshav Menuḥa

kibbutz. In the same years, the Jewish National Fund began its activity and es-tablished training and experimental farms. The draining of the swamps, the irrigation of the dry lands, the planting of forests, and the settling of the Negev are the result of a pioneering and dedicated spirit, and the ability to exploit successfully the advances of modern technology.

Different types of agricultural settlement, some of which are not found anywhere else, were established in Israel to suit its special conditions. The main types are the moshava, the kibbutz or kvutza, the moshav, and the moshav shittuphi.

The moshava was originally an ordinary village based on private land ownership and private enterprise. Many moshavot have expanded into towns. Sixty-four villages may be placed in this category.

The kibbutz is a communal settlement in which all property is collectively owned and work is organized on a collective basis. In return for their labor, its members receive food, housing, clothing, and social services. There are central dining rooms, communal kindergartens, and children's quarters. The kibbutz is governed by the general assembly of all members. The kibbutzim are predominantly agricultural although, in recent years, many of them have embarked on industrial enterprises. Most of the kibbutzim are affiliated with political parties. There are 235 kibbutzim throughout Israel, with populations ranging from 60 to 2,000. The first kibbutz, Degania, was established in 1909.

The moshav is a cooperative small-holders' village based on principles of mutual aid and equality of opportunity. Each member possesses his own land, worked by himself and his family. The purchase of supplies and the selling of produce, however, is carried out cooperatively. The general assembly elects a council which approves all transfers of farms and acceptance of new members. There are 344 moshavim, with populations ranging from 100 to 1,000. The first moshav, Nahalal, was founded in 1921. The moshav shittuphi is a mixture of the kibbutz and the moshav. Like the kibbutz, it is based on collective economy and ownership, but each family has its own house and is responsible for its own cooking, laundry, and child care, as in the moshav. Work and pay are adjusted to individual circumstances. Like the kibbutz, the moshav shittuphi has tended to develop industry, in addition to agriculture, in recent years. There are twenty-two such settlements in Israel, with populations of from 60 to 300. The first one, Kfar Hittim, was established in 1936. Israel's victory in the 1948 War of Independence was due, in large measure, to the agricultural settlements, many of which put up a heroic resistance to the Arab invaders.

In addition to the above, there are still other farms which grow mainly industrial crops and which rely on hired labor. Agricultural education is given on the settlements themselves and in a chain of agricultural schools throughout the country. On the academic level, there is the Hebrew University's agricultural faculty, situated in Rehovot. From the establishment of the State of Israel in 1948 up to 1968, 480 agricultural settlements were established in Israel (many of them along the borders), while the estimated Jewish population involved in agricultural production in 1968 was 274,000. Israel had developed many agricultural exports, of which citrus fruit is first in importance, and its Jaffa oranges are known in many parts of the world.

AKEDAH (binding): Name given to Abraham's intended sacrifice of his son Isaac, which was prevented at the last minute by God's intervention. The episode is described in the 22nd chapter of the book of Genesis. This chapter has had a potent and lasting influence on Jewish thought. Abraham's willingness to sacrifice his most precious possession, his son, gave to the Jewish people the ideal of martyrdom, the readiness to die if necessary for what was called "the sanctification of God's name." Large numbers of Jewish martyrs throughout the ages derived their inspiration and courage from the story of the binding of Isaac. Allusions to the Akedah found their way into the liturgy, and, in time, a whole cycle of synagogue hymns (Piyyutim) grew around it. The account of the Akedah forms the scriptural reading for the second day of Rosh Ha-Shanah, and according to the Talmudic sage, Rabbi Abbahu, the ram's horn *(shofar)* is sounded as a reminder of Abraham's readiness to offer up his son as a sacrifice, and the subsequent replacing of Isaac by a ram which happened to be nearby.

There is also another aspect to the *Akedah*. God's intervention to prevent the sacrifice of Isaac lays down once and for all Judaism's opposition to the ancient practice of child sacrifice. The Bible (Deut. 12:31) warns the people not to serve God in the manner of the surrounding nations: "For every abomination to the Lord which He hateth, have they done unto their gods; for even their sons and their daughters they have burnt in the fire to their gods." When, at times, under foreign influence, this barbaric practice penetrated into Israelite society, the prophets denounced it in the strongest possible terms, regarding it as a savage custom and a hideous aberration. The place where human sacrifice was practiced was Ge-Hinnom, the valley of Hinnom, and this became a synonym for "Hell."

AKIVA BEN JOSEPH (c. 40—c. 135 C.E.): One of the leading sages of the Mishnaic period, Akiva, according to tradition, received no formal education until the age of forty. It was his wife Rachel, the daughter of the wealthy landowner, Kalba Sabbua, who encouraged and persuaded him to study. Under the guidance of the leading scholars of the day who, after the destruction of the Second Temple had gathered together at Yavneh, Akiva rose to become the leading rabbinical authority of his time. Akiva played a leading role in the development of the oral law, regarding every word, letter, and sign in the Bible as the basis for *halakhic* decisions. Akiva was the first to attempt an orderly arrangement of the oral tradition according to subjects. This arrangement was further developed by his pupil Meir, and subsequently codified by Judah Ha-Nasi, as the *Mishnah*. He never lost sight of his humble

beginnings. Thus, he laid stress on love of neighbor, on man's unrestricted liberty of choice, and on the fact that Divine justice is tempered with Divine mercy. According to tradition — doubtless exaggerated — Akiva's school at Bene Berak had a student body of twelve to twenty-four thousand. Akiva, moreover, was a fervent patriot and did all in his power to ease the condition of the people under Roman rule. Together with three other scholars, he participated in a political mission to Rome in order to secure the withdrawal of restrictive regulations against the Jews, enacted by the Emperor Domitian. From about the year 124, relations with the Roman authorities took a turn for the worse, due to the oppressive policy of the Roman Emperor Hadrian. According to the Talmud, Akiva was an enthusiastic supporter of the Bar Kokhba rebellion, proclaiming Bar Kokhba to be the Messiah. It is not certain, however, that he himself took an active part in the revolt. After successfully suppressing the uprising, the Roman authorities carried out a policy of oppression, and brutal massacres of the Jewish population followed. The observance of Jewish law was restricted, and the study of the Torah prohibited. Akiva, believing that without the study of Torah there was no further purpose to living, openly defied the decree. He was arrested and finally executed at Caesarea. According to tradition, the Romans killed him by tearing his flesh from his living body. Despite his agony, Akiva expressed his joy, at being able to die a martyr's death, and, reciting the SHEMA, he died as he reached the words, "The Lord is One."

ALCHEMY: The bid to turn base metals into precious ones like gold or silver. Alchemy was not originally a Jewish science, but its links with Jewish tradition and lore at various periods were numerous.

According to some legends, the secrets of nature were committed to Adam, the first man. He, in turn, passed them on to the Patriarchs, and they went through Moses to Solomon, to whom tradition has assigned several books on alchemy.

A famous Jewish woman alchemist is mentioned during the Hellenistic period in Egypt. Called Maria the Jewess, she is said to have lived and worked in the 1st century C.E., to have invented effective apparatus for chemical experiments, and to have tackled a number of basic laboratory problems.

In the Middle Ages, Jewish writers mention alchemy frequently, while Christian and Moslem alchemists weave Jewish concepts — from the Bible and *Midrash* especially — into their theories. Many Arabic and Latin books on alchemy were translated into Hebrew.

Medieval books on alchemy laid stress on the *Kabbalah,* although their authors seem to have had only a superficial knowledge of that branch of Jewish learning. However, it was precisely the mystery of the *Kabbalah* which seems to have attracted them. Among Christian scholars in the 17th century, for example, the two concepts of alchemy and *Kabbalah* were virtually inseparable. Some links must have existed between the two. The *Zohar,* which is the classical textbook of the *Kabbalah,* contains several passages recalling alchemistic principles, showing that its author actually believed that base metals could be transformed into gold.

Not many names of Jewish alchemists have come down to us. In 1545, nevertheless, Martin Luther warned Duke Joachim the Second of Brandenburg that he should shun alchemy, because the Jews practiced it. In some books, the famous "philosopher's stone" which alchemists eagerly sought is symbolized by a Star of David inside a circle. Baruch Spinoza did not engage in alchemy, but he devoted considerable comment to it; Maimonides was skeptical of alchemy; and Judah Halevi totally condemned it.

ALENU LE-SHABBEAH *(It is our Duty to Praise)*: Opening words of a prayer proclaiming the unity and sovereignty of God. It has been attributed to Rav, the 3rd century sage and founder of Talmudic studies in Babylon. It was originally composed for the additional service of *Rosh Ha-Shanah* where it occupies the important place of introductory prayer to the section known as *Malkhuyot.* From the 12th century on, it began to be used as the concluding prayer to all congregational services on week-days, Sabbaths, and festivals. Before the words beginning "For we bend the knee and offer worship" etc., the original text included the phrase "For they bow down to vanity emptiness, and pray to a god that cannot save." During the Middle Ages, the accusation was leveled against the Jews that these words were meant as a conscious insult to Christianity. In vain did the leading rabbis of the 14th–15th centuries protest against this baseless accusation. It was pointed out that Rav, who edited the *Rosh Ha-Shanah* additional service in which *Alenu* is incorporated, lived in an environment in which there were no Christians at all. Despite this, its recital was prohibited in various places and, in 1703, the cancellation of the "offensive" words was officially ordered, and they are still omitted in the Ashkenazi rite. The Sephardi prayer book, however, has maintained the original text. The *Alenu* prayer is in fact the essence of tolerance and enlightenment, for while in the first half of the prayer Israel acknowledges the selection of Israel for the service of God, the second half is entirely universal, expressing the hope for the day when all idolatry shall have disappeared and God's sovereignty be accepted by all the nations of the earth. Because of its firm proclamation of the Divine unity, the *Alenu* was during the Middle Ages a favorite prayer of Jewish martyrs, who often recited its contents in their moment of agony.

ALGERIA: Algeria, in North Africa, was part of the French Union until 1962. Jews have resided there probably since the days of the Carthaginians, and archeological relics (inscriptions, catacombs, etc.) from the Jewish communities which existed there during Roman times have been unearthed. After the Christianization of the Roman Empire, the position of the Jews deteriorated, but under Moslem rule new communities were established. After the rise of the *Almohades* (extremist Moslems of the 12th century), the open practice of Judaism was temporarily forbidden, but refugees from the Spanish massacres (1391) and expulsion (1492) brought new life to the Algerian community, and it became a leading center of Sephardi life and scholarship. Under Turkish rule from the 16th century, conditions were generally good, and the Jews controlled a high percentage of the country's foreign trade. In the 18th and 19th centuries, Jewish life in Algeria was turbulent, and there were frequent outbreaks of anti-Jewish sentiment. The Cremieux Decree of 1870 conferred French citizenship upon the Algerian Jews, but this did little to reduce the hostility shown them by other segments of the population. During World War II, the Vichy government introduced anti-Semitic legislation into Algeria, and the German occupation caused suffering for many Jews there. More liberal conditions were gradually restored after the war, but the growth of strong Algerian nationalist feelings created fresh difficulties for the Jews.

When Algeria obtained her independence from France, almost the entire Jewish community of 130,000 emigrated. Most went to France; a small number went to Israel. Today, the Jewish population of Algeria numbers only a few thousand.

ALIYAH (Ascent): Term used in ancient times to denote a pilgrimage to Jerusalem from other parts of the country as well as from outside of the land of Israel. According to the Bible, every male Israelite has to make the pilgrimage on foot (aliyat regel) to the Temple three times a year, on the festivals of Pesaḥ, Shavuot, and Sukkot (hence the term pilgrimage festivals, by which they are known). These pilgrimages were outstanding events, and hundreds of thousands participated in them, as testified to by descriptions in the Talmud and in the writings of the ancient historian Josephus. The use of the word *aliyah,* meaning ascent, may stem either from the fact that Jerusalem's geographical elevation literally involves an arduous physical ascent, or it may have the connotation of a spiritual ascent. After the destruction of the Temple, pilgrimages were considered as voluntary acts of piety. Throughout the Middle Ages, pious rabbis and their followers made such pilgrimages from time to time, despite the dangers involved — Naḥmanides in 1266, Obadiah of Bertinoro in 1488, Joseph Karo and the Kabbalists in the 16th century, Judah Ḥasid and 1,500 followers in 1700 — these and others made the strenuous and dangerous journey to the Holy Land. With the rise of the Zionist

An immigrant family arrives in Israel

movement, the term *aliyah* was once again used in connection with the land of Israel and in modern Hebrew the word for immigration is *aliyah,* while an immigrant is an *oleh.*

The word is also widely used to denote the honor of being called to the reading of the Torah. This, too, dates back to ancient times when the Torah was read from an elevated platform, so that whereas one "went down" to conduct the prayers, the reading desk being recessed in the floor, one "went up" to the reading of the Torah. For Immigration to Israel (Aliyah), see ZIONISM and ISRAEL, STATE OF.

ALPHABET: The Hebrew alphabet is derived from the ancient Canaanite alphabet, the world's first known alphabetic script, and like all Semitic languages, it is written from right to left. In the course of its development, the Hebrew script assumed two different forms. The first, the ancient Hebrew script, closely resembled the Canaanite alphabet and was used by the Jews until after the time of the Babylonian Exile. During Second Temple times, the characteristically Hebrew Square Script, still used today, developed from the alphabet of the Aramaic language which was then the most widely spoken language in the Middle East, especially along the trade routes.

The Hebrew alphabet has 22 letters, all of them consonants. Slowly, some of these letters (aleph, heh, vav, and yod) came to be used as vowel indicators. Then, in the 7th–9th centuries C.E., various systems were developed for writing vowels above and below the letters. One of these systems is in general use today, but the addition of vowels had never been an integral part of the Hebrew alphabet, and Hebrew books and newspapers, for example, are still written only with consonants (except for those meant for students who are learning the language). Vowel signs may not be used on the ritual Scrolls of the Law.

Square Hebrew	Sham'al	Nerab	Taima	Ossuaries	Square Hebrew	Sham'al	Nerab	Taima	Ossuaries
א					ל				
ב					מ				
ג					נ				
ד					ס				
ה					ע				
ו					פ				
ז					צ				
ח					ק				
ט					ר				
י					ש				
כ					ת				

Development of the Hebrew alphabet

The specific order of the Hebrew alphabet influenced the Greek alphabet, and the form of European alphabets can be traced back to the Hebrew. Numerical values were eventually assigned to the Hebrew letters, and numbers in Hebrew are indicated by letters of the alphabet. For example, the first letter, *aleph,* equals one; the second letter, *bet,* is two, and so on. The rabbis were very fond of *gematria* — that is, they used to add the numerical values of the letters in a word and then interpret this for mystical purposes or to explain a Biblical passage. In general, the Hebrew alphabet has had a very strong religious significance, and mystical powers were ascribed to the various letters by the kabbalists. The letter combinations which signified the various names of God were held to have special significance, and religious Jews have always avoided writing the full name of the Lord, except when they are writing a Scroll of the Law.

Although for many centuries Hebrew ceased to be a spoken language, it was always used for religious services and rituals. Moreover, the various Jewish communities throughout the world continued to use the letters of the Hebrew alphabet even when writing languages of the countries in which they were living. Thus Yiddish, the most common language of the Jews in the dispersion, was essentially a German dialect written in Hebrew script, and some of the greatest of the medieval Jewish classics were in the Arabic language written in Hebrew letters. The original Hebrew alphabet consisted of capital letters only, but in the course of time various scripts developed — the one popular in eastern Europe becoming the standard Hebrew script which people use today in writing (except in Scrolls of the Law). The printed alphabet, however, is still in the traditional capital letters.

ALROY, DAVID: False Messiah of the 12th century who led a movement whose ultimate aim was the conquest of the land of Israel. David Alroy is a colorful and semi-legendary figure in Jewish history. He lived in the area of northern Iraq and Persia known today as Kurdistan. During the period of the Second Crusade, when the Moslem world was in a state of chaos, Alroy tried to organize the Jews of Persia to help him free Jerusalem from Moslem control. He was one of the most daring of the false Messiahs, but very few historical facts are known about him.

Although many poor Jews followed Alroy, the wealthy people and those who held important positions doubted that he could succeed in raising a general revolt and feared that following him would only harm their high social status. The head (Exilarch) of Babylonian Jewry feared that Alroy would bring disaster on all Jewry, and he threatened him with excommunication unless he disbanded his movement. Alroy was finally assassinated, possibly by his own father-in-law, who, it is said, had been bribed by the Moslem governor.

After Alroy's death, some of his followers continued to believe in him as the true Messiah, and they formed a sect in Persia. The British novelist Benjamin Disraeli (who became prime minister of Britain) made Alroy the hero of a novel, *The Wondrous Tale of David Alroy,* based on the legends surrounding the life of the would-be Messiah.

ALTAR: Structure used in ancient times for the offering of sacrifices. In the Bible, an altar is first mentioned in The Book of Genesis when Noah built one after being saved from the Great Flood. On different occasions, Abraham, Isaac, Jacob, and Moses built altars on which to make "burnt offerings," either as gestures of thanksgiving, or to mark a new covenant with God. Thus, just after giving Moses the Ten Commandments, God spoke and said, "An altar of earth thou shalt make unto me, and shalt sacrifice thereon thy burnt offerings, and thy peace offerings, thy sheep, and thine oxen."

According to the Bible, the altar had to be made of a mound of earth, or of stones which had not been shaped by iron tools. The reason given by the rabbis for the prohibition of iron is that because it was used in weapons of war, it was too much associated with violence and bloodshed, and hence was not fitting material for the construction of a holy place. Another possible explanation is that in the Biblical view, things should be used in the service of God only in their natural state, before they have been interfered with in any way by man. The Bible also warns the people not to follow the pagan custom of planting trees around the altar, and not to climb up to the altar by steps, an act which might immodestly expose the priests' legs.

During the period of the Biblical Judges and Kings, there were many local altars, usually known as "high places." It must be pointed out, however, that the "High Place" *(Bamah)* was a mound or a knoll upon which sacrifices were offered, but not every high place had an altar erected upon it; the knoll itself could take the place of an altar. The Books of Leviticus and Deuteronomy, however, state explicitly that there should be only one altar, regarded as holy by all Jews. The historical books of the Bible, as well as rabbinical tradition, held that only the altar in the Temple at Jerusalem was sacred, and that all other altars were illegal. The Talmud makes an exception for the one-time altar built by Elijah on Mount Carmel in his famous confrontation with the priests of Baal. Elijah's altar consisted of twelve stones symbolizing the twelve tribes of Israel.

The altar served also as a focus for feasts of rejoicing and as a haven for the accused. According to tradition, if a man had accidentally committed murder, he could seek refuge at the altar, whose sacred nature forbade those who might punish him from taking him away. This tradition still exists to some extent even in modern times – hence in America today, one occasionally hears of someone seeking refuge from the police in a church or synagogue.

Since the destruction of the Second Temple in the year 70 C.E., Jews have not had an altar. In the synagogue, its place is taken by the Ark containing the Scrolls of the Law. But the influence of the altar is still alive in Jewish traditions, and the many detailed descriptions of it given in the Bible have been the basis of numerous allegories and mystical speculations which were written down in *Aggadah* or in mystical works.

AMIDAH (standing): Prayer said standing, facing in the direction of the site of the Temple at Jerusalem. In the Talmud, it is designated as *tephillah*, i.e., the prayer *par excellence*, while among Ashkenazim, it is commonly referred to as *Shemoneh Esreh* — eighteen (benedictions). The term *Amidah* is more accurate because the original eighteen benedictions, which rabbinic tradition ascribes to the men of the Great Assembly, were finally edited at Yavneh on the instructions of the Patriarch, Gamaliel II (100 C.E.), who introduced a nineteenth benediction, a prayer "against the heretics," probably aimed originally against the Judeo-Christians. Furthermore, on Sabbaths and festivals the prayer contains seven benedictions, while the *"Musaph" Amidah* on *Rosh Ha-Shanah* has nine benedictions.

The recitation of the *Amidah* is common to all the statutory prayers for both weekdays and festivals. On weekdays, the nineteen benedictions composing it fall into three groups:

1) Praises — Three opening blessings glorifying the everlasting love, eternal might, and infinite holiness of God.
2) Petitions — Thirteen brief prayers for national and individual well-being.
3) Thanksgiving — These three concluding benedictions consist of prayers for the reestablishment of the divine service at Jerusalem, thanksgiving for God's daily wonders, and a prayer for peace and prosperity.

On fast days, an invocation for help in distress is added to the 7th benediction, and it is also permissible to introduce into the 8th benediction prayers for the recovery of an individual from illness. On new moons and festivals (except at *Musaph*) the paragraph *Yaaleh Veyavo* is added to the 17th benediction, and on *Hanukkah* and *Purim,* the passage *Al Hanisim* is introduced in the 18th benediction.

On Sabbaths and festivals, and on every occasion on which *Musaph* is recited, the thirteen intermediate petitions are replaced by one prayer dealing with the specific aspects of the day, and, in the *Musaph* of *Rosh Ha-Shanah,* by three such prayers. The thirteen paragraphs are omitted on these occasions in order that these days should be marked by a happier and more cheerful mood than ordinary weekdays.

In congregational service, except in the evening when it is not repeated, the *Amidah* is first said silently and then repeated aloud by the reader. This custom was originally introduced for the benefit of those who could not say the prayers themselves, and has remained the usage to the present day. When the reader reaches the 3rd benediction, the *Kedusha (sanctification)* is recited, and the priestly blessing is on certain occasions added in the 19th benediction.

Both the latter additions require the presence of a minyan. The meditation *Elohai Netzor* (O Lord, guard my Tongue from Evil), which comes at the end of the *Amidah,* is regarded as an individual prayer and is therefore not repeated by the reader. There is a shorter form of the *Amidah (Havinenu)* attributed to the 3rd century sage, Samuel, which may be recited in cases of extreme urgency in which time is a vital factor.

On Friday evenings, after the *Amidah,* the cantor recites the prayer *Magen Avot.* This is an abbreviated form of the seven benedictions comprising the Friday evening *Amidah* and was originally introduced when synagogues were situated outside towns and it was dangerous to be out alone at night. The recitation of *Magen Avot* enabled latecomers to conclude their prayers and return home with the other congregants.

AMOS: Biblical prophet of the 8th century B.C.E. The book bearing his name has nine chapters and is the third of the twelve minor prophets. At a time when the northern kingdom of Israel was wealthy and powerful, during the reign of King Jeroboam II (784–744 B.C.E.), Amos forecast her doom; when the talented and pious wrote music and made sacrifices to the Lord, he condemned their hypocrisy. As the rich lay on their ivory beds and held their feasts, Amos reminded them of the poor. He was the first of Israel's literary prophets; i.e., one whose writings were collected in a Biblical book. Born in the village of Tekoa, south of Bethlehem, he was a simple herdsman and pruner of sycamore trees with no formal education or aristocratic background. "I am no prophet, neither am I a prophet's son," he used to say, when setting himself apart from the professional prophets and soothsayers of his time. He believed that his message had been given to him by divine revelation and not through any training in the arts of magic and prophecy.

Amos' criticism of the internal corruption of the northern kingdom was harsh and fiery: "Woe to them that are at ease in Zion," he would say, or, "I hate, I despise your feast days." His point was that the Israelites had become too self-satisfied. They had come to feel that being the chosen people was a privilege rather than a moral obligation; they offered their sacrifices and kept their feast days, but had forgotten the real meaning of sacrifice. Amos taught that sacrifice had no importance at all unless accompanied by a sincere desire to lead a more moral life. Again and again he reminded Israel of its moral duties, and he came to be regarded as one of the first men who was able to distinguish morality itself from sacrifices and the ritual acts which were supposed to express moral awareness. Amos proclaimed man's inhumanity to man to be the cardinal sin. This applied not only to Israel, but to all the nations, whom Amos accused of not developing ethical patterns of behavior toward each other. In this sense Amos' prophecy is universalistic. Amos' concern for the poor and the underprivileged has earned him the title "The Great Social Reformer."

Although the burden of Amos' message was the destruction of Israel for her transgressions, he also spoke of the eventual restoration. And in his saying, "Thus saith the Lord unto the House of Israel: seek me, and you shall live," the scholars of the Talmud say that all the commandments of the Bible are summed up.

ANGLO-JEWISH ASSOCIATION: Founded in 1871, it aims to promote the education of Jews in backward areas and advance the Jewish religion through scholarships, financial grants and educational literature. One of its most important institutions is the Evelina de Rothschild school in Jerusalem. Among its activities the Association collects information about religious and social conditions of Jews throughout the world and conducts and publishes research on all aspects of religious and racial intolerance.

ANTI-SEMITISM: Term used to denote the feelings of prejudice and hostility toward the Jews on the part of individuals or organized groups. It is derived from "anti" meaning "against," and "Semites," i.e., the descendants of the Biblical Shem, and was first used in the year 1879 by a little-known journalist, Wilhelm Marr, in a pamphlet containing a violent attack on the Jews.

Hatred of the Jews as such is an ancient phenomenon and finds its classical expression in the Bible in the words of Haman:

> There is a certain people scattered abroad and dispersed among the people in all the provinces of the kingdom, and their laws are diverse from all people, neither keep they the king's laws, therefore it is not for the king's profit to suffer them. (Esther 3:8).

Many a Jew-baiter, ancient and modern, has expressed his anti-Jewish sentiments along lines similar to the above. In the 1st century B.C.E. and the 1st century C.E., anti-Jewish feeling was rife, especially in Alexandria. This was based primarily upon the Jewish rejection of paganism and on the large numbers of pagan converts to Judaism. It was with the rise, spread, and ultimate domination of Christianity, however, that anti-Jewishness began to assume tragic proportions. Throughout the Middle Ages, the basis of Jew-hatred and persecution in the Christian world was theological. The Jew had rejected Jesus, the Messiah, and therefore was cursed and punished by God.

The official policy of the Church was to humiliate the Jew — socially, politically, and economically — but not to destroy him entirely. His existence in a state of oppression was needed in order to show the world how difficult is the fate of those who reject Jesus. The masses, however, were

From Nazi concentration camp, Yad Vashem

unable to understand the intricacies of the Church's hair-splitting, and, to them, humiliation meant rioting and robbery and murder of the Jew, or the anti-Christ, as he was known. The long list of outbreaks against the Jew throughout the Middle Ages was usually accompanied by accusations connected with his rejection of Christianity, such as the libel that Jews used human blood or that they desecrated the Host (the wafer consecrated in the Christian Mass). The Crusaders, imbued with religious zeal, decided before their departure for the Holy Land to wage a much easier war against the infidel Jews of Europe. Throughout this dark period, the Jew was given the choice between baptism or death. If he accepted the former he was granted equality and received into the Christian community. Many of the Middle Ages' greatest Jew-baiters were in fact apostates. The hatred of the Jew during the Middle Ages was primarily directed at his faith, and the object of anti-Jewish violence was to convert the Jews to Christianity. It is true that there was considerable animosity toward the Marranos by the Church and the populace despite their conversion. This was, however, largely due to their being suspected of being insincere Christians and of continuing to practice Judaism in secret. The Inquisition was applied only to Christians suspected of heresy, and the Marranos were regarded by the Church as Christians. The Spanish Jews who refused to convert,

Memorial exhibition at Yad Vashem

even outwardly, could not be touched by the Inquisition and were therefore banished. Up to the modern period, the theological anti-Semitism preached and practiced by some segments of the Church has played an important part in fomenting anti-Jewish feeling. The Christian education received by a child, with its emphasis on the crucifixion of Jesus by the Jews, implants in him a prejudice and animosity which often remains for life. In recent years, however, there have been indications of a changing attitude among some Church leaders, many of whom have placed themselves in the forefront of the struggle against anti-Semitism. Particularly noteworthy in this regard was Pope John XXIII, who convened the Second Vatican Council, which officially absolved the Jewish people of all guilt for the crucifixion of Jesus.

Anti-Semitism in the modern sense, however, is more than religious prejudice. With the rise of the modern nation-state and the subsequent weakening of the Church and religion in general, anti-Jewishness shifted its emphasis from the religious to the racial sphere. In 1853, a Frenchman by the name of Count Gobineau published a book entitled *The Inequality of Human Races,* in which he claimed that civilization was deteriorating because the blood of the aristocracy was being contaminated by the inferior blood of the common people. While he does not mention the Jews, his idea of an Aryan elite as against the non-Aryan middle and lower class found a willing audience, especially in the classical land of medieval, Jew-baiting Germany. His book gained him the friendship of the German philosopher, Nietzsche, whose ideas of the superman and the warrior race may be considered as the cornerstone of the future Nazi state. An English writer by the name of Houston Stewart Chamberlain placed the racial theory on a "philosophical" basis in his book, *Foundations of the 11th Century.* In his view, the Nordic race, blue-eyed, blond-haired, and with pure blood, is represented by the Germans, who are at the summit of humanity, while the Jews are at its lowest possible point. It is no wonder that Houston Chamberlain supported the Germans during World War I. The above "philosophers" of race provided fertile ground for anti-Semites who were only too eager to put their theories into practice. The medieval picture of the stupid, boorish, and uneducated Jew was now transformed into one of a shrewd and wily manipulator, a diabolical creature with superior cunning. In France, Edouard Drumont published a book, *La France Juive,* in which he attempted to show how the Jews would soon dominate France. The book was widely circulated and played no small part in the anti-Semitic outbreaks culminating in the Dreyfus trial. Earlier, an anti-Semitic league had been organized in Germany, whose aim was to deprive the Jews of the vote. From Germany and Austria, anti-Semitism spread to Russia where anti-Judaism had long been rife. At the instigation of Czar Nicholas II, a monk by the name of Sergei Nilus came up with one of the most startling forgeries in history. This forgery professed to show how a group of conspiratorial Jews, the Elders of Zion, planned to conquer the world. The *Protocols of the Elders of Zion* has remained one of the standard weapons in the arsenal of anti-Semitism, despite its having been proven countless times to be a blatant forgery. In Poland, from the beginning of the 20th century, there was an economic boycott of the Jews, interspersed with outbreaks of violence.

After World War I, anti-Semitic propaganda attempted to identify Jews and Judaism with Bolshevism, while the economic depression in many of the countries affected by the war was exploited by anti-Semites to arouse the feelings of the masses. In the United States, the famous industrialist, Henry Ford, conducted an intense anti-Semitic campaign; later, he publicly admitted his errors and brought the campaign to an end.

The zenith of anti-Semitic ideology, propaganda, and indoctrination was reached in Germany with the rise of Adolf Hitler and his National Socialist (Nazi) Party. The ideologist of the party, Alfred Rosenberg, published his book, *The Myth of the 20th Century,* in 1930. Here were formulated all the ideas of the Nordic superman as represented by the Germans, and the myth of pure Aryan blood. The Nazi theory was that the Jew, together with the Slav, was subhuman, and was therefore to be eliminated. Having one Jewish grandparent was sufficient to categorize one as a Jew. Unlike the theological anti-Semitism of the Church, no possibility of conversion existed. Birth, blood, and race were the determining factors in a man's standing. The destruction of European Jewry was to the Nazis part of the mission entrusted to them as the standard-bearers of racial purity.

The defeat of Nazi Germany and the revelation of the horrors of the concentration camps did not, as was hoped, eliminate the scourge of anti-Semitism. The Israel-Arab conflict has shown how quickly dormant feelings of prejudice are able to emerge into the open in times of conflict. While the Arab leaders have claimed time and again that their opposition is not to Jews or Judaism but to Jewish nationalism, their actions have followed the stereotyped pattern of stock anti-Semitism. In Arab countries, Jews have been continually

harassed, accused of disloyalty, and persecuted and expelled. Even the literature of anti-Semitism (such as the *Protocols of the Elders of Zion* and Hitler's *Mein Kampf)* has been widely disseminated in Arab countries.

In the Soviet Union, the situation of the large Jewish population is precarious. The Bolshevik revolution, in which so many Jews were prominent, granted complete emancipation to the Jews, and the constitution of the Soviet Union officially prohibits manifestations of anti-Semitism. Communist hostility toward religion in general led to the establishment of a Jewish section of the Communist party *(Yevsektia),* which was most zealous in its attempt to eliminate religious life. The study of Hebrew was forbidden except as a foreign language, and Zionist sympathy was regarded as a crime against the state. Many Jews, however, reached positions of distinction in Russian society, although they inevitably did so at the price of denouncing their Jewishness. To alleviate Jewish nationalist hopes, the Russians decided to create an autonomous Jewish state in Birobizhan in Eastern Asia, a project which at the outset was stillborn and doomed to failure. Soviet support for the establishment of the State of Israel in 1948 was soon replaced by all-out support for the Arabs and hostility to Zionism. As in the Arab countries, the Soviet leaders are at pains to differentiate between their opposition to Zionism and their lack of anti-Semitic tendencies. However, the lines are thinly drawn, as in the case of the Arabs, and recent open manifestations of Zionist sympathy on the part of Soviet Jews have been violently denounced by the Russian leadership. Russian Jews expressing their wish to emigrate to Israel or identifying themselves with the State of Israel have been summarily dismissed from their jobs and subjected to rigorous social pressure. In Poland, where anti-Semitism was part of the landscape, the anti-Jewish revival has led to the final breakup of the centuries-old Jewish community, many members of which were loyal and devoted Communists.

In the western world since World War II, a large outbreak of anti-Semitism occurred in some of the countries of South America, where many ex-Nazis had taken refuge. In the Argentine for a time, a Nazi organization going by the name of *Tacuara* adopted violent street methods against the local Jewish population. The western democracies, too, have not been free of anti-Semitic outbreaks and attempts to organize anti-Jewish movements. In the main, however, these have been limited in their scope to small fringe groups such as George Lincoln Rockwell's American Nazi Party. Anti-Semitism in the western democracies for the most part manifests itself in social discrimination of various sorts. Many attempts have been made to explain this unique phenomenon. Sociologists, psychologists, religious leaders, and others have analyzed anti-Semitism in its various manifestations, but have been unable to provide a conclusive reason for its appearance. Religious prejudice, economic competition, the psychological fear of the unknown, and the constant need in every society for a suitable scapegoat who can be blamed for all of the society's ills — these and other reasons have been advanced for the continued existence of anti-Semitism. Perhaps the answer lies in the statement attributed to the Christian Socialist, Victor Adler, at a Congress of the Austrian Social Democratic Party held in 1898, "The last anti-Semite will die only with the last Jew."

See also: DREYFUS AFFAIR, HOLOCAUST.

APOCALYPSE (from Greek: disclosure, uncovering): Special type of Jewish literature which flourished from the 2nd century B.C.E. to the middle of the 2nd century C.E. Its characteristic feature is the belief in an imminent day of judgment for the world and the emphasis throughout is on "the end of days" and "last things." Apocalyptic literature must be understood within its historical context. The later Hasmonean rulers had not lived up to early expectation. This was a period of religious turmoil, civil war, and political and social anarchy. With the appearance of the Roman conquerors, disillusionment set in. The fulfillment of the age-old hope of the arrival of the Davidic Messiah seemed doomed forever. In this pessimistic atmosphere, many turned to other worldly ideas for comfort and consolation. The day of judgment was at hand in which all evil was to be utterly and completely destroyed. The prophets of old had also spoken of the "day of the Lord," but, in their philosophy, the concept was never taken to the extreme lengths it reaches in the apocalyptic literature. The apocalypse deals with the revelation of secrets which are beyond the bounds of human knowledge, and employs vivid imagery in which angels, reptiles, and half-man half-beast monsters, all play a part. Attempts are made to calculate the exact date of the coming of the Messiah, and the nature and blessings of the "world to come" are enumerated. Of the books comprising the Hebrew Bible, Daniel contains much material which can be defined as apocalyptic. These sections of the book of Daniel were probably composed at the beginning of the Hasmonean revolt.

The favorite literary device used by the apocalyptic writers was to describe the events of their time in the form of a prophecy by a Biblical personality — long since deceased. Hence the term for all these works: *Pseudepigrapha,* writings under an assumed name. The best known apocalyptic and pseudepigraphic literature is the book of Enoch and the testaments ascribed to the twelve patriarchs. The recently discovered Dead Sea Scrolls also contain literature which is distinctly apocalyptic, such as the *War of the Children of Light against the Children of Darkness.* The apocalyptic writings had a considerable influence on Talmudic literature, and even in the Middle Ages Jews continued to compose apocalypses. The books of the apocalyptic movement contain the first known records of Jewish mysticism.

APOCRYPHA: The body of Jewish religious literature written between the 2nd century B.C.E. and the 2nd century C.E., which was not included in the "canon" (24 books) of the Hebrew Bible. When the rabbis sitting at the Council of Yavneh, about 90 C.E., finally decided on the contents of the Hebrew Bible, they excluded several books of Jewish religious writing which they considered were lacking in divine inspiration. Most of these books, known today as the Apocrypha (from the Greek, "hidden" or "secret") and Pseudepigrapha (Greek, "with false title"), were written after the time of Ezra and Nehemiah — that is, after the time when, according to tradition, divine prophecy had ceased. Unlike the writings which were included in the Bible, there is no original Hebrew or Aramaic text available for many of the apocryphal books. Some were even known to have been written in Greek.

Excluded from the Bible itself, the Apocrypha were also excluded from the attention of most Jewish scholars. After the destruction of the Second Temple (70 C.E.), rabbinical scholars concentrated on the Biblical texts and the oral tradition, feeling it unimportant to devote time to the "minor" works of the small Jewish sects believed to have written the Apocrypha. Many of these writings were, however, incorporated into the Greek translation of the Bible, the Septuagint, and were accepted as sacred by the Christian Church, which preserved them, translating them into Greek, Syriac, Coptic, and other languages. Additional Apocryphal writings were recently discovered among the Dead Sea Scrolls.

The Apocrypha are highly valued today as among the very few remnants of Jewish literature surviving from the Second Temple period. They tell us a great deal about how Jews felt, what they feared and hoped for, and how their religious thinking developed over four of the most critical centuries in Jewish history. For the Christians, these writings are important because of their emphasis on the End of Days and the coming of the Messiah. The themes of the Apocrypha resemble the last section of the Bible (writings), presenting religious and moral teachings, prophecies, historical accounts and legends, and some mysticism. The Pseudepigrapha are almost exclusively devoted to mystical themes. Scholars usually divide the Apocrypha into four main categories: history, legend, prophecy, and wisdom.

Among the historical books are *I Esdras (Ezra)*, which contains Biblical material from *II Chronicles, Ezra,* and *Nehemiah,* followed by a tale about King Darius of Persia and his oath to rebuild the Temple; *I Maccabees,* the history of the Hasmoneans; *II Maccabees,* a partial history of the wars of Judas the Maccabee, styled mainly to inspire Jewish national unity; and *III Maccabees*, about the rule of King Ptolemy IV, the Philopator of Egypt, who wanted to massacre the Jews of Alexandria.

The books of legend include *Tobit,* a folktale demonstrating that piety and trust in the Lord eventually bring their reward; and *Judith,* the story of a brave and beautiful woman who heroically slays Holofernes and saves her town.

From the books of prophecy there is *Baruch,* telling about the sins of the Jewish people which led to their exile, followed by a prayer for forgiveness; and *II Esdras,* reflections on sin, evil, and judgment, set against the background of the Babylonian exile.

Among the books of wisdom are *The Wisdom of Solomon,* which belittles pagan philosophy because it leads to moral corruption, and praises divine wisdom; and

Ben Sira (Ecclesiasticus), a collection of proverbs, wise sayings, and meditations on the Bible.

Other apocryphal books exist which were excluded even from the Christian Bible as lacking in Divine inspiration. They include writings such as *IV Maccabees,* a sermon in Greek attempting to prove that faith in God can make man a hero; *Enoch,* a tale about the marvels of heaven and earth, and a history of mankind; *Jubilees,* a kind of Midrash on the Books of Genesis and Exodus; the letter of *Aristeas,* which tells how the Bible was translated into Greek; and the *Psalms of Solomon,* an imitation of the Biblical Psalms, voicing disillusion over the Hasmonean monarchs, and hopes that the Messiah of the House of David will redeem Israel.

APOSTASY: Conversion from Judaism. This has been a factor in Jewish history, occurring on a significant scale from time to time. During the period preceding the Maccabean revolt, numbers of Jews, notably from the ranks of the aristocracy, abandoned Judaism for Hellenistic culture. The most famous apostate of the Talmudic era was the contemporary of Rabbi Akiva and teacher of Rabbi Meir, Elisha ben Abuyah, referred to after his apostasy as Aḥer — "another one." After the rise of Christianity and Islam, there were periods in which both these faiths indulged in forcible conversion. Thus, in the Roman Empire from the 4th to 6th century, in the Byzantine Empire in the seventh, and especially in Visigothic Spain, there were numerous instances of such conversion, enforced by mob rule. Forced conversion to Islam took place after the rise of Mohammed, and was particularly severe in the 12th century under the Almohades in North Africa and Spain. In Spain, as a result of the violent anti-Jewish outbreak beginning in 1391, there was a mass conversion of Jews to Christianity, while in Portugal in 1496–7, virtually the whole Jewish community was forcibly baptized without even being given the alternatives of exile or death. Both the above events gave rise to the class of secret Jews known as Marranos. Judaism and Jewish sentiment distinguished between those who converted under pressure or by force and those who did so voluntarily and for reasons of convenience and status. Such apostates, unfortunately, arose from time to time and, wishing to impress their Christian masters, often developed a super-zeal for their new religion which they expressed in fanatical hatred of the one they had abandoned. During the Middle Ages, three apostates, Nicholas Donin (Paris, 1240), Pablo Christiani (Barcelona, 1263), and Geronimo da Santa Fe (Tortosa, 1413–14), forced the Jews into public disputations, which obliged Jewish leaders to defend Judaism by describing its advantages over Christianity. These disputations, in which the Jews had no chance of winning, often led to the burning of Jewish books and the enforcement of further anti-Jewish restrictions. Another infamous apostate was Solomon Levi, the Rabbi of Burgos. After the pogroms of 1391, he converted to Christianity and became the Archbishop of Burgos under the name of Paul de Santa Maria. He was a zealous missionary and was responsible for many harsh decrees against the Jews. In the 16th century, another famous apostate, Johan Pfefferkorn advocated the banning of the Talmud. Apostates were active in the spreading of the blood-libel and other calumnies against the Jews. With time, the word *Meshumad* (apostate) became associated in the minds of Jews with treason and persecution. Apostasy was regarded as a despicable act of infamy and desertion.

In Jewish law, however, an apostate, despite his actions, is still regarded as a Jew and most rabbinic authorities are of the opinion that if an apostate repents and returns to Judaism, no formal ceremony of readmission is required.

ARABIA: According to some traditions, Jews settled in the Arabian Peninsula after the destruction of the first Temple in 586 B.C.E. There is, however, no evidence of this, and organized Jewish life dates from the 1st century C.E. onward. For four centuries, these Jews prospered and their numbers grew. Various independent and warlike Jewish tribes are said to have imposed their rule on their neighbors in the Medina area where there was a considerable Jewish population in the 6th and early 7th centuries. Numerous Arabs, including a ruler by the name of Dhu Nuwas, converted to Judaism. Mohammed, who was at first sympathetic toward the Jews, turned against them as a result of their refusal to accept him as a prophet. The Jews of Medina were either annihilated or expelled. The other Jews of Arabia were allowed to remain, on the payment of special taxes. From this time on, the Jews of Arabia were mainly concentrated in the Yemen, Hadramaut, and Aden. The rest were completely assimilated and absorbed into Arab society, so that all their Jewish characteristics vanished. The most important remaining Jewish community was that of Yemen, which managed to survive, albeit in a perpetual state of inferiority and isolation.

See also YEMEN.

ARABS: Semitic people who since ancient times have inhabited the Arabian peninsula and areas adjacent to the land of Israel. The Arabs trace their ancestry to Ishmael, the son of Abraham by Hagar. According to the Bible (Gen. 10), Eber was the forefather both of Abraham and Yoktan, who in turn was the progenitor of the southern Arabs. Between the first centuries B.C.E. and C.E., the Nabatean Arabs, taking advantage of a power vacuum, burst out of the desert and established a powerful kingdom which stretched from Arabia to Syria, and across the Negev to Sinai. They built towns in the Negev and were particularly successful in cultivating its arid regions. Their capital city, Petra, known in antiquity as Sela, was a masterpiece of architecture and planning. The Nabateans spoke and wrote a dialect of the Aramaic language, but also absorbed Greek and Latin culture. They were in evidence for only a few centuries, as the Romans put an end to their empire, and they disappeared back into the desert as swiftly as they had come.

The golden age of Arab history, however, came only after the death of Mohammed (632 C.E.) and the rise of Islam. Within less than one century the Arab empire embraced half of the then known world. By the 9th century when western Europe was sinking deeper and deeper into the Dark Ages, the Arabs had created a dazzling civilization and were the standard bearers of the arts and the sciences. In many of the lands conquered by the Arabs, they were welcomed by the local Jews, who even assisted them in their military campaigns. The Pact of Omar, which discriminated against Jews and Moslems, and according to whose provisions Jews had to pay a special poll tax in return for protection, was not rigidly enforced, and Jews often served with high rank in Mohammedan armies and rose to the highest posts in government service. There were outbreaks of intolerance and persecution, as during the rule of the savage Almohades in North Africa in the 12th century. In general, however, the position of Jews in the Arab world during the Middle Ages was better than in those countries under Christian rule. In Spain in particular, the invasion of the Arabs in 711 brought a new freedom to the Jewish community which, in the course of the following two centuries, became the greatest Jewish center in the world. Personalities such as Ḥasdai Ibn Shaprut and Samuel Ibn Nagrela rose to positions of great influence in Cordova and Granada respectively. Under Arab influence, and at times in cooperation with Arab scholars, Jews devoted themselves to literature, philosophy, and

Israeli Arabs

mathematics. The Arabs revived Jewish interest in the study of classical Greek philosophy, and the Jews thereby became the channel through which classical science reached Europe.

Through lack of unity, the Arab empire began to break up in the 10th century and by the 15th had disappeared under the alternate attacks of the Mongols, Spaniards, and Ottoman Turks. For almost four hundred years, under Turkish rule, the Arabs in the land of Israel and the adjacent territories made no important contribution either culturally or politically. With the exception of the brief reign of the Egyptian viceroy Mohammed Ali between 1831 and 1840, the Arab world was dominated by medieval conditions. In the late 19th and early 20th centuries, Arab nationalism once again began to revive, unfortunately at the same time as the rise of the Zionist movement. During World War I, the Arabs played a minor but important role by rebelling against the Turks under the leadership of Lawrence of Arabia. Their aspirations for independence developed

into a fanatical opposition to colonialism and the Zionist movement. In 1945, with British encouragement, the Arab League was established, consisting of Egypt, Syria, the Lebanon, Iraq, Jordan, Saudi Arabia, and the Yemen. Libya joined in 1953. These states are generally referred to as the Arab states, although many other Moslem countries support the Arab cause. As a result of their decision not to recognize the State of Israel, a state of war has existed for over twenty years. Despite three military defeats, their policy has not changed and their hostility has been encouraged by outside factors, notably the Russians. One of the results of their belligerency has been the tragedy of the Arab refugees. First in 1948, and to a lesser extent in 1967, hundreds of thousands of Arabs fled their homes. In 1948, many of them left at the urging of Arab governments which promised them that they would return in the ranks of the victorious. Some of them emigrated to the West, others found new homes in other Moslem countries, but the majority have remained in refugee camps, depending on international help. The Arab states, rather than make constructive moves to absorb the refugees, have preferred to let them wither in the camps, so that this great humanitarian problem could be used as a political weapon against Israel. The Arab minority which remained in Israel during the 1948–49 war, however, enjoys equal citizenship rights under the law and has eight representatives in the Israeli Parliament. That minority numbered some 300,000 in 1970.

ARAM, ARAMEANS: Warrior tribes which burst into the Middle East (the Fertile Crescent) from about the 15th century B.C.E. on. They are mentioned regularly in Assyrian texts from the end of the 14th century. Although they never succeeded in establishing one large United Kingdom, perhaps because of fierce tribal rivalries, by the end of the 11th century B.C.E. a whole series of independent

Aramean states had been established in upper Mesopotamia. They assimilated the culture and religion of the areas in which they settled and even infiltrated the ruling circles of Babylon. According to the Bible (Gen. 10, 22), Aram and Israel had a common ancestry, and the land of origin of the patriarchs is Aram Naharaim (Aram of the two rivers); i.e., the northeastern area of Mesopotamia. The patriarchs were opposed to intermarriage with the local Canaanite population; thus, Abraham sent his servant Eliezer to his homeland to find a wife for Isaac, and Jacob journeyed northward for the same purpose. The consolidation of the Aramean states in Syria occurred at roughly the same time as the foundation of the Hebrew state in the land of Israel. In the 10th century B.C.E., the Aramean Kingdom of Aram-Zobah in southern Syria attempted, together with other Aramean kingdoms, to check Israelite expansion, and was resoundingly defeated by David. The defeat of Aram-Zobah led to the rise of Aram-Dammesek, so called after its capital, Damascus. The latter was the most important Aramean kingdom in Syria from the 10th to the 8th centuries B.C.E. After the division of Solomon's kingdom, Aram-Dammesek exploited the civil war between Judah and the northern kingdom of Israel to the detriment of the latter. The Aramean wars constitute an important chapter in the history of the northern kingdom. They went on intermittently for 150 years with alternate victories and defeats for both sides. The result was an inconclusive stalemate, but both states were undoubtedly weakened by the perpetual state of warfare. The rise of Assyria with its expansionist ambitions brought about a temporary change. During the 11th and 10th centuries, the Arameans had actually constituted a threat to Assyria, and the latter were hard put at times to defend themselves against the incursions of Aramean bands. It is possible that David's campaigns against Aram-Zobah had given the Assyrians the respite they so badly needed. At any event, when the Assyrian King Shalmaneser III set out on his campaign of conquest in the middle of the 9th century B.C.E., the Arameans and Israelites under King Ahab temporarily united in order to stop him. Such common action, however, was exceptional in the relationships between Israel and Damascus, which were in general bitterly hostile. In the years 735–734 B.C.E., Pekah, King of Israel, and Rezin of Damascus once again united in an attempt to stem the Assyrian advance. The results were fatal to both states, for, in the ensuing campaign of Tiglath Pileser III (733–732), Transjordan and Upper Galilee were severed from the kingdom of Israel. As for Damascus, it was besieged and plundered, its population was exiled, and its existence as an independent state was ended.

The Aramaic language, however, outlived the Aramean states. It spread with varying dialects throughout the Middle East and was, in fact, like English today, the international language of diplomacy. It is the language of the first translation of the Bible; it was the language spoken in Palestine in the late Second Temple period; it was the language of both Talmuds; and more than any other Semitic language, exercised a profound influence on Hebrew. *See also* HEBREW LANGUAGE, SEMITIC LANGUAGES.

ARCHEOLOGY IN THE LAND OF ISRAEL: Archeology is the study of ancient man, as revealed by what he has left behind — the homes he built, the objects he made and used, his writings if he had a written language. Even before archeology could be considered a science, travelers to the Holy Land took an extraordinary interest in such things.

In Israel, interest largely centers on the period and events of Biblical time. But the story of archeology in the country starts very much earlier — at the very dawn of

The Shrine of the Book, Israel Museum

human civilization. More than half a million years earlier, an ape-like man, *Pithecanthropus,* lived by hunting in the Jordan Valley. Apart from Tanganyika (Africa), this is the only spot on earth where his skull fragments have been found, together with tools he shaped from river pebbles: round ones for throwing, "choppers" for cutting and scraping.

When the Ice Age came to this part of the world, the weather farther south was abnormally wet; man sheltered himself from the rain in the caves of Mount Carmel and elsewhere. Each generation camped on the rubbish deposited by earlier inhabitants — their bones, chipped flint tools, crude carvings. Thus a cave floor, dug out in layers, gives us the history of "prehistoric" man. Carmel Man, as he is called, was a cross between an older and less developed breed (Neanderthal Man) and *homo sapiens,* from whom we are all descended. Such a mixture of types had not been found in Europe. But it could have been expected in a land which was always a bridge between three continents.

Finds in and near the Carmel caves indicate that between 10,000 and 7,500 years ago this was also the home of men who emerged from rock shelters to build houses; to gather the early species of wheat and barley; to tame a jackal pup into man's friend and hunting companion, the dog. The next three or four thousand years saw farm animals domesticated; and seed planted, harvested, and ground in stone mortars — which means that porridge and perhaps bread had been added to the diet of meat and fish. Settled villages grew into little towns, such as Jericho on the lower Jordan, which may be the oldest city on earth. The greatest discovery of the late Stone Age was that clay earth mixed with water could be baked into moisture-proof pots. Since styles in earthenware change, the age of a dwelling-site can be judged more or less accurately by the type of pottery, whole or broken, that is found in it.

Ancient remains found in Ashkelon

By 4000 B.C.E., man had learned to smelt copper, as we know from beautiful and useful objects found in scattered places.

Biblical archeology proper begins with the middle Bronze Age (2200–1550 B.C.E.), though there were Canaanite towns in the land before that. From Scripture, we know the names of many towns that have now been excavated: Beisan, Megiddo, Gezer, Ai, Jericho, Hazor, Arad. Each was a city-state, fortified, and probably with a place holy to the gods whose images have also been dug up — the idols against which Scripture warns.

During this period, the land was torn by wars and upset by migrations, such as that of Abraham and his family coming from Ur of the Chaldees in modern Iraq. At first, Abraham lived at Beersheba, shown by excavations to have been a center of settlement in the time of the Patriarchs. Later, the Philistines, a mysterious Aegean people related to the Myceneans of Greece, took over Canaanite cities near the Mediterranean coast. At about the same time, in the 13th or early 12th century B.C.E., the land of Canaan was invaded by several waves of what were probably warlike Hebrew tribes. Many Canaanite towns show layers of burning and destruction dating to the time of Joshua.

The archeological history of the city of Hazor in Galilee is typical. In the time of the Judges, Hazor was the capital of Jabin, the North Canaanite king, whose General Sisera was defeated in battle by the Israelite tribes, an event celebrated by the Song of Deborah. The citadel of Hazor was partially destroyed and repeatedly rebuilt for about two thousand years. Both King Solomon and King Ahab of Israel rebuilt and reinforced its walls. As new towns were built on the ruins of earlier ones, an even-sided, usually flat-topped hill rose above the original place of settlement. The characteristic shape of a Middle Eastern mound or "tel" is easy to recognize. Like the cave floors, it is excavated layer by layer.

The site of Hazor, excavated during five seasons of digging under the direction of Yigael Yadin, has revealed rich remains from many periods. At Ezion-Geber, near present-day Eilat but in Jordan, Nelson Glueck uncovered elaborate furnaces that smelted the copper from King Solomon's mines at Timna.

Other remains have been discovered from the time of the First Temple, including an Israelite sanctuary at Arad, and letters written at the time of Jeremiah, discovered at Lachish.

Exciting discoveries have been made which throw light on the Second Temple period also. Recently the whole area around the Temple in Jerusalem, including vessels that were used in the Temple service, has been uncovered by Benjamin Mazar. The desert fortress of Massada, where a group of Jewish Zealots held out for three years after the fall of the Temple in 70 C.E., was excavated by Yigael Yadin in 1963–1964. Hundreds of volunteers from all over the world helped to clear remarkable palaces

and fortifications built on Massada by Herod the Great, as well as the tragic relics of the Zealots who finally died by their own hands rather than become the slaves of Rome.

Among the finds at Massada were scrolls similar to those from a cave near the Dead Sea. (The Dead Sea Scrolls are a discovery of unparalleled importance and are described in a separate article).

The Roman occupation left behind it fortifications, tombs, statuary, and great open-air theaters at Beisan (Bet Shean) and Caesarea, which have been uncovered. Exploration of the Judean Desert caves (dangerous even for experienced rock climbers), has produced letters from the last Jewish Revolt under Bar Kokhba (132–135 C.E.), together with skeletons, clothing, dried food, and other relics of fugitives fleeing the Roman legions.

But even after this last revolt, Jewish learning flourished. The huge underground burial center of Bet Shearim, with its wall paintings, sculptures, and stone sarcophagi inscribed in Hebrew and Greek, demonstrates the richness of Talmudic times. Many ancient synagogues have also been found, including a partly restored 3rd century building at Capernaum, on the shores of the Sea of Galilee; the beautiful mosaic floor of a 6th century synagogue at Bet Alpha in the Jezreel Valley; and the wonderfully decorated synagogue, not in the land of Israel, but at Dura-Europos in Syria, whose walls vividly depict scenes from the Bible.

Many remains of ancient Christian churches and monasteries survive in Israel. Arab and crusader ruins abound, such as the White Mosque of Ramlah, the knights' refectory at Acre, and crusader castles such as Montfort and Athlit. In Israel, excavating is a profession as well as the hobby of an extraordinarily large and well-informed section of the public — as of course it would be in a country so full of man's history. Archeologists have also discovered many

Remains of Talmudic period synagogue at Baram

remains outside the Land of Israel that are important to the Jewish people — for example, at Elephantine, a fortress island in the Nile near Aswan, which was manned by a Jewish garrison in the 6th century B.C.E., and fine synagogues at Ostia near Rome and at Sardis in Turkey.

See also BET SHEAN, BET SHEARIM, CAESARIA, DEAD SEA SCROLLS, MASSADA.

ARGENTINA: The Jews of the South American republic of Argentina, numbering approximately 450,000, comprise more than half of the Jewish population of Latin America. Most of them live in Buenos Aires, but there are also communities in such other cities as Rosario and Santa Fe. Together, they form the sixth largest Jewish community in the world.

The *Delegación de Asociaciones Israelitas Argentinas* (DAIA) is the representative body of Argentinian Jewry. Other organizations, both Ashkenazi and Sephardi, operate schools and youth groups, and sponsor and participate in social events and philanthropic activities. The library of YIVO (initials in Yiddish for Institute for Jewish Research) is one of the largest and most important Jewish libraries on the continent. There are also two Yiddish dailies, several Jewish publications in Spanish, a Yiddish theater, training seminaries for teachers, and an active Zionist movement.

The first Jews in Argentina were Marranos (Spanish and Portuguese descendants of baptized Jews of the 16th century) who were fleeing the inquisition. Most of them were absorbed into Argentina's Christian population. During the first half of the 19th century, Jewish traders from western and central Europe arrived, and the first Jewish community in Argentina was established in Buenos Aires in 1862. Toward the end of the century they were joined by East European Jews who were fleeing the pogroms in Russia and Poland.

In 1891, Baron de Hirsch organized Jewish immigration and subsidized agricultural settlements in Argentina. Most of the original colonies no longer exist, but they formed the basis for what is still the best organized Jewish community in Latin America.

The last major wave of Jewish immigrants came after World War I when Jews from Mediterranean countries began to arrive. Since then immigration has slowed to a trickle. As in other countries, Jews have played a major role in various spheres of life, producing such noted figures as the poet Carlos Grunberg, and the leader of the Argentine socialist movement, Dr. Enrico Dickman. Early in the 20th century a Jew was elected to the Chamber of Deputies of the National Congress. During the early 1960's a fascist organization calling itself *Tacuara* organized a number of anti-Semitic outbreaks, as a result of which emigration from Argentina to Israel increased.

ARK: The ark of the covenant constructed in accordance with the instructions of God (Exodus 25:10–22) to contain the two tablets of the law which Moses received on

Mount Sinai. Throughout the wanderings of the children of Israel, the ark was carried by the Levites; when the tribe was stationary, the ark was placed in the Holy of Holies inside the Tabernacle, and such was its sanctity that even the High Priest could see it only once a year on the Day of Atonement. The ark symbolized the covenant between God and the children of Israel, hence the term, Ark of the Covenant. After the conquest of the land, the ark was placed in the sanctuary at Shiloh, but from time to time it was removed in order to accompany the Israelites into battle. On one of these occasions, it fell into the hands of the Philistines, but after they had been stricken with plagues, they returned it. David brought the ark to Jerusalem, and during the period of the First Temple, it was housed permanently in the Holy of Holies and never removed. The fate of the ark was wrapped up with that of the Temple, and after the destruction of the latter, the ark does not reappear. It is the subject of many rabbinic legends and sayings.

In the synagogue, the shrine in which the scrolls of the Torah are kept is also called the ark or the Holy Ark, *Aron Ha-Kodesh*. Sephardim refer to it as the *Heikhal* or Shrine. During Talmudic times, it was called *tevah* or chest and was a portable object which was brought into the synagogue only when needed for the service. With the passage of time, however, the ark became the central feature of the synagogue and the subject of much artistic design. For the past thousand years, it has been built into the eastern wall, i.e., the wall facing in the direction of Jerusalem. In western countries, it has become customary to surmount the ark with tablets bearing the Ten Commandments. The eternal lamp *(Ner Tamid)* is arranged in front of or near the ark, and a curtain called *parokhet* generally hangs before it. When, during the course of the services, the ark is opened, the congregation is obliged to rise.

ARMED FORCES, JEWS IN: Although the organizational and fighting capabilities of the modern Israeli Army are frequently spoken of as "surprising" for a people so unused to fighting, Jewish history is in fact rich with stories of military prowess and valor. In Biblical times, Israel was called upon again and again to defend herself on the field of battle. The early Jewish tribal system included mass conscription of every able-bodied male into a form of citizen's army. The units of military organization were the *mishpaḥot* (families) and the *betei avot* (clans). The need for military leadership in the long war against the Philistines was actually responsible for the establishment of the Israelite monarchy, and all the early kings distinguished themselves in battle. By King Solomon's time, Israel had a regular standing army equipped with chariots and augmented by foreign mercenaries. Later, in the period of Ezra and Nehemiah, the nation's defense was once again in the hands of a citizen militia.

The Biblical period gave Israel many heroes and legends, and the individual stories are endless. There was Joshua who led the Israelites to victory over the Canaanites against overwhelming odds; Saul, who defeated the Ammonites, Moabites, Edomites, Arameans, and Amalekites before dying a hero on the battlefield of Mt. Gilboa; King David, the almost legendary boy-warrior who as king secured and expanded Israel's borders through battle. In the book of Kings we read of such heroes as King Zimri who died in the flames of his palace rather than surrender; and King Ahab who, after being mortally wounded, remained standing in his chariot until the evening so that his soldiers would not lose confidence in the successful outcome of the battle — he died hours later, only after victory was assured.

The Maccabean uprising of 165 B.C.E. is one of the most striking cases of military courage and ability in Jewish history. Operating at first in simple guerrilla bands fighting with only the most primitive weapons, the Jews were slowly organized into a regular fighting organization by Judah the Maccabee, and eventually they defeated the Syrians and recaptured Jerusalem. Although Judah is the most famous of the Maccabee fighters, he was only one of five brothers in the Hasmonean family; the other four also distinguished themselves in battle against the Syrians.

In the year 66 C.E. the Jews revolted against Roman rule in the land of Israel and for four years opposed the might of Rome. One group of warriors and their families held out another three years in the Dead Sea fortress of Massada. In a further attempt to throw off the Roman yoke, in 132 C.E. Simeon Bar Kokhba challenged the forces of the Roman Emperor Hadrian. A strong-willed man with a leader's personality and real military talent, Bar Kokhba succeeded in organizing a nearly total popular revolt among the Jews, who were able to hold the best Roman forces at bay for over three years.

Jews often also played a military role outside the land of Israel. From the 6th century B.C.E., Jews served as garrison troops and military settlers under the Ptolemies in Egypt. In the 6th century in North Africa, the warrior-queen Dahia al-Kahinah became a legend. During the Moslem-Christian wars, Jews fought on both sides, and many Marranos (Spanish Jews who were nominal Christians) participated in the Spanish conquest of the New World. A Jewish conquistador, Alonso Hernando, fought against the Aztecs for five years with Cortez and was at the battle for Montezuma's capital. He was burned at the stake in 1528 as a Jewish heretic. In general however, in the Middle Ages Jews were excluded from military service.

Only with the advent of Emancipation in modern times could Jews once again take an active part in military affairs. One outstanding example was the Polish hero Berek Joselowicz, who fell leading a charge against the Austrians.

In World Wars I and II, there were massive Jewish enlistments in all of the Allied armies, and proportionately more Jews fought and died than non-Jews. In World War I the Australian Jew Sir John Monash, was in command of the Australian army in Europe. 400,000 Jews fought in the Soviet forces alone in World War II, including many officers and soldiers who were decorated for distinguished service.

Jews have served in all the American wars since the Revolution, and in World War II, there were over a half-million Jewish soldiers in the various American armed forces — 53,000 of whom were decorated for bravery.

(For a more detailed account of Jewish participation in the two World Wars, see articles on THE JEWISH LEGION and the JEWISH BRIGADE, and for development of the army in Israel see ISRAEL DEFENSE FORCES).

ART, JEWISH: The earliest records of Jewish art are the descriptions of the ornamentation of the Tabernacle in the wilderness, and of Solomon's Temple in Jerusalem. Later, with the growth of prosperity in Samaria, rich animal and floral decorations in metal and ivory (resembling contemporary Phoenician work) began to appear, specimens of which have been discovered in recent excavations. The age of the Hasmoneans and of Herod witnessed a great development in coins, funerary monuments, and buildings, all in the Graeco-Roman style. This tradition was also followed in the synagogues erected in Palestine and elsewhere in the succeeding centuries; of these, massive remains still stand. They were decorated with mosaics (as at Bet Alpha) and frescoes (as at Dura Europos) depicting Biblical episodes and familiar Judaic symbols, such as the etrog, lulav, and menorah. Under Moslem rule and influence, the figurative motifs were

Paintings from Dura-Europos synagogue (ca. 245)

abandoned. In the 9th to 14th centuries, illuminated manuscripts were produced in Egypt, Palestine, and Syria. In these manuscripts, emphasis was placed on penmanship and geometric ornamentation.

Jewish art received a new impetus in Christian Spain, France, Germany, and Italy. French and German synagogues of the 12th century were decorated with wall-paintings. The Passover Haggadah, prayer-books, and Bibles were illustrated with miniatures. With the introduction of printing, woodcuts and engravings were substituted for the illuminations. The illustration cycles created in Prague and later in Venice and Amsterdam were copied in Germany in the 17th and 18th centuries and modified by self-taught limners in Moravia and Hungary. The Scroll of Esther *(megillah)* and the marriage contract *(ketubbah)* were

favorite subjects for illumination. The walls of synagogues in Galicia, Russian Poland, and the Ukraine were decorated with allegorical animals, views of the Holy City, and the zodiac. The furnishings of the synagogues were adorned with carved woodwork. Artists who lived in Jewish quarters often depicted Jews in their art, as, for example, Rembrandt in his painting of Moses holding the Tablets of the Law.

In the 19th century Solomon Hart of England, Moritz Oppenheim of Germany, and the Dutch painter Jozef Israels, turned to Jewish themes. In the late 19th and early 20th centuries Lesser Ury, Herman Struck, and Ephraim Lilien found inspiration in Judaism, particularly in the Zionist cause. The work of Marc Chagall portrays his Jewish village life in Russia, as well as Biblical motifs. Russian village life also

Ornamental wall at Ceramics Musem, Tel Aviv

forms part of the work of Issachar Ryback, and Simon Glatzer. In the Parisian school Mané Katz depicted Jewish subject matter in vivid colors. Arthur Szyk successfully used the old technique of book illumination. The American painters Ben Shahn and Hyman Bloom continued the Jewish tradition. Ben Zion has interpreted Biblical themes with vigor; and Ilya Shorr is an illustrator, painter of still life, and silversmith.

Jewish subjects portrayed in three dimensional sculpture occurred rarely until the 19th century because of the Biblical injunction in Deuteronomy: 4:16–18 against making likenesses of living creatures. Boris Schatz, Jacob Ezekiel, Jacob Guttmann, and Samuel Beer were among the first to deal with Jewish themes in sculpture. Hana Orloff attained unusual power of characterization through simplification of forms.

Sculpture has become an important part of synagogue architecture, especially in the United States, where Reform and Conservative congregations have commissioned sculptors to design their synagogues.

Contemporary Israeli art originated with the founding of the Bezalel School of Arts by Boris Schatz, assisted by E. M. Lilien, in 1906. Its early teachers and artists included Hershenberg, Pann, and the brothers Goldberg. In the course of time, it became a school of arts and crafts directed by Yoseph Budko and later by Mordekhai Ardon. A native style, fostering both Oriental and European traditions, was developed. Israel educated or attracted many artists such as Ardon, Aschheim, Blum, Nahum Gutman, Holzmann, Mokady, Zaritsky, Janco, Levanon, Litvinovsky, Sigart, Yohanan Simon, Steinhardt, Sima, Sobel, Kosonogi,

Artists at work in Israel

Castel, and Rubin, working in oil, gouache, pastel, and water color; while Anna Ticho and Krakauer have drawn chiefly in black and white. Originality is the keynote of the book illustrations of Gutman, Navon, and Stern. Sculpture also begins with Boris Schatz, whose work was primarily in the field of the plastic arts. Important names in this field are Melnikoff, Lishansky, Ben Zvi, and Priver. Abstract concepts can be seen in the work of Sternschuss and Danziger. Public construction has resulted in some unusually striking buildings, such as the Knesset, the Israel Museum, and the Pevsner Hall of the Reali High School in Haifa. Israeli crafts, including textiles, embroidery, silver metalwork, and brassware, show the decided influence of the Yemenite Jews, as well as strong modern lines. Ceramics is an important craft and has attracted such talents as Elspeth Cohen and Penina Harel. Both ceramics and glassware in their utilitarian aspects have been helped by factories devoted to their production in Lapid, Harsa, and Gavish. The artistry in glassware and stained glass in Israel is prominently displayed in one of the pavilions of the Tel Aviv Haaretz Museum and in decorated windows of many synagogues.

See also ISRAEL MUSEUM; CHAGALL, MARC.

ASHKENAZIM: Term now commonly used to refer to Western Jews (or Jews of Western origin, culture, and tradition), as opposed to those from Eastern countries. During the late Middle Ages, it became common to divide world Jewry into two separate categories, the Ashkenazim and the Sephardim. The division was rather arbitrary, based mainly on the geographical location and the language of daily use characterizing the various Jewish communities. The Sephardim usually included those Jews originating from Spain and Portugal, and the Ashkenazim were the Jews of Central and Eastern Europe. For the most part, the Ashkenazim and Sephardim differed only in slight variations in the prayer ritual, in their manner of observing religious customs, and in their way of pronouncing Hebrew.

The Ashkenazim got their name from the word *Ashkenaz,* the term used by scholars of the Middle Ages to refer to Germany. According to the Book of Genesis, Ashkenaz was a great-grandson of Noah. When the Jewish scholars of the Middle Ages worked out their sometimes imaginative distribution of mankind following the Great Flood, they somehow determined that Ashkenaz and his descendants were the ancestors of the people living in what we now call Germany. Thus the Jews living in Germany came to be called Ashkenazim. Following the Black Death plague in Europe (1348–49) and the massive persecution of the German Jews at that time, these Jews migrated and, over the centuries, came to be distributed throughout Europe. And as these Jewish communities were dispersed, the term Ashkenazim took on its more general meaning embracing all the Jews of Eastern and Central Europe. In addition to their prayer ritual and religious customs, the European Jews were united also by their common use of the Yiddish language.

The Billy Rose sculpture garden, Israel Museum

From time to time, there has been rivalry between the Ashkenazim and Sephardim. For example, in 18th century England, the Sephardim were the aristocrats of the community, and if one of their children married an Ashkenazi, the family severed relations with its offending member. In most countries, nowadays, largely as a result of continued intermarriage, the tendency is toward a gradual obliteration of differences.

The same will eventually be true in Israel. At first there was a marked cultural difference between Ashkenazim and Sephardim (and in Israel the latter term was generally used to include all Jews of oriental origin). This even led at times to tension between the two groups. But as the cultural gap is narrowed and as there is growing intermarriage, it seems safe to predict that in two or three generations the differences will disappear. Since the early 1920's in Israel there have been both an Ashkenazi and Sephardi Chief Rabbi because of the differences in customs between the two communities, but here, too, it has been suggested that the time is rapidly approaching when this division will be unnecessary.

ASSYRIA: Ancient empire of western Asia, which flourished from the 20th to the 5th centuries B.C.E. Her fortunes fluctuated, alternating between periods of expansion in the 13th and 10th centuries and intermediate periods of decline. During the first five hundred years of Israel's existence as a people, there was a power vacuum in the ancient Near East, and this enabled the Israelite State to consolidate and even expand without the fear of coming into conflict with a major world power. From the middle of the 8th century, all this changed, because at that time Assyria took the path of empire in earnest. A hundred years previously, the first contact between Assyria and Israel was made when Ahab, king of Israel, joined a coalition of local rulers and fought against the Assyrian king Shalmaneser III (859–824) at the battle of Quarqar in Northern Syria. Although Shalmaneser boasted of a smashing victory, it appears that he was temporarily checked. In the year 746 B.C.E., one of the ablest rulers of ancient times, Tiglath Pileser III, ascended the Assyrian throne. He has justifiably been called the "Empire builder," for, under him, Assyrian arms conquered vast territories and subjugated numerous peoples. Tiglath Pileser was also the originator of the policy of the dispersal, exile, and interchange of conquered populations, hoping thus to prevent local rebellions. The Assyrian war machine in its strategical and tactical policy, as well as the equipment of its armies, was unparalleled in ancient history up till that time. In 735 B.C.E. Ahaz, King of Judah, refused to join an anti-Assyrian coalition in alliance with Pekah, king of Israel, Damascus, Edom, and Philistia. The allies attacked Judah whereupon Ahaz appealed to Tiglath Pileser for help, against the advice of the prophet Isaiah. In the resulting campaign, the Northern Kingdom of Israel lost its territory in Transjordan and Galilee, and the remaining members of the coalition were routed and became Assyrian provinces. Judah, while nominally retaining its independence, was, in effect, an Assyrian vassal state. A further desperate effort by Hosea, King of Israel, to throw off the Assyrian yoke in 726 B.C.E. led to the siege of Samaria by Shalmaneser V, and its capture in 721 by his successor Sargon. The latter exiled 27,900 Israelites and replaced them with a conglomeration of subject peoples from all over the empire. The Northern Kingdom thus ceased to exist.

Assyria was constantly confronted with uprisings and rebellions and was hard put to maintain control of what was now a vast and sprawling empire. In the year 705 B.C.E., King Hezekiah of Judah, at the urging of Babylon, and with the promise of aid from Egypt, participated in what became a general uprising throughout the Assyrian Empire. The Prophet Isaiah opposed the rebellion and regarded Egypt as an unreliable ally, and his view was upheld by subsequent events. The Assyrian monarch Sennacherib subdued his opponents one by one, and, in the years 701 and 700, he defeated the Egyptians, sacked Ascalon, and after capturing all the Judean fortresses including Lachish, he besieged Jerusalem. Only a last minute miracle, in which a plague broke out among the Assyrian forces, saved Jerusalem from inevitable destruction. Assyrian power reached its peak during the reigns of Esarhaddon (681–669) and Ashurbanipal (660–630?), culminating in the total conquest of Egypt. In 652, Manasseh, King of Judah, accused of conspiring against Ashurbanipal, was summoned to Assyria. It seems, however, that he was able to convince the Assyrians of his loyalty. After the death of Ashurbanipal, Assyria declined rapidly and, within the space of twenty years, fell to a coalition of Babylonians and Medes.

ASTROLOGY and **ASTRONOMY**: The pseudo-science of astrology (which assumes and professes to interpret the influence of heavenly bodies on human affairs) seems to be as old as man. Ever since ancient times, astrologers have been claiming that the stars and planets exert an influence on earthly events and individual human lives. The Bible mentions astrology and astrologers several times, but always in negative terms. Jeremiah refers to astrological beliefs as belonging to heathen practice, and, in foretelling Israel's doom because of her wayward behavior, Isaiah mockingly says, "Let now the astrologers, the stargazers, the monthly prognosticators, stand up and save thee from these things which shall come upon thee."

While strictly forbidden by Scripture, astrology has nevertheless always captured the imagination of Jewish scholars, and more than one thinker has succumbed to the lure of its predictions. Thus Rabbi Hanina says in the Talmud that "The planet of a person decides whether he shall be wise or wealthy, and Israel has its planet." This opinion is strongly contested by Rabbi Johanan who quotes Jeremiah's warning against paganism, but his protest is not the last word in Talmudic debate on the subject. Usually, Talmudic scholars restricted themselves to arguing that Israel is beyond the influence of the stars, but agreed that other nations and peoples are indeed subject to such influence.

During the Middle Ages, many rabbis and philosophers studied astrology, and Jews were regarded by most of the Western world as masters of this art. Several Jews served as court astrologers for European kings and princes, especially in Spain. Maimonides stood out among medieval Jewish thinkers in completely condemning astrology, saying, "It is not fitting for Jews to be attracted by these follies. Whosoever believes that they are possible is a fool." Yet, despite such reminders, many Jewish thinkers accepted certain astrological beliefs. The Zohar and other mystical literature discuss various aspects of astrology; and some medieval Jewish customs, such as not starting a project on Mondays or Wednesdays, have their origin in astrology. The universal Jewish phrase for congratulation, *Mazal Tov,* is also of astrological origin, as "Good luck" means "I wish you a good constellation."

The much more serious science of astronomy, which concerns the laws governing the movements of the stars and planets, has attracted the attention of Jewish scholars. The Talmud recognizes the importance of astronomical calculations for determining the New Moon and hence the proper dates for festivals, etc.; and the famous Sage, Samuel, claimed that he knew the paths of the stars as well as the roads of his home town. Talmudic scholars generally agreed with the contemporary view that the earth was the center of the universe, and they further held that the "seven heavens" were placed above the earth as a canopy.

In the Middle Ages, Jewish astronomers translated many important astronomical works from Arabic into Latin and Spanish, and they were the chief authors of the astronomical tables drawn up in Spain during the Middle Ages. In modern times, a number of Jews have distinguished themselves in astronomy, and the development of modern cosmology and astrophysics is largely due to the work of Albert Einstein.

ATONEMENT, DAY OF (Yom Kippur):

The most solemn day in the Jewish calendar, described in the Bible as the Sabbath of Sabbaths. It occurs on the tenth day of Tishri, and is the culmination of the ten days of penitence which begin with *Rosh Ha-Shanah*. It is celebrated as a solemn fast from sunset to sunset. The Bible demands the absolute cessation of labor and the strictest abstention from food and drink. In addition, it is forbidden to anoint the body with oil and to wear leather shoes, while married couples are enjoined to abstain from marital relations. All the prohibitions are designed to invest this day with a purely spiritual nature. Man is at one with his Maker and, in order to be so, he must attempt to free himself from his physical passions and desires. Judaism never accepted the inevitability of sin. Man is able, Judaism affirms, to overcome temptation. If, however, as is only natural, he sometimes falls, he may regain his spiritual stature through genuine repentance. This involves the consciousness of his sins, the courage to confess his guilt, regret for the evil done, and the resolve not to sin again. While man may repent throughout the year, the ten days of penitence culminating in the Day of Atonement were considered especially appropriate for repentance by the rabbis.

Day of Atonement among Amsterdam Ashkenazim (1725)

The description of the Day of Atonement celebration during the Second Temple period has been preserved in the Talmud. The ancient ritual consisted of the selection of a scapegoat symbolically laden with the nation's sins, and its dispatch to the wilderness of Azazel where it met its doom by being thrown from a precipice. Three times did the High Priest make confession of sin; first on his own behalf, then on behalf of the entire Priestly order, and finally for all Israel. The climax of the Temple ritual came when the High Priest entered the Holy of Holies, the only occasion throughout the year in which he was permitted to do so. There, he sprinkled the blood of the sacrifice and made an incense offering. On the Day of Atonement, the High Priest exchanged his golden vestments for white linen, the symbol of purity and humility. It is also the symbol of optimism, for the Day of Atonement is not a sad day nor a day of gloom. It is a solemn day, one of fasting and penitence, which is accompanied by an optimistic conviction that the God of Israel, who is a God of mercy, will forgive the sins of His people. Thus, at the conclusion of the fast, the High Priest gave a banquet at his house where the atmosphere was one of jubilation.

With the exception of the sacrificial ritual, the basic outline of the Temple service has been retained in the synagogue. The services have been deliberately lengthened and embroidered with additional hymns and poetry so as to ensure that congregants remain in the synagogue for the entire day. There are five statutory religious services on the Day of Atonement: in the evening 1. *Maariv;* during the day 2. *Shaharit,* 3. *Musaph,* 4. *Minḥah,* and 5. *Neilah.*

The evening service has become associated with the recitation of *Kol Nidrei* and is often referred to by that name, although, strictly speaking, *Kol Nidrei* precedes *Maariv* and is not part of it. *Kol Nidrei* is a declaration which states that all vows made rashly or unwittingly shall be considered null and void. Originally, the formula referred to vows made during the past year. The medieval Talmudist, Rabbenu Tam, altered the text so as to refer to vows of the forthcoming year. The Ashkenazim accepted his version while the Italian Jews retained the original one. Sephardim and Ashkenazim in the State of Israel combine the two. The origin of the declaration is shrouded in mystery, but most scholars are of the opinion that it dates back to the early Gaonic period. In the 9th century, some of the Babylonian *Geonim* opposed its utterance. *Kol Nidrei* has been the object of attack on the part of anti-Semites who point to its formula as proof that the word of a Jew cannot be trusted if he is so easily able to annul his vows. In fact, as the rabbis have stressed, *Kol Nidrei* refers only to vows made by a man to God; vows which concern another person cannot be arbitrarily cancelled without mutual agreement. With time, *Kol Nidrei* became firmly rooted in Jewish tradition and even endowed with a certain sanctity. The solemn and moving tune with which it is chanted has contributed greatly to its popularity.

The services are distinguished by the recital of confessions. These confessions are, like all Jewish congregational prayer, written in the plural. With one exception, all the sins mentioned relate to man's moral and ethical conduct and not sins of a ceremonial nature.

The reading of the Pentateuch during the morning service deals with the ritual of the Day of Atonement (Lev. 16; Num. 19:7–11) and the Prophetical portion is taken from Isaiah (57:14; 58:14). The additional service is characterized by the inclusion of the *Avodah,* the description of the ritual in the Temple, referred to above, and a moving narration of the martyrdom of ten great sages during the persecutions by the Roman emperor Hadrian in 135 C.E. At *Minḥah,* there is a further *Torah* reading (Lev. 28), and the *Haphtarah* is the book of Jonah with its message of repentance and God's mercy for all mankind. It is considered a special honor to read this *Haphtarah.*

The concluding service for the Day of Atonement is called *Neilah.* Its theme is the impending closing of the gates of heaven and the pleas of the congregation for Divine pardon. The service concludes impressively with the congregational chanting of *Shema Yisrael,* the sounding of the *shophar* and the prayer, Next Year in Jerusalem (in Israel: Jerusalem Rebuilt). The *tallit* is worn at all five services.

The Day of Atonement, say the rabbis, atones only for sins committed between man and God. Wrongs against one's fellow human beings cannot be forgiven until the wronged person has been placated and his forgiveness sought.

AUSTRALIA: Jews were among the earliest settlers in Australia, the first congregation being established in Sydney in 1817. With the founding of the other principal cities such as Melbourne, Brisbane, and Adelaide, further Jewish communities were established. For a long time, the Australian Jewish community was isolated and numerically small. Various Australian governments, however, encouraged immigration in general, and, as a result of this policy, the Jewish population has doubled in the past thirty-five years, numbering today some 70,000. With the increased immigration, especially of European Jews, traditional Judaism was strengthened. Australian Jewish communal life is patterned on that of English Jewry and most of the congregations accept the authority of the Chief Rabbi of the British Empire and are traditional in character. Reform congregations however, have been established in the larger centers. In recent years, Jewish education has made rapid strides, with the establishment of Yeshivot and Hebrew day schools. The Mount Scopus day school in Melbourne is one of the largest of its kind

Sir Isaac Isaacs, Australia's first Gov. General

in the world. There is an active and well organized Zionist movement, and immigration to Israel increased after the 1967 Six-Day War. The Jews of each state have their elected representative body of Australian Jewry, known as the Executive Council of Australian Jewry. Anti-Semitism has never assumed major proportions, and Jews enjoy full equality and citizenship rights. A number of Jews have served as state cabinet ministers, members of parliament, and mayors. The first Australian-born Governor General was a Jew, Sir Isaac Isaacs, as was the commander of the Australian expeditionary force in World War I, Sir John Monash, after whom one of Australia's leading universities is named.

AUSTRIA: While Jews may have reached Austria as early as the Roman period, the first specific reference to them dates to 906, when new Customs Laws gave Jewish merchants equality with their Christian colleagues. During the First Crusade (1096), persecution and the destruction of many communities sent masses of Jews from Germany to Austria, where life remained relatively tranquil. In the 13th century, protection against the enmity of the church and local people was guaranteed by special princely charters in return for which the

Jews paid heavy taxes and dues. From the 14th century, however, the Jews suffered recurrent attacks and persecution. A ritual murder charge in 1420, prompted Albrecht V to burn, baptize, or banish the Jews, confiscating their property. A special badge was imposed from 1592 and, in 1670, the Jews were again banished from Austria. They reappeared in the 18th century, the few "Hofjuden" or "Court Jews" needed to administer the Empire's finances being permitted to settle in Vienna with their families despite Empress Maria Theresa's hostility. On January 2, 1782, her successor, Joseph II, issued his Edict of Toleration, which declared that the disabilities of the Jews were to be gradually removed and that they were to be encouraged to share more equitably in the life of the general population. For all its apparent reversal of contemporary Catholic policy, Austrian Jews were rightly suspicious that the Edict's true purpose was to undermine the Jews' religious traditions and force them to assimilate, although only very wealthy Jews were welcomed as equals by the Christian population. Joseph's successors allowed the Edict's provisions to lapse, making it, in fact, meaningless.

Jews played an important part in the 1848 uprising in Austria. In Vienna, two young Jewish physicians, Adolf Fischhof and Joseph Goldmark, became the chief architects of the revolutionary movement. Thereafter, the community grew in numbers and importance and in 1867 full civil and political equality was granted the Jews. An outbreak of Anti-Semitism sponsored by the Catholic Christian Social Party led by the Mayor of Vienna, Karl Lueger, occurred in 1900. Despite this, the community continued to grow. By 1938, the year the Nazis invaded, it numbered 200,000 and included many of the intellectual and cultural "stars" that made the Vienna of this period so famous. Eighty thousand Jews managed to get out of Austria before the beginning of World War II, but one hundred thousand were annihilated by the Nazis. From the end of World War II, the small Jewish population, numbering approximately 15,000, has enjoyed full equality. One of them, Bruno Kreisky, became Austria's Prime Minister.

AV, NINTH OF (Tishah Be'Av): Fast day commemorating the anniversary of the destruction of the First and Second Temples. This is the only fast besides the Day of Atonement which lasts for twenty-four hours, from sunset to sunset. According to Jewish tradition, the greatest catastrophes in Jewish history occurred on this day. The First Temple was destroyed by the Babylonians in the year 586 B.C.E. on the 9th of Av. The Second Temple was burned about the same date by Titus in the year 70 C.E. Likewise, in the year 135 C.E., the rebellion against Rome led by Bar Kokhba ended with the fall of Betar on the 9th of Av. Numerous tragedies in later Jewish history, including the expulsion of the Jews from Spain in the year 1492, are also said to have occurred on this day. The ninth of Av is accordingly the saddest day in the Jewish calendar, (although according to one legend it will be the birthday of the Messiah). In its restrictions, the fast resembles the Day of Atonement, although there is no prohibition against work. In the evening, the Book of Lamentations is read, and, during the morning service, *Kinot* (dirges which include compositions dealing with tragedies in later Jewish history) are recited. All ornaments are removed from the synagogue, and the congregants sit on low stools or on the floor. A unique feature of the service is that the *tallit* and *tephillin* are not worn at the morning service but at the afternoon service. If the ninth of Av falls on a Sabbath, the fast is postponed to the following day. Since the Six-Day War of June 1967 which resulted in the unification of Jerusalem, the age-old custom of making a pilgrimage to the Western Wall on the 9th of Av has been renewed. Reform Jews do not observe the 9th of Av as a fast day.

AVOT (or *Pirkei Avot;* known in English as *The Sayings* or *Ethics of the Fathers*): A collection of wise sayings by the early rabbis which appears in the 4th order of the *Mishnah, Nezikin.* It is divided into five chapters. The first chapter is meant to illustrate the uninterrupted passing on from generation to generation of the oral tradition received by Moses from God, until it reached the rabbis of the Mishnah who committed it to writing. This is done by presenting wise sayings from great rabbinical teachers over a period of many generations. The remaining four chapters present short maxims, each of which makes some moral point or gives a wise word of advice on how a good Jew should conduct his life. A sixth chapter in a similar strain was added much later. *Avot* does not teach any formal principles of Jewish law, and there are no learned commentaries to explain and elaborate the various sayings. And yet, because it is such a very human book and so richly steeped in the wisdom of the great teachers, it is one of the most loved and respected books of Jewish literature. It is the only work of its kind to be included in the prayer-book, and among Ashkenazi congregations it is read in the synagogue as a part of the Sabbath afternoon service during the summer months. Sephardi Jews read it only as a part of devotion.

BABYLONIA and **BABYLONIAN EXILE:** Ancient empire in lower Mesopotamia (now Iraq). There were two periods in ancient history when Babylonia was a major power and the center of a rich culture. One thousand years divides these two periods, and both of them were followed by a rapid decline. The first is associated with the name of the 6th king of the 1st Babylonian dynasty — Hammurabi (1716–1673 B.C.E., or according to some scholars, 1792–1750 B.C.E.). Under him, Babylonia expanded and became the major power in Mesopotamia. Hammurabi was the author of a code of law which has attracted the interest of scholars because of its similarity to the legal sections of the book of Exodus. After his death Babylonia declined, and in the ensuing centuries was often ruled by foreign kings. At Babylon, there was a famous tower called *E-Temen-An-Ki* (the Temple of the Foundations of Heaven and Earth), and many scholars are of the opinion that the Biblical story of the Tower of Babel, according to which Babylon was the cradle of humanity, has its origins in the existence of this edifice.

The second period of Babylonian ascendancy, and the one which played a vital role in Jewish history, is that of the neo-Babylonian empire. Under the Chaldean prince Nabopolassar (626–605 B.C.E.), Babylonia threw off the Assyrian yoke and, in cooperation with the Medes, stormed the Assyrian capital, Asshur, and in 612 captured Nineveh itself. A counterattack by the Assyrians with the help of Egypt in the year 609 failed, and as a result Assyria was finished. In the year

605, Nabopolassar's son, Nebuchadnezzar, defeated the Egyptians, and Judah thereby came into the Babylonian sphere of influence. Judah's refusal to accept Babylonian hegemony, and her repeated military alliances with Egypt, led to disaster. In 597 Jerusalem was conquered, and the King Jehoiachin, his leading officials, and members of the aristocracy and the army, were exiled to Babylonia. Instead of drawing the necessary conclusions, King Zedekiah, who was under the influence of extremist advisors, repeated the folly of his predecessors. In 589 B.C.E. rebellion once again broke out. Despite temporary Egyptian assistance, Judah was doomed, and in the year 586 B.C.E. the Temple of King Solomon was destroyed by the Babylonian forces and the population of Judah deported to Babylonia. The attempt, encouraged by the Babylonians, to set up a partially autonomous state under Gedaliah was ended by his assassination at the hands of the anti-Babylonian party. The state of Judah had ceased to exist. In Babylonia, the lot of the exiles was not as bitter as had been expected. Despite their yearnings for the land of Israel, the exiles not only managed to exist but also laid the foundations for future developments in Judaism. Under the guidance of such leaders as the prophet Ezekiel, they successfully adapted Judaism to their new conditions and were able partially to fill the gap created by the loss of the Temple. In the opinion of most scholars, it was in Babylonia that the institution of the synagogue developed. The Babylonians seem to have been reasonably tolerant toward the exiles, and in 561 B.C.E. the ex-king,

Bar-Kochba finds, Israel Museum

The Tower of Babel, Byzantine mosaic at Palermo

Jehoiachin, was released from prison and accorded royal honors.

Babylonia's days, however, were numbered. Two factors were mainly responsible for the dissolution of the Babylonian Empire: internal religious disputes and the meteoric rise of the Persian king, Cyrus. In 539, Babylonia fell without a fight, the majority of its citizens actually welcoming Cyrus. By 538, all western Asia to the Egyptian frontier was his.

Cyrus was a tolerant monarch, one of the most truly enlightened rulers of ancient times. He was particularly respectful of his subjects' religious beliefs and assisted in the restoration of temples throughout his empire. Within the framework of the empire, he believed in allowing the subject peoples as much cultural and religious autonomy as possible. It was in accordance with this policy that he issued his famous proclamation allowing those Jews who so desired to return to the land of Israel in order to rebuild the Temple. The vast majority of Jews chose to remain in Babylon, where they had by this time become established both financially and socially. From this time on, Babylonian Jewry's development was parallel to the Jewish settlement in the land of Israel. Babylon itself remained under Persian rule until the conquest by Alexander the Great in 331 B.C.E. After the latter's death, Babylon declined rapidly and within a short period was a heap of ruins which aroused the curiosity of conquerors and travellers.

Babylonian Jewry, on the other hand, continued to thrive under the various regimes which ruled the country, and certain towns had an entirely Jewish population. They produced scholars of the caliber of Hillel and, after the destruction of the Second Temple, they rebelled against the Romans. The revolt was brutally suppressed. With the decline of Palestinian Jewry, Babylonia became the main Jewish center. Men of the caliber of Rav and his younger colleague, Samuel, founded the famous academies of Babylonia, and it was here that the Babylonian Talmud developed and was codified. Under Persian and Parthian rule, the Jews enjoyed a large measure of freedom and autonomy, and at their head was an Exilarch of Davidic descent who was accorded great honor both by the Jews and the ruling authorities. In the 5th century, however, there were persecutions which led to a shortlived Jewish rebellion. From this time until the Moslem conquest, the position of the Jews was insecure.

See also IRAQ.

BALFOUR DECLARATION: Statement of British Middle Eastern policy issued on November 2, 1917, by the British Foreign

Arthur James Balfour

Secretary, Arthur James (Lord) Balfour, on behalf of the British Government (whose Prime Minister was David Lloyd George), in the form of a letter to Lord Rothschild. The Declaration reads:

> Dear Lord Rothschild,
>
> I have much pleasure in conveying to you on behalf of his Majesty's Government, the following declaration of sympathy with Jewish Zionist aspirations which has been submitted to and approved by the Cabinet.
>
> His Majesty's Government view with favour the establishment in Palestine of a national home for the Jewish people and will use their best endeavours to facilitate the achievement of this object, it being clearly understood that nothing shall be done which may prejudice the civil and religious rights of existing non-Jewish communities in Palestine or the rights and political status enjoyed by Jews in any other country.
>
> I should be grateful if you would bring this declaration to the knowledge of the Zionist federation.

This declaration of support for the Jewish national home in Palestine (which applied originally to the country on both sides of the river Jordan) was greeted with enthusiasm throughout the Jewish world. It had been preceded by lengthy negotiations in which Chaim Weizmann played a leading role. The sympathy of the President of the United States, Woodrow Wilson, also helped to influence the British decision. There was opposition, however, from certain leaders of the Jewish community in England, who believed that Zionist aspirations would endanger the position of Jews in other countries. The declaration, despite subsequent differences as to its interpretation between various British Governments and Zionist leaders, may be regarded as a milestone in the struggle for Jewish statehood. It was approved by other allied governments, and in 1922 was incorporated into the Mandate for Palestine granted to Britain by the League of Nations.

See also ZIONISM.

BAR GIORA, SIMON: One of the leaders of the Jewish rebellion against Rome (66–70 C.E.) which culminated in the destruction of the Second Temple. Bar Giora, like most of the Jewish patriots, was basically an expert in guerilla warfare, without possessing any professional military qualifications. The Jewish leadership at the time was hopelessly disunited, and this was one of the factors which led to the eventual defeat. Bar Giora was the leader of a group of extremists, and, in the early stages of the fighting, he helped to defeat the Syrian Governor, Cestius Gallus. After a dispute with the other Jewish leaders in Jerusalem, he set up his headquarters at Massada. His forces conquered large areas of southern Judea and were particularly harsh on settlements suspected of disloyalty to the revolt. At the invitation of the opponents of John of Giscala, he returned in 69 C.E., to Jerusalem, where bitter civil warfare raged until the beginning of the siege by the Roman general, Titus. After the fall of Jerusalem in 70 C.E., he was taken captive and brought to Rome, where he was executed.

BAR-ILAN UNIVERSITY: Israel institution of higher learning founded in 1955 by the American Mizrahi organization and named after the Religious Zionist leader, Rabbi Meir Bar-Ilan. It has a campus of 20 buildings at Ramat Gan, near Tel Aviv, and its object is to produce scholars who are steeped in Jewish tradition while at the same time possessing a sound secular education. Bar-Ilan has branches in Ashkelon and Safad, and in 1970 there were 4,500 students (700 from abroad) and a teaching staff of 550.

BAR KOKHBA, SIMON (Son of the Star, real name Bar or Ben Kosiba): Leader of the rebellion against Rome in the years 132–135 C.E. Very little is known of his life, although the Talmud abounds in tales of his heroism and exceptional valor. He was a nephew of R. Eleazar of Modiin and reputedly of Davidic descent. Even the causes of the rebellion against the Roman Emperor Hadrian are not clear, although the desire to throw off the Roman yoke had been burning in the hearts of many of the people since the destruction of the Second Temple in 70 C.E. The rebuilding of Jerusalem as a Roman city, and restrictions on the study of Torah and the observance of the commandments must have added fuel to the fire. In any event, Bar Kokhba's talents as a leader and military strategist are undoubted, for, in the course of a short time, he organized a nearly total popular revolt and recaptured Jerusalem. In honor of the occasion, he minted coins dated from the time of the "Liberation of Jerusalem" or from the time of "Israel's Redemption." The famous sage Rabbi Akiva enthusiastically supported Bar Kokhba and acclaimed him as the Messiah, although he was not supported by all the rabbis in this. Bar Kokhba was, according to tradition, an autocratic leader who demanded total obedience and discipline, a description which is borne out by letters (recently discovered in the caves of the Judean desert) sent by him to his commanders (some actually bearing his signature). After their initial defeats, the Romans recovered and mounted a counterattack with 35,000 troops under the command of Julius Severus. Slowly but surely they recaptured all the lost territory, including Jerusalem. Bar Kokhba was forced to fall back on his last fortress, Betar, which, according to tradition, fell on the 9th day of Av 135. Bar Kokhba and most of his supporters perished. The revolt was followed by savage reprisals by the Roman Emperor Hadrian. Judea fell into desolation and most of its population was annihilated. Jerusalem was turned into a heathen city

Judean desert caves, site of Bar Kokhba finds

and Jews were forbidden to enter it. The Bar Kokhba rebellion was the last blow for Jewish independence till the struggle for the establishment of the State of Israel.

BAR MITZVAH and **BAT MITZVAH** (literally, a son — or daughter — of the commandment, from the Aramaic *bar,* meaning a son, and Hebrew *bat,* a daughter; and the Hebrew *mitzvah,* meaning commandment): One who is obligated to perform the commandments and is responsible for his actions. The term was originally applied to any adult male reaching his religious majority. This majority was fixed by the Talmudic sages as the age of puberty, which is generally but not exclusively thirteen years and one day.

According to Rabbi Eleazar, when a boy reaches this age the father should recite the blessing *Barukh Shepetarani,* "Blessed is he who has freed me from the responsibility for this child"; since up till that age, the father is legally responsible and liable for the actions of the child. From this time on, the child becomes an adult member of the Jewish community, may be counted in a *minyan,* and is liable for his own actions.

There is no ancient authority or legal basis for the modern usage of the term *bar mitzvah*; that is, the initiation of the child into the observance of the commandments by means of a ceremony conducted in the synagogue and a social celebration held afterward. *Bar mitzvah,* in the modern sense, dates from approximately the 14th century.

The *bar mitzvah* celebration is generally divided into two parts, religious and social. The religious ceremony usually takes place on the first Sabbath after the child's thirteenth Hebrew birthday, and consists of his being called to the reading of the last part of the weekly portion of the Pentateuch, the *Maphtir,* which enables him to chant the *Haphtarah* immediately afterward. In modern times, the custom of addressing the *bar mitzvah* boy in the synagogue has become widespread. The ceremony may, however, be held on any day of the week on which the *Torah* is read. Among observant Jews, one of the first obligations incumbent upon the boy is the putting on of *tephillin.* The first putting on of *tephillin* after the 13th birthday is regarded by some oriental Jews as an occasion for a separate celebration.

The social celebration has in modern times become the occasion for extensive festivities in which the *bar mitzvah* is showered with presents and good wishes. In orthodox circles, however, it is also the occasion for the delivery of a learned discourse by the celebrant on some aspect of Jewish law. This custom dates back to the Middle Ages.

According to Jewish law, girls reach their religious majority *(bat mitzvah)* exactly one year before boys, at the age of twelve years and one day. This too has in modern times become the occasion of a religious and social celebration. In certain orthodox circles, there is opposition to the public participation of girls in religious services, but, despite this the custom has spread to many orthodox synagogues in the western world. Usually a number of girls participate in the ceremony at one and the same time, and, in some communities, the festival of *Shavuot,* the season of the giving of the *Torah,* is considered an appropriate occasion for the holding of the *bat mitzvah* ceremony.

See also CONFIRMATION.

BEERSHEBA: Town in Israel whose connection with the people of Israel goes back to the days of the Biblical patriarchs. Here Abraham made a covenant with Abimelech, and also gave the place its name. Isaac also lived in Beersheba, and Jacob camped there. When the land of Israel was divided among the tribes, Beersheba and its surroundings fell to the portion of Simeon. In the period of the Kings, it was the most southerly settlement in the country — Dan being the most northerly, hence the biblical expression, "From Dan to Beersheba" to designate the extent of the country. Some of the Jews who returned from the Babylonian

A section of modern Beersheba

exile in the 6th century B.C.E. settled in Beersheba. After the destruction of the Second Temple in 70 C.E. it was a frontier post, and the Romans maintained a garrison there. During the later Middle Ages, Beersheba was deserted, and remained so until the latter part of the 19th century, when the Turks made it an administrative center. At the beginning of Israel's War of Independence, Beersheba passed into the hands of the Egyptians, but was conquered by the Israelis on October 21, 1948. Since then, Beersheba has developed rapidly, becoming a wholly Jewish town inhabited mainly by immigrants. It is the largest town in the Negev, and its population in 1969 was 72,000. Many industries have been developed and it is the site of a scientific research institution investigating life in the desert.

BELGIUM: As one of the six provinces of Gaul within the Roman empire, Belgium had Jewish settlers as early as the reign of the Emperor Hadrian. The earliest presence of Jews in the area which constitutes modern Belgium, however, dates from the 13th century. During the Black Death plague (1348–49), the Jews suffered persistent persecution and torture. In 1370, the Brussels community was virtually wiped out as a result of a desecration charge. After the expulsion of the Jews from Spain in 1492, many Marranos settled in Antwerp, forming a secret community which survived various judicial inquiries and produced a number of prominent business leaders, including the banking house of Mendes. Ashkenazi Jews began to arrive during the 18th century, especially after the Union of Belgium and France gave the Jews greater civil and political freedom. When Belgium gained her independence in 1830, the Jews were granted full emancipation. The center of their community was organized in Brussels, although, as the center of the diamond industry in which Jews played an active role, Antwerp remained the largest

community. During World War II, over half of Belgium's 100,000 Jews were deported to the Nazi death camps. Some 43,000 Jews live in Belgium today, centered mainly in Brussels (25,000) and Antwerp (14,000).

BEN-GURION, DAVID (1886 —): Israel statesman. David Ben-Gurion was born as David Gruen in Plonsk, Poland. At an early age, he became an active Zionist and was one of the founders of the Labor-Zionist group, the *Poale Zion* of Poland. In 1906, he immigrated to Israel where he worked as a watchman and an agricultural laborer. He soon achieved political prominence and was chairman of the founding conference of the *Poale Zion* in the land of Israel. After studying law in Constantinople from 1912–14, he returned to the land of Israel, but in 1915 he was among the many new Zionist settlers who were exiled by the Turkish authorities. He made his way to the United States, where he spent three years organizing the American

David Ben-Gurion

wing of Labor-Zionism and encouraging American Jews to settle in the land of Israel. He cooperated with Jabotinsky in the formation of the Jewish Legion, which served under the command of the British general, Allenby. Ben-Gurion himself served under its colors. In 1920, he was one of the founders of the Jewish trade union federation, the Histadrut, and from 1921–1935 he served as its general secretary.

In 1930, he was among the founders of what was to become Israel's dominant political party, *Mapai,* and, by the middle 1930's, Ben-Gurion had attained top leadership in Zionist councils. From 1935–1948, he was chairman of both the Zionist executive and of the Jewish Agency, positions which made him the effective leader of the Jewish community in Palestine. It was during this period that Ben-Gurion came into conflict with the more activist policies advocated by Jabotinsky and his revisionist organization. Much of his Zionist career was to be spent in a no-quarter battle with Jabotinsky and his followers. In 1942, Ben-Gurion was the moving spirit behind the adoption by the Zionist movement of the "Biltmore Program," which called for a Jewish commonwealth in the land of Israel and unlimited Jewish immigration. It was largely due to Ben-Gurion's qualities of leadership, indomitable courage, and determination that the State of Israel came into being. When, after the United Nations partition decision of November 1947, it became clear that the Arabs were preparing a war of extermination against the Jewish population, there were those in the Zionist camp who, fearing the outcome, urged a postponement of the Declaration of the State. Ben-Gurion would not be deterred, however, and on May 14, 1948, he himself read the Declaration of Independence at a meeting of the Council of the People held in the Tel Aviv Museum. Ben-Gurion became Israel's first Prime Minister and Minister of Defense, and in the latter

capacity directed the war effort of the young state, and organized the forces of Israel, which decisively defeated the invading Arab armies.

He held these posts in the various coalition governments until December 1953, when he resigned and retired to the settlement of Sedeh Boker in the Negev. He thus demonstrated by personal example his uncompromising belief that the future development of the State of Israel is dependent on the settlement of the Negev wastelands. The critical events facing Israel in the years 1955–56, however, brought him out of retirement, and in 1955 he returned to the government first as Minister of Defense and then as Prime Minister as well. Under his leadership, the state weathered the second major storm in its short history, culminating in the successful Sinai campaign of November 1956. In 1963, Ben-Gurion again resigned from office, but remained active in political affairs. He became increasingly dissatisfied with the policies of his successors and former colleagues, and in 1965 he led a dissident group which broke away from *Mapai* to form the *Rafi* party. When, at a later stage, the latter decided to rejoin the mother party in order to form the Israel Labor Party, Ben-Gurion disapproved of the move and continued in opposition. In 1970, he officially resigned his membership in the Israel Parliament in order to devote his time to writing. In addition to his political career, Ben-Gurion is a prolific journalist and Bible scholar.

BEN-YEHUDA, ELIEZER (1858–1922): The father of modern Hebrew. He was the most active and productive among those whose efforts resulted in the revival of the Hebrew language.

Ben-Yehuda was born in Lithuania. When he was 20, he went to Paris to study medicine. There he published an article advocating the revival of Hebrew as a living tongue. This idea began to occupy

Eliezer Ben-Yehuda

words to meet modern needs and explained how he derived them. Only part of the dictionary appeared in his lifetime. After his death in 1922, it was completed by his widow, the sister of his first wife (who had not survived many years in the land of Israel), and by other Hebrew linguists who had been inspired by Ben-Yehuda.

In 1890 he founded the *Va'ad Ha-Lashon Ha-Ivrit* (Hebrew Language Council), which helped to establish modern Hebrew terminology.

BEN-ZVI, YITZHAK (1884–1963): Second president of the State of Israel. Ben-Zvi was born in the Ukraine and settled in the land of Israel in 1907. He was a founder of the workers' movement, *Poale Zion,* and a staunch advocate of the idea of Jewish self-defense.

During the First World War, the Turkish government arrested and deported many Zionist leaders, including Ben-Zvi and Ben-Gurion, who both went to the United States. In America, Ben-Zvi helped to organize the Labor Zionist Movement and also joined the Jewish Legion, which was established to fight against the Turks.

After the war, Ben-Zvi was active in the Jewish labor movement in Palestine. For many years he was head of the Jewish National Council that was set up to represent the Jewish settlers while the country was still under the British mandate. After the establishment of the state he was a member of the Knesset until 1952 when he was elected to succeed Chaim Weizmann as President of Israel.

Besides being a statesman and politician, Ben-Zvi was a journalist and scholar. He was particularly interested in the history of the oriental Jewish communities and the history of Jewish settlement in Palestine, and wrote a number of books on these subjects. As a result of his interest in the various communities that make up the people of Israel, he used to hold festive gatherings at his residence on the occasion

more and more of his time and attention. After three years he contracted tuberculosis and had to abandon his studies, but he was determined that his dream would be realized. In 1881 he settled in the land of Israel. On his way there, he stopped off in Vienna, where he married a girl he had known in Russia. At that time other young couples were on their way to the land of Israel, but he was the only husband to demand from his wife that they speak only Hebrew once they reached their destination.

He was very determined and stubborn. His obsession with the Hebrew language dictated his thoughts and actions. When he settled in Jerusalem, his desire to have only Hebrew spoken in his home made it impossible to hire any servants. After his son was born he spoke only in Hebrew to him, but the child had no one with whom he could speak when he went out.

Ben-Yehuda's persistence was one of the chief reasons why Hebrew became the language of the Jewish population in the land of Israel. He gradually won over the teachers and leaders. He even published a Hebrew newspaper. Often Ben-Yehuda had to invent words which had not previously been used in Hebrew. He also began to compile a Hebrew dictionary. He coined

President Yitzhak Ben-Zvi

of the new moon — each attended by Jews originating from a different country. He died in 1963, and his work was continued in the Ben-Zvi Institute which he founded to promote research into the history of Jewish communities in the Middle East.

BENE ISRAEL: Ancient Indian Jewish community whose origin is unknown. Their own tradition claims that they are descended from the lost ten tribes, and that they were shipwrecked on the Indian coast. It is more likely that they are descendants of Jews who emigrated to India in the 5th and 6th centuries B.C.E. from Yemen or Persia. For many centuries, they were cut off from the rest of the Jewish world and in their mode of living, language, and customs assimilated themselves to the Hindus. They nevertheless maintained a distinctly Jewish tradition which included the recitation of the *Shema,* the observance of the Sabbath, and some of the other festivals. They also observed circumcision and some of the dietary laws.

Under British rule, they were concentrated mainly in Bombay, served in the British-Indian army, and entered the professions. During the 18th and 19th centuries, under the guidance of teachers from Cochin and Baghdad, they returned to pure Judaism. They number between eighteen and nineteen thousand, most of whom have immigrated to the State of Israel.

BENEDICTIONS (Berakhot): Expressions of praise or thanksgiving, usually directed toward God, but also applicable to individuals and nations.

According to rabbinic tradition, the blessings were formulated by the men of the Great Assembly (at the beginning of the Second Temple period), and the sage of the Mishnah, Rabbi Meir, asserted that it was the duty of every man to recite one hundred blessings daily. By the third century C.E. all the statutory forms of the blessings had been fixed.

In the prayers, the blessing appears either at the beginning or conclusion of the specific prayer, or both, and contains the formula "Blessed art Thou O Lord." If the blessing appears at the beginning of the prayer, it continues with the words, "Our God King of the Universe," and then enumerates the specific praise appropriate to the particular prayer. The above formula is applicable both to prayers said in the synagogue and to prayers recited in the home, such as the *Kiddush,* but may not be used in prayers which are not obligatory.

Apart from the benedictions connected with the liturgy, there are various other categories of blessings which may be divided as follows:

1) Blessings of enjoyment, which are recited before and after every act of eating and drinking and for the pleasure bestowed upon the senses, such as the smell of flowers or spices. The purpose of these blessings is to acknowledge God as the creator of man's pleasure-providing susceptibilities.

2) Blessings recited before the performance of a commandment, such as the putting on of *tephillin,* the blowing of the *shofar* (ram's horn), and others. The blessing is recited before the *mitzvah* is performed, with the exception of the washing of the hands, where the blessing is recited after the ablution. The purpose of these blessings is to praise God for granting the privilege of carrying out a religious duty.

3) Various blessings of praise and thanksgiving which are recited in response to the appearance of natural phenomena such as thunder, lightning, or a rainbow; on seeing a king, a great scholar, or on hearing good or bad news. On being delivered from danger or sickness, the blessing *Ha-Gomel* is recited in the synagogue after the person has been called to the reading of the Torah; and at the advent of a seasonal festival or on partaking of a fruit for the first time in the year, the blessing *Sheheheyanu* is recited.

The Bible uses the term "benediction" in connection with the blessing bestowed by private individuals as well. Thus, Jacob blessed his sons before his death while Moses did the same to the Children of Israel. In ancient times, great importance was attached to blessings or curses, as evidenced by Jacob's and Esau's struggle over their father's blessing, and by Moses' constant stress on the blessing which accrues to those who observe God's law, and the curse which is the lot of those who violate the commandments.

Underlying the recitation of blessings for various occasions, is a specific Jewish philosophy of life. Judaism does not deny man's right to enjoy life, neither does it reject the physical aspects of life as evil or sinful. Judaism, however, demands that man sanctify the physical. Eating in itself is a physical act with no spiritual meaning or value. By reciting the grace before and after meals, this act is elevated into one of a spiritual nature. Similarly, everyday actions such as getting up, dressing, and even the performance of certain physical acts, are transformed into acts of worship and take on a religious significance through their being accompanied by the recitation of a benediction.

The fact that blessings are to be recited on almost every conceivable occasion and throughout the day serves to bridge the gap between the "holy" and the "profane," thus making the whole of life one continuous act of worship.

BERNSTEIN, LEONARD (1918–): Noted American conductor and composer. At the age of twenty-five, he was appointed assistant conductor of the New York Philharmonic Orchestra, and from 1957–1969 served as its permanent conductor. Bernstein's musical taste and ability range over a wide field, and include both classical music and jazz. He has composed numerous serious works such as the *Jeremiah* and *Kaddish* Symphonies, and has also written the scores for the musical shows *West Side Story, On The Town,* and *Candide.* He has a deep attachment to the State of Israel and has made numerous concert appearances with the Israel Philharmonic Orchestra.

BET DIN (House of Judgment): Jewish court of law. The command to appoint judges and to establish courts of law is mentioned in the Bible (Deut. 16, 18). During the period of the Second Temple, there were three categories of courts: 1) those qualified to deal only with civil matters, comprised of three judges; 2) those dealing with criminal cases, comprised of twenty-three judges; and 3) the Sanhedrin or the Great *Bet Din.* This was the supreme authority for the interpretation of law, and it also appointed the judges of the lower courts. It consisted of seventy-one members and sat in the Chamber of Hewn Stone in the Temple precincts. After the destruction of the Temple, the Sanhedrin was transferred to Yavneh by Johanan ben Zakkai, and remained there until the end of the 3rd century. After the decline of the Jewish center in the land of Israel, it was impossible to reconstitute the Sanhedrin, because it was held that the necessary *Semikha* or Ordination could only be conferred by the scholars of the Holy Land. Nevertheless, wherever Jews settled a *Bet Din,* presided over by the Chief Rabbi or one of the leading rabbinic scholars, was usually established. These local Jewish courts exercised authority in religious matters and in the internal affairs of the Jewish community. In Spain, the rabbinic courts were given jurisdiction by the king even in criminal matters. Although the rabbinical court had the power to enforce its decisions by virtue of the *herem* or excommunication, for the most part its moral authority and the status of the *Dayyanim* (judges) was sufficient to insure the obedience of the Jewish people to its decisions. Until 1764, the Council of Four Lands, the organ of Polish and Lithuanian Jewry, was given juridical powers by the Polish authorities and served as the court of final appeal for Polish Jewry. The emancipation process led to the breakdown of the ghetto and of Jewish communal autonomy. Jews, as equal citizens, were now subject to the authority of the non-Jewish courts.

During the past two hundred years, therefore, the *Bet Din's* authority has largely been limited to voluntary arbitration and matters of Jewish ritual law. In the State of Israel, the status of rabbinical courts has once again risen, and they have exclusive jurisdiction in matters of personal status such as marriage, divorce, and inheritance.

BET HA-MIDRASH (House of Study):
Term used during the Talmudic period for an academy of higher rabbinic learning, generally presided over by a distinguished sage. The sanctity of the *Bet Ha-Midrash* was considered even greater than that of the synagogue. Some rabbis even preferred to pray there, rather than adjourn to the synagogue. In later times there was usually a *Bet Ha-Midrash* attached to the local synagogue or within its precincts. It was used for study and usually contained a suitable rabbinic library. Worshipers would come to synagogue before the services in order to participate in the Talmudic discourse, usually conducted by the rabbi or a learned layman. In some places, individual students spent all their time in the *Bet Ha-Midrash;* in others it was the site of the local *yeshivah.* In Germany, it became known as the *klaus* (from the Latin, *claustrum,* cloister) while in Eastern Europe it was referred to as the *kloiz* and sometimes as the *shtiebel.*

BET SHEARIM: Settlement in Israel in the
western valley of Jezreel, founded in 1936, 3 miles to the east of the ancient town of Bet Shearim, an important center and seat of the Sanhedrin in the 2nd century C.E. Destroyed in the 4th century, Bet Shearim was almost forgotten until excavations, begun in 1936, uncovered the remains of a

In the Bet Shearim catacombs

vast Jewish cemetery. The catacombs of Bet Shearim contain over two hundred sarcophagi with Aramaic-Hebrew or Greek inscriptions referring to the Jews who chose to be buried here during the centuries when Jewish burial in Jerusalem was forbidden by Roman edict. Through the centuries, many of the tombs were looted, but the remaining inscriptions and ornaments furnished a wealth of information on the city's past. Rabbi Judah the Prince, compiler of the Mishnah, lived in Bet Shearim and both he and his sons, Shimon and Gamaliel, are thought to be buried here.

BETHLEHEM: Town $5\frac{1}{4}$ miles south of Jerusalem; population: (1969) 32,000. In Biblical times, Bethlehem was a well-known city, the birthplace of King David and the site of the events narrated in the book of Ruth. The Hebrew name means House of Bread, while the Arabic equivalent, *Beitlahem,* signifies "House of Meat." The Tomb of Rachel, one of the most sacred shrines in Israel, stands at the entrance to the town. The Bible tells us that Rachel, who died while giving birth to Benjamin, was buried "in the way to Ephrath which is Bethlehem."

Bethlehem is sacred to the Christian world as the birthplace of Jesus. In 330 C.E., the Emperor Constantine built the first Church of the Nativity over the cave where Jesus is supposed to have been born and today churches abound in the town.

In 1948, Bethlehem was conquered by Jordanian forces. The Israel army occupied the town in the Six-Day War of June 1967.

BIALIK, ḤAYYIM NAḤMAN (1873–1934): Modern Hebrew poet. Bialik was born in the village of Radi near Zhitomir (in the Russian Ukraine), the youngest of eight children. When he was seven, his father died, and his mother, being unable to support the youngster, brought him to his grandfather. The latter was stern and strict, and many times Bialik cried at the memory of happier days. On the other hand, he received from his grandfather a sound traditional education and the spirit of Jewish piety. After attending the famous Talmudic academy of Volozhin in Lithuania, Bialik made his way to Odessa, then the center of Jewish and Hebrew literary activity. His trip was unsuccessful materially, but his writing caught the eye of Aḥad Haam (Asher Ginzberg), who advised Y. H. Ravnizki, the editor of *Ha-Pardes* (The Garden), to publish Bialik's poem *El Ha-Zippor.* He returned to Zhitomir where he married the daughter of a wealthy lumber merchant and joined his father-in-law's business. In 1900 he was invited to teach in the Hebrew school at Odessa, and from that time on his star began to rise. Together with Ravnizki, his friend and admirer, he published the *Sefer Ha-Aggadah* and established several printing houses. In 1921, he left Russia and, after spending three years in Berlin, transferred his publishing houses to Tel Aviv, where he settled.

Bialik is considered to be the foremost Hebrew poet of the modern age, and one

The town of Bethlehem

of the greatest masters of Hebrew of his generation. His name became a symbol for Hebrew culture, and he is often referred to as the National Poet. This title is most apt. However, Bialik was a national poet not only in the narrow sense of one who sings songs of hope and calls upon the people to rebuild the national homeland. More than any other poet before and perhaps after him, he portrayed the depths of the nation's life and revealed those forces which guaranteed its survival. In his poetry, he gives voice to its joys and despair, to its achievements and failures. In brief, he portrays the nation as it is. At times, he roars in anger with the voice of a prophet; at others, he sings the soft sweet song of nature. After the Kishinev pogroms at the beginning of the century, he wrote *Be-Ir-Ha-Haregah* (In the City of Slaughter), in which he alternately expressed sorrow and anger at the helplessness of the Jewish people. This poem inspired Jewish youth throughout Russia to establish self-defense organizations. In *Akhen Hatzir Ha-Am*

Hayyim Nahman Bialik

(Surely the People is Grass), he is bitterly critical of Jewish society, while the *Megillat Ha-Esh* (The Scroll of Fire) reflects the problem of Jewish spiritual decline against the background of the premature Russian revolution of 1905. In his Hebrew style, Bialik utilized all the various stages of the language's development — Biblical, Talmudic, and modern. He spoke for all Jews, for his writings encompass all the different views and opinions held by the Jews of his generation. In Tel Aviv, Bialik was the center of Jewish cultural life, and people vied with each other in order to attend his famous *Oneg Shabbat*. In Israel, he published children's tales and folk literature and translated some of the classics, including Shakespeare, into Hebrew. As chairman of the *Vaad Ha-Lashon* (Hebrew Language Council) he contributed much to the modernization of the Hebrew language.

The home in which he lived in Tel Aviv is now the Bialik museum.

BIBLE (the term "Bible" is not of Hebrew origin but is derived from the Greek word meaning "a book"): The name was first given, in the 4th century C.E., by the Patriarch of Constantinople, John Chrystosom, to that collection of books considered holy by the Jew. Similarly, the terms "Old" and "New Testament" are of Christian origin and apply to all the books considered sacred by the Christian Church. The Old Testament refers specifically to the Hebrew Bible and, in Christian belief, takes second place to the books of the New Testament. Certain sections of Christianity, however, such as the Calvinists, regard the Old Testament with almost the same importance as the New.

The term most commonly used by Jews for the Bible is *Tanakh,* which has no meaning in itself, but is formed by the initials of the three sections into which the Bible is divided — *Torah, Neviim,* and *Ketuvim.* In modern Hebrew the Bible is called *Mikra* (reading). The first division is

THE BOOKS of THE BIBLE

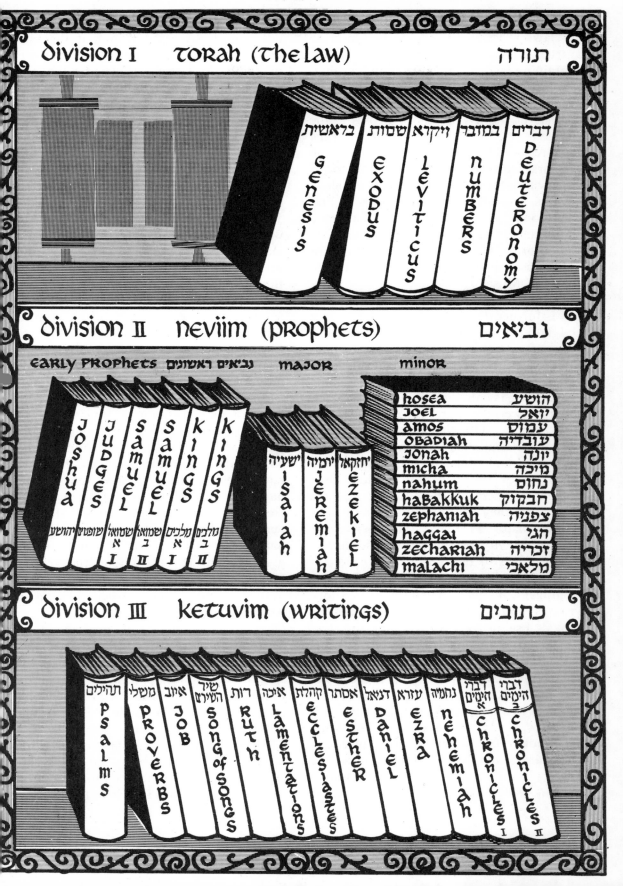

division I TORAH (The Law) תורה

GENESIS בראשית
EXODUS שמות
LEVITICUS ויקרא
NUMBERS במדבר
DEUTERONOMY דברים

division II neviim (PROPHETS) נביאים

EARLY PROPHETS נביאים ראשונים **MAJOR** **MINOR**

JOSHUA יהושע
JUDGES שופטים
SAMUEL I שמואל א
SAMUEL II שמואל ב
KINGS I מלכים א
KINGS II מלכים ב

ISAIAH ישעיה
JEREMIAH ירמיה
EZEKIEL יחזקאל

hosea	הושע
joel	יואל
amos	עמוס
obadiah	עובדיה
jonah	יונה
micha	מיכה
nahum	נחום
habakkuk	חבקוק
zephaniah	צפניה
haggai	חגי
zechariah	זכריה
malachi	מלאכי

division III ketuvim (WRITINGS) כתובים

PSALMS תהילים
PROVERBS משלי
JOB איוב
SONG of SONGS שיר השירים
RUTH רות
LAMENTATIONS איכה
ECCLESIASTES קהלת
ESTHER אסתר
DANIEL דניאל
EZRA עזרא
NEHEMIAH נחמיה
CHRONICLES I דברי הימים
CHRONICLES II דברי הימים

Torah, which is often incorrectly translated as "law." "Teaching" would be closer to a true translation, for the *Torah,* while containing laws, is far more than just that. It is history, legend, poetry, and, above all, moral and ethical teaching. This division consists of the five books of Moses — the *Ḥumash* (in Hebrew) or the *Pentateuch* (in Greek). Their Hebrew names are the very first word or the first important word to appear in the book. The English names — Genesis, Exodus, Leviticus, Numbers, and Deuteronomy — are derived from the Greek and describe the subject matter of the first section of the book. The *Torah* begins with the story of creation and continues to the death of Moses.

The second division is *Neviim* (Prophets), and is further divided into two, the former and latter Prophets. The first part comprises the historical books of Joshua, Judges, Samuel I and II, and Kings I and II. The second part consists of the three major Prophets — Isaiah, Jeremiah, and Ezekiel, and the twelve minor Prophets — Hosea, Joel, Amos, Obadiah, Jonah, Micah, Nahum, Habakkuk, Zephaniah, Haggai, Zechariah, and Malachi. These latter were called minor Prophets not because they lack importance, but because the amount of material they left is much less than that of the major Prophets. The period of greatest activity of the major and minor Prophets was in the 5th century B.C.E.

The third division is known as *Ketuvim* (writings) or as "hagiographa" (holy writings) and is composed of the following books: Psalms, Proverbs, Job, the five Scrolls (the Song of Songs, Ruth, Lamentations, Ecclesiastes, and Esther), and Daniel, Ezra, Nehemiah, and Chronicles I and II.

Books written later, whatever their value might be, were not considered holy and were not received into this collection. There are a number of books known as *Apocrypha,* which means "hidden things" or "put aside." These were kept separate from the holy Scriptures since they were not considered genuine, but at the same time they were not banned, and are even quoted in the Talmud. If a classic is a book that has continuing influence on culture long after it is written, then the Bible is the classic of classics, or, as it is often called, the Book of Books. No other literary work can compete with the Bible in its impact on human civilization. This is partially due to the fact that the Bible has been translated into virtually all languages. The first ambitious translation on record was the Greek version (the Septuagint) made by Jews in Alexandria in the centuries prior to the Christian era. The process of Bible translation has been going on ever since. The translation of the Bible was actually the first literary production of some languages. In addition, Martin Luther's German translation is generally recognized as the chief force in creating the modern German language, and the famous 17th century English authorized version left an indelible stamp on English.

The biblical stories have fascinated generations of children and adults, and, with their simple charm and beautiful prose, never seem to lose their effectiveness. They have a meaning and significance that is eternal. The triumphant song of the Red Sea, David's lament over the death of Saul and Jonathan, and the writings of the great Prophets, rank among the greatest poetry ever written. Moreover, great authors, artists, and musicians have all turned to the Bible for inspiration — and have found it. We think immediately of Milton's *Paradise Lost* and Thomas Mann's *Joseph,* of Michelangelo's *Moses,* many of Rembrandt's finest paintings, and of the music of Handel, Haydn, Mendelssohn, and Stravinsky. The Bible seems to hold something for everyone.

Above all, it has given to the world ideals of democracy and justice. The Negro slave in the United States found comfort in the Bible and put this feeling into song.

The memory of Moses calling on Pharaoh to *Let My People Go* inspired him to fight for his elementary rights as a human being. The Jordan was symbolic of the promised land, of a better future for those who are downtrodden and persecuted. The American revolutionaries, fighting for their independence from England, saw in George III the Pharaoh of their day, and George Washington was their Moses. When the American Supreme Court ruled in the famous Dred Scott decision that a runaway slave should be returned to his master, those who wished to abolish slavery were inspired by the words of the Bible, "Thou shall not deliver unto his master a bondman that is escaped from his master unto thee."

It is true that there are many parts of the Bible which are hard to understand and which even seem harsh and cruel. This problem has occupied the minds of many great Jewish thinkers. While there are undoubtedly parts of the Bible which to the modern mind seem incomprehensible and even offensive, in the main the Bible teaches justice, and the Biblical code contains many ethical and moral values which the world is still very far from practicing. The Bible sees and reflects life as it was and is, and herein lies its beauty and perhaps its hold over people. Even the greatest Biblical character remains human. Abraham, Jacob, Moses, David, and Solomon all at some time or other sin against God or man and are punished. Yet this does not detract from their greatness. The Hebrew Bible knows of no saints: "There is no man on earth who doeth only good and sinneth not." He is able to repent, to regret his wrongdoing, and if his repentance is sincere it is accepted by God, who is, after all, a God of mercy and loving kindness.

During the past hundred years, attempts have been made to question the authority of the Bible on the basis of modern scientific and historical facts. Darwin's theory of evolution, it was said, proved that the Biblical story of creation was scientifically impossible. While it is true that the Bible contains certain statements which, in the light of modern research, can no longer be accepted, it must be remembered that the Bible is not a science textbook and must not be used as such. The story merely stresses the fact that the world did not just come about by chance but was the work of a Supreme Being. This in no way contradicts the theory of evolution: in fact, an examination of the creation chapter will show that there is a definite evolution from one stage to the next until the highest point, the creation of man, is reached.

Similarly, attempts have been made in the light of modern methods of literary research, to determine the authorship of the various books of the Bible. According to the Talmud, for example, Moses wrote the first five books, with the obvious exception of the last eight verses which tell of his death. Modern Bible scholars, especially of the Protestant faith, have tried to prove that the Bible was written by many different authors, and at a much later date than was traditionally believed. These scholars are known as Bible critics and, for a long time, many of their theories were accepted blindly. However, many of the more extreme theories have been disproved as a result of deeper study, which has been made possible through archeology, comparative language, comparative religion, and a more profound knowledge of the ancient Near East. Although in certain instances the Bible critics have made important contributions, the growing trend of biblical scholarship (notably in Israel) is toward a much more conservative attitude than was assumed earlier this century. But it must be stressed that the Bible is neither a science nor a history textbook. Its authorship is to a certain extent not important, for its greatness and enduring value lie in the truths which it teaches. The belief in one God,

Man created in the image of God, freedom as a right for all human beings, love of neighbor and charity, fairness to the foreigner, kindness to animals, love of Israel and the land of Israel — these and hundreds of other teachings which the world still has not accepted are what make the Bible as meaningful today as it ever was.

B'NAI B'RITH (Sons of the Covenant): Jewish fraternal organization, founded in New York in 1843. It is the largest Jewish organization in America, and its many activities include fraternal societies, educational work, philanthropy, fighting anti-Semitism, and sponsoring youth groups. It encourages cooperation and understanding among all sections of the community.

There are branches of B'nai B'rith throughout the world. The B'nai B'rith Youth organization coordinates the activities of several separate youth movements. The Junior Order AZA (the initials for the Hebrew words, *Ahavah,* love; *Zedakah,* charity; *Ahdut,* unity) sponsors a program of cultural, religious, and interfaith service for boys between the ages of 14 and 21. It was founded in 1924, and today there are 600 chapters in the United States, Canada, and Britain. The B'nai B'rith Girls is a corresponding organization for girls. The B'nai B'rith Young Adults is coeducational.

One of the best known activities of the B'nai B'rith is its Hillel Foundations. Its centers on many college campuses provide the Jewish students with a focus for Jewish activities, and they are able to maintain Jewish traditions and services, as part of their general college life. The Hillel Houses offer a large variety of educational and social activities.

Despite its many programs for youth, the B'nai B'rith is not primarily a youth organization. Among its most important divisions is the Anti-Defamation League, which was created in 1913, with a twofold purpose: to prevent anti-Semitism by education, and to fight existing anti-

B'nai B'rith building in Washington

Semitism. In the course of its activities, the Anti-Defamation League has, in a quiet way, made important contributions to the fight against discrimination — not only against Jews — in the United States.

Altogether, the B'nai B'rith today has 900 chapters, with some 350,000 members in the United States. Its motto is: "Benevolence, Brotherly Love, and Harmony," and membership is open to any Jew who supports these concepts.

BOARD OF DEPUTIES OF BRITISH JEWS: The representative body of English Jewry which came into existence in 1760 as a joint committee of the Sephardi and Ashkenazi communities in London in connection with the presentation of a loyal address to George III on his accession. The Deputies' active history, however, dates from the beginning of the 19th century when it first obtained statutory recognition in the Marriage Act and the Registration Act of 1836, the year which saw its first constitution. Relatively small up to the end of the 19th century, it now comprises some

Interior of the Shrine of the Book, general view

450 members, represents all synagogues in Great Britain and the Commonwealth and has taken part in all movements affecting the political and civil rights of Anglo-Jewry, and often, in times of crisis, in affairs overseas.

BRANDEIS, LOUIS DEMBITZ (1841–1941): Justice of the United States Supreme Court and Zionist leader. Brandeis was born in Louisville, Kentucky. He gave early proof of intellectual brilliance, graduating from high school at the age of fourteen and completing his law degree at Harvard before his twenty-first birthday. He had no formal Jewish or religious education and it was only at the age of fifty-four that he made his first real contact with the Jewish community when he was called in to help settle a strike which had broken out in the Jewish-dominated garment industry. It was at this time that he became sympathetic to Zionism and an active campaigner on its behalf. As a result of World War I, European Jewry was divided, and the burden of supporting the Jewish settlements in the land of Israel, in addition to the major political work of Zionism, fell largely on American Jewry. Brandeis gladly accepted the chairmanship of the Zionist Provisional Emergency Committee during these critical years. In 1916, he was elevated to the Supreme Court, and while this inevitably hampered his Zionist activity, it did not affect his devotion to the Zionist cause. On the contrary, Brandeis was impatient with those who claimed that there was a conflict between loyalty to the Zionist cause and American patriotism.

"Every American Jew," he said, "who helps in advancing the Jewish settlement in Palestine, though he feels that neither he nor his descendants will ever live there, will be a better man and a better American for doing so." From 1918 to 1921, he was President of the Zionist Organization of America, and of the World Zionist Organization 1920–1921. As a result of basic differences of opinion with Chaim Weizmann, however, he resigned from both organizations in 1921. He nevertheless remained vitally concerned with Zionism and helped to organize the Palestine Economic Corporation.

As judge, Brandeis was for the legislative freedom of the individual states, but would not allow legislative majorities to threaten the liberties of individual men. He was against monopolies and the "curse of bigness."

BRANDEIS UNIVERSITY: Institute of higher learning in the United States, named after Louis Dembitz Brandeis. It was founded in 1948 as a corporate contribution of American Jewry to American higher education.

The first B.A. degrees were granted in 1952. Today, the university offers masters' degrees and doctorates in seventeen areas of study. It also conducts an institute in Near Eastern studies in Israel. The campus, which is situated near Boston, covers over 270 acres and has over 50 major faculties. Brandeis is coeducational and has a student body of some 2,600 many of them Jewish. Its first president was Abram Leon Sachar, who became chancellor in 1968.

BRAZIL: The first Jewish settlers in Brazil were Marranos from Portugal who, in the 16th century, helped to develop the sugar and tobacco industries. The Spanish conquest of Portugal in 1580, however, led to the introduction of the Inquisition in Spain's overseas territories. This in turn caused many Jews to emigrate from Brazil to territories held by the more tolerant Dutch. The status of Brazilian Jewry depended on the results of the see-saw struggle between Portugal and Holland. The Dutch victory of 1624 led to the granting of full rights to the Jews, but the Portuguese re-conquest thirty years later once more brought with it the Inquisition. Many of the Jews returned to Holland, others established communities throughout the West Indies and in New York, while others were gradually absorbed into the general population.

In 1822, Brazil proclaimed its independence from Portugal and, with that, freedom of religion was restored. Many of the Marranos openly returned to Judaism, and European Jews began to immigrate, establishing communities in Belem, Sao Paolo, Recife, Bahia, and especially in Rio de Janeiro. Immigration increased after World War I, and during the 1930's large numbers of German-Jewish refugees helped to increase the Jewish population. In 1951, a confederation of Jewish organizations was established. This acts as the representative body for the Jews of Rio de Janeiro, Sao Paolo, Porto Alegre, and other smaller communities. In addition to fourteen Jewish newspapers and periodicals, there are 38 Jewish schools with an enrollment of 10,892. The Jews of Brazil are mainly in business and the professions.

BUBER, MARTIN (1878–1965): Jewish religious philosopher. Born in Vienna, Buber studied in various German universities. At an early age, he became a fervent Zionist, and was the editor of the Zionist movement's newspaper, *Die Welt.* From 1916 to 1924 he edited the German monthly, *Der Jude,* and from 1924 to 1933 he was Professor of the Philosophy of Jewish Religion and Ethics at Frankfort on the Main. In 1938, he settled in Israel and was appointed Professor of the Sociology of Religion at the Hebrew University in Jerusalem.

Buber, although not an observant Jew, was a man of deep faith and piety. His religious outlook, which has greatly influenced Christian theology, is best expressed in his *I and Thou.* Religious faith, according to Buber, is a dialogue between man and God. The Bible is the record of the dialogual relationship between Israel and God. Buber was deeply influenced by Hasidism, and, through his writings, he was the first to reveal the inner meaning of Hasidism to West European Jewry.

Martin Buber

Together with Y.L. Magnes, Buber was a passionate believer in and advocate of Jewish-Arab understanding and cooperation.

BURIAL AND BURIAL RITES: Respect and reverence for the dead is an outstanding feature of Jewish tradition. According to the Talmud, it is the religious duty of the heirs to bury the dead. The Bible vividly depicts the importance attached to a decent burial by the patriarchs. Thus, Abraham conducted negotiations with the local Canaanite population in order to buy a burial plot for his wife Sarah. Isaac and Ishmael personally attended to their father Abraham's burial and Joseph, as regent of Egypt, saw to it that his father Jacob was given a state funeral. If there are no heirs, or if the heirs are too poor to pay the cost, the duty of burial falls upon the community. According to traditional Jewish law, the only valid method of disposing of the dead is by placing the body in the earth or in sepulchers. The catacomb system or the construction of burial galleries underground was practiced in Talmudic times, as attested to by the excavations at Bet Shearim in Lower Galilee, and by the Jewish catacombs in Rome. This custom was adopted by the early Christians. The custom of burning the human body after death, known as cremation, is not Jewish, and has been rigidly banned by orthodox rabbinic authorities. Reform Judaism, however, permits the practice.

According to rabbinical law, the burial should take place on the day of death and may be delayed only in honor of the deceased or to enable relatives living at a distance to attend the funeral.

In Jewish communities throughout the world, a special society known as the *Hevrah Kaddisha* (The Holy Brotherhood) is responsible for the granting of a proper burial to deceased Jews. They also perform the ritual washing of the body, the *Taharah*, before the burial. The Jewish burial rites are marked by simplicity. Wrapped in a shroud, the body is borne to the grave on a bier, while the congregation of mourners recites prayers and psalms. In western countries, the body is placed in a coffin, but this is not the custom in eastern countries or in the State of Israel. All those present at the graveside assist in filling in the grave after which the *Kaddish* is recited by the mourners. It is from this moment that the official period of mourning begins. The mourners then pass through two rows formed by those present, the latter reciting the traditional words of comfort, "May the Almighty grant thee comfort and consolation together with all the mourners of Zion and Jerusalem." Jews of priestly descent *(Kohanim)* are forbidden to contaminate themselves by contact with the dead or through proximity to a grave (within 4 cubits). It is therefore customary to bury *Kohanim* either in a front row of graves, or at the end of a row, so as to enable their relatives who are *Kohanim* to attend the funeral. The exhumation of a dead body is permitted only for reburial in a family grave or in the land of Israel.

Jews consider it meritorious to be buried in the land of Israel; thus, there arose the custom of placing some Holy Land soil in the coffins of Jews buried in the diaspora.

C

CAESAREA: Ancient city on the Mediterranean coast of Israel situated approximately halfway between Tel Aviv and Haifa. Originally known as the Tower of Straton, it was a flourishing port in Hellenistic times. Its present name was given it by King Herod, who rebuilt the city, naming it after the Roman Emperor Augustus Caesar. For five hundred years it was the Roman capital in the land of Israel. The strife which erupted between its Jewish and gentile inhabitants in the year 66 C.E. was one

Roman pillars in Crusader wall – Caesarea

of the chief causes of the Jewish rebellion. During the revolt, Caesarea was the headquarters of the Roman legions. After the destruction of the Temple in 70 C.E., Caesarea grew in importance, later becoming the seat of a rabbinic academy. The Crusaders restored and fortified Caesarea in the 12th century, but it was destroyed by the Moslems in 1291 when they put an end to Crusader rule. Much of the extensive area occupied by Caesarea has been excavated in recent years and has yielded Roman, Byzantine, and Crusader remains. In modern Israel, Caesarea has become a major tourist attraction, with the country's only golf course, and a plan to develop it still further is in its initial stages. The Roman theater has been reconstructed, and during the Israel music festival in the summer months, open-air concerts are held there.

CAIN AND ABEL: The two eldest sons of Adam and Eve. Cain was a farmer and Abel a herdsman. One day, when called upon to make their sacrifice to God, Cain brought "fruits of the earth," and Abel brought an animal sacrifice. God, says the book of Genesis, accepted Abel's sacrifice, but rejected Cain's. In his anger, Cain murdered Abel. God punished Cain by putting a curse upon him: "And now thou art cursed from the earth, which hath opened her mouth to receive thy brother's blood from thy hand" (Gen: 4.11). God "set a mark" upon Cain and banished him to wander ever after across the face of the earth, an outcast from human society. He went, we are told, to the land of Nod, east of Eden, and there fathered many peoples.

The struggle between Cain and Abel has been taken to symbolize the age-old rivalry between settled farmers and wandering herdsmen.

CALENDAR: In earliest times, the Israelites used an agricultural, or "farmer's" calendar. Their year began in the fall with the sowing season and ended with the harvest *(Sukkot)*. This procedure is partially described in Exodus 23:16 which says, "The feast of ingathering which is in the end of the year, when thou hast gathered in thy labors out of the field." Only four months are specifically mentioned in the Bible: *Abib* and *Ziv* in the spring, and *Bul* and *Eithanim* in the fall.

Later, Babylonian names for the months were adopted, with the year beginning in the spring. The first month was *Nisan* and this was followed by *Iyyar, Sivan, Tammuz, Av, Elul, Tishri, Marḥeshvan (Ḥeshvan), Kislev, Tevet, Shevat,* and *Adar.* The beginning of each new month, regarded as a semi-festival, was decided by witnesses who watched for the appearance of the new moon and reported it to the Sanhedrin. When this was confirmed, huge bonfires were built on the tops of a series of hills, so that the information was quickly passed throughout the country. This method had several disadvantages. If the skies were cloudy for several days, it was difficult to determine the exact date of the new moon. There was also the danger of a witness giving false testimony, either on purpose or by mistake. Moreover, there was the problem of conveying the information to Jews living outside the land of Israel. Because of this, it became customary for Jews in the diaspora to celebrate certain festivals for two days. The patriarch, Hillel II, who lived in the second part of the 4th century, published the rules of the calendar based on astronomical observation, thus stabilizing it. This is the calendar that is in use to this day. It is divided according to the moon into twelve lunar months of 29 or 30 days each. There are 354 days in this year, eleven less than in a solar year. To compensate for this discrepancy, an extra month is added seven times in nineteen years in the 3rd, 6th, 8th, 11th, 14th, 17th, and 19th years of each cycle. This month is added after the month of *Adar,* and is called *Adar-Sheni.* The Jewish calendar is reckoned from the date of creation which, according to rabbinic calculation, took place in the year 3760 B.C.E. The rabbis therefore settled on this date as the first year of the Jewish calendar. The Jewish year can be determined by subtracting 1240 from the common era date and then adding 5000.

The division between day and night does not depend on the moon, but on the stars. This division is important in determining the beginning and conclusion of the Sabbath and other festivals. When three stars are visible in the sky, night (and the beginning of a new 24-hour period) has officially begun. In a Jewish day of 24 hours, therefore, the night precedes the daytime, and the day officially ends at nightfall.

Ancient agricultural calendar found at Gezer

CANADA: Canada has a very close-knit Jewish community of 270,000. There are 200 Jewish congregations, located mainly in the three largest cities: Toronto, Montreal, and Winnipeg. Most of the congregations are orthodox, but conservative and reform congregations have also been established. The Jews of Canada came originally from many parts of the world. They maintain a comprehensive system of Jewish education which includes 95 Jewish schools, attended by some 40,000 pupils. There are also six yeshivot and two teachers' seminaries. Canada has a strong Zionist movement which goes back to the beginning of the twentieth century when the *Hovevei Zion Society* was formed. Today *Hadassah, Mizrachi,* and Pioneer Women all have active chapters.

Canadian Jewry also has an active Jewish press and an overall representative body, The Canadian Jewish Congress. The Congress was established in 1919 to help Jewish immigrants in Canada, but was disbanded in 1922. However, with the rise of anti-Semitism in the pre-World War II period, it reconvened. Today, it seeks to safeguard the civil and religious rights of Jews in Canada and throughout the world, and, in co-operation with the Zionist organization of Canada, organizes assistance for Israel.

Despite its intensive Jewish activity, the Jewish community has not remained outside the mainstream of Canadian life. Jews have made important contributions to the political, economic and cultural well-being of Canada. Walter Susskind has been conductor of the Toronto Symphony Orchestra, and Ellen Ballon is an accomplished pianist, while Isidore Ascher is known as the first Jewish-Canadian poet. Sigismund Mohr was instrumental in installing electric lights and telephone services in Quebec, and Henry Joseph helped to found the Canadian Merchant Marine.

Although the Gradis family of Bordeaux did much to promote and develop French settlements in Canada, Jews were not allowed to live there under French rule. After the British conquest, a handful of Jews settled in Montreal where in 1768 a congregation was established. As in England, however, their political and civil rights were limited. In 1807, when Ezekiel Hart was elected to the Quebec Assembly, he was barred from office by a law which required all representatives to take an oath on the New Testament. In 1832, however, a law was passed that granted all Jews equal civil rights. This law, sometimes called the Jew's Magna Carta, was enacted 25 years earlier than a similar bill passed in Great Britain, and in 1837 two Jewish magistrates were appointed in Canada.

The year 1881 saw the beginning of a great influx of Jews fleeing the pogroms in Russia. These Russian Jews contributed much to Canada's garment industry, and also developed the Canadian branch of the International Ladies' Garment Workers Union. There were further waves of immigration after World War I and World War II. The latter was comprised mainly of refugees from the holocaust who found that Canada was one of the few countries with liberal immigration laws. Although Canada has experienced anti-Semitism, the Jewish and non-Jewish citizens have usually been able to work and live together in peace. The Canadian Council of Christians and Jews is dedicated to the promotion of this friendship.

CHAGALL, MARC (1887 —): Artist. A native of Vitebsk, he left Russia in 1922, settling in Paris and rapidly making his reputation as one of the leading painters of the surrealist school. His lively fantasy, powerful use of color, and remarkable technical ability give his work a distinctive quality. He has sought his inspiration largely in the life of the East European Hassidim and village communities, and in biblical sources. All his work, however, is colored by his own individual and imaginative conceptions. His is often a world that never was, and yet possesses a special realism in feeling and spirit.

Mosaic wall by M. Chagall in Knesset building

The stained-glass windows at the Hadassah Medical Center in Jerusalem, the ceiling of the Paris Opera House, the frescoes for the Metropolitan Opera in New York, a glass window for the United Nations building, tapestries and mosaics for the Knesset in Jerusalem, and a stained-glass panel for the Vatican audience hall (the first commission given by the Vatican to a Jewish artist), have all contributed to his special status as one of the outstanding artists of our time.

CHARITY: The Hebrew word *tzedakah* means righteousness and was originally used to denote any righteous act or the righting of a wrong. In time, however, it became associated with alms-giving and hence with the English word charity. From the beginning of Jewish history, helping the poor, the needy, and the underprivileged has been one of the fundamental pillars of Judaism. The Bible, in its social legislation, makes provision for the support of those who are unable to support themselves. Thus, the corners of the field *(peah)* must be left unharvested, the forgotten sheaf must not be retrieved, and the vines and olive trees must not be gleaned too carefully. They are to be left for the poor, the widow, and the alien; i.e., for those who have no harvests to gather. The Prophet Isaiah, like all the Prophets, exhorts the people of Israel to be charitable. "Deal thy bread to the hungry and that thou bringest the castout poor to thy house. When thou seest the naked that thou cover him, and that thou hide not thyself from thine own flesh" (Is. 5, 8:7). The use of the word *tzedakah* implies that the relief of poverty is not an act of philanthropy but a duty, an act of justice.

The rabbis of the *Talmud* broadened the concept of charity still further. They distinguished between *tzedakah* and *gemilut ḥasadim* (deeds of loving kindness). The latter they say is a higher form of assistance to the needy. While *tzedakah* is limited to the giving of money to the poor, deeds of loving kindness (which include visiting the sick, comforting the mourner, burying the dead, and even giving a loan to one who is temporarily in need) may be applied to the rich as well as the poor. Furthermore, while *tzedakah* can be performed only with men's material possessions, *gemilut ḥasadim* demands the service of the heart and the mind. Finally, *tzedakah* can be performed only for the living, but *gemilut ḥasadim* for both the living and the dead. It is in the latter sense that *gemilut ḥasadim* is considered, together with the study of the *Torah* and the service of God, to be one of the three pillars upon which the world rests (Avot 1:2). The medieval scholar and philosopher Maimonides (1135–1204), lists eight degrees of charity, one higher than the other. At the highest rung of the ladder is the giving of assistance by helping a man to help himself; e.g., by means of a loan, by going into partnership with him, or by finding him a suitable job. This is the true concept of *gemilut ḥasadim,* for it avoids the embarrassment of the recipient at receiving something for nothing. He maintains his dignity and is spared the natural shame of one who feels he is receiving charity. Maimonides also stresses the desirability of the givers and the recipients being unknown to each other. Although *gemilut ḥasadim* as defined above is considered a higher form of charity, charity in the classical sense of giving to the poor and needy is one of the greatest *mitzvot* that a human being can perform. Throughout the ages, the Jewish people have had special institutions for the purpose of helping the underprivileged. During the *Mishnaic* period, a charity box existed in every community, and from it the town poor were given money for fourteen meals a week. The administration of charity was in the hands of three distinguished members of the community known as *gabbaei tzedakah*. Special importance was attached to the assistance of poor brides, the burial of the dead, and the ransoming of Jewish captives. Despite the poverty of the average

Jew during the ghetto period, most communities maintained an elaborate system of charitable institutions.

In the 19th century, Jewish philanthropic activity began to take on the vast dimensions for which it has earned world-wide repute. Philanthropists such as Sir Moses Montefiore (1784–1885) exerted their influence for the alleviation of Jewish suffering throughout the world. In the United States, the names of Guggenheim, Warburg, Schiff, and Rosenwald became symbols of Jewish philanthropic endeavor. The persecution of Russian Jewry in the late 19th and the beginning of the 20th centuries led to unprecedented relief work on an organized basis.

As a result of World War I and its tragic consequences for Central and East European Jewry, the American Jewish Joint Distribution Committee, popularly known as the "Joint," came into being. During its first years, it was mainly concerned with assisting East European Jews who had been affected by the First World War. This assistance was expressed not only in monetary contributions, but also in the giving of medical care, vocational assistance, and rescue work following anti-Semitic outbreaks. With the rise of Nazism, its efforts were concentrated on the rescue of German Jewry, and on the outbreak of war, the Joint made desperate efforts to save as many European Jews as possible. Since the establishment of the State of Israel, the Joint, as part of the United Jewish Appeal, has played an impressive role in assisting with the absorption of immigrants and the development of the State. Its activities in Eastern Europe have at times been permitted by the Communist regimes, but, in general, the Joint is regarded with suspicion and hostility.

In addition to those in the United States, Jewish communities in countries where they enjoy full equality have spared no effort in their assistance to Israel.

Jewish charitable work is not confined to Jews only. The rabbis laid down the principle that charity should extend to non-Jews also. Wherever Jews live, they generally associate themselves with philanthropic work of the larger non-Jewish community, whether it be in the sphere of child welfare and care for the aged, in the sponsoring of educational foundations, or in the manifold social work that is the characteristic feature of modern society. The increasing assumption of welfare activities by the state may alter the direction of Jewish charitable activity, but the principles of *tzedakah* and *gemilut hasadim* will remain the very warp and woof of Jewish communal life.

CHINA: According to legend, the settlement of Jews in China dates from the 1st century C.E. The first Jews known to have gone to China arrived about the year 1,000, perhaps having come from Persia. In the 13th century, Marco Polo mentions a number of influential Jews at the court of Kubla Khan. At that time, special taxation was imposed on them as dissenters. The only historic community was at Kai Feng Fu, where a Jewish mandarin helped to build the synagogue in the 17th century. This community gradually assimilated into Chinese society, and, by the end of the 19th century, had virtually disappeared. In the early 20th century, Sephardi communities were established in the port towns of Shanghai and Hong Kong. After World War I, there was an influx of Jewish refugees, some of them ex-prisoners of war. The Jewish community of China reached its peak during World War II when large numbers of refugees from Europe managed to find sanctuary there. During this period, the Jewish population numbered some 26,000. The community managed to survive the anti-Semitic restrictions introduced by the Japanese in the years 1941–1945, but, after the war, most of the Jews continued on to the United States, South America, and, after 1948, to Israel.

Those remaining emigrated when the Communists came to power, so that the only Jewish community extant in China today is that of the British Crown Colony of Hong Kong.

CHOIRS: According to the Bible, (I Chron. 15:16–24), King David chose 4,000 Levites for the musical service, which, in the Temple, was both instrumental and choral. During the Second Temple period, the choirs consisted of a minimum of twelve adult singers, who were accepted for the Temple choir after going through a period of training between the ages of 25 and 30. After the destruction of the Temple, the rabbis prohibited all music as a sign of mourning, but in the opinion of most rabbinic authorities this did not apply to synagogue choirs without instrumental accompaniment. The induction of the leader of Babylonian Jewry, the Exilarch, was conducted by a ḥazzan and a male voice choir. The modern synagogue choir originated in Italy during the Renaissance, and in many Ashkenazic congregations, the ḥazzan was often accompanied by a bass and a boy soprano. In modern times, i.e., from the 19th century, the institution of the choir has been the subject of much controversy.

Reform Judaism introduced the mixed choir with instrumental accompaniment in the form of an organ. Orthodoxy vehemently opposed this innovation, and in more extremist circles the choir was derided. In most modern Orthodox synagogues, however, services are conducted by a ḥazzan and a choir without instrumental accompaniment. Ḥasidism from the outset preferred unaccompanied congregational singing in which all the worshippers participated equally. This has remained a characteristic feature of Ḥasidic prayer.

CIRCUMCISION: The Covenant of Circumcision *(Milah* ot *Berit Milah).* Ceremony performed on a Jewish male child on the 8th day after birth. It owes its origin to the Patriarch Abraham who was commanded by God to undergo circumcision as the sign of his covenant with God. Hence, each Jewish father, at the ceremony, blessed God "who has sanctified us by His commandment and commanded us to enter our sons into the covenant of Abraham." Circumcision, which involves the removal of the foreskin, was practiced by many ancient peoples, as it is to this day by various tribes in Africa and Asia. Its significance as an initiation rite is thus universal. With the people of Israel, however, the practice took on a particular religious significance. During the wanderings of the children of Israel in the wilderness, circumcision was temporarily neglected, but this omission was repaired by Joshua before the conquest of the land (Josh. 5:2–9). During the Hellenistic period, prior to the Maccabean revolt, numbers of assimilated Jews attempted to conceal the fact of their circumcision, especially because of their participation, naked, in the athletic contests in the gymnasium. But, generally speaking, circumcision has been one of those commandments which the people of Israel carried out even when the rite was forbidden on pain of death, as during the reign of the Roman Emperor Hadrian.

The circumcision ceremony is performed on the 8th day after birth even if it falls on the Sabbath or the Day of Atonement. Postponement is permitted only when the health of the child would be endangered. If two male children in the family have died as a result of the operation, it would seem that there is a tendency in that family

Circumcision instruments

to continued bleeding; i.e., hereditary hemophilia. In such a case, and this is the only exception made, any further male children born need not be circumcised.

The circumcision ceremony is regarded as a festive event and is celebrated with a festive meal *(Seudat Mitzvah)* after the operation. In Gaonic times, the ceremony was held in the synagogue and in some places this custom still prevails. The three main participants in the ceremony are the *mohel,* who performs the operation; the father, who recites the blessing; and the *sandak* who holds the child on his lap during the operation. According to rabbinic tradition, there is also an invisible participant, the Prophet Elijah, who is the patron of circumcision. The chair on which the child is placed is therefore known as the Chair of Elijah.

Jewish circumcision is a complete and effective surgical operation, and, for this reason most modern communities ensure that the *mohel* is adequately qualified and that the operation is performed with antiseptic precautions. Orthodox Judaism frowns on the use of a medical doctor who is not, in addition, an observant Jew. Reform Judaism adopts a more lenient view in this regard. In addition to an eight-day-old child, all male converts to Judaism have to undergo ritual circumcision.

COINS: No coins, as such, existed among the Israelites in the early Biblical period. Gold was weighed out according to a silver standard, called a *shekel,* but this *shekel* was a weight rather than a coin.

Coins have been discovered that are from the 5th century B.C.E., the period of Persian rule in the land of Israel, but it is uncertain whether they are Jewish or Persian. They bear the inscription *yahud.* On one side of the coin is an owl, and on the other, the head of a man. Jewish coins from the Hasmonean era can be identified with more certainty. From the first period there are small copper coins with a Hebrew inscription "Johanan the High Priest and the Assembly of the Judeans." On the other side of the coin is the horn of plenty. Alexander Yannai (103–76 B.C.E.), the first Hasmonean prince to use the title of king on his coins, also imprinted an anchor on them. This was perhaps to symbolize the expansion of his kingdom to the shores of the Mediterranean. His inscriptions are in Greek and Hebrew. Coins from the period of Mattathias Antigonus (40–37 B.C.E.) bear a seven-branched candelabrum.

No Hebrew inscriptions have been found on coins from the time of King Herod (37–4 B.C.E.). His royal portrait appears on the coins from his non-Jewish provinces, but is absent from the coins in his Jewish provinces. This reflects Jewish opposition to the making of images. The period preceding the destruction of the Second Temple has yielded a very large collection of coins. Again, only Hebrew inscriptions appear on the Jewish coins. Thus, one coin carries the imprint of a chalice, and on the other side a stem with three flowers,

Coins of the State of Israel

the abbreviation for the year, and the words "Jerusalem the Holy." Many copper coins have also been found bearing pictures of vine leaves, date palms, citron, and fruit baskets. The fall of Jerusalem in 70 C.E. marked the end of the Jewish coin, at least temporarily. Instead, Roman coins were minted, symbolizing the Roman victory over the Jews. These showed a weeping Jewess under a palm tree, in bonds, with hands tied. To reinforce the image, the inscription read *Judea Capta* (Captured Judea).

Jewish coins again appeared during the second rebellion against Rome, the Bar Kokhba Rebellion (132–135). This produced the last series of independent Jewish coins until the modern rebirth of the State of Israel. Due to a shortage of metal, the Jews of this period sometimes used Roman coins and merely placed their stamp over the Roman. Many musical instruments appear on these coins, as well as a building with a four-pillared front, perhaps symbolizing the hope for the rebuilding of the Temple. During the period of the British Mandate in the land of Israel, coins with Hebrew inscriptions were again made, although by the British and not by the Jews. They bore inscriptions in Hebrew, Arabic, and English and contained the initials "EY" *(Eretz Yisrael)* beside the word "Palestine."

With the independence of Israel, a new monetary system was created. It is based on the pound *(lira;* plural *lirot)*, which on one side bears the Israel seal of the candelabrum, as did the coins of Alexander Yannai. This is surrounded by two olive branches, symbolizing peace. The word "Israel" is inscribed in English, Hebrew, and Arabic. The other side says in Hebrew only, "One Israeli Pound." This pound is equal to 100 *agorot,* or "cents." These are minted in various denominations such as 5, 10, and 25, corresponding to American nickels, dimes, and quarters. Each carries a symbol: a lyre, wheat representing bread,

palm trees, flowers. These smaller coins bear only Hebrew and Arabic inscriptions. Unlike the pound, they bear no English writing.

Israel today also issues paper money. These bills bear pictures of the people of Israel: factory workers, scientists, and fishermen. They are also inscribed in the three languages of the State — Hebrew, Arabic, and English.

COMMANDMENTS, 613: According to an early rabbinic tradition, there are 613 commandments in the five books of Moses. 248 of them are positive ("Thou shalt..."), and 365 negative ("Thou shalt not..."). This division is said to correspond to the 248 bones and 365 muscles of the human body, as well as to the 365 days of the year. Since no count of all the laws in the five books of Moses yields precisely this number, various scholars have attempted to enumerate the list of commandments. As a result, several different versions have appeared. The medieval Jewish scholar and philosopher Moses Maimonides wrote a book devoted to the subject entitled *The Book of Precepts,* and, in his introduction, he devises various rules according to which the commandments should be counted. In addition to the division between positive and negative precepts, the sages of the Talmud and later Jewish scholars made further distinctions. Rational commandments, for whose observance a logical explanation exists, and which would have been instituted by human society even if the Bible had not enjoined their observance, are known as *mishpatim* (ordinances). On the other hand, there are commandments for whose observance no reason exists or can be found, but which must nevertheless be accepted without hesitation as a decree of God. These are called *hukkim* (statutes). In addition, there are commandments regulating conduct between man and God, and between man and man, commandments applicable only to the land of Israel, commandments which must be observed at a specific time or which are contingent upon a particular period, and commandments the observance of which is not limited in time or place, but is permanent.

The commandments are generally referred to as the *taryag mitzvot,* the numerical value of the Hebrew letters T. R. Y. G., being 613.

The word *mitzvah,* which originally was used in a technical sense to denote a commandment, has in the course of time received the meaning of a worthy or meritorious deed. It is also used to describe an honor received in the synagogue.

CONFIRMATION: Religious ceremony for boys and girls (14–16) introduced by Reform Judaism. It originally replaced the bar mitzvah ceremony and took place at a later age, thirteen being considered too immature for the assumption of Jewish responsibilities. It was also in accordance with Reform Judaism's policy of placing women on an equal footing with men. Orthodox Judaism opposed this innovation on the grounds that it was a non-Jewish custom "having no root in Israel," and because of Orthodoxy's negative attitude to the participation of women in the synagogue service. In the course of time, however, this latter opposition diminished, so that in many Orthodox synagogues, especially in the western world, the bat mitzvah ceremony has become an integral part of the synagogue ceremonial, usually being held when the girl reaches the age of puberty; i.e., twelve years and one day. The tendency in modern Reform, on the other hand, has been to practice both bar mitzvah and confirmation, the latter serving the purpose of extending the child's career in the religious school.

CONSERVATIVE JUDAISM: One of the three religious movements within American Judaism (the other two being Reform and Orthodox). It developed in the United States during the 20th century, but derived its inspiration from the 19th century Historical School of Judaism in Europe, one of whose chief exponents was Zacharias Frankel (1801–1875). This school of thought arose as a counter-reaction to the Reform movement and insisted on the preservation of historical Judaism in its traditional form. The importance of Jewish nationhood, the land of Israel, the Hebrew language, and the observance of the *mitzvot,* principles rejected by early Reform, were reaffirmed by Frankel and his followers. At the same time, however, the Historical School accepted the need for the development, reinterpretation, and adaptation of Jewish law to changing conditions. In the United States, the forerunners of this school of thought, which was to become Conservative Judaism, were Isaac Leeser, Marcus Jastrow, Alexander Kohut, and others.

The rise of Conservative Judaism was facilitated by the mass immigration of Jews from eastern Europe to the United States in the last quarter of the 19th century. Reform Judaism, which had previously been in the ascendancy, had little in common with these immigrants, the majority of whom came from a traditional background. The founders and early leaders of Conservative Judaism, too, had their spiritual roots in the traditional Judaism of pre-World-War-I East European Jewry. The Jewish Theological Seminary, under the leadership of Solomon Schechter (1850–1915) set the tone. Schechter set up a faculty of scholars and teachers of international renown. Chief among these were Louis Ginzberg, Alexander Marx, Israel Friedlander, and Israel Davidson. Their international standing established the seminary as a central pillar of Jewish scholarship in America. In 1913, Schechter also organized the association of Conservative congregations in the United States, known as the United Synagogue of America, which today numbers some 800 affiliated synagogues in the United States and Canada; while as early as 1900, graduates of the seminary had formed an alumni association which in 1940 was reorganized as the Rabbinical Assembly of America.

Conservative Judaism stresses the maintenance of Jewish tradition and its observances on the one hand, but, on the other, regards Judaism as dynamic and progressive, as being in a state of continual development. This has led to considerable tension within the movement regarding religious change and innovation. For the most part, Conservative Judaism has opposed extreme changes in traditional observances, but it has permitted certain modifications of Jewish law with regard to the sitting together of men and women during worship, and in the wording of the traditional Jewish marriage document, the *Ketubbah*. These modifications have been violently opposed by Orthodox Judaism. As opposed to Reform, Conservatism accepts the authority of the *Halakhah*, of traditional Jewish law, believing that any changes made must be within the framework of that law. Nevertheless, Conservative Judaism has never been dogmatically defined, and this has been both its strength and its weakness. The tension between the forces of change and the forces of Conservatism has led to a variety of customs and practices within the movement. There are congregations in which the organ, mixed pew, and mixed choir have been introduced, whereas in others the practice both in form and in liturgy is close to Orthodox.

Because of a basically flexible and tolerant attitude, all the various forces have remained within the ranks of Conservative Judaism. In fact, every effort has been made to keep congregations which have deviated from tradition within the movement. The Reconstructionist movement is a case in point. Founded by the first principal of the Jewish Theological Seminary's teachers' institute, Mordecai Kaplan, this movement has attracted adherents from Reform and purely secular groups as well as from Conservatism itself. Kaplan formulated his philosophy in his *Judaism as a Civilization,* published in 1934. Reconstructionism calls for freedom of, for, and from religion as such. It advocates the acceptance of variety and freedom in religious practices, and urges the development of new ceremonial patterns in keeping with the facts of Jewish living in modern times. The concept of *Torah* is broadened to include ethical culture and the arts. God is defined as the power which makes for salvation and which helps the Jew make the most of his life. The Reconstructionist movement has often been referred to as a fourth religious party in American Judaism. But the Reconstructionist members of the Rabbinical Assembly continued to work within the framework of Conservative Judaism, and Kaplan was granted the freedom to continue with his independent thinking and teaching at the Jewish Theological Seminary even by those who disagreed most radically with him. The Conservative movement has, from the outset, been staunchly Zionist, and the concept of the Jewish people occupies a prominent place in the philosophy of the Reconstructionist movement. While supporting the development of the State of Israel and encouraging immigration, it has nevertheless also stressed the importance of the diaspora communities. The cultural Zionism of Aḥad Ha'am has greatly influenced Conservative thinkers who have applied that concept to the religious sphere, talking in terms of a spiritual nationalism which unites the Jewish people.

One of the most significant trends in the congregational system of the Conservative movement has been the development of the Jewish center. The first such institution was founded by Kaplan in 1918 with the purpose of reviving the traditional concept of the synagogue as a place of worship, study, and fellowship. This pattern was adopted by the United Synagogue as a whole and has been imitated in various forms by the other religious groups. In recent years, Conservative Judaism has begun to extend its activities to the State of Israel and also to other countries in the diaspora.

CONVERSION TO JUDAISM: The process whereby one is admitted into the Jewish faith. The English word "proselyte" is derived from the Greek translation of the Biblical word *ger* which originally meant a stranger or a sojourner, but has come to indicate one who accepts Judaism. Throughout Jewish history, there have been periods in which converts were accepted and even sought, and there have been other times when conversion to Judaism was actively discouraged. Thus, the sage Rabbi Eleazar ben Pedat was of the opinion that the Jewish people were dispersed so that they could spread Judaism among the gentiles. Rabbi Helbo, on the other hand, proclaimed that converts are as grievous as a scab on the skin. It seems that historical and external circumstances often played a large part in the shaping of Jewish attitudes to the problem of conversion, so that it is impossible to define a fixed Jewish viewpoint on the subject.

The rabbis distinguished between two types of converts, the half-convert known as *ger toshav* (the settler) or *ger ha-shaar* (the proselyte of the gate), and the full convert known as *ger tzedek* (the righteous proselyte). The first, while accepting the principle of monotheism and its corollary, the seven laws given to Noah, did not accept the ceremonial and ritual obligations imposed by Judaism. He was entitled to economic and social equality and had equal rights before the courts. The *ger tzedek* (which is now the only type of convert to Judaism) is the one who wishes to be admitted as a member of the Jewish people because of a sincere desire without ulterior motives to adopt Judaism. Once he has been through a period of preparation involving intensive study, he is circumcised (in the case of men), and immersed in the ritual bath, the *mikve* (in the case of men and women). Once accepted, the convert is considered a Jew in the full sense of the word, and it is forbidden to annoy or insult him by reminding him of his past. On the contrary, he is singled out for special blessing in the Amidah prayer.

Immediately before and after the destruction of the Second Temple (70 C.E.), the rabbis fostered missionary activity among the pagans. According to the ancient historian, Josephus, there were large numbers of converts in Roman and Greek society, even among the aristocracy. A whole royal house, that of Adiabene, converted to Judaism, while among the outstanding rabbinic sages, Rabbi Meir, Shemaiah, Avtalyon, Akiba, and the translator of the Bible into Aramaic, Onkelos, are all said to have either been converts or descendants of converts. The Idumean people were forcibly converted in Second Temple times, and from them came the famous King Herod. When early Christianity began to have some success among the Greek and Roman converts to Judaism, and when it was suspected that the Romans were purposely planting spies in the form of converts, the previously sympathetic attitude turned to one of antagonism. This bitter historical experience may have prompted the negative attitude of some of the rabbis as expressed by the statement of Rabbi Helbo, quoted above. Moreover, after Christianity became the official religion of the Roman Empire, conversion to Judaism was made an offense punishable by death. This was the prevalent situation throughout the Middle Ages, and, as a result, Jewish rabbinic authorities wanted to avoid bringing unnecessary dangers upon themselves and their communities by encouraging or practicing conversion. A prospective candidate was discouraged, and it was pointed out to him that Judaism was a persecuted faith and the nation of Israel downtrodden and oppressed, so that it was foolhardy and dangerous to identify with them. Nevertheless, throughout the Middle Ages there were numbers of non-Jews who converted to Judaism despite the danger involved. Among the converts were the Arabian tribal king Dhu Nawas in the 6th century and the leaders of the Khazar people in Russia in the eighth. There were many converts to Judaism among the tribes of North Africa, and in modern times it has been estimated that half the Jews of North Africa are descendants of Berber converts. In western Europe there were occasional converts to Judaism even among the clergy, notwithstanding the danger to which they and those who received them were subjected (many of them were put to death by the Church). In the 19th century, there was a widespread conversion to Judaism among the Russian peasantry and in Transylvania, while at the same time an entire group of converts was living at Safed in the land of Israel. In recent years, a body of converts from San Nicandro in Italy emigrated en masse to the State of Israel.

In modern times, especially with the rise of Reform Judaism, the question of conversion has aroused much controversy and debate. The problem has been aggravated by the rising number of persons wishing to convert to Judaism for personal reasons, in particular, in order to marry a Jew.

Orthodox Judaism, which is traditionally suspicious of insincere converts, tends to move cautiously and even to discourage conversion unless sincerity of motive is proved. Reform, on the other hand, has a more liberal and lenient approach to the problem. In the State of Israel, where conversion is under the jurisdiction of the Orthodox Rabbinate, the question of Reform conversion has generated much public debate.

Whatever the varying shades of opinion with regard to conversion, Judaism, unlike Christianity, does not regard missionary activity as a matter of life and death. The Talmud states specifically that the righteous men of all nations have a share in the world to come. It is therefore unnecessary to undertake conversionist activity, as in the case of Christianity, in order to "save souls."

COSTUME: Throughout the ages, Jews have tended to adjust to the style of clothing and fashions of their place of residence. The Bible lays down three basic regulations concerning dress. They are: 1. not to wear *shaatnez,* clothing woven of wool and linen; 2. to wear *tzizit,* fringes upon the four corners of one's garment; and 3. not to wear the clothing worn by the opposite sex. Evidence from ancient monuments, however, seems to indicate that the dress of the Hebrews in Biblical times did not differ from that of other Semitic peoples. During Talmudic times, the rabbis stressed the importance of wearing distinctive Jewish clothing in order to differ in costume from the gentiles. The later Jewish commentators, however, explain the prohibition of dressing like the gentiles as referring to clothing which has an idolatrous connection or to clothing which is peculiarly distinctive of the gentiles. The introduction of the Jewish badge by both Islam and the Church during the Middle Ages is proof that without the badge it was impossible to distinguish between Jews and non-Jews. In addition to the badge, the pointed hat (often called *Judenhut* or Jew-hat) was considered to be specifically Jewish. Jews settling in a new country would often continue to wear the distinctive clothing of the inhabitants of their previous country. In the Moslem countries of North Africa, Jews were forbidden to wear bright colored clothing, so the habit of wearing a black robe and skull cap developed. During the late Middle Ages, Polish Jews adopted the costume which had at one time been worn by the Polish

Yemenite Jewish woman

nobility, consisting of a long ungirdled coat known as a *caftan* and a fur-trimmed hat called a *shtreimel*. The Ḥasidim added a girdle in order to distinguish between the upper and lower portions of the body, and in certain cases knee-breeches and buckled shoes. This costume was later endowed with a sacred character and is worn to this day in Ḥasidic and ultra-Orthodox circles.

In western countries there has never been any distinctive Jewish garb. The rabbinic codes, however, warn against ostentation and exaggerated extravagance in matters of dress. The scholar is especially enjoined to be meticulously tidy.

CREATION: Judaism is based on the belief that the universe was created by the one, Almighty, and all-righteous God, as described in the opening chapter of the book of Genesis. This idea, which was later accepted by the other monotheistic religions, Christianity and Islam, is the unique product of the Jewish genius. The origin of the universe has always exercised a fascination for the mind of man, and long before the advent of the Jewish people on the scene of history, other ancient nations and religions had their own account of how the world and man were created. Some modern scholars have attempted to show that the Biblical version of creation was influenced by the earlier Babylonian mythology. An examination of all other accounts of creation, however, whether Babylonian, Phoenician, Greek, or Roman, reveals a wild, cruel, and pagan setting. Thus, Assyro-Babylonian mythology describes the creation as the result of a vicious conflict between rival gods, the various elements comprising the universe being parts of the corpse of the defeated God. In its simplicity and purity of religious thought, the Biblical account of the six days of creation is unparalleled. While the fact of creation was never doubted, the actual manner in which the world was fashioned and the process whereby the universe came into existence was left as an open question. This gave thinkers and philosophers much leeway for the presentation of their ideas. The Talmudic sages regarded speculation about the origin and nature of the universe, known as *Maaseh Bereshit* (the act of creation), as a dangerous exercise and limited its study to a select, spiritual elite. Most of the rabbis of the Talmud and, after them, the medieval Jewish philosophers accepted the principle that God created the universe out of nothing. Others, however, under the influence of the Greek philosopher, Aristotle, who proclaimed the theory of the eternity of matter, held that the universe was fashioned from formless matter which had preceded all existence. In the Talmud, the possibility that our world was preceded by other worlds is not excluded. Throughout Jewish history, with the exception of

,fundamentalists who take every word of the Bible literally, the tendency on the part of most Jewish scholars has been to interpret the creation chapter with some flexibility. From Philo of Alexandria in the 1st century C.E., Moses Maimonides in the 12th century, and Moses Mendelssohn at the beginning of the modern period to Jewish scholars of our own day, Jewish thinkers have sought to reconcile Judaism and philosophy, and Judaism and science. For this reason, and because of the non-literal approach to the creation chapter, modern scientific discoveries — especially the theory of evolution — have never posed a danger to the fundamental principles of Judaism. On one principle, however, Judaism stands firm and uncompromising– the world is no product of chance, no mere accident, but an act of divine will. Whether God achieved His purpose through a process of evolution or not is immaterial. Judaism in all its different manifestations, whether Orthodox, Conservative, or Reform, affirms that behind the orderly development of the universe, there must be a cause, a Supreme Power — in brief, a God, one and all-powerful. Only thus can the origin of life, mind, conscience, and the human personality be explained. In the final event, however, the Bible is not a scientific textbook, and the Biblical account of creation is to be read for its moral and religious message rather than for the acquisition of scientific knowledge.

CRUSADES: Holy wars undertaken by Christians from Europe to liberate the Holy Land from Moslem rule. The First Crusade was proclaimed in 1095 by Pope Urban II. While the basic motive for the Crusades was undoubtedly sincere, and many of the Crusaders were pious men bent on freeing the Land of Israel from the "infidels" and turning Jerusalem into a Christian shrine, many others were adventurers whose real interest was the quest for booty, fame, and slaughter.

Long before the Crusaders reached the Holy Land, they ran out of supplies and did not hesitate to plunder the countryside through which they passed. As for the Jews, it seemed preposterous to many Crusaders to journey so far to the Holy Land to fight the infidels there, while leaving untouched the infidels — i.e., the Jews — at home. The Crusaders therefore fell upon one defenseless Jewish community after another. Such famous Jewish Rhineland communities as Speyer, Mainz, Worms, and Cologne were wiped out and similar attacks took place in Prague. In the Holy Land itself, the Jews were massacred along with the Moslems when Jerusalem was captured in 1099. When the Second Crusade was proclaimed in 1147, all who joined were freed from the obligation of paying any debts owed to Jews. Once more, massacres occurred and this time the infection spread to northern France. In some cases, local authorities and churchmen attempted to protect the Jews, the most outstanding in this respect being Bernard of Clairvaux, who preached in their favor. Consequently, the number who were martyred was less than during the First Crusade. The Third Crusade in 1187 was led by Richard the Lionhearted of England, Philip Augustus of France, and Frederick I of Germany. This time, the well-established Jewish community of England was affected. The Jews of York suffered a particularly merciless slaughter. Subsequent Crusades were supported with less and less enthusiasm on the part of the masses and Jewish suffering diminished accordingly. As late as 1320, however, there was an outbreak of violence in the South of France and Northern Spain, accompanying the so-called "Shepherds' Crusade."

The Crusades ushered in a new era of unparalleled suffering and unmitigated violence for the Jews. Outbreaks had occurred before 1096, it is true, but never before on such a vast scale. Tens of thousands of Jews were murdered and many Jewish communities destroyed. Moreover, the enormous losses of property they sustained drove the Jews deeper into the business of money-lending, thereby providing their neighbors with an additional pretext for hating them. By opening up new trade routes with the East, the Crusades also served to displace many Jewish merchants by depriving them of what had been a monopoly. The Crusader "Kingdom of Jerusalem," covering varying areas of the Holy Land survived for some two centuries, leaving many remains that can still be seen today.

CZECHOSLOVAKIA: Before the establishment of the Czechoslovak Republic in 1919 by the Union of Bohemia, Moravia, Austrian Silesia, Slovakia, and Carpatho-Russia, the history of the Jews in this area was tied up with the history of the Jews in the Austro-Hungarian Empire to which these provinces previously belonged. Jews lived in Bohemia as early as the 10th century, the main settlement being in Prague. During the Crusades, they suffered severe persecution and until the 16th century their position was precarious. From the 16th–18th centuries, Prague enjoyed a golden age and was considered one of the most important Jewish centers in the world. Its "Judenstadt," as the Jewish quarter was called, contained synagogues, a printing press, and other autonomous institutions. Great Talmudic and Bible scholars made Prague their home, as did many Jews fleeing from persecution in Eastern Europe. In 1744, the Empress Maria Theresa decreed a general expulsion of the Jews, but this was never entirely enforced and was revoked in 1749 on payment of a heavy tax. From 1781–1919, the history of the Jews of Czechoslovakia merged with that of Austria. Under the Czechoslovak Republic, Jews enjoyed full equality, although immediately after World War I there were some anti-Semitic outbreaks inspired mainly by German elements in the population. As a result, the Jewish population which had previously supported all German cultural institutions drew closer to the Czechs. In 1935, there were 357,000 Jews in Czechoslovakia but with the Nazi occupation in March 1939 there began a campaign of systematic annihilation. Large numbers managed to emigrate, but of those remaining, only 42,000 survived the holocaust. During Israel's War of Independence, Czechoslovakia was a source of much-needed military equipment and between 1945–53, 24,000 Czech Jews immigrated to Israel. The attitude of the Communist regime soon changed, however, and in 1952 a number of Jews prominent in the regime were purged and put on trial. The Slansky show trial — named after the main defendant — had strong anti-Semitic undertones and was openly anti-Zionist. The subsequent years saw limitations placed on Jewish cultural and religious activities similar to those in other Communist countries. The brief rule of Alexander Dubcek brought a more liberal attitude but this was curtailed by the Russian invasion of August 1968.

There are only 12,000 Jews in Czechoslovakia today.

DANIEL: Ninth Biblical book of *Ketuvim* (Writings), the third section of the Bible. The book contains twelve chapters which may be divided into two distinct sections. The first six chapters record the adventures of Daniel and his three friends, Hananiah, Mishael and Azariah (renamed Shadrach, Meshach and Abednego), Judean exiles carried to the court of King Nebuchadnezzar. Because of his success in interpreting the king's dreams, Daniel rises to a position of authority at court and his friends are made provincial governors. His success arouses the jealousy of the Babylonian astrologers and advisers at court and they conspire against the interlopers. For refusing to obey the king's command to worship a golden idol, the three friends are condemned to be thrown into the burning fiery furnace. Miraculously they are saved. Their bonds fall from them and they walk unharmed in the center of the fire, proving to the king and his counselors the power and the glory of the God of Shadrach, Meshach and Abednego.

Daniel also predicts the madness and downfall of Nebuchadnezzar and, at the great feast given by Belshazzar, is the only one who can interpret the mysterious

Story of Daniel in old mosaic near Jericho

writing on the wall that foretells the doom of the Babylonian empire.

Daniel maintained his high position at the court of the Persian conqueror Darius, the king who reluctantly had him thrown into the lions' den for continuing to worship his God in the face of a royal interdict. Again, Daniel is saved by the angel of God who keeps the lions' mouths shut all night so that Daniel can walk out unscathed in the morning "and no hurt was found upon him because he had trusted in his God."

The following six chapters (7–12) contain visions which seem to relate to ancient times but most probably refer to the great world powers of the time the book was written — during the Maccabean revolt of 165 B.C.E., in the opinion of most Bible scholars. For fear of Antiochus' agents, names are not mentioned, but to the people of that time, the "four beasts," the ram, the goat, and the other visions clearly fitted the events of their own time.

All the stories of the Book of Daniel were designed to hearten the Jews against the persecutions of Antiochus Epiphanes and to encourage them to uphold their traditions, whatever the cost.

Most of the second section is written in Hebrew, while the earlier chapters are in Aramaic. Some scholars believe that this section was written before the later chapters. The Book of Daniel is, in all probability, the latest of the Old Testament Books.

See also: APOCALYPSE.

DAVID: Second king of Israel, ruled from 1007–967 B.C.E. Born in Bethlehem, the youngest son of Jesse, David's life story is told in the Bible from the 16th chapter of the first book of Samuel to the opening chapter of the Book of Kings.

David was a shepherd and a skilled musician. He was brought to King Saul's court to calm the king when he was suffering one of his fits of depression. Another story tells us that David won fame by killing the Philistine giant Goliath. He then became Saul's armor-bearer and later one of his commanders. He married Saul's daughter, Michal, and won the undying friendship of Saul's son Jonathan. However, as David's popularity with the people grew, Saul became insanely jealous. Obsessed with the idea that David was conspiring to overthrow him, the king resolved to kill him. David was forced to flee to the wilderness of Judah where he was joined by his kinsmen and fugitives and distressed persons of all types. There he led the life of an outlaw, desperately seeking to stay out of reach of King Saul who spared no effort to trap him.

In desperation, David took his six hundred men and went over to the Philistine king, Achish, who gave him the town of Ziklag, expecting that he would make as much trouble for Israel as possible. Instead, David and his force attacked the Amalekites and other Bedouin tribes who were harassing Israelite shepherds, sending Achish false reports to persuade him that they were actually raiding Judah. The defeat of Israel by the Philistines on Mount Gilboa and the death of Saul and his three sons in battle, much as it grieved David, nevertheless presented him with a unique opportunity. He returned to Judah, settled in Hebron and was there elected King by the elders of Judah. In the meantime, Saul's general, Abner, had taken Saul's surviving son, Eshbaal, to Maḥanaim in Transjordan and proclaimed him king.

However, Eshbaal had no real authority. Later he quarreled with Abner, who then transferred his allegiance to David. Eshbaal lasted only two years, after which he was murdered by two of his officers. With no one left to further the claims of the house of Saul, the people flocked to David in Hebron and acclaimed him King over all Israel.

David *by Bernini, Museum Borghese, Rome*

David's first step was to rid the country of the Philistine menace. In a series of brilliantly fought battles, he succeeded in

destroying Philistine military power. Thus
freed of external danger, David was able
to devote himself to the consolidation of
his throne. He conquered the Jebusite city
of Jerusalem and, by bringing the ark of
the covenant from Kirjat-Jearim where it
had remained for more than a generation,
he made clear his intention of making
Jerusalem the political and religious capital
of the state. During David's reign, the
conquest of Canaan, begun in the days of
Joshua, was finally completed. Moreover,
he waged war against the Ammonites and
defeated their allies, the Aramean tribes
who had come to their aid. It was during
the siege of the Ammonite capital Rabbath
Ammon that David, who had remained
in Jerusalem, took another man's wife,
Bathsheba — the wife of Uriah who was at
the front. This affair blackened his name
and brought down on his head a stinging
rebuke from Nathan the Prophet.

David rounded out his military conquests
by attacking Moab and Edom in Southern
Transjordan and conducting a successful
campaign against the Aramean king,
Hadadezer, in revenge for his support of
the Ammonites. David's conquests made
Israel the strongest power in the area. No
longer a disorganized group of tribes, but
a complex state under a crown, Israel had
become the center of an empire that, by
ancient standards, was of quite respectable
size. From the Red Sea in the south, it
stretched north and eastwards to the
Euphrates and in all that area its power
was, for the moment, unchallenged.

David's latter years were far from
peaceful. The question of the succession
understandably led to bitter internal rivalry
among his sons, a situation that was not
improved by his being an indulgent parent.
Years of constant intrigue, violence and
even outright rebellion followed. His favorite son, Absalom, turned against him,
and it was with difficulty that the rebellion
was put down, the death of Absalom
plunging David into the depths of grief.

Then his son Adonijah, next in line for
the succession, attempted to seize the
throne. Only after the pleading of
Bathsheba, supported by Nathan the
Prophet, did the old king at last intervene
to have her son, Solomon, proclaimed
king in his stead.

David reigned for forty years: seven
and a half in Hebron and thirty-three
in Jerusalem. The memory and symbol of
David remained vivid in Jewish thought
and folklore. The kings of Judah were
all descended from him and, traditionally,
the Messiah must also be his descendant.
So many stories and legends were woven
around his personality that it is no wonder
that, in the popular phrase, *"King David
lives!"* David was also known as "the
Sweet Singer of Israel" because of the
tradition that he was the author of the book
of Psalms. Whether or not he did compose
any of them, the Laments for Saul and
Jonathan and for Absalom suggest that he
was adequately qualified as a poet.

DAYAN, MOSHE (1915–): Israeli soldier
and statesman. Dayan was born in the
first kibbutz, Deganya, of which his father
was one of the founders. When he was
six, the family left the kibbutz and were
among the founders of the first *moshav* in
Israel, Nahalal. At twelve, Dayan took
part in Jewish self-defense activity against
plundering Bedouin groups. He acquired
his first basic military training from the
British captain, Orde Wingate, who trained
Jewish commando units undertaking
reprisal actions against Arab marauders
and guerrilla bands. As a member of
the *Haganah,* the Jewish self-defense
organization, Dayan helped found its elite
section, the Palmaḥ. In 1939, he was
arrested by the British authorities but was
soon released in order to take part in
British military action against the pro-Nazi
Vichy regime in Syria. It was during this
campaign that he was wounded and lost an
eye. In the Israeli War of Independence,

Moshe Dayan

DEAD SEA (Hebrew, **Yam Ha-Melaḥ** — the Salt Sea). Southernmost and largest of the lakes in the land of Israel. Situated 1,292 feet below sea level, it is the lowest spot on the surface of the earth. Its length is 48 miles, its maximum width 11 miles and its total area 390 square miles. Its average depth is 462 feet, although in places it is as much as 1,320 feet deep. It lies within the Jordan depression, between the mountains of Moab on the east and the Judean Hills on the west. According to geologists, however, in ancient times the Dead Sea covered a far larger area, extending eighty miles north and sixty-two miles south of its present shores. The water of the Dead Sea, derived mainly from the Jordan and Arnon rivers, has an exceptionally high saturation of various salts and other minerals, which make it a major source of potash and bromine compounds. These salts are extracted by the Dead Sea Works at their plant at Sodom, to the south of the sea. The therapeutic virtues of the

he commanded the unit which drove the Syrian army out of the Jordan Valley and in August 1948, he was appointed commander of the Jerusalem region. In 1953, he was named Chief of Staff of the Israel Army and given the rank of Major General. In this capacity, he was the architect of Israel's victory over the Egyptian Army in the 1956 Sinai campaign. Dayan left the army in 1958 and, in 1959, was elected to the Knesset as a *Mapai* (Labor Party) deputy. From 1959–64, he served as Minister of Agriculture. The split between David Ben Gurion and his former colleagues found Dayan on Ben Gurion's side and in 1965 he left the government to join the *Rafi* party and serve as one of its Knesset members. On the eve of the Six-Day War of June 1967, a government of national unity was formed and, by popular demand, Dayan was given the portfolio of Minister of Defense. After the successful conclusion of that war, Dayan became responsible not only for defense but also very largely for the administration of the territories taken by Israel during the war.

Salt formations on the Dead Sea

waters are also exploited, especially at the springs of En Bokkek. Fish cannot live in the Dead Sea water, which destroys practically all organic life — hence the name, Dead Sea. No trace remains today of the five "cities of the plain" of Abraham's time (Sodom and Gomorrah, the wicked cities God destroyed; Admah; Zeboiim; and Zoar), but a peak of Mount Sodom is still called "Lot's Wife." Ein Gedi, midway along the Western shore, has had a flourishing community since before David's time.

DEAD SEA SCROLLS: Ancient scrolls, fragments, and manuscripts discovered in 1947 and in subsequent years in caves along the western shore of the Dead Sea. Archaeological exploration of a ruin in the vicinity of the caves called Khirbet Qumran unearthed an ancient settlement, the inhabitants of which were probably the authors and scribes of the scrolls. One of the most important archaeological discoveries of the century, the Dead Sea Scrolls and their relationship to the sect of Qumran, are the subject of intense discussion and debate among scholars. All the scrolls and manuscripts have not yet been deciphered and analyzed, and it is still impossible to reach dogmatic conclusions on their significance or the identity of the inhabitants of Qumran. But on the basis of the research to date, the Dead Sea Scrolls cast new and additional light on the period preceding the destruction of the Second Temple. Radiocarbon tests and ancient coins found in and around Khirbet Qumran indicate that the site was lived in from the time of the Maccabean ruler John Hyrcanus (135–104 B.C.E.), although there is evidence of an earlier occupancy. As a result of an earthquake in the year 31 B.C.E., the settlement was temporarily abandoned. Soon afterward, it was resettled and lived in until its final destruction in the revolt against Rome (67–70 C.E.).

The scrolls themselves are of inestimable value for several reasons. Primarily, they provide us with the oldest known manuscripts of the Hebrew Bible, including two complete copies of the book of Isaiah and fragments of every other book with the exception of the book of Esther. Since the oldest versions previously known date from the Middle Ages, the authenticity of the traditional Hebrew text (the Masoretic text) may be judged by a comparison with the scrolls. While such a comparison reveals numerous differences here and there, especially with regard to the book of Samuel, which is closer to the Greek version than to the traditional one, the differences are of a minor nature so that the scrolls generally justify a conservative approach to biblical studies. Of special interest are the Sectarian writings; i.e., those scrolls that pertain to the life of the sect and its world outlook. Among these are the Manual of Discipline, the Scroll of the War of the Sons of Light and the Sons of Darkness, and the Scroll of Thanksgiving Psalms. One scroll, written on copper, contains a cryptic guide to buried treasure. In addition, there are numerous commentaries on biblical books, each commentary *(pesher)* explaining the biblical text in terms of the history of the sect and its special standpoint. The sect made its home in this desolate part of the world out of a deep dissatisfaction with the ruling priestly caste in Jerusalem, the desire to pursue its own principles and practices, and a genuine belief in isolation as a means of achieving spiritual elevation. The teacher and perhaps the founder of the sect, known as the teacher of righteousness, is spoken of with reverence; his opponent and persecutor, called the "wicked priest," is denounced. The members of the sect saw themselves as the Children of Light in contrast to their enemies, the Children of Darkness. The struggle between the forces of good, represented by the sect, and the forces of evil, their enemies, would, after a series of

Students examining the Dead Sea Scrolls, Shrine of the Book

indecisive battles, culminate in the triumph of the Children of Righteousness. The Qumran sect lived an extreme other-worldly existence, being even more particular in matters of ritual purity than were the Pharisees. Admission to their ranks was achieved only after a prolonged period of probation and trial. They considered themselves to be members of a special community which was both of this world and a part of the coming heavenly world, a concept reminiscent of the New Testament idea of the "Kingdom of God." Their attitude toward the Torah and its commandments was rigid and uncompromising and they rejected the calendar accepted by the rest of the Jews. They therefore considered festivals celebrated in Jerusalem as profane, since in their view they were not held on their appointed days. Like the early Christians, they awaited the imminent arrival of the Messiah.

Several theories have been suggested as to the origin of the sect, but that it was a Jewish religious sect is beyond doubt. Most scholars tend to the view that it was either identical with or closely related to the Essenes. The description of the latter given by the ancient historian Josephus, and the statement by Pliny the Elder that an Essene settlement flourished on the north-western shore of the Dead Sea, tend to confirm this judgment. The Dead Sea Scrolls, in the opinion of many scholars, throw a new light on the origins of Christianity which, far from being a unique phenomenon, is now shown to be rooted in Judaism, albeit of a sectarian nature. It has even been suggested that John the Baptist, the forerunner of Jesus, was a member of the Qumran sect, or was close to it. A number of the scrolls are now in the permanent possession of the State of Israel and are housed in the Shrine of the Book at the Israel Museum.

See also: ESSENES, MASORAH.

DEBORAH: Judge and prophetess who, together with Barak the son of Abinoam, inspired the tribes of Israel to rally and fight the Canaanite king, Jabin of Hazor, and his general, Sisera (Judges 4). Before this victory, the tribes of Israel had been unable to conquer the Valley of Jezreel against the military superiority of the Canaanites, expressed in the use of chariots, which the Israelites did not possess.

Victory was won when a torrential rainstorm bogged down the Canaanite chariots and enabled the Israelite infantrymen to slaughter the occupants. The victory was celebrated by Deborah with a song of praise (Judges 5) which is regarded as one of the oldest pieces of Hebrew poetry. It is recited in the synagogue as the prophetical reading when the story of the crossing of the Red Sea constitutes the Pentateuchal reading.

DIASPORA: Greek word for "dispersion," generally used to refer to all the countries outside the land of Israel where Jews live. The Hebrew word *galut* meaning "exile" is not quite the same, as it implies a forced dispersion, whereas diaspora may be voluntary. Since the establishment of the State of Israel and the resultant opportunity given to all Jews to return to their ancestral homeland, the Diaspora

Dead Sea Scroll fragments, Shrine of the Book

may no longer be defined in terms of an enforced exile, but rather as the voluntary dispersion of the Jewish people referred to in Hebrew as *tephutzot*. This does not apply to those countries in which Jews are discriminated against and whose regimes do not permit their immigration to the State of Israel. For such communities Diaspora remains, in its classical sense, a *galut*.

Whatever meaning the term received in later Jewish history, historically the Diaspora is the product of military defeat and enforced exile. The conquest of the Northern Kingdom of Israel by the Assyrians in the year 721 B.C.E. led to the deportation of the vast majority of the Ten Tribes of Israel that constituted the population of that State. All subsequent rumors, legends, and reports as to their whereabouts are unreliable and they were doubtless assimilated into their new surroundings. The second large movement of Jews out of the land of Israel took place in the years 597 and 586 B.C.E., when King Nebuchadnezzar deported them to Babylon. A few years later, after the assassination of Gedaliah, numbers of Jews fled to Egypt. In Babylon, the Jews established a vital community and even when Cyrus, the Persian conqueror, permitted them to return to their homeland, the vast majority chose to remain in Babylon. From there they spread throughout the Persian Empire. After the conquests of Alexander the Great in the 4th century B.C.E., Jews settled throughout Asia Minor and the Greek islands. During the period of the Second Temple, Alexandria in Egypt became the center for hundreds of thousands of Jews. The Jewish centers in Babylon and Egypt thus thrived and developed spiritually and culturally and, in all probability, the numbers of Jews there exceeded those in the land of Israel. They nevertheless maintained strong links with the Jews in the Holy Land which was still regarded as the main center of the Jewish people. The destruction of the Temple by the Romans in 70 C.E. and the suppression of the Bar Kokhba revolt in 135 C.E. brought Judean independence to an end and with it the dispersion of the Jews increased in all directions. There was hardly a place throughout the Roman Empire where Jews did not settle. Tens of thousands were captives carried to Rome where they were sold as slaves. Many, however, were either redeemed by their fellow Jews or liberated by their masters. In general, the Jews of the Roman Empire were granted citizenship rights and a certain amount of internal autonomy. During the Roman Imperial period Jews settled in North Africa, Spain, northern France and the Rhineland. The Christianization of the Empire, however, drastically worsened their lot. Even after the destruction of the Temple, great centers of Jewish learning existed in the land of Israel, but these too declined, especially after the Emperor Constantine proclaimed Christianity the official religion of the Empire. Babylonian Jewry, on the other hand, first under the Parthian rulers and then under Islam, became the main center of Jewish scholarship. The authority of its leaders was recognized throughout the Jewish world. The Babylonian Diaspora retained its pre-eminence for close to seven hundred years, declining during the 10th and 11th centuries until it finally disintegrated physically and spiritually. The focus of Jewish life moved to Spain where, since the Moslem invasion of 711, the Jews had enjoyed a large measure of freedom. The Spanish Diaspora produced some of the greatest figures of Jewish medieval history. Jews achieved prominence in almost every sphere of life as theologians, philosophers, mathematicians, poets, astronomers, statesmen, and physicians. The massacres of 1391 sounded the death knell of the community and, with the promulgation of the expulsion decree of 1492, the last Jews fled from Spain. The exiles succeeded in founding new communities and strengthening those already established in Turkey, the land of Israel, Italy, and North Africa. Many Marranos were among the early pioneers in South and North America. The center of gravity for the Jews, however, now shifted to the continent of Europe, in particular to eastern Europe. This shift had already begun in the 12th and 13th centuries when the persecutions of the time of the Crusades had forced the Jewish communities of France and Germany eastwards to Russia, Poland and Lithuania. These communities, together with other Jewish settlements in central and western Europe, became the center of Jewish life and scholarship. By the latter part of the 19th century, 80 percent of world Jewry lived in eastern Europe. But the persecutions that began then, in the second half of the 19th century, prompted far-reaching changes in the physical make-up of the Diaspora, with hundreds of thousands of Jews fleeing westwards from central and eastern Europe to the countries of western Europe, and other countries of the western hemisphere.

The European Diaspora was almost entirely wiped out by the Nazis between 1940–45, the only sizeable communities remaining being those of the Soviet Union and, on a smaller scale, in France. The Jewish population of the Soviet Union numbers $2\frac{1}{2}$ to 3 million but, because of its enforced isolation, it is unable to play a major role in Jewish life. The Western Diaspora has accordingly assumed a major role in the life of the Jewish people outside the land of Israel. This is particularly true of the Jewish community of the United States, which is the largest in the world and, together with the state of Israel, has assumed leadership of the Jewish world.

DIETARY LAWS: Biblical and rabbinical regulations governing the food which a Jew may or may not eat. The permitted and forbidden foods are enumerated in the biblical books of Leviticus (ch. 11) and Deuteronomy (ch. 14). These may be divided into three categories: 1) cattle or beasts, 2) birds, and 3) fish. Of the first category, only those which meet the following double test may be eaten: They must have a divided hoof which is completely cloven or split, and must chew the cud. This especially excludes the pig, which does not chew the cud. Animals and beasts permitted for food are known as "clean" cattle or "clean" beasts; those prohibited are known as "unclean." A number of birds are mentioned in the Bible as forbidden, but no general rule is given and many of those enumerated are impossible to identify. The birds prohibited are mainly birds of prey. Because of the uncertainty involved, however, only birds that are traditionally known to be "clean," may be eaten, such as the hen, goose, or turkey.

The rule governing marine life is that only fish that have fins and scales may be eaten. Thus, oysters, lobsters, crabs, and eels are prohibited.

Insects and reptiles are prohibited with the exception of certain kinds of locusts mentioned in the Bible. In addition, the products of unclean cattle, beasts, birds, and fish such as their milk, eggs, or caviar prepared from the roe of the sturgeon, are also prohibited. Moreover, those parts of the fat of clean animals which were burnt on the altar in the days when sacrifices were offered may not be eaten. Such fat is called *helev* and must be removed by the process known as porging. Blood may not be part of the Jewish diet in any form. It is considered to be the life force of the animal and hence unfit for human consumption. Similarly, a blood speck in an egg renders it unfit. The blood of fish, however, is permitted. This prohibition against eating blood led to two special requirements: a special method of slaughtering the animal known as *shehitah* and the special preparation of meat for cooking. *Shehitah* is the act of ritual slaughter and only this act renders an animal or bird fit for consumption according to Jewish law.

Fish do not require *shehitah*. The slaughtering of the animal is performed by a specially qualified and observant Jew known as a *shohet*. It consists of the slashing of the gullet and the windpipe with a meticulously prepared knife which is examined by the *shohet* before the slaughtering so as to ensure that it is sharp and has no blemish. The slightest dent in the knife disqualifies the slaughtering. This method of slaughter ensures the maximum drainage of blood while the minimum amount of pain is inflicted on the animal. In various parts of the world attempts have been made to ban the Jewish method of slaughter on the alleged grounds that it is cruel to the animals. This humanitarian concern for animals has often been a cover for anti-Semitism and for attacks on the Jewish religion. Scientific evidence, offered by both defenders and critics of *shehitah,* acknowledges the effectiveness of this method. Leading Jewish and non-Jewish authorities point out that an animal loses consciousness immediately after cutting his jugular vein so that this is, in effect, the kindest method of slaughter.

Once the animal has been slaughtered, the *shohet* examines its state of health for any signs of disease. If any are found, he pronounces the animal unfit for consumption. Although the major part of the animal's blood is drained by *shehitah,* further precautions must be taken before the meat may be cooked. It is soaked in water for thirty minutes and then covered on all sides with salt which is removed after an hour by rinsing. The process of salting ensures the removal of any blood which may have remained after the *shehitah.* Any bird or animal permitted by Jewish law and which has undergone the process of *shehitah* and salting, is called *kasher.* A bird or animal that is not permitted by Jewish law, or has not been ritually prepared, is *terefah.* The word *terefah,* meaning torn, originally referred to an animal mauled by a wild beast. Now it

has been extended to mean any kind of food forbidden by Jewish law.

Meat and Milk. Aside from the rules and regulations governing animals permitted for food and their slaughter, the Jewish dietary laws were extended still further to include the actual cooking and eating of the food. The most distinctive of these rules are those concerning the separation of milk and meat. The verse "Thou shalt not cook a kid in its mother's milk" is repeated three times in the Bible. This, say the rabbis, is to teach that it is forbidden to cook, eat, or benefit from (by selling it) a mixture of milk and meat. Traditional Judaism insists on rigid adherence to this law. Thus, every Jewish household is expected to have separate sets of cutlery, crockery, pots, and pans, one for meat dishes and the other for milk. After eating meat, it is obligatory to wait a period of time before eating milk foods. Custom varies as to the length of time (one hour, three hours, six hours) which should elapse. After eating dairy foods, however, a shorter period is sufficient before eating meats. If meat and milk are eaten together, it is not only a violation of the law, but the utensils in which the mixture was cooked are also considered *terefah,* and may not be used again without undergoing a process known as *kashering.* Although the vast majority of the dietary laws apply only to animal foods, there are a number of biblical commandments about vegetable products and fruits as well. Thus, it is forbidden to eat the fruit of a tree during the first three years after planting. This prohibition, known as *orlah* (forbidden fruit) was extended to the fourth year as well, after the destruction of the Temple.

In addition, the new corn of each yearly crop, known as *hadash,* may be eaten only after the second day of Passover when, in Temple times, the *omer* was brought as a wave offering. Produce from which the tenth part for the Levites (tithe) was not yet set aside is known as *tevel,* and was forbidden in the land of Israel during Temple times. A further prohibition applicable only in the land of Israel is the sowing of different kinds of seeds together. This is known as *kilayim*. A special class of forbidden food is wine used for idolatrous worship. This prohibition was later extended to include any wine prepared or even touched by a non-Jew.

Many attempts have been made to give a rationalistic explanation for the Jewish dietary laws. At one time, it was claimed that their observance was introduced for health reasons and that all foods prohibited according to Jewish law contain ingredients which could create unhealthy symptoms in the human body. The modern adherents of the dietary laws, while not denying the above possibility, regard it as of secondary importance. Their purpose is specifically ordained in the Bible, they say: "For I am the Lord who brought you up out of the land of Egypt to be your God: Ye shall therefore be holy, for I am holy" (Lev. 11:45). The Bible thus clearly states that the purpose of the dietary laws is to attain the ideal of holiness. Judaism does not demand from man that he abstain from the physical pleasures of the world. On the contrary, he who neglects his health and physical well-being is considered a sinner. Food is not only a necessity but is given to man for his pleasure and enjoyment. On the other hand, man is expected to discipline himself and to exercise control over his physical desires and appetites. By so doing, he attains the ideal of holiness which, as has been seen, is the primary goal of the dietary laws. "The dietary laws," says Maimonides, "train us in the mastery of our appetites; they accustom us to restrain the growth of desire, the indulgence in seeking that which is pleasant, and the disposition to consider the pleasure of eating and drinking the end of man's existence."

In modern times, the Reform movement has allowed the entire *kasher* code to lapse, regarding it as obsolete and outdated.

Conservative Judaism, with its historical approach, emphasizes the code's importance for the distinct survival of the Jewish people. The Orthodox insist on the scrupulous observance of the laws of *kashrut*.

DISPUTATIONS: Organized debates between the adherents of different faiths in which the parties concerned seek to prove the superiority of their own religion. Such debates are mentioned in Talmudic and Midrashic literature, and are said to have taken place between rabbis and Samaritans and, during the Graeco-Roman period between Talmudic sages and Pagan philosophers.

With the rise of Christianity as a missionary religion, religious disputations assumed a different character. Christianity, in its zeal for converts, felt an urgent need to prove its superiority over all other faiths, particularly Judaism. The first recorded disputation between Christian and Jew is Justin Martyr's dialogue with Tryphon the Jew. During the period of the Crusades such public debates became increasingly unsafe for the Jews, who thereby exposed themselves to the charge of blasphemy. From then on, Jews increasingly avoided such confrontations, knowing that they were not being held in a spirit of free inquiry and debate. The church, on the other hand, not only encouraged such disputations but turned them into public spectacles, held in the presence of popes and royalty. Furthermore, the representative of Christianity was often an apostate Jew who, in his zeal to impress his masters with his devotion to his new faith, would stop at nothing to prove not only the inferiority of Judaism but also its hostility to Jesus. This included distorting the Old Testament and Talmudic texts. The Jewish representative, on the other hand, was usually restricted to the defense of Judaism against a specific charge, and was warned against any attack on Christianity. Of all these medieval disputations, three were outstanding: 1) The disputation of Paris in 1240, in which Christianity was represented by the apostate Nicholas Donin and Judaism by R. Jehiel of Paris. As a result of the debate, the Talmud was publicly burned. 2) The disputation of Moses ben Naḥman (Naḥmanides) with the apostate Pablo Christiani held at Barcelona in 1263. The chief subject of the debate was the Jewish Messiah concept and Naḥmanides shattered his opponent's arguments with such dignity and courage that the Spanish king awarded him a sum of money. Nevertheless, Naḥmanides was forced to flee Spain and seek safety in exile. 3) The disputations of Tortosa in 1413–14 was the longest and most spectacular of all. The Christian representative was the apostate Geronimo da Santa F'e (formerly Joshua Lorki), and he faced twenty-two distinguished but intimidated rabbis. Held in the presence of the entire Papal Curia, it was organized with all the outward trappings of public entertainment and with the purpose of bringing about a mass conversion of Jews.

Later, less formal and provocative disputations took place in various parts of Europe. In the years 1757 and 1759, however, the Catholic church in Poland organized two disputations in the medieval spirit, between rabbinic spokesmen and the leaders of the dissident Frankist movement.

In modern times, a more enlightened attitude to Judaism by Jewish and Christian scholars has led to objective study and comparison of both faiths without resorting to the polemics of disputations.

DISRAELI, BENJAMIN (Earl of Beaconsfield) (1804–1881): British statesman and novelist. Of Italian Jewish descent, Disraeli was baptized at the age of 13 by his father, who had become estranged from Judaism. His first novel, *Vivian Gray,* written at the age of twenty-two, earned him a brilliant reputation as a writer.

In 1828–1831 he traveled through the Mediterranean, including Cyprus and the land of Israel. The visit to the Holy Land had a profound effect on him, and his novel *Alroy,* based on the legendary false Messiah of the 12th century was undoubtedly influenced by the visit. Despite his baptism, Disraeli never attempted to disown his Jewish past. On the contrary, he took pride in it and never ceased to proclaim his sympathy with and admiration for the Jewish people. His opponents often made sneering allusion to his Jewish background, and these contributed to his defeat in his first attempt to enter Parliament. In 1837, however, he was elected and despite initial failures, slowly became accepted as the leader of the right wing of the Conservative Party. In Parliament too, he was the champion of Jewish emancipation and, in reply to a taunt by one of his opponents, he said, "Yes, I am a Jew, and when the ancestors of the right honorable gentleman were brutal savages in an unknown island, mine were priests in the Temple of Solomon."

After serving in various Conservative governments as Chancellor of the Exchequer and Leader of the House of Commons, he became Prime Minister in 1868 and again from 1874–1880. Disraeli fostered Great Britain's vision of empire. During his six years in office, Queen Victoria, one of his ardent admirers, was proclaimed Empress of India; Britain acquired a controlling interest in the Suez Canal; and Cyprus was made a British protectorate. Probably his greatest personal triumph came at the Congress of Berlin which concluded the Russo-Turkish war and from which Lord Beaconsfield (the title had been bestowed in 1876) returned, bringing, so he said, "peace with honor."

DIVORCE: Process by which the marriage bond is dissolved. Divorce is an ancient institution in Judaism and the Bible makes provision for its occurrence: "When a man taketh a wife and marrieth her, then it cometh to pass, if she find no favor in his eyes, because he hath found some unseemly thing in her, that he writeth her a bill of divorcement and giveth it in her hand, and sendeth her out of his house" (Deut. 24:1). It can be seen that in ancient times, the right to divorce rested only with the husband who could exercise this right even against the wishes of his wife. In the course of time, however, attempts were made to liberalize the law, ensuring greater equality for the woman and the protection of her rights. Thus, in the 1st century C.E., the sage Simeon ben Shetah introduced the *Ketubbah*. This document, which is read even today at Jewish wedding ceremonies, sought to put a check on arbitrary divorce by stipulating certain legal payments and obligations which the husband must fulfill in the event of divorce. Its purpose, therefore, was to discourage husbands from hasty divorce. At the same time, there was a fundamental difference of opinion on divorce between the rabbinic schools of Hillel and Shammai. The school of Shammai claimed that a marriage could be dissolved only in the case of immoral conduct on the part of the wife, while the school of Hillel argued that divorce should be permitted if domestic harmony was no longer possible. Judaism, throughout the ages, has followed the principle of Hillel. Not that it is indifferent to the tragedy involved in breaking up a home — on the contrary, "The very altar weeps for one who divorces the wife of his youth," says the Talmud. The process involved in obtaining a divorce or *get* as it is called, is a purposely long, drawn-out, and protracted one so as to give the parties every opportunity to think the matter over carefully. The Rabbinical Court to this day tries every expedient to dissuade the husband and wife from going through with the divorce. Judaism, however, in contrast to other faiths, agrees that if life in the home has become unbearable for all concerned, including the children, then the termination

of the marriage is in the nature of the lesser of two evils.

However, even following the reforms of the Talmudic Rabbis, it remained almost impossible for a woman to sue for divorce and she remained liable to divorce against her will. In the 10th century, the great rabbinic sage, Gershom Ben Judah, issued a decree establishing that no man can divorce his wife without her consent. Since then this has been a firm principle of Jewish divorce law. With a few very special exceptions it is the husband who gives the divorce, of his own free will, with the consent of the wife. The divorce bill is written and issued by the court at the husband's bidding. The wording follows an ancient form and any mistake, either in the wording or even in the spelling of the names, renders the document invalid. It is signed by two witnesses and handed to the woman by the husband in their presence. The husband may, however, hand over the divorce through his specially appointed agent. Civil divorce proceedings must be supplemented by a religious divorce. Without the *get,* neither of the parties is able to remarry in a synagogue. Jewish religious courts generally insist on a civil divorce before proceeding with the religious dissolution of the marriage. Although the uniform aim of Jewish law throughout the centuries has been in the direction of greater equality for women, numerous problems remain which as yet have not been solved. Chief among these is that of the *agunah,* the woman whose husband has merely vanished, and whose fate or whereabouts nobody knows. Learned rabbis have sought and are still looking for a solution to this question which, because of war or as a result of the Nazi holocaust, continues to cause particular hardship. Another problem arises with the refusal of one of the parties to give a divorce. Reform Judaism has eliminated these problems by accepting civil divorce as final and Reform rabbis will officiate at marriages of people divorced by the laws of the state without requiring a traditional Jewish divorce. The Conservative rabbinate attempted to deal with this problem in 1953, by introducing a revised *ketubbah,* in which both husband and wife agree, before marriage, to place any future domestic difficulties before a National Rabbinic Court.

DREYFUS AFFAIR: The center of the affair was the charge of treason brought against a Jewish-French captain on the French Army's General Staff, Alfred Dreyfus (1859–1935). In 1894 the French Intelligence Service discovered that military secrets were being sold to the Germans by a member of the French General Staff. Despite the lack of any conclusive evidence, Dreyfus was accused, tried by a military court, and convicted. He was publicly degraded, stripped of his rank, and sentenced to life imprisonment on Devil's Island, a disease-ridden penal settlement off the coast of French Guiana. Dreyfus' protestations of innocence were of no avail.

To his family and many liberals in France, it was clear that Dreyfus had been framed. The French army, supported by right-wing circles, both generally anti-Semitic, had singled out Dreyfus, the only Jew on the General Staff, as a scapegoat. When evidence proving Dreyfus' innocence came to light, it was suppressed by the French Defense Minister and the army. Upholding Dreyfus' guilt became a matter of prestige. The honor of the French military establishment was at stake. Thus, when Major Picquart, head of Intelligence at the War Office, uncovered the real traitor, another officer named Major Esterhazy, Picquart was transferred to Tunis, imprisoned and later dismissed from the army. Esterhazy was tried in 1898, but acquitted. The famous novelist Emile Zola intervened on Dreyfus' behalf, publishing an open letter to the French government entitled *J'accuse* (I accuse) in the liberal newspaper *l'Aurore.* The letter was an attack on the army

General Staff, accusing them of perverting justice. Zola was sentenced to prison for libel and fled to England.

Further investigation revealed that the head of the espionage bureau, Colonel Henry, had forged the evidence against Dreyfus. Threatened with arrest, Henry committed suicide. Esterhazy fled. France was now divided into Dreyfusards and anti-Dreyfusards. Anti-Jewish riots occurred in various parts of the country. French liberals, however, succeeded in keeping the case alive and in attracting international attention to it. A retrial took place before a military court in 1899, in an atmosphere of country-wide tension bordering on civil war. To the amazement and disbelief of all, Dreyfus was once again found guilty, although this time with extenuating circumstances. His sentence was reduced to ten years imprisonment, instead of life, but a few days later, the President of the Republic granted him a free pardon.

It was clear that the army had acted solely to protect its own prestige and had unhesitatingly played on feelings of anti-Semitism to maintain its position. Dreyfus continued to assert his innocence but only in 1906 did a superior court at last pronounce him completely innocent on all charges. He and Picquart were reinstated in the army. Dreyfus retired, but returned to the ranks on the outbreak of World War I and served with distinction, finally retiring with the rank of Lieutenant-Colonel.

The Dreyfus affair made a deep impact in France and had a lasting effect on the Jewish people. Theodor Herzl was sent to report the trial for the Viennese newspaper *Neue Freie Presse* and found his existing Zionist convictions confirmed. If anti-Semitism could break out so easily in the most enlightened country in Europe, then the only solution for the Jews lay in the establishment of their own Jewish State. Herzl went on to found the Zionist movement while in France the gross miscarriage of justice in the Dreyfus Affair contributed to the separation of church and state and to the rise of the Socialist Party.

DUBNOW, SIMON (1860–1941): Historian, essayist, and social philosopher. Born in White Russia, Dubnow studied the works of Moses Mendelssohn and other leading Jewish thinkers. After being refused admission to a university, he continued his studies in languages and philosophy on his own, devoting himself especially to the study of Jewish history. As a writer, Dubnow inherited the mantle of the great German-Jewish historian of the 19th century, Heinrich Graetz, but Dubnow stressed the history of East European Jewry and gave a prominent place to social factors in the shaping of events. Despite his emphasis on socio-economic rather than religious factors, Dubnow's devotion to the cultural heritage of the Jewish people was unquestionable. In 1890, he went to Odessa where he spent the thirteen happiest years of his life. Odessa was a center of Jewish cultural activity and some of Jewry's most prominent writers, thinkers, and Zionists were gathered there. In the company of Mendele Mocher-Seforim, Aḥad Ha'am, Shalom Aleichem, and other personalities, Dubnow matured into an illustrious scholar and public figure. In 1903, he left Odessa, settling subsequently in Vilna, Saint Petersburg, Berlin, and Riga. The solution to the problem of the Jews in the Diaspora which he proposed was the idea of Diaspora autonomism. According to this theory, the Jews represent a nation spiritually and culturally, but not politically. Jews, therefore, while remaining citizens of the countries in which they lived, must nevertheless be granted the freedom and autonomy necessary for their cultural and spiritual development. During the early Nazi period, and after the outbreak of World War II, Dubnow's friends, students, and admirers begged him to flee from Riga to safety, but he stayed on, to be murdered by the Nazis at the end of 1941.

Dubnow's main works are a ten volume *Universal History of the Jewish People,* a history of the Jews in Russia and Poland and a history of Ḥasidism.

Simon Dubnow

DYBBUK (Attachment): The soul of a dead sinner which attaches itself to a living person and refuses to leave. This form of transmigration is mentioned in both late kabbalistic folklore and in Ḥasidic literature. The *dybbuk* could only be removed by the proper use of the divine name. Many Ḥasidic rabbis were believed by their disciples to have had the power of removing a *dybbuk*. A popular play on the subject, *The Dybbuk,* was written by S. An-Ski in 1916.

EBAN (Even), ABBA (Aubrey) SOLOMON
(1915–): Israeli politician and diplomat.
Born in Cape Town, South Africa, he
studied at the University of Cambridge,
where he specialized in Middle Eastern
languages and literature. From 1946,
Eban worked in the political department
of the Jewish Agency and was a member
of the Jewish Agency delegation to the
U. N. in 1947–48. When the State of
Israel was admitted to the U. N. in May
1949, Eban was appointed its permanent
representative and served in that capacity
until 1959. Concurrently, from 1950–59,
he was Israel's Ambassador to the United
States. Since 1959, he has been a member
of the Israeli Cabinet, first as Minister
without Portfolio, and then, from 1960–63,
as Minister of Education and Culture.
From 1963–66, he was Deputy Premier
and in 1966 he succeeded Golda Meir as
Foreign Minister. During the crisis preceding the June 1967 Six-Day War, Eban
led Israel's diplomatic efforts to avert war.
In addition to his talents as an orator and
as the spokesman of his people — not for
nothing is he known as the "man with the
golden tongue" — Eban is also a noted
linguist. He has written a history of the
Jews entitled "My People" and most
recently a second book entitled "My
Country: The Story of Modern Israel."
A selection of his speeches to the United
Nations also appeared in book form.

ECCLESIASTES (Heb: **Kohelet**): The
fourth of the five scrolls *(Megillot)*
contained in the third section of the
Bible — *Ketuvim* (writings). Its opening
words announce that it was written by
"the Preacher, the son of David,"
traditionally identified with Solomon.
The book's twelve chapters consist of
meditations on human life and society
which make it part of biblical wisdom-
literature. The opening declaration, "Vanity
of vanities, all is vanity," sets the tone
for the book, which is generally pessimistic
in tone. Having tasted of life to the full,
the author finds that "there is nothing
new under the sun." All is empty, meaningless, and, above all, transitory. Thus
one should eat, drink and enjoy as much
pleasure as possible in the time allotted
by God. Everything has been decided in
advance, therefore no effort is worthwhile
since nothing can be changed. Man has
no choice but to reconcile himself to the
absence of justice in the world. The last
few verses, which many scholars believe
are a later addition, provide a more
conventional conclusion: "Fear God and
keep His commandments."

Abba Eban

Because of the contradictions in the book and because its essentially pessimistic outlook is so foreign to the general trend of Jewish teaching, some early rabbis wished to exclude it from the scriptures. However, the fact that its author describes himself as "The Preacher *(Kohelet),* son of David" assured its inclusion. Modern scholars are of the opinion that the title is a pen name, and that Solomon, who ruled over Israel during its period of greatest glory, could not have written such a pessimistic work. Moreover, the language bears a close resemblance to Mishnaic Hebrew. They therefore prefer to ascribe its composition to the 3rd century B.C.E. The book of Kohelet is read in the synagogue on the intermediate Sabbath of the festival of *Sukkot,* or, in the absence of an intermediate Sabbath, on *Shemini Atzeret.*

EDUCATION: From earliest times, Judaism has stressed the importance of education as a means of ensuring the continuity of its ideals and beliefs. The Bible makes no specific mention of organized educational institutions and all indications point to the parent as being largely responsible for the education of his children. Of Abraham, it is said (Gen. 18:19), "For I know him, that he will command his children and his household after him that they shall keep the way of the Lord." The verse in Deuteronomy (6:7): "Thou shalt teach them diligently unto thy children," has often been quoted as the basis of parental responsibility in the sphere of education. The findings of archaeology point to widespread literacy among the people of Israel during the biblical period. Toward the end of the First Temple period, there is evidence that formal religious instruction was given by the Levites. A new impetus was given to education by the return of the exiles from Babylon. Under the leadership of Ezra, public readings of the Torah were instituted, accompanied by explanations. This period saw the

emergence of a non-priestly class of scholars and scribes known as the men of the Great Assembly, who devoted themselves to the exposition of the Torah and the development of the oral tradition. An educational reform was accomplished by two sages who established schools, Simeon ben Shetah for boys between 15 and 17, and Joshua ben Gamala for boys from the age of six. By Talmudic times, the future pattern of Jewish education was already established in the land of Israel, and from there it spread to the Diaspora. Elementary education was given in the school *(bet sepher)* and higher rabbinic education in the *Bet Midrash.* These institutions were later paralleled in Europe by the *Heder* and the *Yeshivah* respectively, the first serving as a preparation for the latter. In Babylon the academies instituted the unique system of adult education known as *Kallah.* This was a biannual seminar held during the months of Adar and Ellul and attended by scholars and students from all over Babylonia. Such education, however, was restricted to boys and men, the rabbis being opposed to formal education for girls although there were women both in the Talmudic and medieval periods whose knowledge and learning were acknowledged by the rabbis. The extent to which Jews indulged in secular education seems to have been influenced by the given situation of each community. Even in Talmudic times there were rabbis opposed on religious grounds to the study of secular subjects. The Talmud itself, however, contains much that could be categorized as secular learning — for example, astrological and philosophical speculation. The Golden Age of Spanish Jewry witnessed the appearance of scholars who occupied themselves not only with Talmudic studies but with mathematics, philosophy, Hebrew and Arabic grammar and, as in the case of Moses Maimonides, medicine. In Renaissance Italy, the scope of Jewish learning widened to include philosophy and even Latin.

It was then that Jews began to enter universities. In the 15th century a *Talmud Torah* for girls was established in Rome. At the famous Talmud Torah of the Sephardi community of Amsterdam in

Arab boy in Israeli school

Talmudic study, even to the extent of neglecting the Bible. The old system was brought to the west by eastern European immigrants, and only in recent times has it begun to undergo modification. Some of the *Yeshivot* in the United States and Israel, which to this day follow the eastern European pattern, are still opposed to their students' receiving a secular education. The importance of education in Jewish life is such that the subject even now generates bitter controversy. When the leaders of the 19th century Enlightenment movement advocated drastic reforms in Jewish education so as to include secular subjects, there were violent reactions by the traditionalists who feared that the Jewish content would be superseded and gradually eliminated. With the emancipation of Jewish communities throughout the world and the spread of universal education in the western world, the traditional system of Jewish education went through a severe crisis, and the rabbis were unable to stem the tide of secularization. Hebrew school, (*Talmud Torah* or *Ḥeder,* by whichever name it went), was relegated to a second

Studying in Yeshivah

Yemenite children in Israeli school, Lachish

the 17th century, Spanish and Latin were taught and the highest class spoke only Hebrew. In the ghettos of eastern Europe, however, Jewish education was limited to the old system, typified by the *Ḥeder* and the *Yeshivah.* All the emphasis was on

class status and was able to give only a very elementary Jewish education which for the most part ended after bar mitzvah. In some places, Jewish education was limited to once a week and given the most non-Jewish name of "Sunday School."

In recent years, however, Jewish education has undergone a revival. This is in no small part due to the rise of the Zionist movement, the renaissance of the Hebrew language, and the establishment of the State of Israel. At the same time, moderate Orthodox leaders realized that secular education was not only an inevitable process but even desirable in order to graduate rabbis capable of confronting modern atheism, and they began to search for a synthesis between the old and the new. The lack of a contradiction between the two had been clearly stated by the leader of German Orthodoxy in the 19th century, Samson Raphael Hirsch (1808–1888), whose basic maxim was *Torah im Derekh Eretz* — i.e., religious study together with secular knowledge.

Of late, the trend has been to revert to Jewish day schools or parochial schools in which a comprehensive Jewish education is given side by side with a general education whose syllabus is in accordance with the requirements of the civil education authorities. The day school movement has spread to most of the countries of the Diaspora, with the exception of the Soviet Union where religious instruction in general and Jewish education in particular have been suppressed. Despite the above-mentioned revival, it is nevertheless thought that about one-half of the 1,800,000 Jewish children in the western world receive no Jewish education whatsoever.

See also: HASKALAH. For education in Israel, *see* ISRAEL, STATE OF.

EGYPT: Jewish history, from its beginnings, is closely tied to Egypt and Egyptian culture. Abraham and his wife Sarah visited Egypt, and Jacob left Canaan to join his long-lost son Joseph, who had reached a position of great authority in that country. The slavery of the children of Israel and the subsequent Exodus were the crucial events in the emergence of the people of Israel. Thereafter, it seems as if Israel's leaders intended to sever all connections with Egypt. The book of Deuteronomy (17:16) speaking of the appointment of a king says, "But he shall not multiply horses to himself, nor cause the people to return to Egypt." In the ancient Near East, however, Egypt was for centuries either the dominant power or was contending for supremacy with her rivals to the north, such as the Hittites, the Assyrians, and the Babylonians. It was impossible, therefore, to escape her influence or avoid coming into contact with her. The conquest of the land of Canaan by the tribes of Israel coincided with a period of decline in the power of Egypt and the destruction of her main rival, the Hittites. This decline continued during the reigns of David and Solomon. The latter married an Egyptian princess, receiving territorial concessions from her father as a dowry. Egyptian cultural influence continued to be strong, however, and there are certain parts of the Bible such as the book of Proverbs which show a marked resemblance to similar Egyptian writings. After the death of Solomon, the Egyptians, who had in the meantime recovered, actively encouraged the rebellion of Jeroboam and the ten tribes, and Pharaoh Shishak later invaded Judah and Israel.

In her struggles with Assyria and Babylonia, Egypt used Judah as a political tool, encouraging her to rebel, promising her aid, but usually failing to keep these promises. The prophets Isaiah and Jeremiah both opposed military alliances with Egypt in their time, but the pro-Egyptian party at the Judean court always seemed able, through intrigue and conspiracy, to prevail. The result was the open rebellion of King Zedekiah against Babylon. This time, Egyptian troops did appear momentarily to assist the beleaguered Judeans, but they were speedily disposed of by the more powerful Babylonians, who were thus free to conquer Jerusalem and destroy the First Temple. Numbers of Judeans fled to

Egypt, including the prophet Jeremiah. From there, he issued his last prophecy warning his fellow exiles against adopting Egyptian religious customs. The exiles evidently integrated well into Egyptian life and even served in the army. From about the year 590 B.C.E. and throughout the Persian period, the island fortress of Yeb (also known as Elephantine) on the Nile opposite Assuan, near the Egyptian-Ethiopian frontier, was manned by Jewish soldiers. They built their own temple, which was destroyed by an Egyptian mob but subsequently rebuilt with the permission of the Persian governor. The conquests of Alexander the Great and the Hellenization of his Empire led to an influx of Jews into Egypt, some coming voluntarily, others perhaps as prisoners of war. There now began the golden age of Egyptian Jewry, and it is estimated that the Jewish population at this time numbered one million. The main center was Alexandria, and it was there that the great philosopher Philo expounded his theory of Judaism. Being so close to the Hellenistic way of life, it was necessary for men such as Philo to find a middle road between Judaism on the one hand and Greek customs on the other.

This Hellenistic influence gave rise to the need to translate the Hebrew scriptures into Greek, both for those Jews who no longer felt at home in Hebrew and for the gentile world as a whole. The result was the first Greek translation of the Bible, known as the Septuagint, made in the reign of Ptolemy Philadelphus (285–247 B.C.E.). The Septuagint has had enormous influence; to this day, Bible scholars regard its study as essential. Strongly anti-Jewish feelings grew up among the Greek population, caused partly by the economic success of many Jews, and also by the spread of Judaism among the pagan population. In the year 38 C.E., riots broke out in Alexandria, and the two factions, pagans and Jews, appealed to Rome. The Romans attempted to establish order by rebuking both sides, but this merely encouraged them to take the law into their own hands. After the destruction of the Temple in 70 C.E., many refugees fled from the land of Israel to Egypt, and there, in the year 115, a rebellion broke out against Rome which developed into a war of extermination against the pagans. The rising was put down with the utmost severity. The Jews of Egypt never recovered from this blow. The Christianization of the Roman Empire led to a further deterioration in their position, and in 415 there were riots in Alexandria instigated by the Bishop Cyril, and masses of Jews were driven to baptism.

After the Moslem conquest in 640, Jewish life in Egypt revived. The community retained almost no trace of the Hellenistic past; its way of life was Arab in character. Moslem rule, with periodic exceptions, was relatively tolerant, and the community was able to establish academies of learning and even produce a scholar and leader of the stature of Saadyah Gaon. When Maimonides arrived in Egypt during the second half of the 12th century, he found there a congenial atmosphere and a community worthy of his leadership. After the Turkish conquest in 1517, the community maintained itself, although culturally its greatest achievements were behind it.

In more recent times, the Zionist struggle was at first viewed sympathetically in Egypt, being regarded as part of the anti-colonial movement, but the Israel-Arab wars changed the status of Egyptian Jewry drastically. Today that ancient community has virtually ceased to exist. In 1947, there were 90,000 Jews in Egypt. A great exodus took place following Israel's War of Independence until, in 1955, there were only 30,000. In the wake of the Sinai campaign (1956), the Egyptian ruler, Nasser, expelled thousands more and requisitioned their property. By 1966, only 2,500 remained and, at the outbreak of the 1967 Six-Day War, most of the males were arrested. The once mighty Jewish community of Egypt numbered only about one thousand in 1969.

EICHMANN TRIAL: Judicial proceedings conducted in Jerusalem from April-December 1961, against Adolph Eichmann (1906–1962). Eichmann had been head of the Central German Emigration Office and during World War II was head of the Jewish section of the Gestapo, the German secret police. As such, he was responsible for the mass deportations of European Jews to the Nazi death camps where millions were killed. Along with other Nazi war criminals, Eichmann escaped after Germany's surrender in 1945 and made his way to the Argentine where he lived and worked under another name. After a manhunt lasting fifteen years, he was discovered working for a water-supply company. When the Argentine Government refused to agree to his extradition, he was abducted by Israel agents and taken to Israel. When David Ben-Gurion, then Prime Minister of Israel, announced that Eichmann was a prisoner in Israel, it caused a sensation throughout the world and led to angry diplomatic exchanges with Argentina. The Argentine Government claimed that its sovereignty had been violated, but owing to the exceptional nature of the case, the matter was resolved and good relations between the two governments restored.

The trial of Adolph Eichmann was held before three judges and received worldwide publicity. Hundreds of journalists followed the proceedings and they were also filmed. The case for the prosecution was presented by the Israel Attorney General, Gideon Hausner, while Eichmann was represented by a well-known German lawyer, Dr. Servatius. A succession of witnesses vividly recreated the grim and terrible story of the destruction of six million Jews by the Nazis, and of Eichmann's key role throughout the entire tragic history. The trial served to remind the world, Jewish youth in and out of Israel included, of the worst

Adolph Eichman at his trial

outburst of genocide and bestiality in human history. It strengthened the resolve of the Jewish people that such events must never be allowed to recur.

After four months of argument and counter-argument, the court recessed and, when it reassembled, rejected the main defense plea that Eichmann was only a cog in the machine and had only acted under orders from his superiors. The court was convinced of his central role in the destruction of European Jewry.

Under a special law enacted by Israel's Parliament in 1950, known as the Nazi and Nazi Collaborators Punishment Law, Eichmann was sentenced to death. After an unsuccessful appeal to the Israel Supreme Court, he was hanged, his body cremated and his ashes scattered into the sea.

EILAT: Southernmost town of the State of Israel; population (1970): 12,100. There was a town at Eilat in the biblical period, also known as Eilot. The Book of Kings relates that "King Solomon built a fleet of ships at Ezion-geber, which is near Eloth on the shore of the Red Sea." Amaziah and Uzziah, kings of Judah, also realized the importance of Eilat as the gateway to Africa and the East, but during the reign of Ahaz, the town was captured by the Arameans and became an Edomite city.

Eilat on the Red Sea

Under the Arabs it flourished again, but was destroyed by the Crusaders at the beginning of the 12th century.

During the period of the British Mandate, the British developed the nearby port of Akaba, while the area which is now Eilat was occupied only by a small mud-brick police station. Eilat was captured by the Israel army on March 10, 1949 in the last operation of the War of Independence. Eilat's strategic position makes its development and security of supreme importance to Israel. Situated at the northern extremity of the Red Sea, Eilat stands at the head of a gulf enclosed by two mountain ranges: Sinai on the west and the Mountains of Edom in Jordan on the east. Thus the Gulf of Eilat is bounded by four countries: Jordan, Israel, Saudi Arabia and Egypt. At the entrance to the gulf lie the Straits of Tiran, controlled until 1956 by Egyptian guns which prevented free navigation and hampered Israel's trade with Africa and the Far East. In the Sinai campaign of 1956, the Israel Army conquered the Egyptian coast of the gulf, but withdrew under U.N. and U.S. pressure, in return for the guarantee of free navigation. A U.N. force was stationed at Sharm el Sheikh, the fort controlling the straits. For ten years, the trade from Israel's southernmost port expanded, while the town of Eilat grew steadily. Its population increased and thousands of tourists, attracted by the climate and exotic scenery, turned Eilat into one of Israel's most popular holiday resorts. Skin diving among tropical fish and coral reefs added to its other attractions.

Nasser's closing of the Straits of Tiran in May 1967 was the last straw in the series of events leading up to the Six-Day War.

At the end of the war, the Egyptians had been ousted from their previous positions and Israel controlled the whole of the western coast of the gulf right down to the Straits of Tiran. Since the war, an oil pipeline has been laid between Eilat and Ashkelon.

EINSTEIN, ALBERT (1879–1955): Physicist and mathematician. Born in Ulm, Germany, he studied in Zurich, Switzerland, and worked for a time in the patent office in Berne. During the years 1902–9, while serving as a professor in Zurich and in Prague, Einstein published a number of works laying the foundations for his theory of relativity. The general theory of relativity was published between 1913–16. Hailed as the greatest advance in physics since Newton's discovery of the theory of gravity, Einstein's theory paved the way for vast developments in atomic physics.

In 1914, Einstein became director of the Kaiser Wilhelm Institute of Physics in Berlin and Professor of Physics at the Prussian Academy of Sciences. The Nobel Prize for physics was awarded him in 1921.

When Hitler came to power in Germany in 1933, the Nazis burnt his books and Einstein emigrated to the United States. He was appointed professor of theoretical physics at Princeton University and, in 1940, became an American citizen.

Einstein was a supporter of the Zionist cause and took a keen interest in Israel's scientific progress and academic institutions, especially the Hebrew University. In 1952, when Israel's first President, Chaim Weizmann, died, Einstein was invited to be a candidate to succeed him, but he gratefully and modestly refused the honor. Throughout his life, Einstein remained an ardent democrat and a supporter of humanitarian causes.

EL AL (Upwards): Israel's National Airline. Founded in 1949, it made its first commercial flights to Rome and Paris, and from 1951, to New York. Later it expanded to other countries, including South Africa. In 1958, El Al was one of the first companies to purchase the Bristol Britannia turbo-prop airliner. As a result, transatlantic traffic was doubled and economic success followed. El Al was then able to compete with other airlines in service and equipment. Its airline fleet is today composed entirely of Boeing jets: two medium-range 720's and eight long-range 707's, with two giant Boeing 747's now brought into service. After the June 1967 Six-Day War, Arab guerrilla groups made a number of unprecedented attacks on El Al aircraft and passengers, committing hijackings and brutal assaults with machine guns and other deadly weapons. Thereafter, El Al took a number of security measures to insure the safety of its aircraft and passengers. Although the Government of Israel is the majority shareholder in El Al, the airline is run on a private enterprise basis, and pays its way without relying on subsidies.

ELAZAR, DAVID: Lieutenant General. Ninth Chief of Staff of Zahal (Israel Defense Forces).

David Elazar

Born in Yugoslavia in 1925, he immigrated to Israel in 1940. He enlisted in the Palmach in 1946 and during the War of Independence was company commander of the "Har-El" Brigade which played a vital role in opening the road to Jerusalem. Elazar commanded the forces which attempted to relieve the besieged Old City.

An El Al Boeing 747

In 1948 he was appointed Commander of the "Spearhead Battalion" which penetrated into the Sinai Peninsula in the closing stages of the War of Independence.

During the Sinai Campaign (1956), he was in command of an infantry brigade operating in the Gaza Strip. In 1957, he was transferred to the Armored Corps and contributed much to the development of armored tactics and strategy.

During the Six-Day War Elazar commanded the Northern Front and was responsible for the brilliant campaign in which the Israeli Army captured the Golan Heights.

In 1969 he was appointed Chief of the Operations Branch of the General Staff and on January 1, 1972 succeeded Lt. General Haim Bar-Lev as Chief of the General Staff.

ELDAD HA-DANI (the Danite): Well known traveler of the late 9th century. He visited communities in North Africa and Spain, and excited their imagination with his tales of the life and customs of the Lost Ten Tribes.

Claiming to be himself of the tribe of Dan, he reported that it, with Asher, Gad, and Naphtali, ruled over a large area in Africa. The laws and customs which he described differed in many details from rabbinic tradition.

His account aroused varying reactions, ranging from enthusiastic acceptance to extreme skepticism. One North African community actually consulted the Babylonian Gaon Tzemaḥ as to the reliability of Eldad Ha-Dani's fantastic story. In retrospect, it is possible that his claims and tales were based on the experiences of the black Jews of Ethiopia, the Falashas.

ELIJAH: Israelite prophet of the 9th century B.C.E. He appeared on the scene at a critical period in Israel's history, when spiritual disintegration threatened the nation. Omri, King of Israel, made an alliance with Tyre as part of a policy of improving relations with neighboring states, and sealed the pact with the marriage of his son, Ahab, to the Tyrian princess, Jezebel. A priestess of the Canaanite god, Baal, god of Tyre, Jezebel sought to replace Israel's monotheistic religion with his cult as the official religion of Israel. Wholesale apostasy threatened and the true prophets of God who dared resist were mercilessly persecuted. At this moment, Elijah, who came from Gilead in Transjordan, appeared in Israel and took up the defense of the faith. He spoke the word of God regardless of the consequences and very soon had become public enemy number one in Jezebel's eyes. The most dramatic act of his career was his confrontation with the priests of Baal on Mount Carmel. Here, in front of the assembled people, he challenged them to prove their god's real power. As their efforts went unanswered, he mocked and derided their helplessness. You are "limping with two different opinions," he accused the people and urged them to decide once and for all which was the true God. In response to Elijah's prayer, God sent fire from heaven to consume the sacrifice he offered and at the sight, the people cried out spontaneously, "The Lord is God." There followed a massacre of the false prophets and priests of Baal. When Jezebel learned what had happened, she was filled with rage and Elijah had to flee for his life.

As the prophet of the one God, Elijah was also the uncompromising champion of social justice. When Jezebel engineered the execution of the innocent Naboth on a trumped-up charge so that her husband could take possession of his vineyard, Elijah unhesitatingly confronted Ahab with the words, "Have you murdered and also taken possession?" and he prophesied, "In the place where dogs licked up the blood of Naboth shall dogs lick your blood." When the time came for Elijah to die, we are told (II Kings, ch. 2), he appointed Elisha, his disciple, to succeed him and then was carried up to heaven in a fiery chariot. The personality of Elijah takes a prominent place in Jewish legend. The prophet Malachi (ch. 3:23) proclaims that Elijah will be the one to prepare the way for the coming of the Messiah, and will unite the hearts of the fathers with the hearts of the children. Thus he is depicted as the great redeemer, wandering from place to place and bringing relief to the suffering people of Israel. During the Passover *Seder,* a fifth cup of wine is filled for the prophet Elijah, and the door is opened so that this redeemer may enter.

As the Angel of the Covenant, in the prophecy of Malachi, he has become associated with the covenant of circumcision. The chair used in the ceremony was called the "Chair of Elijah." At the termination of the Sabbath, it is customary to sing the popular hymn, *"Eliahu Ha-Navi,"* which is also associated with Elijah's traditional role as the announcer of the Messiah's coming. Elijah also figures in Christian and Moslem legends.

ELIJAH BEN SOLOMON ZALMAN OF VILNA — THE VILNA GAON

(1720–1797): A rabbinical authority and one of the great leaders of East European Jewry. Born in Lithuania, he was early recognized as a child prodigy. Legend has it that at the age of seven, he perplexed his rabbinic instructors by the depth of his questions and his skill in Talmudical subjects, and that by the age of nine, he had completely mastered the entire range of rabbinic literature. From 1740–45, he traveled among the Jews of Poland and Germany after which he settled in Vilna, where he founded his own academy. The Gaon of Vilna refused to accept public office, but the community, realizing his greatness, granted him a small pension from a fund left by one of his ancestors. This was barely sufficient to support his family, but Elijah was satisfied to live in poverty, as long as he was independent and not forced to interrupt his studies.

The Gaon of Vilna brought about a revolution in rabbinic studies. He rejected the method of *pilpul* prevalent in the rabbinical academies. This method, which led to endless debate, hair-splitting arguments, and verbal gymnastics, he considered harmful. Instead, believing that simplicity is the best criterion of truth, he substituted a critical approach in which the text was analyzed as it stood. All his efforts were directed to finding out the true meaning of the words.

Furthermore, unlike his contemporaries, he stressed the importance of the Bible as the basis of all later rabbinic literature, and he studied Hebrew grammar in order to understand the language in which the scriptures were written. Even more radical was his study of the secular sciences: mathematics, geometry, astronomy, and algebra. His attitude to these sciences was that although they had no real value in themselves, their study helped throw light on the Torah. He was, however, opposed to philosophy, and even went so far as to criticize the great medieval scholar, Moses Maimonides, for too much indulgence in that sphere. Elijah's authority was unquestioned, and as the leader of Lithuanian Jewry, he led the fight against the Ḥasidim, ordering their excommunication and the destruction of their literature. This opposition checked the spread of Ḥasidism in Lithuania. At the age of sixty, he set out unaccompanied for the Holy Land, but for unknown reasons, returned before reaching his destination. The Gaon did not create a movement but he left many books and still more disciples who carried his ideas into practice. Chief among these disciples was Rabbi Ḥayyim of Volozhin, founder of one of the most famous rabbinic academies in eastern Europe, where study was conducted, to a great extent, in the spirit of the Gaon.

ELISHA: Israelite prophet of the 9th century B.C.E., the disciple and successor of Elijah. His life story is told in the second

book of Kings. The battle against the idolatrous Omri Dynasty to which Elijah had
dedicated his prophetic career was brought
to a successful conclusion by Elisha. Unlike
his master, however, who lived the life of
a recluse, only making rare appearances in
order to preach the word of God, Elisha
was continually in the public eye and lived
and worked among a band of men, probably his disciples, known as the sons of
the prophets. It was one of these sons of the
prophets whom Elisha sent to appoint Jehu
king of Israel. The latter then proceeded to
carry out a purge against the royal family,
killing Ahab's son, Ahaziah, and having
Jezebel thrown from a window. In the resulting bloodbath, all who were in any way
connected with Ahab were put to death.

Elisha frequently appears in the Bible as
the healer of sickness and even as reviving
the dead. He was one of the people and saw
his task as bringing comfort to the poor and
the needy. Of no biblical personality are
so many miracles related as of Elisha. His
prophetic activity lasted some sixty years.

EMANCIPATION: The achievement
(often incomplete or temporary) of equal
citizenship and other rights for Jews in
their various countries of dispersal, and the
elimination of all forms of discrimination
against them. Although the actual process
of emancipation began in the 18th century,
signs of change in the attitude of many
thinkers toward the Jews were already
apparent in the late 17th century. The
religious wars between Catholics and Protestants had disillusioned many people, and
there was a general tendency toward religious tolerance. At the same time, nation-
states were beginning to develop and to
assert their independence from the church.
Furthermore, a new interest in Judaism
and the Old Testament grew up which,
if not always sympathetic, nevertheless
gave Christians a new insight into Jewish
literature and teaching. As early as 1714,
John Toland, an Englishman, advocated

the full emancipation of the Jews. During
the course of the 18th century, the question
of Jewish emancipation was one of the
controversial issues of the day and was
debated in virtually every country in Europe.
Arguments for and against were waged furi-
ously, to be repeated time and again during
the debates of the next hundred years.

The opponents of emancipation claimed
that the Jews were unassimilable, that their
separate beliefs would always prevent them
from mixing with the gentiles and that, if
given more opportunities, they would exploit the non-Jew economically. Against
this, the supporters of emancipation claimed
that the negative qualities of the Jewish
people were the result of persecution and
forced separation, and that if granted equal
rights, the Jews would assimilate and
become useful citizens. In support of their
view, they pointed to men like Moses
Mendelssohn, who overcame the disadvantages of his ghetto background to
become one of the foremost German philosophers of his time. Moses Mendelssohn,
it must be pointed out, was certainly not
in favor of assimilation, although many of
his followers in the "Enlightenment" movement became estranged from traditional
Judaism. There were those among the
Jews as well who feared that emancipation
would lead to assimilation and were therefore opposed to the breakdown of the
ghetto, which despite its disadvantages had
ensured the preservation of Jewish tradition.
The majority of Jews in western Europe,
however, greeted emancipation with
enthusiasm.

The emancipation process in the Anglo-
Saxon countries was fairly rapid and,
interestingly enough, came more by way
of evolution than revolution. In England,
in fact, efforts to bring about Jewish
emancipation by way of legislation failed
or met with intense opposition. Only in
1858 was a Jew legally able to sit in
Parliament. Over a hundred years before
that, however, Jews were living in freedom

in England with no anti-Jewish restrictions or ghetto system. Jews occupied positions of importance in most spheres of life, so that the law permitting a Jew to become a member of Parliament was the culmination and not the beginning of Jewish emancipation in England.

Similarly, in the United States the process was carried out almost inadvertently, so that George Washington in his letters to the Jewish and other groups could speak as if equality were already an established fact. It must be remembered however, that the American Declaration of Independence of 1776 stipulated specifically that no religious test should be required as qualification for any public office.

On the continent of Europe, the process was conducted formally and in a blaze of publicity and declarations. The French Revolution and the Declaration of the Rights of Man of 1789 set the tone for other countries. Yet in France there was strong opposition to Jewish emancipation, not only among rabid anti-Semites, but also among members of the enlightenment who believed that the Jews could not be assimilated. The French National Assembly debated the Jewish question for nearly two years. Only in September 1791 was full equality finally granted to French Jewry, the understanding being, at all times, that the Jews in return would cast aside their "vulgar habits" and outdated traditions in order to become Frenchmen in the full sense of the word. Napoleon was not satisfied with the pace of Jewish assimilation, so he called an assembly of Jewish notables and attempted to revive the Sanhedrin. He also reorganized the existing Jewish communities into a new "consistorial" system under close state supervision. The purpose behind all these moves was to accelerate the absorption of the Jews into the new French society.

The ideals of the revolution were carried all over Europe by the armies of the Republic. Wherever French troops appeared, Jewish emancipation followed, by force if necessary. Thus, in Holland in 1796, in the various Italian cities in 1796–1798, and in those parts of Germany which came under French influence, the equal rights of the Jews were ensured.

The defeat of Napoleon led to a reaction in Europe against the ideals of the revolution and against the Jews as well. Those Jews who had lulled themselves into believing that complete equality was around the corner were shocked out of their lethargy by the ensuing avalanche of anti-Semitism. The clock, however, could not be turned back, and the Jew who had tasted a bit of freedom was no longer prepared to let it escape him. He now fought back and produced men such as Gabriel Riesser in Germany who refused to "apologize" for the Jew but demanded Jewish rights as an integral part of human rights due to all German nationals. Jews played a leading part in the revolutionary events of 1848 in Germany, Austria, and Italy. The general picture is that of a seesaw: progress followed by reaction, followed by progress, and so on. Many Jewish thinkers became disillusioned with emancipation when they realized that the price which had to be paid was too high, namely, the giving up of Jewish identity. Others were shocked by the recurrent waves of anti-Semitism, even in countries like France which had led the way in the fight for emancipation. The Dreyfus trial and the anti-Semitic roar of the mobs led Theodor Herzl to the conclusion that emancipation was an unattainable dream, that anti-Semitism was too deep-rooted in the Christian heart and that, therefore, the only solution to the Jewish problem lay in the Zionist ideal — that is, in Jewish statehood.

In eastern Europe, the position of the Jews was for the most part intolerable. Tsarist Russia made no secret of her intention of making life untenable for her large Jewish population. Constantin Pobedonostsev, Procurator of the Holy

Synod, is said to have defined the objective of imperial policy: that one-third of Russian Jewry emigrate, another third become Christian, and the final third perish. Little wonder then that many Russian Jews came to the conclusion that only a change of regime by revolution could alleviate their lot, and they joined revolutionary movements — liberal, socialist, and communist.

The 20th century has brought the biggest shock and disillusionment in the events of the Nazi period. German Jewry, which had felt so secure as a result of its emancipation, was wiped off the map, and the lesson was not lost on Jews throughout the world. Moreover, in place after place, the Jew has been selected as the scapegoat, and his position has been undermined in many countries where he has had a long history and seemed to be living in safety.

In Russia since the revolution, Jews have been free on the surface, but the condition attached to that freedom is the abandonment of Judaism. At the first sign of Jewish religious or nationalist stirrings, the repressive machinery of Soviet Russia moves into action. Recent events in the Soviet Union and her satellites have confirmed the continuing existence of a basic suspicion toward the Jew and have shown the existence of anti-Semitism even in regimes that officially disclaim it.

In the democracies, the big question is emancipation — at what price? Will the Jews in the West survive as Jews, or will they lose their identity and tradition and be swallowed up by their surrounding cultures?

No definite answer can be given to the above question, for the process of emancipation, begun over two centuries ago, has not yet ended. As long as a modicum of discrimination exists, it seems as if the Jew will cling to his heritage, albeit weakly. The question as to whether he will do so in an idyllic Utopia completely free of anti-Semitism cannot be answered, for such a condition does not exist in the Diaspora.

ENGLAND: There is no evidence of the existence of a Jewish community in England prior to the Norman conquest (1066). Communities were thereafter established in London, York, Bristol, Lincoln, Oxford, and Canterbury. During the First and Second Crusades, the Jews of England escaped the persecution which their co-religionists on the continent suffered, although in 1144 the first recorded ritual murder accusation was brought against them in Norwich. The gradual welding of the Norman and Anglo-Saxon elements of the population into one nation encouraged the rise of English nationalism and the subsequent awareness of the "strangeness" of the Jews. This and a hostile clergy, as well as resentment at Jewish financial activities, all combined to change the situation drastically. The Third Crusade and the coronation of Richard the First were followed by mob attacks on the Jewish communities of London, Norwich, and particularly York in 1190. The damage done to Jewish property and the subsequent loss of revenue to the state prompted the establishment of a unique institution known as the exchequer of the Jews. Through this, a tight measure of control was exercised over Jewish financial activities, and during the reigns of John (1199–1216) and his successor, Henry III (1216–1277), the Jews of England were systematically bled dry. Parallel to these developments, there took place throughout the 13th century further

Baron Lionel de Rothschild in British Parliament

massacres and ritual murder accusations. When Edward the First ascended the throne in 1272, he found an exhausted and impoverished Jewry, and, after, vainly attempting to reorganize it, ordered its expulsion in 1290. During the following centuries, England was free of professing Jews. The church, however, maintained a *Domus Conversorum,* or house for converted Jews in London for the benefit of apostates arriving from overseas.

At the beginning of the 17th century there was a community of secret Jews or Marranos in London, which was broken up in 1609 but was followed soon after by further "secret" settlers. The victory of Oliver Cromwell and his puritan revolution, with its ideals of religious tolerance and sympathy toward the Old Testament, provided fresh hope for the readmission of the Jews. In 1655 the famous Dutch rabbi, Menasseh ben Israel (1604–1657), was invited to White-hall and received graciously by Cromwell himself. However, the opposition of the church, merchants, and others to the readmission of the Jews was too intense, and Cromwell decided to take no action. Instead there now began a policy of turning a blind eye to the presence of Jews in England and even informally permitting them to practice their faith. The original Marrano Jews were reinforced by immigrants from Holland, Germany, and central Europe who established their first synagogue in London in 1690. In 1753 an attempt to pass through Parliament an act granting naturalization to the Jews, known as the "Jew Bill," failed, but the process of Jewish settlement continued. There was no ghetto system, no very important restrictions on their activity, and no violence against their person. Great financiers such as Sir Solomon de Medina, Sampson Gideon, the brothers Goldsmid, Nathan Mayer Rothschild, and the great philanthropist Sir Moses Montefiore played an important part in English public life. Finally, in 1858, Lionel de Rothschild was admitted to Parliament without having to take the oath on the New Testament.

The readmission of the Jews to England is a classic example of the success of an evolutionary process proceeding gradually and informally. From 1881, a strong influx of Russian Jews fleeing persecution greatly increased the numbers of the Jewish community, and large Jewish communities were established not only in London, but also in Manchester, Leeds, Glasgow, and other cities. During the 1930's, numbers of German-Jewish refugees came, and this latest influx led to a weak and short-lived anti-Semitic movement. The Jewish population of England and northern Ireland now numbers approximately 420,000. They are well-organized and centralized, being represented in spiritual matters by the Chief Rabbi, and in civic affairs by the Board of Deputies of British Jews.

Widespread British sympathy for the Zionist movement was an important factor in the issuing of the Balfour Declaration and the subsequent British mandate under which the Jewish National Home was established in the land of Israel. Unfortunately, in her efforts to avoid a clash with the Arabs (who were in a position to threaten interests considered vital to the British Empire), Britain adopted a policy that was regarded by the Jews as a betrayal of her original promises. The high hopes of the Balfour Declaration deteriorated into open warfare in the land of Israel between the Jewish community and the British administration. During this time, British Jewry stood squarely behind the Jews of Israel, despite the accusations of a dual loyalty.

Eventually Britain turned the question of the land of Israel over to the United Nations and withdrew from the country. Before long, normal relations were established between the sovereign states of Israel and Great Britain.

ESHKOL (SHKOLNIK), LEVI (1895–1969): Israeli statesman and Prime Minister.

Born in the Ukrainian town of Oratovo, he immigrated to the land of Israel in 1914 and worked as a laborer in Petah Tikvah. After serving in the Jewish Legion during World War I, he helped to establish one of the first and most famous kibbutzim: Deganiah Bet. In the years that followed, he played an important role in the Jewish labor movement and was one of the founders of the *Histadrut* (National Labor Federation) and the Israel Labor Party, *Mapai.* His economic, administrative, and diplomatic talents soon brought him into the leadership of the Jewish community, where he was especially active in the sphere of land settlement and immigration. He played a vital role in the creation of the *Haganah,* the Jewish self-defense organization and, after the establishment of the State of Israel in 1948, he was made Director-General of the Israel Defense Ministry.

In 1949, he was elected to Israel's Parliament and served as the head of the settlement department of the Jewish Agency during the period of large-scale immigration. In 1951, he joined the Government as Minister of Agriculture and Development, becoming Minister of Finance the following year. In this latter capacity, he guided the young state through its initial period of economic difficulties, making numerous trips abroad on behalf of the Jewish Agency and Israel Bonds. He also put forward various proposals for the rehabilitation of Arab refugees and was one of the architects of Israel's technical aid program for the developing countries of Africa and Asia.

On Ben Gurion's retirement in 1963, Eshkol became Prime Minister and Minister of Defense. Despite the subsequent rift with his former colleague, Eshkol was a conciliator and strove for national unity. Under his leadership, the various Israeli labor groups united to form the Israel Labor Party and, on the eve of the 1967

Levi Eshkol

Six-Day War, a national unity government of all the major parties was formed. Much of the success of that period was due to measures taken under Eshkol's direction. Just before the war, Eshkol relinquished the Defense Ministry to Moshe Dayan. After the war, Eshkol succeeded in holding the different strands of the coalition together, believing that national unity was essential for Israel's survival. He was noted for his skill as a conciliator.

ESSENES: Jewish religious sect which, like the Pharisees and Sadducees, flourished during the last two centuries B.C.E. and up to the destruction of the Second Temple in 70 C.E. The origin of the name is still a puzzle, although it has been suggested that it is derived from the Syriac *hasya* meaning pious. They were of an extreme ascetic nature, living in isolation and sharing all their possessions. In matters of ritual and Sabbath observance, they were stricter than the Pharisees, and they also stressed the importance of frequent ritual bathing. They rose very early for their prayers and encouraged long periods of silence. The ancient historian Josephus mentions at least two distinct groups among the Essenes, one practicing celibacy and the other permitting marriage. To become a member, a candidate had to go through a rigorous probation period, and it was forbidden for an Essene to pass on the teachings of his sect to an outsider.

Until recently, the main sources of information on the Essenes were Josephus and Philo of Alexandria (both 1st century C.E.). The discovery of the Dead Sea Scrolls stimulated further debate on the question, and a number of scholars are of the opinion that the sect described in the scrolls must have been the Essenes. According to Pliny, the Essenes lived in a community located on the Northwestern shore of the Dead Sea, a description which fits the location of the ruins at Qumran where the scrolls were discovered. Only further research into the Dead Sea finds will render a final decision possible.

The sect was not entirely cut off from political affairs and took part in the rebellion against Rome. After the destruction of the Temple, however, nothing further was heard of them.

See also: DEAD SEA SCROLLS.

ETHIOPIA: Country in Northeast Africa whose population is derived partially from Semitic sources. It has been surmised that Ethiopia is identical with the biblical Cush. The royal house claims descent from King Solomon, who, according to Ethiopian tradition, had a son called Menelik by the Queen of Sheba, hence Ethiopia's royal title, Lion of Judah. The old Ethiopic language, also known as *Ge'ez,* is a Semitic dialect closely related to South Arabian. The official religion of the country is Christianity, but as interpreted by the Abyssinian church, it contains many heathen and even

Jewish elements. Tribes of black Jews known as Falashas live in Ethiopia. The origin of the Falashas is shrouded in mystery and all sorts of theories have been propounded, including descent from Solomon and the Ten Lost Tribes. The first genuine information on their existence came to light at the end of the 15th century. They lived together in village communities and their main occupations were and are handicrafts and agriculture. In appearance, habits, and language, they are no different from their neighbors. They practice a primitive form of Judaism based on a literal interpretation of the Old Testament, but their knowledge of Hebrew is scanty, their scriptures being written in *Ge'ez.* They observe the biblical festivals but have no Ḥanukkah or Purim. It is almost certain that they were far more numerous and powerful at one time but have been weakened by war and Christian missionary activity. This would explain the presence of Jewish elements in official Abyssinian church practices. From 1904, the French Jew Jacques Faitlovich visited Ethiopia regularly, and as a result of his efforts, committees were established in Europe and America to bring the Falashas back into the orbit of traditional Judaism. Since the establishment of the State of Israel, numbers of young Falashas have been brought to Israel, undergone a period of intensive study, and returned as teachers to their communities. The number of Falashas is uncertain, and has been put at between 12,000 and 20,000.

EXODUS: Second of the five books of Moses, known in Hebrew as *Shemot* (names) after the second word of the opening sentence. Of its forty chapters, fifteen deal with the history of the Israelites in Egypt and their triumphant Exodus. The other main events described in the book are the revelation at Mount Sinai and the building of the Tabernacle in the wilderness. The book contains many of the

Exodus scenes from a Spanish Haggadah

fundamental principles of Judaism, including the Ten Commandments (Ch. 20) and the commands concerning the Sabbath and the three pilgrimage festivals. The laws contained in Ch. 21, 22, and 23 form the basis of Talmudic criminal and civil law.

No other event was so enshrined in Jewish history as the Exodus from Egypt. It marked the beginning of Jewish nationhood, and such was its importance that the Bible makes mention of it in no less than one hundred and sixty passages. The Exodus is mentioned daily in the recitation of the *Shema* and on Sabbaths and festivals in the Kiddush prayer, aside from its annual commemoration in the festival of Passover.

Historically, scholars are divided as to the exact date of the Exodus, opinions varying between the 15th to the 13th century B.C.E., with opinion now favoring the later date. The desperate efforts of the survivors of the Nazi holocaust in Europe to reach the land of Israel after World War II was compared to the Exodus, and one of the ships carrying "illegal" immigrants to the land of Israel was called "Exodus 1947." The callousness of the British in returning these desperate refugees to Germany was an important factor in creating a climate of world opinion favoring the establishment of the State of Israel.

EZEKIEL: Biblical prophet of the 6th century B.C.E.; younger contemporary of the prophet Jeremiah. The book bearing his name is the third of the three major prophets. He was a member of the priestly family of Zadok, and is said to have been among the clergy deported to Babylon in company with King Jehoiachin in 597 B.C.E. His prophetic career, which began five years after his arrival in Babylon, extended for at least twenty years. He was one of the leaders of the Jewish exiles and the outstanding prophetic figure of the Babylonian exile.

The book of Ezekiel has forty-eight chapters, which may be divided as follows: 1) 1–24, containing prophecies of rebuke and warning of the impending destruction of the Temple; 2) 25–32, prophecies against the wicked Gentiles; 3) 33–39, prophecies of consolation and comfort after the destruction; and 4) 40–48, Ezekiel's vision of the redemption of the people and the reconstructed Temple.

The most remarkable section of the book is its opening chapter in which the prophet vividly describes God's revelation, in which He showed Ezekiel the divine throne-chariot *(merkavah).* This vision, one of the most outstanding in the prophetic literature, became the basis for an entire branch of Jewish mysticism known as *Maaseh Merkavah,* and also influenced the apocalyptic literature and in a later period, the *Kabbalah.* His prophecies concerning the destruction of the Temple are harsh and uncompromising. The evils of the past, he maintains, can no longer be atoned for; God's judgment has been given and the decree of destruction is irrevocable. Those in Jerusalem and Babylon who still believe that God will not allow His sacred Temple to be destroyed are deluding themselves with false hopes. As if to demonstrate his point, Ezekiel would commit strange acts by which he hoped to bring home to his listeners the truth of his words. Thus, on one occasion, he made a hole in the wall of his house and crawled through it at night carrying his baggage on his back, in order to act the part of one going into exile. When some of the exiles asserted that they were not responsible for what had happened and claimed that they were suffering for the sins of their fathers, Ezekiel rejected this charge out of hand and laid down the doctrine of individual responsibility.

"What mean ye, that ye use this proverb concerning the land of Israel, saying: the fathers have eaten sour grapes and the children's teeth are set on edge?... The soul that sinneth, it shall die" (Ch. 18).

After the destruction of the Temple, however, Ezekiel's prophecies of doom give way to those of hope and consolation. He graphically illustrates Israel's regeneration through the vision of the valley of the dry bones (Ch. 37). No more inspiring message could have been given to the despairing exiles to revive their national will to live.

The last eight chapters contain Ezekiel's vision of the renewed Temple, its worship, the people, and the land in the new era of redemption. According to the Talmud, the book of Ezekiel was at one time in danger of being excluded from the books of the Bible because certain passages seem to contradict the teachings of the Torah. According to tradition, the book of Ezekiel, while composed by the prophet himself, was finally edited by the men of the Great Assembly. Bible scholars, however, have been divided as to the exact dates of Ezekiel's prophecies.

EZRA: Priest, scribe, and religious reformer of the 5th century B.C.E. His story is told in the book bearing his name,

Ezekiel's visions: Dura-Europos Synagogue (ca. 245)

appearing tenth in the third division of the Bible, *Ketuvim*. The books of Ezra and Nehemiah were originally one unit, the division into two separate books dating only from the 15th century. The book of Ezra contains ten chapters. The first six relate the story of the return of the Jews from the Babylonian exile to the land of Israel, and the rebuilding and inauguration of the second Temple. The last three chapters deal with Ezra's mission. The continuation of his career may be found in the book of Nehemiah. Many scholars are of the opinion that the books of Ezra, Nehemiah, and Chronicles are the work of one author.

Approximately sixty years after the first group of exiles had left for the land of Israel under Zerubbabel, word reached Babylon of the physical hardships suffered by the returnees and their spiritual laxity which expressed itself in neglect of the commandments and intermarriage with the Samaritans. Ezra, a scribe at the court of the Persian king Artaxerxes I received the latter's permission to proceed to the land of Israel in order to help stabilize the situation. Armed with the necessary royal authority and accompanied by 1,754 returning exiles, he arrived in Jerusalem bearing the sacred vessels of the Temple. Two months later, on the feast of Tabernacles, Ezra read from the five books of Moses to the assembled masses. He then carried out his program of religious reform which culminated in a covenant of the people in which they agreed to keep the Torah, observe the Sabbath and the Sabbatical year, pay their Temple dues, and reject intermarriage with gentiles. Those who had already married out of the faith were persuaded to divorce their wives. The Talmud credits Ezra with the introduction of many laws and of the square Hebrew script. He is also traditionally considered to be the founder of the Great Assembly. The rabbis state that "Ezra would have been worthy of receiving the Torah for Israel, had not Moses preceded him." If Moses was Israel's founder, it was Ezra who rebuilt its spiritual foundations and gave Judaism the form in which it was to survive throughout the centuries.

Scholars are divided as to the exact date of Ezra's arrival in Jerusalem as well as the relation of Ezra's activity to that of Nehemiah. Undoubtedly the work of both men was vital and they complemented each other. Nehemiah, it seems, occupied himself with secular affairs and the political well-being of the returnees; while Ezra dedicated himself to their spiritual life. According to the ancient historian Josephus Ezra died and was buried in Jerusalem. There is, however, another tradition which locates his grave on the Shatt-el-Arab by the banks of the Tigris.

FAMILY AND FAMILY LIFE: From its inception, Judaism has stressed the family unit as the central pillar of the social structure. The duty of building a home and rearing a family is expressed in the phrase "Be fruitful and multiply" (Gen. 1:28), which is regarded as the first of the 613 commandments of the Torah. In contrast to classic Christianity (Catholicism), which regarded marriage as a necessary evil and the state of celibacy as the ideal, Judaism condemned the celibate as a sinner. "O Lord God, what wilt thou give me seeing that I go childless," was Abraham's despairing cry. Earthly possessions were worthless to him unless he had a child who could carry on his name and work after him. This has been the outlook of Judaism throughout the ages. In addition to the raising of children, woman is to be the "helpmate" of man, in the words of the Bible. The secondary goal of the institution of marriage, therefore, is companionship.

The ancient Israelite family centered around the father, i.e., it was patriarchal. The husband was the master or lord of his wife. The father had absolute authority over his children, over his married sons if they lived with him, and over their wives. The members of the family had an obligation to help and protect one another. While polygamy was permitted in ancient Israel, it is clear that the most common form of marriage was monogamy. The story of the creation of the first two human beings (Gen. 2:21–24) presents monogamous marriage as the will of God. Abraham had at first only one wife, Sarah, and it was because she was barren that he took her handmaid Hagar. After Sarah's death, he took another wife, Keturah. The taking of a concubine was a permitted practice in the ancient Near East, especially if the wife was barren. The concubine, however, never had the same rights as the lawful wife. Jacob, on the other hand, married two sisters, Leah and Rachel, each of whom gave him a handmaid as well. The book of Deuteronomy (Ch. 21:15–17) recognizes bigamy as a legal fact. Gideon had many wives and the kings sometimes kept a large harem. Polygamy, however, did not make for peace in the home. A barren wife was despised by her rival, and was then jealous of one with children. The husband's preference for one of his wives made this rivalry more bitter. It is noteworthy, however, that the books of Samuel and Kings, which cover the entire period of the monarchy, do not record a single case of bigamy among commoners with the exception of Samuel's father. This trend toward monogamy is even more marked during the Talmudic period. Out of 2,800 teachers mentioned in both the Babylonian and Jerusalem Talmuds, only one is stated to have two wives. In other words, the famous decree of Gershom Ben Judah in the 10th century, outlawing polygamy among Ashkenazi Jews once and for all, was merely the culmination of a process which had been taking shape for hundreds of years. Among Oriental Jews, however, polygamy has been known up to modern times and is only ending with their arrival in Israel where it is illegal.

In the eyes of the rabbis, the Jewish family rested on three religious principles: 1) The responsibility of the father to teach

Four generations of Bukharan family in Israel

his children, boys more intensively than girls, the moral laws of the Torah; 2) The fact that even though the father's legal responsibility for a girl ends at the age of twelve years and six months and for a boy at the age of thirteen years and one day, he is still, as the head of the family, morally responsible for their actions; 3) The belief that the duty of honoring parents is equivalent to the duty to honoring God. The obedience of children to their parents is unconditional, the only exception being if the parents urge the child to violate one of the commandments, in which case the word of God has precedence.

These principles governed the pattern of Jewish family life in the Middle Ages and in later periods. The family was the central pivot of Jewish life, and the home, a sanctuary. During long periods of persecution and suffering, the celebration of the Jewish Sabbath and the festivals within the family unit was undoubtedly one of the factors responsible for Jewish survival. Excesses such as infidelity, alcoholism, and wife-beating which often characterized the non-

Jewish environment, were conspicuously absent in Jewish society. The medieval Jewish scholars Rabbenu Tam (Rashi's grandson), and Rabbi Meir of Rothenburg said of wife-beating, "This is a thing not done in Israel." The official code of Jewish law, the *Shulḥan Aruch,* states that it is the court's duty to punish a wife-beater and to excommunicate him. If this does not help, he is to be compelled to divorce his wife.

This family solidarity continued after the children had married and left home. For example, it was considered a duty to take care of aged parents.

From the period of the emancipation, and especially in recent years, the previously close bonds of Jewish family ties have loosened. The neglect of Jewish observances and assimilation of the Jew into the non-Jewish environment has led to an increase in divorce and a dwindling of internal solidarity. The long line of Jewish tradition, however, still serves as an influence to higher standards of morality.

FASTS: Aside from the Day of Atonement and the fast of the 9th of *Av,* which are the subject of special articles, there are a number of statutory fast days which, unlike those two, last only from sunrise to sunset. They commemorate a tragic event in Jewish history and are observed as days of mourning and repentance with complete abstention from food and drink.

They are: 1) The 17th day of *Tammuz* which commemorates the breach in the walls of Jerusalem by Nebuchadnezzar and Titus; 2) the 3rd of *Tishri* commemorating the assassination of Gedaliah, governor of Judea; and 3) the 10th of *Tevet* commemorating the beginning of the siege of Jerusalem by Nebuchadnezzar. To these, the fast of the 13th of *Adar,* known as the Fast of Esther, was added later. With the exception of the Day of Atonement, all fasts which fall on a Sabbath are postponed, generally to the Sunday following. The Fast of Esther, however, is put back to the previous Thursday.

After the destruction of the Second Temple, a number of public and private fasts were added. The former were mainly instituted in times of calamity such as drought, and their purpose was to prevent the "evil decree" by prayer, fasting, and repentance. A whole section of the Talmud, the tractate of *Ta'anit,* is devoted to the regulation of these fasts. Among the private fasts instituted were the fast of the firstborn on the 14th of *Nisan,* (the day before Passover), the fast of a bride and groom on their wedding day, the fast on the anniversary of the death of a parent *(Yahrzeit),* and the fast after a bad dream. Some extremely pious Jews fast every Monday and Thursday. Fasting is prohibited on the Sabbath (the Day of Atonement excepted), on festivals and their intermediate days, on the new moon, and on Ḥanukkah and Purim.

The Jewish concept of the value of fasting is best expressed in the words of the prophet Joel (2:13): "Rend your hearts and not your garments," and in the portrayal of the true fast in Isaiah 58, read as the *Haftarah* on the morning of the Day of Atonement. Fasting is not an end in itself and has no inherent value. It enables the faster to direct his heart to the spiritual values of life, to repent the evil deeds he has committed, and to resolve to show more charity and loving-kindness toward his fellow human beings.

FIRSTBORN: In the Ancient Near East, the firstborn was regarded as the spiritual and material heir of his father. It was he who inherited the spiritual tradition of his father and was the main beneficiary in his will. The importance of this spiritual birthright is reflected in the story of Jacob who persuaded his brother Esau to sell his birthright for a mess of pottage (Gen. 25:31–34). There are a number of other cases in which the firstborn had to forego this privilege. Thus Ham loses it to Shem, Ishmael to Isaac, Esau to Jacob, Reuben to Judah, and Manasseh to Ephraim. It would seem that the inheritance of the spiritual birthright also depended on merit, and if the firstborn were not worthy, it could be transferred to another of the sons. In the case of the material heritage, however, the Bible (Deut. 21:17) lays down specifically that the firstborn son of the father is to be allotted a double portion of the inheritance. The father was not entitled to disinherit the firstborn. He could, however, dispose of his property during his lifetime if he wished others, and not the firstborn, to be the main beneficiaries. The rabbis disapproved of this step, however.

In commemoration of the redemption of the firstborn, on the night of the Exodus when Egyptian firstborn were slain, Israelites are enjoined to dedicate all firstborn men and beasts to the service of God (Ex. 13:1–16). In fact, until the erection of the Tabernacle in the wilderness, and the establishment of the hereditary priesthood, the firstborn formed the priestly class and were responsible for religious services. According to some traditions, this privilege was taken away from them and handed to the Levites as a punishment for their participation in the worship of the golden calf. The only way a firstborn child could be freed from this dedication to God was by a process of redemption in which his father paid a priest a ransom of five shekels or its equivalent in goods. Jews still observe this custom in the ceremony known as *Pidyon Haben* (redemption of the firstborn) held on the 30th day after birth. The short ceremony in which the father gives a *kohen* (priest) the equivalent of five shekels in modern currency is accompanied by the recitation of an appropriate prayer formula. As opposed to the law of inheritance, the command concerning the redemption of the firstborn applies only to the firstborn son of the mother — in accordance with the Biblical verse: "Whatsoever openeth the womb." Similarly, on the basis of this verse, a son born after a previous miscarriage or as a result of a Caesarean section, is also exempted from the obligation of redemption. Sons of priests or Levites need not be redeemed since they are dedicated to the service of God by virtue of their being priests or Levites.

In the case of animals, the firstborn, if they were without blemish, i.e., "pure," were eligible for the altar, and were sacrificed. The firstborn of an ass was either redeemed or destroyed. After the destruction of the Temple, the rabbis ruled that the firstborn of animals should be left to pasture and no benefit derived from them.

In commemoration of the sparing of the Israelites' firstborn on the eve of the Exodus, the fast of the firstborn was instituted for the 14th of *Nisan*. It became customary on that day, however, for firstborn sons to participate in a *"Siyyum,"* a feast held to celebrate the completion of a study of a section of the Talmud. Such participation exempts the firstborn from the obligation of fasting. In the State of Israel, the laws of inheritance are according to Ottoman law with no special privileges accorded to the firstborn.

FLAG: According to the Bible, each one of the twelve tribes carried a banner which, in the view of the rabbis, had as its emblem the blessing accorded them by Jacob (Gen. 49) and Moses (Deut. 33), and the color of one of the precious stones contained in the High Priest's breastplate. Later on, the Maccabees are said to have borne a banner with the initials of the words "Who is like unto Thee among the Gods, O Lord" *(Mi Kamokha Ba-elim Adonai),* from which they drew their name, Maccabee.

The emblem of the State of Israel, the seven-branched candelabrum or *menorah* was one of the most prominent symbols of the Jews in Temple times. As to its flag, the *Magen David* or Shield of David, its origin is obscure. It consists of two superimposed equilateral triangles forming a

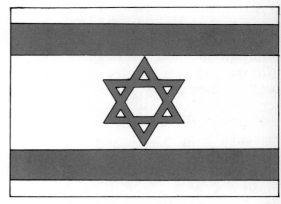

Flag of the State of Israel

star or hexagram. It has been discovered in ancient excavations, but for the most part in non-Jewish environments.

In the *Kabbalah,* the *Magen David* figures as a mystic symbol. But it developed as a distinctive Jewish symbol only in the 17th century. The Zionist movement chose as its flag a *Magen David* set off by two broad blue horizontal stripes upon a white background, said to have been inspired by the *Tallit.* This flag was adopted by the State of Israel.

FOUR QUESTIONS: The questions asked by the youngest child at the Passover *Seder* commencing with the words *"Mah Nishtanah —* Why is this night different from all other nights?" The questions are motivated by the natural curiosity of the child, who on this night observes customs and practices which seem strange to him. The questions provide the father with the pretext for the reading of the Haggadah which contains the answers to the questions, beginning with the words "We were slaves unto Pharaoh in Egypt."

FRANCE: Jewish communities existed in France during the period of the Roman Empire. With the rise of Christianity, however, and the subsequent triumph of the church, their position deteriorated. The first period of French-Jewish life came to an end in 629 when King Dagobert expelled Jews from all territory under his control in central and northern France. In southern France, under the protection of the Visigothic nobility, the Jews prospered, and in the 8th century under Charlemagne, Jewish settlement in France expanded. In the 11th and 12th centuries, France was the center of intensive rabbinical learning, producing some of the most illustrious Talmudic scholars of the Middle Ages including Rashi and the Tosaphists. The development of the feudal system, however, deprived the Jews of most of their lands, and the growth of a Christian merchant class lessened their economic importance. As a result they were forced increasingly to turn to money-lending.

The First Crusade of 1096 marked the beginning of a period of persecution and anti-Jewish legislation. The blood libel became common and in 1240, after a forced disputation in Paris at which the Jews had to defend their beliefs, the Talmud was burned. This persecution brought about a decline in culture and learning and, under Louis IX (1226–70), the position of the Jews deteriorated further. In the 14th century, a series of expulsions took place in 1306, 1321 and, finally, in 1394. After this date, only small numbers of Jews remained, concentrated mainly in Provence. After their expulsion from Spain, however, Jewish refugees and Marranos reached the south and west of France. When Alsace and Lorraine passed from German to French rule, in the mid-17th century, the Jewish population of France grew once more, due to the presence of a large Ashkenazi community in that area. The French revolution with its motto of liberty, fraternity, and equality brought emancipation and equal citizenship rights to the Jews of France — but not before a long and uphill struggle. The French Assembly debated the matter at length, and there was much opposition to extending the Rights of Man to the Jews. At last, on September 27, 1791, the Jews

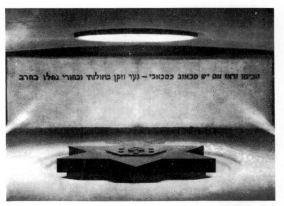

Paris: Memorial to Jewish victims of the Nazis

were finally emancipated. Before long, however, reaction set in, due in part to the anti-Jewish activities of the Alsatians. Napoleon, impatient with the slow progress of Jewish assimilation, called an assembly of Jewish notables in 1806 and established a Sanhedrin one year later. As a result of these gatherings, Napoleon decided to introduce the same type of religious organization among the Jews that he had established among the Christians.

Subsequently, however, the status of French Jewry improved. Indeed, the emancipation achieved in France encouraged the Jews in other European countries to aim at a similar status. In the 19th century, French Jewry, together with the Jews of England, took a leading part in philanthropic activity and in the alleviation of Jewish suffering. The *Alliance Israélite Universelle* was established in 1860 for this purpose. Toward the end of the 19th century, there was again an anti-Semitic reaction which culminated in the Dreyfus Affair. But at the same time French Jewry was strengthened by a large influx of Jewish refugees from eastern Europe, particularly after the First World War. The Jews of France now enjoyed complete freedom, and a number of them, such as Leon Blum, René Mayer and later on, Pierre Mendes-France, achieved political distinction and occupied the highest ministerial offices. The conquest of France by Nazi Germany and the establishment of the puppet Vichy regime, exposed French Jewry to the danger of annihilation. Anti-Jewish legislation was enforced and anti-Semitism was rife. 90,000 Jews were deported from France to the death camps. After the war, the community once again recovered. With the granting of independence to Algeria, the majority of Algerian Jews immigrated to France so that by 1970 the Jewish population exceeded half a million, with Paris their main center. From the 1950's, relations between France and Israel were extremely cordial and the two countries cooperated in military, economic, and political spheres. This policy, however, was abruptly terminated by General de Gaulle on the eve of the June 1967 Six-Day War.

FRANK, ANNE (1929–1945): Dutch-Jewish girl, killed by the Nazis, whose diary achieved worldwide fame. Born in Frankfurt, Germany in 1929, she immigrated to Holland together with her family when Hitler came to power in 1933. With the German conquest of Holland and the subsequent deportation of Jews, the Frank family, together with four other Jews, went into hiding in Amsterdam. They were concealed and fed in a secret attic by non-Jewish friends at great danger to themselves. It was in this atmosphere that the fourteen-year-old girl wrote her diary which extends from June 14, 1942, to August 1, 1944. All the tensions, fears, and even occasional feuds of this trapped group are described in simple but beautiful language, in which the author displays remarkable literary ability and psychological insight. Throughout the diary there is an air of optimism which is strengthened by the young girl's yearning for freedom which, she believed, would inevitably come. This optimism increased after the Allied invasion of France in June 1944 and after the attempt on Hitler's life in July of that year. But on

August 4, 1944, the Nazis discovered the secret hiding place. Anne was first detained in a concentration camp in Holland but was later sent to Auschwitz and from there she went to Bergen Belsen where she died in March 1945. The diary was discovered in the secret attic after the war and its publication made a deep emotional impact on hundreds of thousands of people. It has been translated into many languages, dramatized on the stage, and made into a motion picture. The house in Amsterdam where she was hidden has been made into an Anne Frank museum.

FRANKFURTER, FELIX (1882–1965): U.S. jurist and Associate Justice of the Supreme Court, 1939–62. From 1914–39, he was a professor at Harvard Law School and acted as adviser to successive American presidents. Frankfurter was a member of the "liberal" school, concerning himself with labor laws and civil liberties. Many of his students occupied prominent positions in the New Deal administration of President Roosevelt.

Frankfurter was associated with the Zionist Movement, and in 1919 he was a member of the American Jewish delegation to the peace conference at the end of World War I.

FREUD, SIGMUND (1856–1939): Psychologist and founder of psychoanalysis. Freud had originally experimented with the treatment of mental disorders and neuroses through hypnosis. He then developed the method known as "free association" by which the patient is required to speak out openly whatever comes to his mind. This approach laid the foundation for psychoanalysis and Freud's subsequent work. Freud laid much stress on the importance of one's earliest associations and experiences in the shaping of character and as a cause of mental disorders. Dreams are also, according to Freud, a means of getting a glimpse into

Sigmund Freud

a person's subconscious. His attitude to Judaism, and to religion in general, was negative. In three of his best-known books, *Totem and Taboo* (1913), *The Future of an Illusion* (1928), and *Moses and Monotheism* (1939), Freud develops the idea that religion is an illusion and a childish desire for a father substitute; that the day must come when men will rid themselves of it and learn to stand on their own feet. Because of its repressive nature, religion is the cause of much internal conflict and disorder.

Freud lived most of his life in Vienna where he was a professor of neurology. The German invasion of Austria in 1938 forced him to leave for London where he died in 1939.

GALICIA: A province of central Europe on the northern slopes of the Carpathian Mountains. Until 1772, it was part of Poland, but in that year Poland was partitioned, and Galicia, with its 200,000 Jews, was annexed by Austria. Life under Austrian rule was, in effect, no easier than life under the Poles. On the surface, however, certain steps were taken which gave the appearance of attempting to alleviate the discriminatory position of the Jews. Thus, under Joseph II (1780–1790), legislation was introduced for the establishment of elementary and high schools for Jews, for the introduction of military service, and the acquisition of family names, while land and financial support were granted those Jews willing to enter agriculture. However, these measures were in reality aimed at the enforced assimilation of the Jews, for they were accompanied by a severe limitation of rabbinical authority and the abolition of communal autonomy.

Especially high taxes on marriage licenses, on kosher meat, and on synagogues were introduced. Jews were forbidden to use Hebrew or Yiddish in official documents, and Galician Jews were allowed to stay in Vienna for no more than fourteen days, for which a special tax had to be paid. In the city of Lvov, the ancient ghetto was maintained. Though supported by a minority of "enlightened" Jews, the vast majority recognized the reforms for what they were, a transparent attempt to "civilize" the Jews and to lessen their "harmfulness." The reforms failed and, in fact, served only to impoverish an already poor population. At the beginning of the 19th century, Galicia became the arena for the battle between Ḥasidism and its opponents, the *Mitnagdim*. In this battle, Ḥasidism was triumphant, and Galicia remained, until the Nazi holocaust, a Ḥasidic stronghold. In the middle of the 19th century, however, the Hasidim and *Mitnagdim* tended to unite to fight what they considered an even greater danger, the *Haskalah* or Enlightenment Movement. Concurrently, the struggle for Jewish emancipation proceeded, and despite the violent opposition of all segments of the population, Poles, Germans, and Ukrainians, progress was made. In the 1850's, legal limitations on Jews in the liberal professions were removed and finally, with the Austrian constitution of 1867, Jews were granted complete political and civil equality. The second half of the 19th century saw a period of reaction, in Galicia as in the rest of Europe. Polish patriotic and nationalist groups tended to be extremely anti-Semitic. A "Christian Social Party" was founded, and advocated a total economic boycott of the Jewish population. Excesses against the Jews, including pogroms, occurred. Sections of the Catholic Church openly supported these trends. The Jewish community itself was internally divided. Certain sections advocated assimilation and there was, at first, a great deal of sympathy among Jews for the Polish Nationalistic movement. A smaller group supported the aspirations of the Ukrainians. Added to this was the split between the different religious groupings so that Jewish political influence, on the whole, decreased. Disillusionment with the Polish Nationalists set in when they adopted an anti-Semitic platform and

Jew in Galicia

initiated an economic boycott of the Jews. This prepared the ground for the emergence at the turn of the century of Jewish Nationalist, Zionist, and Socialist tendencies. Immigration to the United States and western Europe increased. During World War I, the Jews of Galicia suffered from the repeated invasions by Russia and Austria. As part of the peace settlement of 1919, Galicia was once again returned to Poland and its Jewish community shared the vicissitudes and ultimate destruction of Poland's ill-fated Jewry at the hands of the Nazis.

GALILEE: Northern part of the State of Israel. Covering an area of 1,414 square miles, it extends from the Valley of Jezreel in the south to the Lebanese border in the north, and from the Jordan Valley in the east to the Mediterranean in the west. According to the Bible, it was assigned to the tribes of Naphtali and Asher. After King Solomon's death and the resultant division of the kingdom, it was part of the northern kingdom of Israel. As such, it was conquered by the Assyrian King Tiglath-Pileser in 732 B.C.E. During the late Second Temple period it was reattached to Judea, and under Herod became one of the three administrative districts into which the country was divided. During the rebellion against Rome (66–70 C.E.), Galilee was placed under the command of Josephus who, without offering serious battle, defected to the Romans. It was in Nazareth of Galilee that the founder of Christianity, Jesus, was reared and much of his preaching and spiritual activity took place in the vicinity of Lake Kinneret (the Sea of Galilee). After the destruction of the Temple in 70 C.E., Galilee became for a time the center of Jewish settlement and scholarship. The academies of learning at Beth Shearim, Sepphoris, and Tiberias produced numerous great scholars, and the fruits of their labor was the Jerusalem or Palestinian Talmud, completed at Tiberias in approximately 400 C.E. The ensuing centuries of Persian, Arab, and Crusader rule were centuries of desolation and spiritual barrenness, although Jews continued to live in the area. In the 16th century, Safed became the world center of Jewish mysticism, and an effort was made by Joseph Nasi to establish an autonomous settlement at Tiberias. The resettlement of Galilee in modern times began with the founding of Rosh Pinah in 1882. The first *kibbutz,* Deganiah, was established on the banks of Lake Kinneret in 1909, and since then, the process of development has continued unabated

During the 1948 War of Independence, the entire area of Galilee was captured by the Israel Defense Forces. The draining of the Huleh swamps in the 1950's made northern Galilee one of the most fertile and beautiful parts of the State of Israel. New settlements and cities were established and the population grew. The mountains of Upper Galilee reach 3,724 feet at their highest point, Mt. Meron. Because of its scenic beauty, Galilee has become a major tourist attraction.

GALILEE, SEA OF (Yam Kinneret, i.e., Lake Kinneret): One of the two lakes formed by the Jordan River and one of the most beautiful sights in the land of Israel. In the Bible it is called the Sea of Chinnereth, but in later times the name was changed to *Ginnosar,* hence the form Lake of Gennesaret found in the New Testament, which also uses the names Sea of Galilee and Sea of Tiberias (the town of Tiberias was founded on its shores in the 1st century C.E.). The lake acquired sanctity in Christian tradition through the activities of Jesus and his disciples in the area.

great irrigation projects, the National Water Carrier, provides for pumping the waters of the lake to the arid Negev. After Israel's 1948 War of Independence, the lake was under Israel sovereignty, but the eastern heights were controlled by the Syrians, who lost no opportunity to bombard the Jewish settlements below them and to attack the Israel fishermen as they fished in the lake. It was only in the 1967 Six-Day War that the heights were captured by Israel, and these attacks ceased.

The Sea of Galilee lies 680 feet below the level of the Mediterranean; its length is 13 miles, its width opposite Tiberias $5\frac{1}{2}$ miles, its circumference $32\frac{1}{2}$ miles, and its maximum depth 156 feet. In Hebrew thought and music, the lake has acquired a romantic aura, and many are the poets who have been inspired by its beauty.

View of Sea of Galilee

View of Mt. Sussita and Ein Gev

Beginning in 1909 with the first *kibbutz,* Deganiah, many Jewish settlements have been established on the shores of the lake. In modern times, Tiberias has grown and, with it, the area of Lake Kinneret, which has become a popular tourist, holiday, and health resort. One of Israel's

Especially famous is the song, *V' Ulai* (Perhaps), by the poetess Rachel.

GAON (Excellency; Pride; Eminence): Title given to the heads of the Babylonian academies of Sura and Pumbedita from the end of the 6th to the end of the

12th centuries. The title is an abbreviation of their full designation, *Rosh Metivta Geon Yaakov,* i.e., "Head of the academy which is the Excellency of Jacob." During this period, Sura and Pumbedita produced the intellectual and rabbinic leadership not only for Babylonian Jewry but for the whole Jewish world. The rivalry between these two great rabbinic centers was often decided by the caliber of the man who headed the academy. Thus, there were periods when Sura was pre-eminent and vice versa. The authority of the Babylonian *Geonim* was acknowledged throughout the Jewish world, and they were virtually inundated with queries about Jewish law sent from Egypt, North Africa, Israel itself, and other centers. The answers to these queries gave rise to a vast literature known as *Responsa.* Among the famous leaders of the Sura Academy were Amram Gaon (856–874), the compiler of the first prayer book, and Saadyah Gaon (appointed 928), one of the greatest Jewish figures of the early Middle Ages. Under him, Sura reached its zenith. Saadyah not only occupied himself with Talmudic studies but was one of the first Jewish scholars to formulate a philosophy of religion. It was Saadyah too who led the battle against the growing Karaite movement. The rival Pumbedita Academy reached the height of its fame during the late 10th and early 11th centuries under the successive leadership of Sherira Gaon and his son, Hai. It is to the former that we owe much of our knowledge of the period, through a letter known as the Epistle of Sherira Gaon. This was written in response to a question from the Jews of Kairouan in North Africa. In it, the writer traces the chain of Jewish tradition and scholarship from the early Mishnaic period to his own day.

Even when the two academies were transferred to Baghdad at the end of the 9th century they retained their distinctive names. At the same time, an attempt to rival the Babylonian institutions was made in Israel where the head of the academy there also used the title *Gaon.* This Palestinian gaonate, however, only lasted a short time, and never achieved the distinction and authority of its Babylonian rival. The influence of the Babylonian Academies and the *Geonim* lasted until the beginning of the 13th century. By that time, Babylon's place in the Jewish world had been superseded by new centers of Jewish life in North Africa, Spain and France.

In later usage, the term *Gaon* came to be used for a rabbinic scholar of particular brilliance. Thus the famous leader of 18th century Lithuanian Jewry, Elijah of Vilna (1720–1797), is often referred to as the *Vilna Gaon.*

GARDEN OF EDEN (Heb. **Gan Eden**): Traditional site of the story of Adam and Eve as related in the second chapter of the book of Genesis. According to the Bible, it was watered by a river which divided into four streams, the Pishon, Gihon, Tigris, and Euphrates. This led numerous scholars to conjecture as to the exact geographical location of the garden. Some placed it in the fertile valley of the Tigris-Euphrates Rivers, others suggested a more eastward location. The medieval Jewish scholar-philosopher, Moses Maimonides, regards the story as allegorical. In later rabbinic literature, the Garden of Eden, perhaps because of its connection with the tree of life and its description as an ideal place, became the designation for the abode of bliss, reserved for righteous souls after death. In this sense, as the world to come, it is mentioned in the memorial prayer. In modern Hebrew usage, a *Gan Eden* is the equivalent of the English expression, "a veritable paradise."

GENIZAH (Heb. **Hiding**): According to Jewish law, it is forbidden to destroy holy books and utensils which are no longer useable. The custom arose therefore of placing such articles in special store-houses or depositories such as the foundations and attics of synagogues, or of burying them in the ground. Hebrew writings so deposited are called *Shemot* (names), because they contain the "names" of God which should not be destroyed. The discovery of such *Genizot* in various parts of the world, especially in the Middle East, led to the recovery of valuable manuscripts and shed much light on various periods of Jewish history. The most famous *Genizah* was discovered in the Fostat Synagogue near Cairo, built in the year 882. In 1897, Solomon Schechter transferred thousands of leaves and manuscripts from this *Genizah* to the Cambridge University Library. Among others, he recognized part of the last Hebrew version of the book of Ecclesiasticus. Thousands of other documents cast fresh light on the religious and social life of Egyptian and Palestinian Jewry in the early Middle Ages. A large amount of the rabbinical correspondence carried on by the Babylonian *geonim* was also contained in this *Genizah*. Other *Genizot* were subsequently discovered in a number of oriental communities, but none were quite as important and illuminating as the Cairo find. Another type of *Genizah* was used by the Dead Sea sect who successfully hid and thus preserved documents in Judean caves.

GERMANY: The earliest evidence of Jews in what are now the Republics of East and West Germany, dates back to the Roman Imperial period. During the 8th and 9th centuries, the Carolingian rulers welcomed Jews as traders and merchants, and by the 10th and 11th centuries, large Jewish communities existed in the Rhineland towns of Mainz, Speyer, Worms, Cologne and others. Conditions were relatively tolerable and an intense intellectual and spiritual life, particularly in the sphere of Talmudic study, was pursued.

The First Crusade in 1096, however, resulted in the massacre of thousands of Jews throughout the Rhineland, and initiated an era of persecution and suffering which justifies Germany's reputation as the classical country of medieval Jew-baiting. The continued existence of the Jewish community was largely due to the fact that Germany was not one united kingdom but a series of petty states all competing with one another. It was thus impossible to expel or persecute the Jews in an organized and coordinated manner, on the decision of the sovereign, as happened in England, France and Spain. Driven out of one area, the Jews could find another German state which would receive them, thus preserving the continuity of the Jewish settlement. The standard accusations leveled against Jews during the Middle Ages — such as the ritual murder charge and the stealing of the sacred wafer (known as the Host) — were regular occurrences in medieval Germany. At the beginning of the 14th century, a fanatic named Rindfleisch whipped the populace into a frenzy with an account of how he had seen Jews crush the wafer in a mortar, after which he led a howling mob through Jewish quarters on a murder spree. In the ensuing massacres, some 20,000 Jews are estimated to have lost their lives. A few German towns, such as Ratisbon and Augsburg, protected their Jewish population. In 1336–37 two nobles wearing leather patches on their arms (and therefore called *Armleder*), led hordes of pogromists in a campaign of murder and destruction of Jews and their property. This time, some of the authorities reacted more forthrightly and even punished the murderers. The height of German-Jewish suffering during the Middle Ages came in 1348–49 during an outbreak of the plague known as the Black Death. Jews were accused of having caused the plague by poisoning the wells. The mass slaughter which followed was unprecedented both in geographic extent and in the number of its victims. Once again, some city councils attempted to protect the Jews but this time the mobs, whipped into a frenzy by their superstitious fears and beliefs, were determined to carry out their mission of vengeance without interference. This Black Death Massacre almost spelled the end of organized Jewish life in large sections of Germany. During the initial stages of the Protestant Reformation, there seemed to be a chance of improving the position of the Jews. Martin Luther, like Mohammed before him, hoped that by showing more tolerance toward the Jews, they would support him and thus become more amenable to conversion. When his hopes were disappointed, he turned against them with an intense hatred. After the religious wars of the 17th century, disillusionment with both the Catholic and Protestant religions prompted a slightly more tolerant attitude. At the same time, the nation-states of Germany began to develop economically and militarily, and many of them employed Jews as financial advisors, particularly as buyers of military equipment. This led to the emergence of a small but privileged class of Jews known as Court Jews. These latter were often granted the right to establish new communities. With the growing strength and expansion of Prussia in the 17th century, Jewish communities sprang up in the areas under its domination. By the 18th century, the question of Jewish rights had become the subject of bitter public debate. On the Jewish side, the struggle was led by Moses Mendelssohn, supported by a number of enlightened gentiles. Such was the respect in which Mendelssohn was held as a man of deep learning and culture, that he was granted the status of a "privileged Jew." Nevertheless, despite his efforts, the majority of the Jewish population continued to suffer from severe discrimination. The French revolution and the conquests of Napoleon brought equality and emancipation to the Jews of western Germany, but with Napoleon's defeat, there was a reaction marked by anti-Jewish riots in 1819. By this time, however, the Jews, who had had a taste of freedom, were no longer prepared to sit back and watch their hard-earned achievements taken from them. They supported various liberal and humanitarian groups and played no small part in the revolutions of 1830 and 1848. The unification of Germany under Bismarck in 1871 and the new German Imperial constitution brought complete political and civil emancipation for German Jews, but until World War I, in 1914, this equality was purely theoretical. Social disabilities and restrictions remained. Almost no Jew was able to secure high office in the government, army, or even in the universities. An active anti-Semitic movement began in 1878, and in 1891 there was a ritual murder allegation. Despite this, Jews had begun to enter the mainstream of German life with brilliant success. In every sphere — literary, cultural, and scientific — Jews made an important contribution. Germany also became the center of a new scientific approach to Judaism. The attempt to adjust religion to modern life resulted in the birth and growth of Reform Judaism. The outbreak of World War I witnessed an outpouring of patriotic fervor among German Jews. Thousands of Jewish soldiers fought with distinction in the German Army, and many were decorated for their services. The Jewish chemist Fritz Haber made discoveries that enabled Germany to overcome the blockade imposed by the allies.

Under the Weimar Republic, the last vestiges of Jewish discrimination were removed, and the Jews of Germany attained great achievements in all spheres. This phase ended quickly with the rise of Adolf Hitler and his National Socialist party. With his rise to power began the most ruthless campaign in history to deprive the Jews of their possessions, their livelihood and, eventually, their lives. The Nuremberg laws of 1935 had as their purpose the total exclusion of Jews from all spheres of life. The riots of November 1938, which resulted in the burning of synagogues and the sacking of Jewish businesses, made life unbearable and ended the possibility of maintaining organized Jewish life. Thousands of refugees made their way to England, the United States, and particularly to the land of Israel where they provided a rich addition to the already growing Jewish community. The majority of German Jewry, however, was trapped by the outbreak of World War II, and their fate was tied up with that of European Jewry in general. In September 1941, the wearing of the Jewish badge was enforced, and soon thereafter the deportations to the extermination camps began. The Jewish population, which in 1938 was over half a million, was totally decimated. After World War II, there was a noticeable reluctance on the part of Jews to return to the land which had engineered the destruction of 6,000,000 of their brethren. Many Jews from East European countries nevertheless went to Germany which was now divided into the Federal Republic of West Germany and the East German Democratic Republic. In 1968, there were 30,000 Jews in Germany, living mainly in Berlin, Frankfort and Munich. 1,500 lived in East Germany. However, there is a preponderence of old people in the community, the young ones tending to leave. Despite the fact that there are still anti-Semitic manifestations from time to time, the various German governments have gone out of their way to improve Germany's image in the world by denouncing the Nazi crimes of the past. In 1952, a reparations agreement was signed whereby West Germany agreed to pay 822 million dollars compensation to the Jewish people for the material losses suffered by German Jews during the Nazi period. The West German Government also showed a measure of understanding for Israel's struggle to survive the onslaughts of Arab hostility. Diplomatic relations between Israel and the Federal Republic were established in 1965.

GHETTO: Jewish quarter. The origin of the name has been the subject of much conjecture. The generally accepted explanation is that it derives from the decision adopted by the Senate of Venice in 1516 that the Jews of that city reside in the houses adjacent to the cannon foundry, which in Italian is *gheta*. That decision bestowed the name ghetto on the system of separate Jewish quarters in other countries as well. This separation was not always enforced, as is popularly believed. The tendency on the part of Jews to live together is an ancient one. For religious, economic, and social reasons, Jews often congregated together in their own Jewish neighborhoods. The oldest and most persistent ghetto in Europe originated before the rise of Christianity in Rome's Trastevere District, where numerous Jewish freedmen (slaves released by their masters) lived.

The enforced separation of Jews resulted from the Lateran councils of 1179 and 1215 at which the church forbade contact between Christians and Jews. In certain parts of Spain, Jewish quarters called *Juderia* were established, and in Germany, Austria, and Bohemia there were *Judenstädte* — or Jewish quarters. Prague's *Judenstadt* was especially famous, and within its confines, the Jews enjoyed a great deal of autonomy, even having their own town hall.

The *Ghetto Age* in its more humiliating form commenced with an instruction issued by Pope Paul IV in July 1555, that all Jews must reside in separate quarters where they were not allowed to own property. Soon after, ghettos were established throughout Europe. The typical ghetto in Germany, Austria, and Bohemia consisted, as a rule, of a main street with a synagogue at one end and a cemetery at the other. The entire ghetto was walled, with one gate

Ghetto of Frankfurt (15th cent.)

which served as exit and entrance. It was a town within a town, enjoying a considerable degree of autonomy and a vigorous spiritual and intellectual life. It was at the same time overcrowded and subject to frequent fires. The ghetto system, moreover, was often accompanied by discriminatory measures such as the wearing of a Jewish badge, and the inhabitants were never safe from anti-Jewish outbursts and pogroms. Despite the humiliations involved, in the long run segregated living benefited Jewish social and communal life, and it was only at the beginning of the 18th century that the perpetuation of the ghetto system elicited protests from Jewish leaders. The French Revolution heralded the end of the ghetto although it was not finally abolished until Rome united with the Kingdom of Italy in 1870.

European ghettos were revived in World War II by the Nazis. Their aim, however, was not the establishment of permanent separate quarters for the Jews. The ghettos of Warsaw, Lublin, Lodz, Minsk, Vilna, and many others were used as concentration points in which the Jews were assembled before being transported to the death camps. Hundreds of thousands of Jews were crammed into tiny areas, isolated, and starved to break their spirit before extermination. The population of the Warsaw Ghetto rose to 450,000 while the Ghetto of Lodz had 200,000 Jewish inmates. Despite their desperate situation, the Jews maintained religious and cultural institutions, and finally, when news began to filter through of the fate of their brethren transported to the concentration camps, some of them rebelled. The rebellion of the ghettos in 1943 is one of the noblest pages in the history of Jewish heroism.

The Warsaw Ghetto was liquidated in 1943, after heavy casualties had been inflicted on the Nazis by the defenders. The remaining ghettos were eliminated soon after.

GOD: Judaism has no specific definition of God. Neither in the Bible nor in rabbinic literature is any attempt made to prove the existence of God. The ancients apparently had no doubts on the question. The existence of a Supreme Being who created the world and everything within it is taken for granted from the very first verse of the Bible, "In the beginning, God created the heavens and the earth." This is not a subject for debate. An atheist, one who denies the existence of God, is not only unknown but inconceivable to the authors of the books of the Bible. There are references in Talmudic literature to heretics and to the *Kopher Ba-Ikar* ("he who denies the root principle") but this refers to one who claims that God does not intervene in the affairs of the world which He created. The oft-quoted rabbinic phrase "There is no judge and no judgment" also refers to those who, while acknowledging God's existence and the fact that He created the world, nevertheless are of the opinion that He has no further interest in what happens to His creation. Similarly, the verse in the Psalms (141) "The fool hath said in his heart, there is no God," also refers to denial of God's intervention in human affairs.

The ancient world was deeply religious and the concept that everything in nature was controlled by supernatural powers was common to most peoples. Archaeology has revealed highly organized religious frameworks of god, temple and priests in nearly all the societies of the ancient world. One such society was Abraham's ancestral city, Ur of the Chaldees, situated at the southern end of the Euphrates River.

In the main, however, ancient religion was polytheistic, i.e., believing in the existence of many gods; and pagan in that it made gods of actual, finite things, beings, and natural forces. The ancient Near Eastern texts are full of the names of vast numbers of gods. They tell of their wars, loves, and jealousies to explain of events and natural forces beyond the comprehension of primitive man. For all practical purposes, the ancient peoples were idol worshippers. There were, it is true, occasional glimpses of higher religious truth, but these remained only glimpses. The remarkable Egyptian Pharaoh Amenophis IV attempted to reform Egyptian religion by worshipping only the sun, under the name of *Aton,* and embracing the new philosophy of *maat,* the principle of truth. He changed his name to Ikhnaton, but with his death, the priests of the old religion reasserted themselves. The reformation was a failure and Ikhnaton was branded a criminal by his own people. Into this god-intoxicated world, Judaism made its entrance and its unique contribution to civilization — monotheism, the worship of one infinite God.

The God of the Bible is the one and only God, creator of the physical universe, ruler of all men and nations. He is capable of all things at one and the same time. He is distant, yet near, a God of wrath but also of mercy. He punishes but also forgives. He has no human or manly qualities; no body, no relatives, no human needs.

He must not be depicted in painting or sculpture for He is above and beyond all material representation. Yet He speaks to man through revelations and through the prophets, His specially chosen messengers.

All this is taken for granted by the biblical writers and, later, by the rabbinic sages. In discussing those who will have no share in the world to come, the rabbis mention those who deny the resurrection of the dead or the divine origin of the Torah. The atheist is not mentioned, because such a person was inconceivable to the rabbinic mind.

It was only under the impact of Greek philosophy and the clash between Judaism and Hellenism that Jews were impelled to look for proofs of God's existence. The problem arose especially in the 1st century B.C.E. in the large Jewish community of Alexandria, where the Jewish scholar and philosopher Philo developed his theories. During the Middle Ages too, following the Arabs' rediscovery of Greek philosophy, Jewish, Christian, and Moslem thinkers all claimed that God's existence could be proved rationally. Three main proofs were postulated: 1) the cosmological, i.e., the argument of the "first cause." Everything in nature can be traced to an earlier cause, but what is the origin of the first cause? Obviously some pre-existent, supernatural being — God; 2) the ontological, which claims that God must exist since, if not, how did human beings come to think of Him?; and 3) the teleological, or argument from design. Everything in the universe, the solar system, the human body, plant life, etc., shows evidence of design and there can be no design without a designer. The designer must be God.

Moses Maimonides (1135–1204), the greatest Jewish thinker of the Middle Ages, wrote a special work, *Guide for the Perplexed,* in an attempt to reconcile seeming contradictions between faith and philosophy. So strictly did Maimonides view the unity and spiritual nature of God that he taught that whoever believes that God can actually be described in human terms, is a heretic. When the Bible describes God in such terms, for instance, as sitting on His throne or talking to men, it does so in order to make it easier for ordinary people to comprehend the complete spirituality of God and to understand and believe in His power. This is called anthropomorphism — describing God in human terms. Furthermore, Maimonides was of the opinion that one cannot ascribe positive attributes to God. One cannot say what God is, because He is indefinable. One can only say what God is not. To say that God exists does not really say anything about God, it merely denies the possibility of His not existing. This strictly spiritual definition of God makes the Jewish rejection of the Christian trinity imperative. To speak of God as being divisible into three is a blemish on His unity, and to speak of His having a son is to assign physical attributes to God, as the pagans did to their gods. God has no wife or female counterpart by whom He has children. Another medieval thinker, Jehuda Halevi, was opposed to the above philosophical abstract speculation and preferred to see God as the Lord of History and to stress His rule over nations, especially Israel.

Jewish monotheism also rejects the identification of God with nature (pantheism). The great Jewish philosopher Spinoza (1632–1677) was excommunicated by the Amsterdam Bet Din for teaching that the universe, in its entirety, was God. This view, in contradiction to the idea of God's being above all that He has created, opposes the theory of man's responsibility to a higher being and denies the existence of God in the ordinary sense of the word.

In the modern age, the medieval "proofs" of God's existence have been rejected as inadequate. God's existence, it is generally held, cannot be proved either mathematically or philosophically. Judaism, while adhering basically to the strict monotheistic approach outlined above, has been influenced by and has in turn influenced contemporary thought. Immanuel Kant (1724–1804), the central figure in modern German and general philosophy, was convinced of the existence of God because of the prickings of conscience, the "voice of God" within man. "Two things," he said, "fill the mind with ever-increasing wonder and awe the more often and the more intensely the mind of thought is drawn to them: the starry heavens above me and the moral law within me." It is interesting to note that the late Chief Rabbi of the land of Israel, Abraham Isaac Kook (1865–1935), also believed that by obeying the moral law, men were actually doing the will of God without necessarily being aware of it.

The founder of the *Hasidic* movement, Israel Baal Shem Tov (1700–1760), under the influence of the mystical *kabbalah,* taught that God, like food, cannot be proved or conveyed, only experienced and tasted. In this connection, he was fond of quoting the verse from the book of Psalms, "Taste ye and see that the Lord is good."

Moses Mendelssohn (1729–1786), pioneer of the German enlightenment and fighter for Jewish emancipation, was convinced of the rationality of Jewish belief. There is, according to Mendelssohn, no conflict between reason and belief. Judaism, said Mendelssohn, has no dogmas, and its main principles such as the existence and unity of God, His providence, and the immortality of the soul are known to man by reason and are merely reaffirmed by Judaism.

In recent years, the existentialist movement has won many adherents. The Danish theologian Kierkegaard coined the phrase "the leap of faith" to express the idea that God must be encountered, that it is impertinent to attempt to prove His existence. The Jewish existentialist school is represented by Franz Rosenzweig (1886–1929), Professor Martin Buber (1878–1965), and their disciples. Buber was deeply influenced by Hasidism and his philosophy sees religious faith as a dialogue between man and God. The most radical modern conception of God in Jewish circles has come from the Reconstructionist movement of Professor Mordechai Kaplan. He defines God as "the power that makes for salvation." His approach tends to "depersonalize" God. God should not be thought of as a "person" but as the totality of relationships, tendencies, and agencies which, together, make human life worthwhile. This is the extreme opposite to anthropomorphism — ascribing human characteristics to God, as discussed earlier.

In general, most Jewish thinkers and scholars have tried to avoid both extremes— too much humanizing on the one hand and too much depersonalization on the other. The God of Judaism is the Supreme Being, the creator of the universe, Lord and ruler of history, the one and only God who, despite being infinitely above His creation and creatures, is at the same time interested and involved in His handiwork and is, therefore, approachable to man through prayer and good deeds.

GOLDMANN, NAHUM (1895–): Zionist and communal leader. After studying at German universities and working in the German Foreign Office during World War I, from 1922–34 he was one of the editors of the German Encyclopedia Judaica. In 1933, he became chairman of the Zionist Actions Committee and from 1935–39 represented the Jewish Agency at the League of Nations in Geneva. After Stephen Wise's death, Goldmann became chairman of the executive of the World Jewish Congress and in 1953 was made its president. From 1935–68, he was president of the World Zionist Organization. Goldmann played a vital role in the negotiations with West Germany which led to the signing of the Reparations Agreement in 1952, by which payments were made to Israel and World Jewry in recognition of the material damage inflicted on the Jews by the Nazis. Goldmann was long the most influential world Jewish leader but his original approach to many problems frequently led to controversy.

GOLEM (Shapeless matter): An automaton, usually in human form, into which life was breathed by the magical use of one of the divine names. In the Talmud there appear various stories of the creation of a *golem*. The German Hasidic (Pietist) movement of the 12th and 13th centuries developed the *golem* legend, and in the writings of one of the movement's leaders, Eleazar of Worms (1160–1238), we even find recipes for the creating of the *golem*, which was regarded by them as an ecstatic experience. The being which emerged became the servant of its creator, but also possessed the Frankenstein-like power of causing destruction and ruin. The ability to create a *golem* was attributed to various rabbis, and the most famous legend of all is associated with Judah Low ben Bezalel of Prague, also known as *Maharal*. In Yiddish, the word *golem* is used for a stupid person.

GRACE BEFORE AND AFTER MEALS: Before partaking of food of any kind, it is obligatory to recite a benediction. The full grace, however, is only recited after a meal which has included bread. Before eating, the hands are washed and the blessing "Blessed Art Thou O Lord . . . who hast commanded us concerning the washing of the hands" is said. A piece of bread is then taken and the blessing "Who brings forth bread from the earth . . ." recited.

The obligation to recite grace is derived from the verse: "Thou shalt eat and be satisfied and bless the Lord thy God for the good Land He hath given you" (Deut. 8:10). If three or more males over the age of bar mitzvah eat together, they say grace as a group, one of them inviting the others to join him in thanking "Him of Whose bounty we have partaken." This custom is ancient, and the formula is found in the Mishnah. On weekdays, some communities recite Psalm 137 before the grace, and on Sabbaths it is customary to recite Psalm 126. The grace itself consists of three ancient blessings to which a fourth was later added. They are: 1) *Birkat Ha-mazon,* thanksgiving to God for his bounty; 2) *Birkat Ha-aretz,* the national blessing in which the Almighty is thanked for the land of Israel, for redeeming His people from Egyptian bondage, and for His laws and commandments; 3) *Boneh Yerushalayim,* a plea for the rebuilding of Jerusalem; 4) *Ha-tov Veha-meitiv,* a blessing added after the destruction of the Temple. The supplications commencing *Haraḥman* ("The all-merciful") are a later addition and vary in number in different rites. There are also insertions for the Sabbath, New Moon and festivals, Ḥanukkah and Purim, circumcision and wedding meals, and the consolation of mourners. A shorter form of grace is recited after partaking of certain kinds of fruit or cake. It consists of only one benediction but this benediction contains all the main themes of the full grace, outlined above.

GRAETZ, HEINRICH (1817–1891): German historian and Biblical scholar. Graetz received a traditional Yeshiva education but at the same time absorbed secular learning privately. At first he was a follower of the Orthodox leader Samson Raphael Hirsch, but gradually drifted from his master as he began to adopt a rationalist-scientific approach toward Judaism. Unable to get along with large groups, his attempts to enter public life as rabbi and as school director were unsuccessful. In 1854, he was appointed lecturer in Jewish history at the newly founded Breslau Rabbinical School. Graetz's main contribution to Jewish scholarship is his monumental eleven-volume history of the Jews. This pioneering work, unique in its time,

aroused much debate and some hostility. Christian historians were upset by his open and bitter attacks on the Christian treatment of the Jews. Orthodox Jews, on the other hand, were dismayed at Graetz's contempt for Jewish mysticism and the Hasidic movement. He also paid too little attention to economic and social factors in his historical analysis. Nevertheless, the work was received with acclaim by all who recognized its brilliant and original scholarship, and to this day it is regarded as a standard textbook for all students of Jewish history.

GREAT ASSEMBLY (Knesset Ha-Gedolah): Body which constituted the spiritual leadership of the people of Israel from the beginning of the Second Temple period until approximately 200 B.C.E. Its beginnings have been traced to the Great Assembly of the people presided over by Ezra, as described in the 8th chapter of the book Nehemiah. This body, which is variously estimated to have been composed of 85 or 120 sages, bridged the gap between the end of the prophetic period and the beginning of the rabbinic period.

According to the opening *Mishnah* of *Pirkei Avot* (Ethics of the Fathers) three basic principles guided their work: 1) be slow in giving judgment; 2) raise up many disciples; and 3) put a fence about the Torah. The men of the Great Assembly brought about a silent religious revolution which democratized Jewish spiritual life and its institutions. This consisted of the transference of religious authority from the hereditary priesthood to the scribe, the man of letters. It is to their credit that from this time on, scholarship achieved uncontested supremacy among the people of Israel. The development of the oral tradition which was to characterize later rabbinic Judaism was due in no small measure to the men of the Great Assembly. Thus, many of the observances and regulations which govern Jewish life to this day were attributed to them by the rabbis. The institution of the *Amidah* to be recited thrice daily, the benedictions before and after meals and before the performance of a commandment, the *Kiddush* and *Havdalah*, the reading of the Torah on Mondays and Thursdays, and the inclusion of certain books in the Bible — these and many other customs have been assigned by rabbinic tradition to the men of the Great Assembly.

HADASSAH: Women's Zionist Organization of America, founded in 1912 by Henrietta Szold. Initially, its primary aim was the improving of health conditions in the land of Israel. In 1918, it sent a medical unit there which played a vital role in laying the foundations of the Jewish community's health services. The unit's program included the establishment of welfare centers and training schools for nurses. Hadassah introduced such concepts as preventive medicine by educating the population to understand its health needs. The health programs introduced and fostered by Hadassah were later incorporated in the health services of the State of Israel. One of Hadassah's crowning achievements was the establishment in 1939 of the Hadassah Medical School and Hospital attached to the Hebrew University in Jerusalem. This medical center, situated on Mount Scopus, is the most modern in the Middle East. It was cut off by the Arabs during the 1948 War of Liberation, and its facilities were abandoned. As a result of the 1967 Six-Day War, however,

Hadassah Medical Center

the path to Mount Scopus was liberated. The medical center reopened, its facilities reactivated. In the meantime, however, a magnificent new medical center had been built by Hadassah at Ein-Kerem near Jerusalem. In the early 1930's, Hadassah began to broaden its activities and embrace other spheres of Zionist endeavor. Youth Aliyah and the establishment and support of youth villages became other major activities. During and following the Nazi persecution, Hadassah also concentrated on the alleviation of suffering among Jewish refugees. Hadassah is now the largest Jewish women's organization in the world, with a membership of 320,000. Together with its junior branch for young women between the ages of seventeen and twenty-five, Hadassah maintains an extensive program of Jewish education, culture, and welfare work, both in the United States and in Israel.

HAIFA: Israel's third largest city and main port. Although it is mentioned in Talmudic literature of the 3rd century, and was of some importance during the Middle Ages when it was defended by Jews and Arabs against the Crusaders, Haifa's importance in modern times began only in the second half of the 19th century. During the Turkish period, it was exceeded by the port of Acre, but the sanding-up of Acre harbor and the growth of Zionism gave Haifa the impetus which stimulated its development. Under the British mandate, Haifa grew in importance and its deep-water harbor, completed in 1933, made it one of the most important ports in the Eastern Mediterranean. This importance was enhanced by the fact that it was the terminal point of the oil pipeline from Iraq. In April 1948, Haifa was captured by forces of the Haganah, and the Arab population fled almost in its entirety.

Since the establishment of the State of Israel, Haifa's population has grown to 215,000. In addition to being Israel's main port, it is also one of the country's main centers of industrial development. In recent years, it has seen the development of glass, textile, and fertilizer plants. Haifa is the home of the Israel Institute of Technology, known as the Technion, and a branch of the Hebrew University. The city, originally built at the foot of Mount Carmel, has spread to the top of the mountain and along the coast in both directions. An electric subway called the Carmelit connects the lower city to the top of Mount Carmel, where some of Israel's finest residential suburbs are situated. From the top of Mount Carmel, a magnificent panorama over Haifa Bay unfolds. At night, the scene is enhanced by the thousands of sparkling lights glittering all around the bay. Haifa is the holy city of the Bahai sect, originally from Persia. The golden dome of the Bahai Temple, set amid beautiful gardens, is one of the city's major landmarks. Haifa is also the main gateway for immigration into Israel by ship.

ḤALUTZIM (Pioneers): The name given to young men and women dedicated to the building of the land of Israel, particularly through agricultural settlement. This ideal developed especially in the period of the Second Aliyah, before World War I, and spread after the war, under the guidance and inspiration of Joseph Trumpeldor. Agricultural training centers were

View of Haifa

Early pioneers in Degania

Ḥanukkah *lamp (15th cent.)*

established throughout Eastern and Central Europe, and in them young pioneers were given intensive preparation in both agricultural work and communal living prior to their immigration to the land of Israel. These farms were called *Hakhsharah,* the Hebrew word for preparation. In 1924, a world organization, *He-Ḥalutz,* was established, and in the 1920's and 1930's the pioneering ideal spread to Western countries. Many youth movements whose ideals included forming agricultural settlements, particularly the *kibbutz,* became affiliated with *He-Ḥalutz.* During the Nazi period, the various *Ḥalutz* movements participated in resistance groups, and the Warsaw Ghetto uprising was largely directed by these groups. Although the war decimated the European *Ḥalutz* groups the ideal was continued by the various youth movements in England, South Africa, the United States and South America. Among the youth movements who still practice the ideal of *Ḥalutziut,* as defined above, are *Habonim, Hashomer-Hatzair,* and *Bene Akiva.*

ḤANUKKAH (Dedication): Eight-day Jewish festival celebrated from the 25th day of *Kislev* till the 3rd day of *Tevet.* The story of its origin is told in the first book of Maccabees. Antiochus Epiphanes, the Syrian king, attempting to force the

Jews to accept the Greek way of life known as Hellenism, had forbidden the study of the Torah and the observance of its commandments. On the 25th of *Kislev* in the year 167 B.C.E., he defiled the Temple by setting up a pagan altar and offering sacrifices to Zeus Olympias. He then sent officials throughout Judah to enforce the restrictive decrees. When they came to the village of Modiin, the priest Mattathias, together with his five sons, rebelled and fled to the hills. From there, they conducted guerrilla warfare against the king's forces which, as their numbers grew, blossomed into a full-scale war of liberation. After three years, the rebels, under the command of Judah the Maccabee, the most illustrious of the five sons, won a temporary victory. On the 25th of *Kislev* 164 B.C.E., exactly three years after the Temple's desecration, Judah entered it and rededicated it to the service of God. There, according to the legend, he found only one cruse of pure oil with the seal of the High Priest, which would normally have lasted for only one day. A miracle occurred, however, and the oil lasted for eight days. The Talmud, in its only reference to Ḥanukkah, ignores all mention of the military struggle, dwelling solely on the miracle of the oil. Hence, the major Ḥanukkah ceremony performed in the synagogue and the home is the lighting of the eight-branched *menorah* which has often been the object of artistic design. One light is kindled on the first night, and an additional one added each succeeding night. The lighting of the Hanukkah lights is preceded by the recitation of two blessings and is followed by the singing of hymns. Chief among these is *Maoz tzur* which, judging from the acrostic of the first letter of each verse, was written by Mordecai, an unknown poet belonging most probably to the 13th century. The whole episode of the Maccabean struggle is related in the 5th verse, and its rousing tune, which in all likelihood was adapted from an old German folk-song, is well-known throughout the Jewish world. In the synagogue, the special psalms of praise and thanksgiving, *Hallel* (Psalms 113–118 and Psalm 136), are recited each day of the festival, and there are special readings of the Torah taken from Numbers (ch. 7), which deal with the daily gifts offered by the princes of the twelve tribes at the dedication of the altar in the wilderness. The *Haphtarah* on the Sabbath of Hanukkah is taken from the book of Zechariah (ch. 2:14 to ch. 4:7) which includes the vision of the golden candlestick. If there happens to be a second Sabbath of Hanukkah the *Haphtarah* read is from the first book of Kings (ch. 7:40–50), which describes the various ornaments in King Solomon's Temple. In the *Amidah* prayer, and in the grace after meals, a special paragraph is inserted. It begins with the words *Al hanissim* (for the miracles) and it gives an account of the Hanukkah story. Hanukkah is also known as the Feast of Lights, a name given to it by the ancient historian Josephus. Special games became associated with Hanukkah, especially one associated with a spinning-top called *dreidl* (Yiddish) or *sevivon* (Hebrew). In recent years Hanukkah has attained a new popularity in the United States and in Israel. In the United States, it has become accentuated as a sort of Jewish counterpart to Christmas — with considerable gift-giving. In Israel it has become significant because of its association with the Maccabeans and their tradition of heroism and valor. One of the central observances is the relay of a torch from Modiin to the home of the President of Israel.

HAPHTARAH (Conclusion): Portion from the prophetical books of the Bible read in the synagogue on Sabbaths, festivals, and fast days after the reading from the five books of Moses. There is no historical data concerning the institution of this custom. Some think that the prophetic reading goes back to the days of Antiochus Epiphanes who in the year 168 B.C.E. prohibited the reading of the five books of Moses as part of his campaign of persecution against the Jews. In its place the Jewish authorities instituted the reading of at least twenty-one verses from the Prophets, corresponding to the seven men who were called to the reading of a minimum of three verses each of the Torah. Even when the reading of the five books of Moses was resumed after the Maccabean victory, this custom continued. Most scholars reject the historical theory and are of the opinion that the prophetic reading came about by virtue of the importance of the prophets in their own right. These readings were considered a suitable conclusion to the reading of the five books of Moses. Hence, the word *Haphtarah,* meaning conclusion.

Whatever the exact origin of the *Haphtarah,* there is always some point of contact between the portion of the week (the *Sidrah*) and the Prophetic selection. Some portions are chosen because of their appropriateness to a particular festival or special Sabbath. As with the reading of the Torah, the *Haphtarah* is changed in a special way according to the traditional musical signs or *trop.* The reader of the *Haphtarah* is also called to the reading of the last verses of the portion of the five books of Moses which is known as *Maphtir*. In Sephardi communities, the *Haphtarah* is read by a child, and in Ashkenazi ones by a member of the congregation or by a boy celebrating his bar mitzvah. It is preceded by one benediction, and on its conclusion followed by four.

See also: ACCENTS, BIBLE, PROPHETS.

ḤASIDISM: Revivalist religious and social movement founded by Israel Baal Shem (1699–1761). Baal Shem himself left no written testament; thus, knowledge of him is confined to the vast literature of stories and legends related by his followers (*hasidim* — pious ones). Ḥasidism was a rebellion against the somewhat unemotional Talmudic Judaism of the time, which glorified as its hero one who at the age of five was able to recite by heart the most difficult tractates of the Talmud. Delving into the depths of the Talmud was, and still is, the hallmark of rabbinic Judaism. The legendary stories about the

Celebration at Ḥasidic village in Israel

Baal Shem lead us to the conclusion that he was comparatively unversed in higher rabbinic learning. Instead of spending his time in the *Bet Hamidrash* engrossed in the complicated intricacies of Talmudic studies, he preferred to pass his time under the green trees of the forest, where he felt closer to God. It was through nature that Baal Shem reached his spiritual maturity. He taught tolerance, humility, compassion, and optimism. The most ignorant of men, even if he be illiterate or unable to read the standard prayers, is nevertheless able to pray to God through song or by expressing what is in his heart. In the eyes of those rabbis who came into contact with him, Baal Shem was an ignorant boor. To his disciples, he was a saint. The unlearned and persecuted masses of Jewry, too, especially in Volhynia and Podolia, were ripe for the advent of such a personality. In addition to persecution from the church and to pogroms, the internal state of the Jewish community was one of chaos, due to the tyrannical and sometimes corrupt leadership of its heads. Moreover, a serious spiritual vacuum had been created by the realization that the notorious Shabbetai Tzevi (1626–76) was a false Messiah and that the movement named after him, Sabbatianism, was a threat to the very existence of Judaism. Baal Shem's stress on simple faith, good intentions, and the emotion of the heart was therefore calculated to find a response. The fact that he was considered a *Baal Shem* — a Master of the Name (in other words, a person able to work miracles through the use of one of the Names of God, an idea which the modern mind may reject), was to East European Jewry of the 18th century an added source of attraction. On his death his disciples, led by Dov Beer of Mezhirich, undertook vast missionary work on behalf of the new movement. They met with great success and even succeeded in penetrating some of the strongholds of rabbinic learning.

The movement and different sects of Ḥasidism were founded. Certain groups even showed a tendency to return to the path of rabbinical learning. Such a school of rationalist Ḥasidic thought was that of *ḤABAD* (after the initial letters of the three words *ḥokhmah* — wisdom; *binah* — understanding; and *daat* — knowledge) founded by Shneur Zalman of Lyady.

The stress for the most part, however, was on the personality of the Ḥasidic leader, the *tzaddik* (saint). This emphasis contained within it the roots of decay, for while the personality of the leader had from the outset been at the very core of Ḥasidism, in time the movement developed into a veritable worship of the *tzaddik*. Different dynasties of Ḥasidism were set up with the *tzaddik* (also called *rebbe*) at the head, and leadership passing from father to son. Ḥasidim who were not privileged to live in the *tzaddik's* place of residence did their utmost to make as many pilgrimages to him as possible. Hanging on his every word, their idolization reached such proportions that it was even considered a *segullah,* a sign of good fortune, to eat of his leftovers known as *shirayim*. While most of the *tzaddikim* were pious, there were naturally those who unscrupulously set up luxurious "courts" financed by their adherents who considered it a *mitzvah* (a meritorious deed) to be able to serve the *tzaddik*.

The leaders of rabbinic Judaism obviously could not allow the Ḥasidic phenomenon to spread unopposed. There were elements within Ḥasidic thought, such as the attitude to the study of the Torah, their laxity towards the fixed hours of prayer, their general dress and conduct, and — above all — their idolizing of the *tzaddik* which were foreign to the mainstream of Jewish thought. The conflict broke out with great vehemence in many localities. In 1772, the *Gaon* Elijah of Vilna, the outstanding leader of Lithuanian Jewry, led the opposition, called *mitnaggedim,* in an organized persecution of the new movement. Then, in 1784, the *mitnaggedim* prohibited ritual slaughter *(sheḥitah)* by a Ḥasid. As late as 1800, fanatical opponents of Ḥasidism tried to convince the Russian government it should suppress the new movement. The conflict was sharp, accusations and counter-accusations were made, and great bitterness was engendered throughout Lithuania. With time, however, the opposition abated, and during the 19th century the Ḥasidim who had, except for minor changes in the customs, never intended breaking from Jewish law, joined hands with the *mitnaggedim* to combat the movement called *haskalah* or enlightenment. The Ḥasidic movement which had started out as revolutionary, like so many others before and after it, became staid, often decadent, and conservative. Far from being a force for change, Ḥasidism became one of the most fanatical and stubborn defenders of fundamentalist Orthodoxy.

During the Nazi holocaust, all the Ḥasidic centers in Russia and Poland were destroyed. A few of the *tzaddikim* escaped, however, and re-established their courts. Among these were R. Joseph Isaac of Lubavitch *(ḤABAD* Ḥasidism based in New York, with branches in Israel and other countries), R. Aaron Rokah of Belz, and R. Abraham Mordecai of Gur, whose centers were re-established in Tel Aviv and Jerusalem respectively. There are still thousands of Ḥasidim throughout the world, and they have preserved some of the original characteristics of the movement which made it such an interesting phenomenon. Among these are an ardent faith, and the service of God with joy and ecstasy. Interest in Ḥasidism has revived in recent years. This is due partly to the writings of the scholar Martin Buber, who related Ḥasidic thought to the modern world, the popularity of Ḥasidic music and tales, and the missionary activity of the *ḤABAD* Ḥasidim.

HASMONEANS: Priestly dynasty founded by Mattathias of Modiin. The name may be either a family name or derived from a place name. Mattathias and his five sons, Judah the Maccabee, Jonathan, Simon, John, and Eleazar, led the revolt in 166 B.C.E. against the Syrian king, Antiochus Epiphanes, whose policy of enforced Hellenization demanded the abandonment of Jewish tradition and religion. The revolt culminated, in 164 B.C.E., in a great victory for Judah the Maccabee and the rededication of the Temple. The Syrian ruler was by then prepared to grant the Jews religious freedom but the Hasmoneans were no longer satisfied with that alone. What had started as a struggle for religious freedom now became an all-out battle for political independence. One by one, the Maccabean brothers fell in the service of their people. The only one to survive was Simon. In the year 147 B.C.E., he succeeded in obtaining exemption from the payment of Syrian taxes — which was tantamount to independence — arranging for the liquidation of the Syrian garrisons in Judea, and laying the legal foundations for rule by the new Hasmonean dynasty. Simon was confirmed by the people as hereditary high priest and general in 142 B.C.E. and, following his assassination in 135, he was succeeded by his son John Hyrcanus. John Hyrcanus ruled for thirty-one years (135–104 B.C.E.). His reign began with war with the Syrian king, Antiochus Sidetes, during which Jerusalem was taken after a long siege. However, the death of Antiochus and consequent decline of Syrian power enabled Hyrcanus to consolidate his position and extend the borders of the Hasmonean state.

During Hyrcanus' reign, severe disputes arose involving the Pharisees and the Sadducees. While religious freedom had been the initial objective of the Maccabean revolution, it had given rise to the desire for political independence. John Hyrcanus' ambition led him to wars of conquest, the employment of heathen mercenaries, and, worst of all, the forced conversion of conquered peoples to Judaism. The Pharisees were opposed to the concentration of both priestly and politico-military leadership in one man and urged John Hyrcanus to relinquish the priesthood. This led to a breach between the Pharisees and the royal house. Relying on Sadducee support, Hyrcanus began to hound the Pharisee leaders and revoke their laws. The two parties emerged bitter rivals, and the conflict between them dominated the political and religious scene during the remainder of the Second Temple period. When John died, his son Aristobulos assumed power. Though his rule lasted only one year, until 103 B.C.E., he behaved like a despot for that period, treating the Itureans as his father had the conquered Idumeans. It was also Aristobulos who took the step of proclaiming himself king, a title not previously used by the Hasmoneans. His brother, Alexander Janneus (103–76 B.C.E.), who succeeded him, governed as both high priest and king. Throughout the twenty-seven years he ruled, he waged one war after another. Like his father, he relied only on the support and advice of the Sadducees. Not only were the Pharisees deprived of all influence and responsibility in the Sanhedrin; they were persecuted with a ferocity that drove them to despair and to call for help from the hated Syrians. Alexander, it is said, showed his contempt for Pharisee customs during a Succoth festival by pouring the water libation at his feet, instead of on the altar. The congregation, outraged at this insult to what was to them a sacred custom, spontaneously pelted the king with the *etrogim* (citrons) they were carrying for the festive occasion. The royal bodyguard responded with a charge into the tightly packed mob and hundreds were killed. In the ensuing persecution of the Pharisees, thousands were forced to flee the country.

The gulf between the king and the **Pharisees** (who were supported by the majority of the ordinary people) grew so wide that when after six years of futile civil war the king asked the Pharisee representatives what he could do to regain their sympathy, they had only one answer: die.

Eventually, of course, he did, to be succeeded by his widow Salome Alexandra (76–67 B.C.E.). She made peace with the Pharisees and restored them to preeminence in the Sanhedrin. Understanding that the people were tired of the endless wars of conquest and were disillusioned with the Hasmoneans, she ensured that her reign was a period of relative calm and tranquility. After her death, however, the Hasmonean dynasty rapidly declined. Her two sons, Hyrcanus and Aristobulus, fought over the throne and in the ensuing chaos the Romans intervened to restore "peace." They never left. From the year 63 B.C.E., Judea was a Roman province and all major officials, including the high priest, were appointed by the Romans. Herod, an Idumean in origin who married the Hasmonean Mariamne, ruled as a Roman puppet and destroyed the last surviving members of the Hasmonean family — including his own wife and sons. The dynasty, which had begun with such promise and won such loyalty and affection from the people, ended in ignominy. They had drifted further and further away from the original ideals that had inspired the revolt and, in so doing, lost all the popular support they had once enjoyed.

See also: PHARISEES AND SADDUCEES.

HA-TIKVAH (The Hope): Israel national anthem, originally adopted as the hymn of the Zionist movement at its first congress in Basle. The author of the poem was Naphtali Herz Imber (1856–1909), a poet, Zionist, and writer who took an interest in musical folklore.

Much has been made of the fact that the opening theme of *Ha-Tikvah* is practically

---

HATIKVAH

The National Anthem

כָּל עוֹד בַּלֵּבָב פְּנִימָה	So long as still within our breasts
נֶפֶשׁ יְהוּדִי הוֹמִיָּה,	The Jewish heart beats true,
וּלְפַאֲתֵי מִזְרָח קָדִימָה	So long as still towards the Easts,
עַיִן לְצִיּוֹן צוֹפִיָּה,	To Zion, looks the Jew,
עוֹד לֹא אָבְדָה תִּקְוָתֵנוּ	So long our hopes are not yet lost —
הַתִּקְוָה מִשְּׁנוֹת אַלְפַּיִם,	Two thousand years we cherished them —
לִהְיוֹת עַם חָפְשִׁי בְּאַרְצֵנוּ,	To live in freedom in the land
בְּאֶרֶץ צִיּוֹן וִירוּשָׁלַיִם.	Of Zion and Jerusalem.

Ha-Tikvah

identical with a theme in the tone poem, *Die Moldau,* by the Czech composer Smetana, but in fact the *Ha-Tikvah* melody can be found in a great number of folk songs and musical works. It is one of the "wandering melodies" which appear in many forms and variations. Thus it can be found in a setting of the *Yigdal* prayer, in Basque folk songs, in German nursery songs, at the beginning of Mahler's *Song of a Wayfarer,* in *Ḥazzanut* (cantoral music), and in various other musical compositions.

HAVDALAH: A ceremony at the termination of Sabbaths and festivals. The word *Havdalah* means "differentiation," and the theme of the prayer is praise of God who distinguishes between holy and profane, between light and darkness, between Israel and the Nations, and between the Sabbath and the six days of creation. A form of the *Havdalah* is also inserted in the *Amidah* of the evening service. It is not clear whether *Havdalah* originated in the home or the synagogue. According to Jewish tradition, it was instituted by the men of the Great Assembly. The *Havdalah* is recited over wine or any liquid (except water) and is accompanied by benedictions over spices and over the light of a plaited candle. The spice box in particular has been the object of much artistic endeavor. If a

Spice box for Havdalah *ceremony*

festival follows the Sabbath, a special form of the *Havdalah* is incorporated in the *Kiddush*.

After the *Havdalah,* it is customary in many homes and communities to sing the hymn *Ha-Mavdil* (He who Distinguishes) and the well known song *Eliahu Ha-Navi.* The mention of Elijah is based on the belief that his arrival to proclaim the advent of the Messiah will occur on a Saturday evening after the conclusion of the Sabbath.

HEALTH: Jewish law strictly enjoins man to preserve and take care of his health. The verse in Deuteronomy (ch. 4:9) "Only take heed to thyself and keep thy soul diligently," is explained by the rabbis as urging man to do everything in his power to preserve his life, and not commit any act which might be injurious to his physical well-being. The Talmud lays down various rules and regulations all aimed at the prevention of danger to life. Thus it is forbidden to drink liquids which may be contaminated, nor should one enter a ruined building which is in danger of collapse. In the opinion of the rabbis, whoever endangers his life violates a positive commandment. In the words of Moses Maimonides, "If one says 'I want to endanger my life, what concern is it to others,' disciplinary flogging is to be inflicted upon him." Man is created in the image of God, and therefore his life

is not his own to do with as he pleases. Man's life is the property of God, and any act which endangers a human life is a transgression of His will. Arising out of this concept, the doctrine of *Pikuah Nefesh* was formulated by the rabbis. This states that life takes precedence over everything and in the case of danger to health, it is not only permitted to violate a commandment, but one is obligated to do so, and he who hesitates is a sinner. Accordingly, *Pikuah Nefesh* takes precedence over the most important commandments, even over the Sabbath and the Day of Atonement. If a physician feels that fasting on the Day of Atonement would injure a person's health, that person is forbidden to fast; and if he disregards the doctor's advice, he is regarded as having transgressed the holy day. The only exception to the above rule is when a violation of the three cardinal sins — idolatry, immorality and the shedding of innocent blood — is involved. In the latter cases, one must rather sacrifice one's life than transgress. The principle of *Pikuah Nefesh* is not only applicable to the individual but to groups and nations. During the Maccabean war, the policy was adopted that Jewish soldiers may fight back on the Sabbath if attacked. Danger to the existence of the state is also regarded as being in the category of *Pikuah Nefesh.* Thus, in the State of Israel where the public observance of the Sabbath is regulated by law, services essential to the health and safety of the individual and the state as a whole are maintained.

HEBREW LANGUAGE: Hebrew belongs to the Canaanite branch of the group of Semitic languages. Biblical Hebrew was a literary language, rich in poetry and idiomatic expressions, but after the Babylonian exile it began to decline slowly. This was largely due to the influence of Aramaic, the language of officialdom and commerce throughout much of the Middle

East, which was spoken by many Jews. The decline was hastened by the rise of Mishnaic Hebrew, which, dealing as it did with matters of everyday life, lost much of the poetic coloring and style of biblical Hebrew although it gained in flexibility and precision. After the destruction of the Second Temple in 70 C.E., the use of Hebrew declined. The ensuing Talmudic period was characterized by the use of Greek and, in particular, Aramaic, as evidenced by both the Palestinian and Babylonian Talmuds. About the year 500, a literary revival of Hebrew took place thanks to the activities of the author of the synagogal poetry known as *Piyyutim*. These poets made daring innovations in Hebrew grammar, and contributed to its widespread use in written form throughout the Middle Ages. The rabbis of the Talmud invested Hebrew with a sacred character, and in rabbinical literature it is known as the "Holy Tongue." This no doubt contributed to the tendency in the Middle Ages to confine the use of Hebrew to prayer, study, or correspondence of a religious nature. The Spanish Jews sometimes preferred the use of Arabic even in their theological writings. When Hebrew was used, it was often for poetry and in the style of classical biblical Hebrew. Only in the 19th century did scholars, especially those belonging to the *Haskalah* movement, begin to apply Hebrew to modern circumstances. They wrote all sorts of works in the language, from novels to scientific textbooks, but they were hampered by the fact that the language had not been spoken for so long, and their usages were frequently artificial.

With the rise of modern Jewish nationalism, the modern period of Hebrew began. Eliezer ben-Yehuda (1858–1922) devoted himself to making Hebrew the modern vehicle of communication among Jews in general, and in the land of Israel in particular. His activities were bitterly opposed by religious extremists who regarded Hebrew as the Holy Tongue, not to be profaned by everyday use. To this day, the members of *Neturei Karta* refrain from using Hebrew and in many of the *Yeshivot* (rabbinical academies) which follow the East European tradition, Yiddish is still both the language of instruction and the vernacular.

In 1921, however, Hebrew became one of three languages recognized by the British authorities of mandatory Palestine and in 1948 it became the official language (together with Arabic) of the State of Israel. With the rise of modern Hebrew in Israel, its use gradually expanded in the Diaspora where it is taught in Hebrew schools, although not widely spoken. The Hebrew day school movement has contributed greatly to the raising of the standard of Hebrew among Diaspora youth.

Modern Hebrew is a combination of all the previous stages of development through which the language passed, but it has absorbed from each stage only those elements which suit it. It is strongly influenced by modern European languages, and, in some cases, European words are used. New words, especially of a technical nature, are constantly being introduced either by giving old words new meanings or just by forming new words. In this connection, important work is being done by the Academy of the Hebrew Language in Jerusalem.

The Hebrew alphabet contains twenty-two letters comprised of consonants only. The consonants (the "root") carry the meaning while the vowel points *(nekudot)* which are a later invention designed to facilitate reading, provide the form. Different vowel systems, such as the Babylonian, Palestinian, Samaritan, and Tiberian were introduced at various times but the last, which represents Palestinian pronunciation in the 9th century C.E., is the only one still in use. In pronunciation, as in writing, there is a distinction between

Ashkenazi and Sephardi, with subdivisions within these two main groups. These differences are mainly in the vowel sounds and in accentuation. The pioneers of modern Hebrew and subsequently the State of Israel chose the Sephardi pronunciation. As a result, the trend toward this usage is increasing throughout the world today, even in many Ashkenazi synagogues.

HEBREW UNIVERSITY: Israel's largest and best-known academic institution. The idea of establishing a Hebrew university was first suggested by Hermann Schapira even before the establishment of the Zionist movement. The latter, however, made the idea an essential part of its platform and at the 11th Zionist Congress in 1913, at the urging of Chaim Weizmann, a formal resolution was passed and a committee elected to implement the project. The cornerstone was laid on Mount Scopus overlooking Jerusalem in 1918, and the university officially opened by Lord Balfour in 1925. Since then, the Hebrew University has played a major role in training the country's intellectual and academic leaders. As a result of the 1948 War of Independence, the Hebrew University was cut off from the State of Israel, and access to Mount Scopus denied by Jordan.

From 1954–58, a new campus was built in western Jerusalem (at Givat Ram) housing all faculties except those of agriculture, in Rehovot, and medicine and dentistry, in the Hadassah-University Medical Center at Ein Karem.

With the reunification of Jerusalem after the June 1967 Six-Day War, the Mount Scopus facilities were again reactivated. Accommodation for 10,000 students is being planned there. The Hebrew University has over 15,000 students. Some 3,000 come from abroad and several hundred are Arabs. Partially supported by the Government of Israel, the main part of the university's budget is derived from fees and from supporters throughout the world who belong to "Friends of the Hebrew University" groups. For the first twenty-five years of its existence, the university's fortunes were guided by Judah L. Magnes. Since 1968, the President has been Israel's former ambassador to the United States, Abraham Harman.

In addition to its Jerusalem campuses, the University is also academically responsible for the Haifa University, and the embryonic University of the Negev in Beersheba.

Hebrew University campus, Jerusalem

HEBRON: One of the world's most ancient cities, situated some eighteen miles south of Jerusalem. According to the biblical account, the Patriarch Abraham bought a burial ground from Efron the Hittite. This spot, the cave of Machpelah, which contains the tombs of Abraham, Isaac, and Jacob and their wives, Sarah, Rebekah, and Leah, is one of the most holy and sacred shrines in the land of Israel. Hebron was King David's capital before he took Jerusalem and it was here that he was proclaimed king. During biblical times, Hebron was one of the cities of refuge and a Levitical center. After biblical times, it was captured by the Edomites, recaptured by Judah the Maccabee, and then destroyed by the Romans. There was a Jewish community in Hebron during the Byzantine period and later under Arab rule. The Arabs regard Hebron as sacred because of the tomb of Abraham. Over the cave of

View of Hebron

Machpelah, they built a mosque surrounded by a wall. During the later Middle Ages, Hebron, together with Jerusalem, Safed, and Tiberias, was regarded by the Jews as one of the four holy cities of the land of Israel. In the main, it was regarded as a religious center, and in 1925 the famous Lithuanian Rabbinical Academy of Slobodka was transferred there. In 1929, violent anti-Jewish riots broke out, assuming the dimensions of a pogrom. Many of the town's seven hundred Jews were massacred while the rest fled. A small number returned in 1931, but after further Arab riots in 1936, the Jewish community ceased to exist. During Israel's War of Independence, Hebron was annexed by the Kingdom of Jordan but during the Six-Day War, June 1967, it was captured by Israeli forces, enabling Jews to visit the sacred shrines of their ancestors once again. A number of Jews have again settled in Hebron whose population in 1968 was 38,350.

HEROD (known as "The Great"; 73–4 B.C.E.): King of Judea. When the Maccabean ruler, John Hyrcanus (ruled 135–104 B.C.E.) conquered the territory of Idumea (Edom) he forced the inhabitants to convert to Judaism. As a result, Herod's father, Antipater, was nominally Jewish. He intrigued his way into a position of influence by exploiting the civil war between the last Maccabean rulers and rivals, the brothers Hyrcanus II and Aristobulus. Antipater, moreover, utilized the internal wars between the rival Roman leaders, Pompey and Caesar, for his own benefit. Having ingratiated himself with Caesar, Antipater was granted Roman citizenship, and his sons were appointed district governors. Herod was assigned to Galilee and in this capacity, he distinguished himself by the savage suppression of an uprising of Jewish patriots against the Romans. Called before the Sanhedrin to give an account of his actions, Herod showed his contempt for that body by appearing before the judges surrounded by a guard of armed lieutenants. By a combination of relentless energy, ability, tireless ambition and a certain measure of charm, Herod was able to win the support of successive Roman rulers even though previously he may have supported their rivals. Despite his intrigues, Herod's path to the throne was full of obstacles. The Maccabean Antigonus, whom the masses of the people and even certain Roman generals supported, made every effort to halt Herod. Rome's great rival, Parthia, supported Antigonus, and at a time of Roman weakness, invaded the Holy Land. Herod managed with difficulty to escape and made his way to Rome where in 37 B.C.E. he was appointed King of Judea by the Roman Senate. Antigonus, the last prince of the Hasmonean dynasty, was besieged in Jerusalem, defeated, and after horrible tortures, put to death. Herod succeeded in ingratiating himself with the new Roman ruler, Augustus, who regarded him as a useful ally and returned to him most of the territory previously taken from Judea by Marc Antony under the influence of Cleopatra. Herod's power depended on the support of Rome. In turn, he had to support Rome in his foreign policy. His policies were energetic, but he was detested by his subjects. All political activity was suppressed, and a regime of repression introduced. The army was conscripted largely from foreign levies and hired mercenaries. Herod understandably did not trust his Jewish subjects, who retained their ancient loyalty to the Hasmoneans. Herod's pathological suspicion of plots against him led him to eliminate even his closest associates. His wife — the Hasmonean Mariamne, whom he loved dearly but who despised him — was put to death as were their two sons, Alexander and Aristobulos.

Herod was a great builder and his projects were of economic benefit to the state. The building of the port of Caesarea named after Augustus was one of Herod's greatest achievements. Over the ruins of Samaria, Herod built Sebaste — the Greek for Augustus. His crowning achievement, however, was the rebuilding of the Temple, making it one of the most beautiful shrines in the ancient world. An indication of its magnificence shines through both in the pages of Josephus and in the excavations undertaken in Jerusalem in recent years. Outside Palestine too, he financed ambitious construction projects which enhanced his reputation among the Romans. Nothing, however, that Herod could do was able to enhance his standing with his people. The exorbitant taxation, the dictatorial and repressive system, his loyalty and admiration for Rome coupled with his total strangeness to Pharisaic Judaism, made the breach between him and his subjects inevitable. In his will, he divided his kingdom among his three sons.

HERZL, THEODOR (1860–1904): Founder of political Zionism and the Zionist movement. Born in Budapest, the only son of a wealthy merchant, Herzl received his preliminary secular education as well as a somewhat skimpy Jewish education, in that city. At the age of nineteen he moved with his family to Vienna, where he enrolled in the law faculty of the university. He was prominent in Austrian student societies, from one of which he resigned in protest against its anti-Semitic tendencies. Herzl received his doctorate in 1884 but soon after decided to devote himself entirely to writing. He achieved prominence as an essayist and writer of light plays. In 1892, Herzl was sent to Paris as the correspondent of the most important Viennese newspaper, *Neue Freie Presse*.

By virtue of his education and upbringing, at first Herzl may have shared the conventional view of most westernized Jewish intellectuals of his time, that progress and emancipation were very close at hand for the Jews. His experience at the university and the rising anti-Semitism in France even before the Dreyfus trial impressed him considerably. In his play, *The New Ghetto,* Herzl makes the point that even the most assimilated of Jews live in an invisible ghetto in the gentile world. The Dreyfus trial and the accompanying hysterical anti-Semitism of the French mobs cured Herzl of whatever illusions he may have cherished about Jewish emancipation. He was now convinced that only a Jewish state would solve the Jewish problem. His ideas were presented in *Der Judenstaat* (The Jewish State), published in February 1896, which was received with astonishment and hostility by some and acclaim by others. Herzl attempted to interest prominent personalities such as Baron Maurice de Hirsch in his scheme and when this failed he turned to the Jewish people. The result was the first Zionist Congress, originally scheduled to be held in Munich but, because of the opposition of the Jewish community, held in Basle, Switzerland, on August 29–31, 1897. It was attended by over 200 delegates from all over the Jewish world. At this congress, the Zionist Organization was established under the leadership of Herzl, and the aims of Zionism defined as follows: "Zionism strives to establish a homeland for the Jewish people in Palestine secured by public law." Herzl was a firm believer in what came to be called political Zionism and was impatient with the slow colonizing efforts then being made. He embarked upon a series of political negotiations which led him to the Turkish Sultan, the German Emperor, the Pope, the Russian Interior Minister, and the British Government. In the midst of all this intensive Zionist activity, he wrote his utopian novel *Altneuland* (Old-New Land), in which he predicted the society in the future Jewish state in Israel. All Herzl's international negotiations led to nothing; indeed, his only success in the international arena

Theodor Herzl

nearly wrecked the Zionist movement. This was the offer made by the British government in 1903 for a Jewish self-governing settlement in Uganda, East Africa. Herzl was at first inclined to accept the proposal, insisting that he regarded the offer not as a substitute for the land of Israel, but as a preparatory step. The proposal led to a bitter debate and fierce opposition, especially from the Russian Zionists, led by Menaḥem Ussishkin, who accused Herzl of deviating from the Basle program. The Uganda affair caused Herzl much grief and aggravated his already severe heart condition. Worn out by his exertions, Herzl died prematurely on July 3, 1904. In his will, Herzl requested that he be reinterred in the land of Israel by the Jewish people. Forty-five years later, on August 17, 1949, by an act of Israel's Parliament, the Knesset, an Israeli Air Force plane brought his remains to the Jewish state where they were buried on Mt. Herzl in Jerusalem.

HILLEL (called "The Elder," 1st century B.C.E.): Mishnaic sage who lived at the time of King Herod. He was born in Babylonia and tradition has it that he was a descendant of King David. When still a young man, Hillel went to the land of Israel to study under the famous sages Shemaiah and Avtalyon. He pursued his studies under conditions of dire poverty. One story relates that for lack of funds, he climbed to the skylight of the academy to overhear the discussions within and was snowed under by one of the Holy Land's rare snowfalls. Such was his success that he became a member of the Sanhedrin and subsequently its president. Together with his colleague Shammai, he was the first to give shape to the Oral Law and laid the foundations of future rabbinic studies. He enumerated seven principles by means of which the biblical text may be analyzed and legal conclusions drawn, and the future codification of the *Mishnah* was largely based on his work. In contradistinction to Shammai, Hillel tended to adopt a more lenient approach in matters of Jewish law, and, when the economy of the country and the welfare of its inhabitants demanded the adjustment of a biblical law, Hillel did not hesitate to do it. Thus, the law of Shemittah states that in the seventh year, all debts are canceled. When Hillel saw that this would prevent people from lending money, thus harming the needy as well as the wealthy, he instituted the Prosbul which enabled creditors to recover whatever sums had been borrowed from them. Similarly, in his human relations, Hillel exhibited tolerance and understanding. A famous anecdote relates that once a heathen came to Shammai and mockingly asked him to teach him the Torah while he stood on one leg. Shammai drove him away with his measuring rod. He then went to Hillel, who answered him, "What is hateful unto thee, do not do unto thy neighbor. This is the whole Torah. Go and study it, the rest is commentary." Although there were only a few differences of opinion between Hillel and Shammai, these grew in time, and the years following were characterized by a large number of legal disputes between their disciples known respectively as the Schools of Hillel and Shammai. Both these schools followed the traditions of their masters, but in about the year 100 C.E., a rabbinic decision was taken that, with only a few exceptions, the law should be in accordance with the School of Hillel.

HOLLAND (Netherlands): The area now known as Holland had Jewish inhabitants as early as the 13th century. Their situation and status was similar to that of the Jews of medieval Germany, and there are records of persecution, expulsion, and the usual standard accusations made against Jews during that period.

The history of Dutch Jewry proper begins with the Dutch Declaration of Independence from Spain and Portugal at the end of the 16th century. Marranos, fleeing the Inquisition, found a haven in Amsterdam. Synagogues were established and freedom of worship granted. Holland thus became a great center of Spanish culture as well as of Jewish life. Jews also played a prominent role in Holland's overseas expansion and some became influential members of the Dutch West India Company. A number went to Brazil where they established the first Jewish community on the American continent and supported the Dutch against Portugal. Thanks to the tolerant atmosphere, Dutch Jewry was able to reach a high standard of Jewish and general culture at this stage of its history. They were admitted to universities, and produced such intellectual rebels as Uriel Acosta and Baruch Spinoza. The Dutch rabbi Menasseh ben Israel went to England in an attempt to negotiate the formal readmission of Jews to that country. In the middle of the 17th century, German and Polish Jews augmented the existing Sephardi community although the two groups remained formally separate. By the close of the 17th century, the Amsterdam community, numbering some ten thousand, was the greatest in western Europe. The French Revolution and the subsequent occupation of Holland brought to Holland, as elsewhere, full emancipation for the Jews. In Holland, however, this was a mere formality, and even after Napoleon's downfall, there was no anti-Jewish reaction as was the case in most countries where Jewish emancipation had been enforced by French arms. The Jews of Holland were distinguished from those of other lands by the fact that no political or intellectual differentiation separated them from the non-Jewish population. Holland was the first country in the modern world to admit Jews to Parliament and other high positions. From 1815, Jewish Ministers of Religion, like their Christian colleagues, were paid by the state. Despite the growth of other large western communities and the decline of the Sephardi community, Holland remained a vital center of Jewish life right up to the outbreak of World War II, when it numbered approximately 150,000. Even then, Holland was one of the few countries where both the leadership and the populace opposed the Nazi's annihilation program of Jews. Numbers of Dutch gentiles risked their lives to save Jews, and in February 1941 a general strike on their behalf took place in Amsterdam and other cities. No amount of goodwill, however, could stand in the way of the Nazi extermination machine which accomplished the destruction of the overwhelming proportion of Dutch Jewry. The Jewish population today numbers some 25,000, centered mainly in Amsterdam.

HOLOCAUST (Shoah): Systematic annihilation of six million European Jews by Nazi Germany. When Adolf Hitler came to power in Germany at the head of his National Socialist (Nazi) party in January 1933, the Jewish population of Europe was 9,500,000. Twelve years later, when Nazi Germany surrendered, that number had been reduced to 3,500,000. In his book, *Mein Kampf,* written in prison, Hitler already had made his ideas on race abundantly clear. The German people were part of the "Aryan" master race and it was their duty to subdue all *Untermenschen* (subhumans) such as the Slavs and the Jews who were racially inferior. These racial ideas were not new but Hitler and his supporters, often aided by the *Gestapo* (Secret State Police) took them to previously unheard-of lengths. In September 1935 the Nuremberg race laws were passed. These deprived the German Jews of their citizenship, relegating them to the status of "subjects." They also served to drive the Jew out of the German economy by excluding him from most of the professions

Dutch Rabbi *by Rembrandt*

in which he had been occupied. Signs such as "Jews not admitted," "Jews enter this place at their own risk," began to appear in grocery stores, hotels, most public places, and even at the entrances to towns. Jews who ventured into the streets were subject to beatings and mass hooliganism. This culminated in the "Crystal Night" of November 1938, when Jewish shops were looted and synagogues burned throughout Germany. Twenty thousand male Jews were at that time placed in special concentration camps such as Dachau and Buchenwald which had originally been established for opponents of the regime.

Some Jews foresaw the disaster to come and made every effort to leave Germany escaping mainly to Palestine, western Europe, Great Britain, and North and South America. Most of the Jews arrested before 1938 were allowed to emigrate on the surrender of most of their property. In this way, during the 1930's tens of thousands of energetic and talented immigrants arrived in Israel where they played no small part in the development of the country. The majority, however, chose to stay, preferring to close their eyes to the inevitable conclusion. Their fate was bound up with that of European Jewry in general. In a speech to the German Parliament (Reichstag) on January 30, 1939, Hitler prophesied that a new world war would be marked by the extermination of the Jewish race. The outbreak of war presented him with the opportunity of fulfilling his own prophecy. After the German conquest of Poland, three million Jews found themselves under German control, and later, with the extension of German rule to eastern Europe, the Balkans, the Baltic countries, White Russia, the Ukraine, and Western Europe, the number exceeded seven million. The Nazis were now free to carry out what they called the "final solution" to the Jewish problem. On July 31, 1941, the Nazi Marshal Herman Goering sent the following directive to Reinhard Heydrich, head of the Central Security Office of the Reich: "I herewith commission you to carry out all preparations with regard to... a total solution of the Jewish question in those territories of Europe which are under German influence." In fact, the mass killings had begun almost with the war itself. Jews had been herded into overcrowded ghettos containing populations ranging from several thousands to the half-million in the Warsaw Ghetto. This move facilitated the easy assembling of Jews for transportation to the death camps.

Mass execution of the Jews was first carried out by *Einsatzgruppen* (Special Action Groups), meaning, in plain language, extermination squads. Following the German combat troops, and for the most part with the cooperation of the German Army, they would round up thousands of Jews, order them into pits which they themselves were sometimes forced to dig, and then machine-gun them. These executions were supplemented by pumping carbon monoxide fumes into trucks filled with victims. 1,400,000 Jews were thus murdered by 3,000 members of the Special Action Groups.

However, the "efficient" Germans were not satisfied with these relatively clumsy methods. German ingenuity found the answer to the problem of mass murder and the mass disposal of bodies — the gas chamber and the incinerator. Special camps with special installations were set up. German science had found the means to murder the greatest number of people in the shortest possible time — prussic acid or zyklon B. German industry competed for the privilege of building the "novel" installations. The post-war Nuremberg trials of German war criminals and the trial in Israel of the notorious Adolf Eichmann, kidnapped from Argentina by Israel agents, have provided us with the "statistics" and details. The names will live in infamy — the death camps for Jews transported in cattle trains from the various ghettos of eastern Europe and from all areas where the Nazis succeeded in setting foot. The greatest number — 1,500,000 including 400,000 Hungarian Jews — perished at Auschwitz. In other death camps in the Polish sector, such as Treblinka, Belzec, Maidanek, Sobibor, and Chelmno, 2,000,000 Jews were exterminated.

At Auschwitz, the Nazis did their work to the "sound of music." The freshly arrived Jews would be divided into two groups. Those who were fit for forced labor would work until their weakened physical condition made them ready for the gas chambers. Those who were feeble, and young children and infants, would be immediately dispatched to the gas chambers. At the entrance, which bore the sign "Bath," the unsuspecting victims would sometimes even be given a towel, thus leading them to believe that they were about to have a shower for delousing purposes. To the strains of light music they marched to their deaths. Once they were inside, the realization would dawn on them that there were neither showers nor drains, and that, in any case, it was impossible for 2,000 people at a time to shower there. It was too late, for the iron gates would be sealed and the gas vents opened. The process took fifteen to twenty minutes, after which special crews called *sonderkommando* took over. These were Jewish male inmates who were promised their lives and adequate food in return for "clearing up the mess" and disposing of the bodies in the crematoria. They too were inevitably sent to the gas chamber and replaced by new teams. The Nazis wanted no survivors who could tell tales. As if this were not enough, before cremation the bodies of the victims were plundered, gold teeth were extracted, and hair cut off to be used in the mattress industry. Afterwards, the ashes of the cremated bodies were utilized for fertilizer.

From 1943, the mass annihilation of European Jewry was a well-known fact in Germany and in the neutral and allied countries. Almost nothing was done to try to save those who could still be saved. There were, it is true, periodic protests, and numbers of gentiles risked their lives in order to save individual Jews. These have received a special place of honor at *Yad Va-Shem,* the monument to European Jewry in Jerusalem. For the most part, however, the world was a passive spectator, and in some cases actually cooperated with the Nazis. Among those who did were the Ukrainian police and peasants, whose hatred of the Jews rivaled that of the Nazis themselves.

It is little wonder then that for the most part, the Jewish victims — in the face of Nazi strength — were unable to resist. Their heroism was, for the most part, that of the spirit, which manifested itself in the singing of *Ani Maamin* (I Believe) as they went to their death. However, many acts of heroism and resistance occurred. In some of the ghettos and extermination camps, Jews organized revolts, knowing well they were foredoomed to failure. Many Jews succeeded in joining partisan groups and participated in sabotage operations. Toward the end, when word of the fate of their brethren began to trickle back to those still alive in ghettos, they rebelled and refused to board the transport trains. The best known of those rebellions is the revolt of the Warsaw Ghetto, which broke out on April 18, 1943. For several weeks, a few thousand Jews, practically without arms and without assistance, fought the might of the German army. The final tragic result was never in doubt, but the fighters were determined to struggle to the bitter end and not to surrender.

The Warsaw Ghetto revolt, together with other ghetto revolts as well as partisan activities, marked the first time in almost 2,000 years that Jews had lifted up their arms in national military combat.

See also: ANTI-SEMITISM; EICHMANN, ADOLF; WARSAW GHETTO; YAD VA-SHEM.

HOLY PLACES: There are numerous sites and shrines throughout the Land of Israel which are sacred to believers of the three faiths — Judaism, Christianity, and Islam. The sanctity of these shrines may be attributed to their being connected with major events or personalities in the history of the three faiths, or with incidents in the Old and New Testaments or the Koran. As such, they are regarded with reverence by millions of people throughout the world, and are centers of pilgrimage for the devout. Some of these shrines are sacred to the adherents of more than one faith and

Church of the Holy Sepulchre, Jerusalem

for the adherents of Christianity and Islam. The major Christian sites — mostly associated with events in the life of Jesus — are situated in Jerusalem, Bethlehem, and Nazareth. They include the Church of the Holy Sepulchre, the Sanctuary of the Ascension, and the Tomb of the Virgin in the Jerusalem area; the Church of the Nativity, the Milk Grotto, and the Shepherds' Fields in the Bethlehem area; the Church of the Annunciation in Nazareth and various churches and sites in the vicinity of the Sea of Galilee. The most

The Western Wall, Jerusalem

have, as a result, been the cause of friction, even war. The proposal to "internationalize" Jerusalem is motivated by the desire to protect the sacred shrines, more concentrated in Jerusalem than at any other place, from the ravages of war. Between 1948 and the June 1967 Six-Day War, the Jordanian Government did not honor its obligation to allow free access to Jews to visit their holy places in Jerusalem and in other areas under its rule. Since June 1967, not only have Jews been able to visit their sacred shrines, but the Israel Government has scrupulously maintained this same privilege

Mosque of Omar, Jerusalem

important Moslem site is the Temple area in Jerusalem known as *Haram-es-Sharif* — the Venerable Sanctuary. It includes the Mosque of Omar, also known as the Dome of the Rock, and the Aksa Mosque. The burial place of the Patriarchs at Hebron, the Cave of Machpelah, is sacred to Moslems as well as Jews, a mosque having been built on the site.

The principal Jewish holy sites are: 1) the Western Wall in Jerusalem, which is part of the ancient Temple compound, 2) Rachel's Tomb outside Bethlehem, and 3) the above-mentioned tomb of the Patriarchs in Hebron. For almost 2,000 years, until 1967, Jews were denied unrestricted access to these sites. In addition, there are numerous sites and tombs throughout the country traditionally associated with certain Biblical and Talmudic personalities. The most famous of these is the tomb of Simeon Ben Yohai at Meron, the scene of pilgrimage and celebration on the festival of *Lag Ba'Omer*.

HUNGARY: While there are indications, through tombstones and other objects, of the presence of Jews in Hungary from the Roman period until the 10th century, very little is known of this early settlement. That Jews antedated the Hungarian period, however, is certain. The Crusades did not affect them as violently as other communities, and in fact brought Jews from other countries to Hungary. During the reigns of Andrew II (1220) and Bela IV (1235–70), Jews enjoyed a large measure of toleration and were employed as tax-collectors and minters of coins, despite the opposition of the church. The situation changed for the worse in the 14th century, and especially during the period of the Black Death plague in 1348 which the Jews were accused of having caused by poisoning the wells. There was an expulsion in 1349, followed by a further one in 1360. In both cases, the Jews were recalled a few years later. The 15th and 16th centuries witnessed a number of ritual murder accusations against Jews. When the Turks conquered the southern part of Hungary in 1526, conditions improved for the better; but with the Hungarian reconquest in the North in 1686, the expulsions, oppression, and restrictions on Jewish economic activity were pursued with vigor. Despite this, the Hungarian Jewish population increased, especially as a result of Jewish persecution in other centers such as the expulsion from Vienna in 1670. Under Maria Theresa, the already heavy taxation of Jews was made still heavier. On the other hand, Joseph II (1780–1790) believed that the Jewish problem could best be solved by assimilation and the granting of civil rights. Jews were permitted a large measure of economic freedom and the Jewish badge was abolished. On his death, however, these rights were nullified.

As in other parts of Europe, Jews participated in the national rebellion of 1848. A Jewish regiment fought under the Hungarian leader, Louis Kossuth, who favored emancipation. In 1867, full emancipation was granted, but this led to a split in the Jewish community. The Orthodox group claimed that the emancipation decrees endangered their religious convictions, and in 1871 they organized a separate community. The rise of modern anti-Semitism in the last decades of the 19th century once again set the clock back, and culminated in a charge of ritual murder brought against the Jews of Tisza-Eszlar in 1882. Hungarian Jewry nevertheless continued to play an important role in the life of the country and in World War I they more than did their share. After the war a Communist regime was set up with a Jewish Bolshevik named Bela Kun at its head. Although the regime only lasted 132 days, some Jews were sympathetic toward it. A resultant anti-Semitic period can be partly attributed to this. Intense reaction set in and the number of Jews permitted to attend universities was limited.

The culmination of the long history of Hungarian anti-Semitism came with the Nazi occupation and the establishment of ghettos and concentration camps. Over 400,000 Hungarian Jews were murdered by the Nazis, and the community never recovered. Under Communist rule, Jewish religious and cultural life has continued but to a far lesser extent than previously, when Hungarian Jewry produced great rabbis and intellects. There has of late been an upsurge of interest in Judaism and the State of Israel on the part of Hungarian Jewish youth. The general trend, however, is toward conformity. The Jewish population presently numbers some 70,000.

IRAQ: The area now occupied by Iraq was, in ancient times, part of Babylonia and then Persia, so that the early history of the Jews there is tied up with that of Babylonia and Persia. After the Moslem invasion of 637 C.E. which was welcomed by the Jews, Jewish cultural life flourished. The overall leader of the community, the Exilarch, was a revered figure in non-Jewish as well as Jewish circles, and the spiritual leaders, the *Geonim* who were at the head of the academies of Babylonia, extended their influence throughout the Jewish world. Disputes and rivalry, however, between the Exilarch and the *Geonim* often led to internal friction and a consequent weakening of the community. Less friendly and sometimes hostile rulers were quick to exploit such developments to the detriment of the Jewish community. The internal disintegration was hastened from the 8th century onward by the growth of the dissident Karaite movement.

In the 9th and early 10th centuries, there was a revival under the *Geonim* Saadyah, Sherirah, and Hai, but with the cessation of the *gaonate* and the closing of the academies Iraq lost its central position in the Jewish world. Under Moslem rule, the position of the Jews seems to have been relatively stable and secure. The discriminatory measures laid down by the Caliph Omar were not aimed only at Jews, and in any event were never strictly enforced. In the 10th century, Jews were admitted to state offices and many achieved prominence as physicians, scholars, scientists, and bankers. When the medieval Jewish traveler Benjamin of Tudela visited the area in the 12th century, he found a number of communities with up to 15,000 inhabitants.

The Mongol conquest in the second half of the 13th century led to a new upsurge of Jewish cultural activity. The Mongols regarded all men as brothers and did not differentiate between believers and non-believers, Christians, Jews, or Pagans. Under the Mongols, a number of Jews became court officials, court physicians, court astronomers, and even viziers of the great Mongol Persian Empire. There is little information concerning the fate of Iraqi Jewry from the 14th century until the Turkish conquest of 1534. Under the Turks the Jews seem to have improved their economic condition despite occasional maltreatment at the hands of corrupt local officials. With the defeat of Turkey in 1917 and the arrival of the British, Jews gained a foothold and were at times dominant in commerce and the professions. However, when Iraq was granted its independence in 1932, the situation changed drastically. There was a spate of anti-Jewish rioting, and in 1941, when Rashid Ali attempted to bring about a pro-Nazi coup, hundreds of Jews were killed. Iraq participated in the Arab invasion of Israel in 1948 although her army did not acquit itself very well. Unlike Jordan, Egypt, and the Lebanon, Iraq refused to sign an armistice agreement with Israel. Anti-Zionism speedily became anti-Semitism and the Jews of Iraq found themselves in an unbearable situation. Accordingly, in 1950–51, in a spectacular operation called *Ezra and Nehemiah,* the overwhelming majority of Iraq's Jews — some 125,000 — were flown to Israel. Those who remained suffered severe discrimination after the June 1967 Six-Day War, when the public hanging of a number of so-called Zionist spies led to an international outcry. Iraq's Jewish population, centered mainly in Baghdad, now numbers less than 3,000.

ISAIAH (Yeshayahu): The first biblical book in the section of latter prophets. It contains sixty-six chapters. Although historically the prophecies appear to belong to at least two periods, traditional scholars have explained this by ascribing to Isaiah the ability to predict future events. The medieval Spanish scholar Abraham Ibn Ezra was the first to suggest the possibility (now generally accepted, even by most Orthodox scholars) that the book of Isaiah is the work of two authors.

The first Isaiah lived in the 8th century B.C.E. and prophesied from the year of King Uzziah's death (742 B.C.E.) until the year 701 B.C.E. and possibly later. Judging from the ease with which he approached the king, he was of good family and possibly even of noble descent. His prophecies are contained in the first thirty-nine chapters of the book. Despite his ties with the ruling establishment, throughout most of his life Isaiah opposed the court, and at times rebuked it in the sharpest terms. The rise of the Assyrian Empire served as the background to his prophecies, and he regarded Assyrian domination as the inevitable will of God who rules over history. It was futile therefore to attempt to oppose Assyrian might by alliances with Egypt or other states. Isaiah's advice was not heeded, and he lived to see the destruction of the Northern Kingdom of Israel and the near capture of Jerusalem by Assyrian forces, a disaster averted only by a last-minute miracle. Isaiah was imbued with the sense of justice common to all the prophets. He launched furious attacks against the corruption of the wealthy classes; no one, not even the priests or the king, was spared by his lashing tongue.

To him, it was hypocritical to offer sacrifices unless they were accompanied by the pursuit of justice, mercy, and equality for all. In a famous parable (Ch. 5), Isaiah likens the people to a well-tended vineyard which nevertheless produces rotten grapes instead of good ones. Isaiah prophesied the coming of God's day of judgment, the Assyrians being cast as the instrument of that judgment. God alone, in His own time, would give the signal for Assyria's downfall. According to the Talmud, Isaiah was murdered by the godless King Manasseh.

Chapters 40–66 are assigned to the second or Deutero-Isaiah. They begin with the famous words "Comfort Ye, Comfort Ye, my People," and their author obviously witnessed the events leading to the downfall of Babylonia at the hands of Cyrus. Unlike the first Isaiah's dire prophecy of judgment, the second Isaiah's message is one of hope, comfort, and redemption. His theme is the salvation of God as reflected in Israel's return to Zion. Chapters 52, 53, and sections of other chapters contain the prophecies concerning the "suffering servant" which the Christian church later interpreted as referring to Jesus, but which, in Jewish tradition, refer to the people of Israel.

Some modern Biblical scholars and critics have suggested that chapters 56–66 are the work of a third prophet whom they call the third or Trito-Isaiah.

ISRAEL DEFENSE FORCES (Tzva Hagana le-Israel, abbreviated to **Tzahal):** Army of the State of Israel. The Israel Defense Force was established in 1948 at the height of Israel's War of Independence and the struggle to repel the Arab invaders. It grew out of a merger of several pre-state underground organizations — the *Haganah,* the *Irgun Tzevai Leumi* (National Military Organization) and the *Lohamei Herut Yisrael* (Freedom Fighters of Israel), the *Haganah* being the largest of the three.

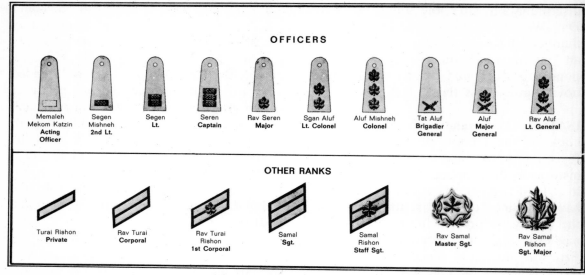

Military ranks in Israel Defense Forces

Although many of its soldiers had seen action in the ranks of the Jewish Brigade during World War II, the I.D.F. at the outset was more of a partisan guerrilla force equipped to operate underground, not to wage modern warfare. All this changed during the War of Independence and by the time victory had been won and the armistice agreements signed, early in 1949, the I.D.F. had been transformed into a regular army. In the ensuing years, this army was expanded and trained to meet the needs of the young state with its abnormally long and complex frontiers, surrounded by enemies whose desire to destroy Israel grew with the years.

The I.D.F. has three sources of manpower: the permanent force, the conscripts, and the reserves. All able-bodied men and women are liable for military service at the age of eighteen, men being called up for three years and women for two. Married women are exempted. Exemption is also granted to women on grounds of religious conviction. Israel's women soldiers serve in all three arms of the forces as non-combatant personnel, replacing men who are thus freed for duty in combat. After their term of national service, men and single women remain on the reserves until the ages of 55 and 34 respectively. Until they are 40, men report for 31 consecutive days of training annually, and, from then till they are 55 for 14. In time of emergency, however, the length of service may be extended. Soldiers wishing to serve a longer period or to make the army their career, may sign on the permanent force.

The ranks in the I.D.F. with their English equivalents are as follows:

Rav-Aluf — Lieut.-General, *Aluf* — Major-General, *Tat-Aluf* — Brigadier, *Aluf-Mishneh* — Colonel, *Segan-Aluf* — Lieut.-Colonel, *Rav-Seren* — Major, *Seren* — Captain, *Segen* — Lieut., *Segen-Mishneh* — 2nd. Lieut., *Rav-Samal* — Sgt.-Major, *Samal* — Sergeant, *Rav Turai* — Corporal, *Turai* — Private.

All three arms of the forces — land, sea and air — are under the command of the General Staff, which is headed by the Chief-of-Staff who has the rank of *Rav-Aluf*, the only serving officer of that rank. In addition, it includes the three Major Generals who command the northern, central, and southern regions into which the country is divided, the Commanders of the Air Force and Navy, and the Chiefs of the General Staff manpower, logistics, and intelligence branches. The Chief of Staff is subordinate to the Minister of Defense and, as in the United States, the President is Commander-in-Chief of the whole defense force. The training of officers is carried out by a network of military schools and academies. Within the framework of the I.D.F. are two unique units which many developing countries have adapted for their own needs. They are the *Naḥal* (Pioneering Fighting Youth) and the *Gadna* (Youth Corps). *Naḥal* combines soldiering with pioneering. After a few months of intensive military training, the men and women of the *Naḥal* are assigned to a border settlement or to the establishing of a new settlement in a strategic area. While working the land they live under army discipline. The *Gadna* is an organization

for boys and girls aged 14–18 in which basic training is provided within the framework of their high school education. It includes agricultural service on various settlements and annual trips around the country to enrich the youngsters' knowledge of the land. Three times in twenty years — 1948, 1956 and 1967 — Israel's army has been forced to do battle in defense of the country. Between these major wars, numerous reprisal raids and countless "smaller" battles took place. Despite the inevitable loss of life, the army has emerged victorious from all its trials. Foreign military observers have expressed the view that, man for man, the I.D.F. is one of the finest fighting forces in the world. A number of factors

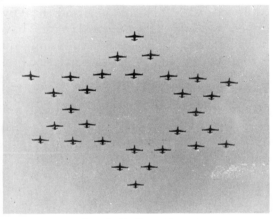

Israel Air Force flypast

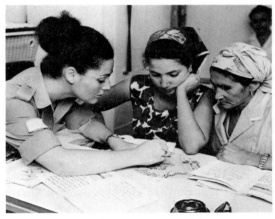

New immigrants studying Hebrew

Israeli reserves on call-up

At an Air Force base

have contributed to Israel's military victories in the face of overwhelming Arab superiority in numbers and equipment.

First, the I.D.F. is a people's army in the sense that all Israel's citizens serve in it for the major part of their lives. Israel's mobilization system, among the most efficient in the world, ensures the swiftest possible call-up of the reserves in time of danger. Units can be equipped and made completely operational in a short time. In this way, Israel is able to muster all its able-bodied manhood. The Israeli citizen-soldier knows that he is fighting for the existence of his land and the values it represents. This knowledge has imbued him with the necessary determination to fight until victorious.

Second, Israel's military leadership, understanding the importance of high morale, has always endeavored to see to it that the soldiers' basic needs are taken care of. Furthermore, despite the tight discipline characteristic of any military framework, there is a basic informality between officer and ordinary soldier. The Israeli soldier knows that in the event of war his commanding officer will not be standing in the rear, binoculars in hand, as in other armies, but will be the first to endanger himself, leading his men forward with the cry "Follow me!" He also knows that in the event of his being wounded, no effort will be spared to rescue him even under enemy fire and at great risk. This relationship has contributed to a team spirit unparalleled in any other army.

Third, Israel's military planning has always been based on the principle of attack as the best form of defense. Being a tiny country, Israel cannot afford to let its enemies strike the first blow. This would necessitate defensive action without sufficient territory and space into which to withdraw. The principle of striking first and fast has paid off handsomely in the past. The use of élite armored and paratroop units, supported by what is generally accepted as one of the most efficient Air Forces in the world, all working together in concerted, hard-hitting thrusts, has always broken the enemy's defenses in a relatively short time. The best example of this method was given in the June 1967 Six-Day War when the Israel Air Force destroyed the combined air forces of the enemy in a matter of hours, and then gave air support to the army and infantry who broke the enemy's front and their will to resist. After the war, the I.D.F. found itself holding a static defense line, something unusual in view of the "attack mentality" described above. Nevertheless, the military initiative was by and large maintained by Israel. In addition to the army and air force, the small Israel Navy has been streamlined in recent years and equipped with fast-moving and heavily-armed torpedo vessels. Its exploits have been marked by the same daring and inventiveness that have characterized all branches of the army. In addition to all the above, the Israel Defense Forces fill an important role in education and civic training. Much of the difficult task of welding the diverse elements of the population into one homogeneous whole is carried out within the framework of the army. New immigrants are taught Hebrew and no soldier leaves its ranks without completing a basic education. The army has also developed popular entertainment groups and issues a wide range of publications.

ISRAEL INDEPENDENCE DAY: Israel's national holiday, falling each year on the fifth day of the Hebrew month of *Iyar,* the day on which the state was proclaimed. The day is also celebrated festively throughout the Jewish world. In Israel, the high point of the celebration was until recently the military parade and display held each year in one of the large cities. At present, the occasion is celebrated with public rejoicing, dancing in the streets, fireworks,

Proclamation of the State of Israel, 1948

Independence Day Parade, Jerusalem

Independence Day Parade, Jerusalem

bonfires, and the annual award of the Israel Prizes. An authoritative and definitive religious attitude to the day has not yet been established, but special synagogue services are held and the *Half-Hallel* recited. The Reform rabbinate proclaimed Israel's Independence Day to be a full religious festival.

ISRAEL, KINGDOM OF: The northerly of the two kingdoms into which King Solomon's realm was divided after his death. It comprised ten tribes: Ephraim, part of Manasseh, Issachar, Zebulun, Naphtali, Asher, and Dan; and in Transjordan, Reuben, Gad, and the other part of Manasseh. The schism resulted from an assertion of the tribal independence which David and Solomon had repressed but not obliterated. It was encouraged and brought to a head largely by the oppressive policies pursued at first by Solomon himself. After Solomon's death, the ten tribes, led by the dissident Jeroboam, approached Rehoboam and offered him their allegiance in return for a lightening of the heavy burden of taxes and forced labor imposed by his father. Rehoboam's elder statesmen advised him to accept, but the young king impetuously rejected their counsel, followed the advice of his young lieutenants and answered Jeroboam, "My father chastised you with whips, but I will chastise you with scorpions." His words provoked a rebellion and the Northern Kingdom of Israel came into being, with Jeroboam as its first king. Israel was larger and wealthier than Judah and wielded greater military power. She was, however, far less stable than the latter and except for brief periods her internal affairs were marked by chaos and anarchy. She was easily influenced religiously and morally by the surrounding Canaanite population, and from the very beginning idolatry made inroads into the monotheistic faith of Israel. This internal instability is demonstrated by the fact that during the two hundred and ten years of its existence Israel had nineteen kings from nine separate dynasties. Ten of these died violently while seven ruled for less than two years. Judah, on the other hand, maintained the Davidic line throughout the whole of her history.

Only with the accession of Omri in 876 B.C.E. did the Northern Kingdom achieve a period of stability. He established a dynasty which held power for three generations, successfully resisted the powerful Aramean kingdom of Damascus, and established friendly relations with the Phoenicians. The building of the new capital, Samaria, was begun by Omri and completed by his son Ahab (869–850 B.C.E.) who continued his father's policies.

Under the Omri dynasty, the feud with Judah which had continued on and off for fifty years, since the division of the kingdom, was brought to an end. Judah and Israel entered into a period of political, economic, and military cooperation to the benefit of both states. On the other hand, the alliance with Phoenicia led to the severe religious crisis between Elijah the prophet and Ahab's Phoenician wife, Jezebel, who attempted to enforce the worship of Baal throughout the kingdom. The dynasty of Omri was brought to an end by the blood purge conducted in the year 842 B.C.E. by the general Jehu with the encouragement and blessing of the prophet Elisha, Elijah's successor. The Jehu dynasty lasted almost a century but it inaugurated a period of weakness and internal confusion. This was the period of the ascendancy of Damascus, and Israel was virtually one of its vassal states. An era of resurgence began with Jehu's grandson, Jehoash (801–786) and culminated in the long and prosperous reign of Jeroboam II (786–746). Under Jeroboam, the northern boundaries of Israel were pushed back to where they had been during Solomon's reign, and the Arameans were decisively defeated. The economy of the country flourished, resulting in an unprecedented era of prosperity. It also led, however, to a moral and social disintegration. As indicated by the vivid prophecies of Hosea and Amos, corruption was rife, and the number of poor and underprivileged grew rapidly. Injustice was rampant, and the greed of the wealthy knew no bounds. No means were disdained in the pursuit of gain and pleasure. Such a society was doomed to disintegrate and on the death of Jeroboam it did, so completely that within the space of twenty-four years the kingdom had ceased to exist. The rising power of Assyria had set out on the path of conquest and under the brilliant empire builder Tiglath Pileser III seemed unstoppable. Israel now entered a period of decay with no less than five kings in ten years. Moreover, these so-called rulers attempted to resist the Assyrian advance by forging a series of alliances with the surrounding states. When Judah refused to participate in such an alliance, she was attacked by Pekah of Israel and Rezin of Damascus. In desperation, Ahaz, the king of Judah, called upon Tiglath Pileser for help, which the latter was only too ready to provide. In the resulting campaign (734 B.C.E.), the kingdom of Israel lost two-thirds of its territory, including Galilee and Transjordan. The decimated kingdom, comprised only of Samaria, held out for a further ten years, stumbling from one blunder to another. The last king, Hoshea (732–724), rebelled against Tiglath Pileser's son Shalmaneser. This was Israel's suicide. Despite three years of heroic resistance, Samaria was finally captured by Shalmaneser's successor, Sargon II in 721 B.C.E. Most of its inhabitants were deported to Upper Mesopotamia and Media. There they were assimilated and ultimately lost their identity, while new emigrants from Mesopotamia were brought into Samaria.

ISRAEL, LAND OF (Eretz Yisrael): Name given in rabbinical literature to the land in Asia which, according to the Bible, was promised by God to Abraham and his descendants. The area which became designated as the land of Israel, however, was inhabited long before the arrival of the tribes of Israel and is referred to in ancient documents by various names. For the Sumerians, it was a part of *Kur Martu-Ki* meaning the land of the west. The ancient Akkadians called it *Mat Amuru* — the land of the Amorites. The Egyptians used the name *Retenu,* the meaning of which is not clear, and in the 15th century B.C.E. the name Canaan appears in a cuneiform document. The name Palestine, still used by the Arabs *(Falastin)* and the majority of Christians, derives from the Latin *Palaestina.* It was used by the ancient Greeks and by the Romans, and owes its origin to the Philistines who at one time occupied the southern seaboard of the country. Curiously enough, it became the standard name for the land of Israel centuries after the Philistines had disappeared from the historical scene.

To the Jews, however, it has always remained the land of Israel or the Holy Land. The conception of "Palestine" as an independent geographical or historical unit in fact owes its origin to the time when the whole country was in the possession of the people of Israel.

The unique geographical location of the land of Israel, at the juncture of two continents, Africa and Asia, has made it from time immemorial a strategic and political prize, whose domination was the ambition of rival world powers. Major trade routes between Asia and Africa ran through the land of Israel from the earliest times. Warring nations such as Egypt and Assyria met on the battlefields of the land of Israel. This foreign rivalry posed then, as it does today, serious problems for the leaders of the nation. More than once, Israelite sovereignty and independence was violated because of it.

The borders of the land of Israel have varied with the changing political conditions. There were times when the land of Israel, in its entirety, was the national territory of the people of Israel. On the other hand, in times of political, economic, and military weakness, large sections of the country were sliced away and given to other nations. A glance at a map will show, however, that certain geographical divisions in the area can readily be called "natural boundaries" and historically, most nations who sought to conquer the land, aspired to possess the territory within this area. These natural divisions are: 1) the Mediterranean coast in the west; 2) the western outskirts of the Syrian desert in the east; 3) from the great bend of the Quasimaya river along the northern edge of the Iyon valley to the southern foothills of Mount Hermon in the north, and 4) *Nahal Mizraim* (The Brook of Egypt; in Arabic *Wadi' l' Arish,* not the Nile) and the road descending from El Arish to the Gulf of Elath in the southwest, and in the southeast, the road leading from Elath to Maon in Edom, the railway line as far as Edrei and the southeastern borderline of the Hauran mountains.

The biblical boundaries as promised in God's covenant with Abraham and his descendants are larger than the natural boundaries, reaching to the Pelusium arm of the Nile delta in the south, and to the Euphrates opposite Aleppo in the east. At no time were both the natural and biblical boundaries occupied in their entirety by the people of Israel. During the reigns of David and Solomon, however, the territory conquered approximated the natural boundaries, and in the north reached the Euphrates.

The land of Israel is divided into four natural belts, stretching from north to south, almost parallel to each other. These consist of 1) the coastal plains, 2) the western mountains, 3) the Jordan valley, and 4) the Transjordan Plateau.

The coastal plain extends from the Wadi El Arish in the south to the Quasimaya river in the north and is twice interrupted: by the Carmel promontory and by the ladder of Tyre. Its average width is 20 kilometers (about 14 miles) but in the south it is 50 kilometers (30 miles) wide in parts. In the Haifa area, it is no wider than 3 kilometers (2 miles). The western mountains, from the mountain of Elath to the Quasimaya River, average 55 kilometers (33 miles) in width. The largest and deepest valley that cuts through them is the Valley of Jezreel.

The Jordan Valley stretches from the Valley of Iyon in the north to the Gulf of Elath in the south. It reaches a width of 20 kilometers (14 miles) in the vicinity of Jericho, while between Northern Samaria and Gilead it is no more than 5 kilometers (3 miles) wide. The Transjordan Plateau, consisting of the area east of the Jordan Valley up to the Syrian Desert, extends from the foothills of Mount Hermon in the north to the Gulf of Elath in the south. The land of Israel has a Mediterranean climate comparable to that of Spain, southern Italy, or Greece. There are, however, regions with a tropical temperature such as the Jordan Valley and the basin of the Dead Sea, while the Negev and the Steppe of Transjordan have a nearly continental climate. There is no clear-cut division into four seasons. The months from May to October are hot and completely rainless while the rest of the year is rainy and cool. There are, however, considerable regional differences, partly caused by the differences in elevation. This makes it impossible to speak of a single climate in the whole country.

History

Evidence of prehistoric man's life has been discovered in the Jordan Valley and in the Carmel Caves. Archeological excavations have further shown that as early as the Stone Age organized city life existed in Jericho, in the vicinity of the Yarmuk River, in Beersheba and in other places in Israel. The earliest recorded inhabitants, however, were the Canaanites, from whom the land originally took its name. These Semites settled in the land somewhere between 3000–2500 B.C.E., developed towns, and substituted bronze for flint. According to the Bible, there were seven Canaanite tribes. With the exception of the period in which the mysterious Hyksos dominated both Canaan and Egypt (1730–1500 B.C.E.), the land was organized into a series of petty, warring city-states under Egyptian domination. It was the Israelite invasion, however, which gave the land its political unity and historical significance. The process of conquest, starting with the military campaigns of Joshua, was slow and painful. The loosely united Jewish tribes were not sufficiently strong, even when they acted together, to conquer Canaan, nor, later, to ward off the attacks of the much more powerful Philistines. This situation prompted the establishment of the monarchy, first under Saul, then under David. David succeeded in putting his kingdom on a firm footing with a properly organized administration imposing the rule of the central government. Making Jerusalem his capital, David completed the process of conquest and extended the frontiers of the country. In his day, and during the reign of his son Solomon the territory of the kingdom extended beyond the natural boundaries of the land of Israel to encompass almost all the biblical boundaries. For a short time Israel was the most powerful country in the area. Solomon's lavish expenditures and heavy-handed treatment of his subjects, however, led to widespread discontent. Upon his death, the kingdom split into two: the Northern Kingdom of Israel, comprising the ten tribes, and the Southern Kingdom of Judah (and Benjamin). The two kingdoms alternately fought each other, coexisted peacefully, and even cooperated at times. They were, however, bereft of international prestige and with the exception of temporary periods when they were able to extend their frontiers northward and southward respectively, they were, in the main, defensive vis-a-vis their immediate neighbors and the rising power of Assyria. The Northern Kingdom finally succumbed to the might of Assyria in the year 721 B.C.E. Its population was dispersed and interchanged with foreigners, subsequently known as Samaritans. Because of its greater geographical isolation and its healthier spiritual climate, Judah was able to hold out longer. She too, however, finally fell to the armies of King Nebuchadnezzar of Babylon who destroyed the Temple of Solomon in the year 586 B.C.E. and exiled the population to Babylon. An attempt to renew organized political life as a vassal

state of Babylon under Gedaliah, a member of the old royal house, was prematurely ended by his assassination in the year 582 B.C.E. In the year 539 B.C.E., the Persian conqueror of Babylon, King Cyrus, gave permission to all the exiles so desiring to return to the land of Israel in order to rebuild the Temple and to set up an autonomous center under Persian rule. The returnees, some forty thousand in number, were greeted by desolation and the hostility of their Samaritan neighbors. It was only with the arrival of Ezra and Nehemiah that the new settlement was firmly established. They refused the Samaritans' offer of cooperation, for fear of a negative religious influence on the returnees. They further forbade intermarriage with Samaritan or other "women of the land" and demanded strict obedience to the Torah from the people of Judah. Nehemiah did much to strengthen the walls and defenses of Jerusalem.

Henceforth, Judah was a Persian province ruled over by the High Priest in Jerusalem. The situation remained basically the same after the conquest of Persia by Alexander the Great of Macedon and the subsequent division of his empire on his death. Judah was subject first to the Ptolemies of Egypt and then to the

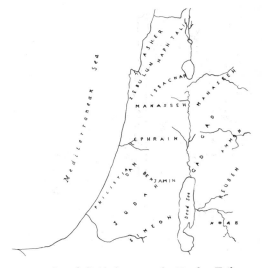

Israel divided among the Twelve Tribes

Seleucids of Syria. It was the attempt by one of the latter—Antiochus Epiphanes—to "hellenize" the country, both culturally and spiritually, that led to the Maccabean revolt of 165 B.C.E.

With the success of the rebellion, full Jewish independence was restored under the rule of the Hasmoneans for the first time since 586 B.C.E. Their rule was confirmed as a monarchy during the reign of Aristobulos and his brother Alexander Yannai. Through a series of costly but successful military campaigns, the latter extended the country's borders. However, his reign also saw a civil war with the Pharisees and finally, internal dissension caused by rival Hasmonean claimants to the throne gave the Romans the opportunity to take control of the land of Israel. From the year 63 B.C.E. the country became part of the Roman Empire. Nominally it was administered first by members of the Hasmonean dynasty, then by the house of Herod and, later, at different times directly by the Romans themselves. The revolts of the Jews against the Romans (66–70 C.E. and 132–135 C.E.) led to the destruction of the Second Temple in Jerusalem (70 C.E.), the devastation of the country itself, and to the extermination of a large part of its inhabitants. Nevertheless, after the year 135 C.E., Jewish life continued to flourish, especially in Galilee under the spiritual leadership of the "patriarchs," the presidents of the Sanhedrin whose authority was recognized by the Roman government. This was a period of intense intellectual activity, reflected in the Mishnah and the Palestinian Talmud.

The Christianization of the Roman Empire proclaimed by the Emperor Constantine brought this to an end. The Patriarchate was abolished, the Jews mercilessly persecuted, and the land of Israel increasingly made the focus of Christian piety. The Byzantine rulers adopted even more repressive policies so that the tiny Jewish population was reduced to an insignificant minority without any rights whatsoever. Roman rule lasted in the land of Israel for 700 years, to be finally brought to an end by the Arab conquest. In a bitter campaign lasting from 633 to 640, the Arabs, led by the Caliph Omar and his generals, conquered the country. Under the Moslems, the role of the Jews was insignificant and the country was the scene of perpetual conflict between rival Moslem sects, some of whom were tolerant to the Jews, and others, such as the Fatimides, who were repressive. The Crusader "liberation" of Jerusalem in the year 1099 was celebrated with a savage massacre of both Moslems and Jews. They established a European-style feudal state, built monasteries and churches, but did nothing toward the development of the country. In 1187, Sultan Saladin defeated the Crusaders at Hittin in lower Galilee and recaptured Jerusalem. In 1291, the last Crusader fortress at Acre fell to the Egyptian Mamelukes who ruled the land of Israel for the next two hundred years.

Toward the end of the 15th century, particularly after the Spanish expulsion in 1492, Jewish life in the land of Israel revived. Safed emerged as a great center of Jewish learning and mysticism, and numerous scholarly luminaries were atracted to this center. The Turkish conquest in 1517 made a promising start and brought a period of peace and prosperity. Suleiman the Second (the Magnificent) was sympathetic toward the Jewish population, and it was with his blessing that Don Joseph Nasi attempted to establish an autonomous Jewish center in Tiberias, unfortunately without success. Emissaries from the four holy cities, Jerusalem, Hebron, Safed, and Tiberias, traveled abroad seeking Jewish financial support for the local communities and institutions of the land of Israel. However, the Turkish administration soon sank into apathy and corruption. In spite of the efforts of competent local leaders such as the Druse Emir Fakhi ed-Din in the 17th century, or the Bedouin Sheikh Taher el-Amr in the 18th, there was little attempt to develop the country. The Turks saw the land of Israel as a remote and unimportant province whose sole value lay in the revenue that could be extracted from it. Between 1831 and 1840, the land enjoyed a period of prosperity under the honest rule of an Egyptian, Muhammed Ali, and his son, Ibrahim Pasha. Then their regime was overthrown by Turkey with the assistance of England, Austria, Prussia, and Russia. Nevertheless, during that period technology, transportation, and communications had been modernized. Thereafter, more and more tourists visited the Holy Land and construction and development made rapid strides. Religious institutions of all faiths were widely established and new settlers became more common. The restrictions on Jewish settlement in Jerusalem were lifted and with the support of the great philanthropist Sir Moses Montefiore, the first Jewish suburb was established outside the walls of the Old City. With the immigration of Russian Jews in 1882 (the *Biluim*), the modern period of Jewish settlement in the land of Israel began.

Turkish rule was terminated with her defeat in World War I. The administration of the land was given to Great Britain under a League of Nations Mandate. From then on, the history of the land of Israel was bound up with the Zionist struggle for a Jewish state, which culminated triumphantly in 1948 with the establishment of the State of Israel.

See also: ZIONISM, ISRAEL.

ISRAEL, STATE OF: Sovereign Jewish State proclaimed on May 14th, 1948.

Making of the State

From the time of the November 1947 United Nations decision to partition the land of Israel until the proclamation of the state, feverish preparations were made to meet the inevitable Arab onslaught. Irregular bands of Arab guerrillas sowed terror and created havoc wherever they could. As the date of the announced British evacuation drew near, the Arab states made it clear that they would violate the U.N. decision and attack the young state. Friendly governments and even some Zionist leaders, fearing a slaughter of the Jewish population, urged the postponement of the declaration. David Ben-Gurion, sensing that history had presented the Jewish people with a unique opportunity, rejected this advice and went ahead with the proclamation of Israel's Declaration of Independence. The following day, Israel was attacked from all sides by hostile Arab armies. Chief among these was the British-trained and led Arab legion from Transjordan. Although soldier for soldier the other Arab forces, including the Egyptian army, were no match for the Israelis, their tremendous superiority in armor, artillery, and fighter planes made the outcome seem a foregone conclusion. Indeed, things went badly for the Israelis in the beginning. Despite the valiant resistance of the southern Jewish settlements, the Egyptians advanced to within thirty miles of Tel Aviv. The Old City of Jerusalem fell after a heroic and desperate battle, and the New City was besieged. The infant army of Israel was desperately short of arms, ammunition, and trained manpower. The elite Palmach shock troops were moved from place to place, and the lines were thinly stretched. At times, as in the case of the attack on the Latrun police station, immigrants fresh off the boat, without any knowledge of Hebrew, were given a "crash course" in the use of rifles and thrown into the battle. Yet, to the amazement of the world, the Israelis held out.

All the people of Israel, with the support of world Jewry, rallied to the defense of the young state. The various underground groups that had been fighting the British joined hands with *Zahal (Tzva Haganah le-Israel),* the new defense force of Israel, and were eventually absorbed by it. Arms were procured from every possible source. Especially helpful were the thousands of rifles and some Messerschmidt planes received from Czechoslovakia. The Israel Army was now able to go over to the offensive, and in a number of brilliant operations succeeded in clearing the Egyptians from the Negev desert (except for the Gaza Strip). But for the armistice negotiations, they would in all probability have annihilated the Arab armies entirely. Negotiations were held on the Greek island of Rhodes with U.N. Under-Secretary Ralph Bunche acting as mediator. Armistice agreements were reached with all the Arab invaders with the exception of Iraq, who refused to recognise the cease-fire. The Israel Army had successfully emerged from its severe test, leaving the territory in Israel's hands far larger than that allocated to her by the partition plan. The price paid, however, was the flower of Israel's youth — over 5,000 dead and many more maimed and wounded.

Immigration and the Law of Return

Despite the war and the severe economic difficulties, the task of development and immigration went ahead. At its inception, Israel's Parliament, the Knesset, passed a unique law — the Law of Return. Under its provisions, any Jew so desiring would receive Israeli citizenship the moment he set foot on Israel soil. Within the first three years, Israel's Jewish population doubled from 650,000 to 1,300,000 through mass immigration. The immigrants included survivors from Nazi concentration camps and other refugees from eastern and central Europe, refugees from such Arab countries as the Yemen and Iraq, immigrants from North Africa, and smaller numbers from western Europe and the affluent Western countries. The task of settling this vast mass of largely underprivileged Jews with little or no means evolved upon the Israel Government, the Jewish Agency

From Metulla to the Sinai

(which after the establishment of the state dealt mainly with matters of finance and immigration), and, of course, the Jewish people. The problem was not only economic but also social. Here for the first time in 2,000 years the Jewish people were meeting once again. Different customs and beliefs adopted over the centuries from the

the many faces of Israeli towns

environment surrounding them made the Jews of this melting pot assemblage seem at times foreign to each other. Furthermore, there were always more problems for the newcomer than for the established veteran. Israel, however, was committed to mass immigration. It was her very lifeblood and the cardinal principle of Zionist ideology.

Gradually, seemingly insuperable obstacles were overcome and many early mistakes corrected. Special *ulpanim* were established where intensive Hebrew courses were given. New development towns were built and populated largely by immigrants. The schools, youth villages, and, above all, the army, played an important part in the colossal task of converting a heterogeneous mass into a united nation. The tide of immigration ebbed and flowed. From 1952 to 1960, it averaged 33,000 a year. During the next few years, there was a large increase, followed by a sharp drop in 1965–1967. This was partly because the reservoir of emigrants from lands in which they were persecuted (but nevertheless allowed to emigrate) had dried up. The number of Jews immigrating to Israel from the affluent western countries, where they enjoyed full civil rights, had been relatively few. After the Six-Day War of June 1967 however, the graph showed a vast increase in western emigration. Most of these new immigrants were motivated not by persecution in their countries of residence but by a voluntary decision to share in the upbuilding of the Jewish State. Special privileges, which have always been granted to immigrants in the spheres of housing and loans, have been greatly extended. At the beginning of 1969, Israel had a total population of 2,841,100 consisting of 2,434,800 Jews, 300,800 Moslems, 72,150 Christians, and 33,300 Druze and others. These numbers do not include the Arab population of the territories occupied in the Six-Day War (with the exception of reunified Jerusalem).

Development

The story of Israel's development is one of meteoric progress, and in almost all spheres, lines on the graph have spiralled upward. In addition to the three major cities of Jerusalem, Tel Aviv, and Haifa (populations 275,000; 384,700; and 212,000 respectively), there are a number of towns such as the one-time Tel Aviv suburb of Ramat Gan (130,000), Beersheba (72,000), and Holon (80,100), which have blossomed; and villages such as Petah Tikvah and Rishon Le-Tzion that have become towns. Now development towns such as Dimona in the Negev, and Kiryat Shemonah in northern Galilee have been built from nothing. Eighty-two percent of Israel's population lives in the cities, towns, and townships, while 18 percent lives in the various forms of agricultural settlements — the *kibbutz,* the *moshav,* and the *moshav shittuphi.*

Industrialization has proceeded apace and, for a country with relatively few natural resources, Israel's economic growth is unparalleled, rivaling that of some of the most highly industrialized nations.

Education

The demands of modernization and technology have accelerated the need for better education. Accordingly, existing educational institutions have been expanded and new ones have been established. In spite of the heavy burden of immigration, defense, and development, a complete educational system from kindergarten to university has been built up, and scientific research is of a remarkably high standard. There are about 800,000 pupils and students in educational institutions, as compared with 140,000 in 1948–1949. Primary education is free and compulsory, and under a law of 1969 the school-leaving age is to be gradually raised to sixteen by 1975.

The Hebrew University of Jerusalem has over 15,000 students; the University of Tel Aviv 9,700; and the religious university, Bar-Ilan, 4,500. The Israel Institute of Technology, known as the Technion, is situated in Haifa. The Weizmann Institute of Science in Rehovot has a staff of some 1,200, of whom 370 are scientists. Branches of the Hebrew University have been established in Haifa and Beersheba, and will develop into independent institutions.

Government

Despite her trials and tribulations — the inevitable birthpangs of a developing society — and periodic setbacks, Israel has from the outset maintained a democratic system of government. The Knesset is elected by universal suffrage, according to proportional representation. The voters choose between national party lists of candidates, seats being allocated in proportion to the number of votes obtained by each list. The weakness in this system lies in the fact that the citizen votes for the party and not for the individual candidate. The system also leads to a plethora of political parties and makes it virtually impossible for one party to govern. Indeed, all Israel's governments since the establishment of the state have been coalitions. In recent years, the tendency has been toward mergers, both on the left and the right wing of the political spectrum.

The head of state in Israel is the President who is elected by the Knesset for a period of five years, and may be re-elected for one further term. The first President was Dr. Chaim Weizmann; the second Yitzhak Ben-Zvi; and the third, Zalman Shazar.

As in most democracies, the independence of the courts is guaranteed by law. Judges and magistrates are appointed by the President on the recommendation of an independent nominations committee. There are magistrates courts, district courts, and the highest court in the land, the Supreme Court. In addition to these, each of the major communities has its own religious courts — Rabbinical (Jewish), Moslem, Druze, and Christian. Marriage and divorce in the State of Israel come under the exclusive jurisdiction of these religious courts.

Israel's Arab minority, which has grown considerably since 1949, is accorded equality before the law and in Parliament (where there are eight Arab representatives), and shares in the democratic process. Although Israel's conflict with her Arab neighbors places them in an ambiguous position, they have for the most part shown loyalty to the state and, before and during the Six-Day War, many Israel Arabs volunteered to help the war effort as blood-donors and by replacing farm-laborers called to the army. Despite her magnificent achievements, Israel is confronted with numerous internal problems — social, religious, and economic.

Unfortunately, she has been unable to devote herself entirely to the building up of a model society because of the continual external danger to her very existence. The security problem is at the very root and core of Israel's being.

Security Problem

During the early years of the 1950's, hopes for a peace settlement were raised by the overthrow of the corrupt regime of King Farouk in Egypt by a group of officers led by General Naguib and Colonel Nasser. The latter, who soon became the strong man of Egypt, at first seemed to be more interested in the modernization of his country than in conflict with Israel. However, these hopes were soon dashed. Not only was the attitude of belligerency continued, but it soon became clear that Nasser, at the head of the Arab world, was actively planning a "second round," in which he hoped to achieve what the Arabs had failed to do in 1948. The Suez Canal, despite United Nations resolutions to the contrary, was closed to Israel shipping. The Straits of Tiran, Israel's only outlet to the Indian Ocean, was sealed by the placing of cannons at Sharm el-Sheikh, and raids across the frontier were intensified.

In 1955, Nasser made a huge arms deal with the Soviet bloc, which completely altered the balance of power in the Arab states' favor. Organized commando groups known as *fedayin* now began to penetrate deep into Israel territory, sowing terror and bloodshed among innocent citizens. In addition, Nasser, in a fit of anger at the British and American refusal to finance the Aswan High Dam, decided to confront the western powers by nationalizing the Suez Canal. Behind Nasser stood the Soviet Union, which had reversed her originally sympathetic policy toward Israel into one of undisguised hostility. When Nasser, together with King Hussein of Jordan, set up a unified Arab command aimed at encompassing Israel militarily, Israel decided to act.

On October 29, 1956, Israel's defense forces, under the command of Moshe Dayan, moved into the Gaza Strip and the Sinai Peninsula, and routed Egypt's forces east of the canal. The blockade of the Straits of Tiran was lifted and access to the Indian Ocean assured. At the same time, Britain and France, for reasons of their own, attempted to take the canal by force. In the eyes of many, Israel's just struggle was unfortunately identified with the two Western powers, especially with France, who had supplied Israel with much-needed military equipment. Charges of collusion were leveled at Britain, France, and Israel. Under the extreme pressure of the U.N., especially the Soviet Union and the United States, Israel was forced to withdraw from all occupied territories. A United Nations force was set up to act as a buffer between Israel and Egypt. It was stated specifically by Israel and many member states at the U.N. that all armed incursions into Israeli territory should cease, and that there should be no attempt by Egypt to hinder freedom of navigation. Unfortunately, this "agreement" or promise was never documented, but was merely verbal. The essential element for peace was still lacking — the recognition on the part of the Arab states of Israel's right to exist. The gravity of this defect became only too evident ten years later.

The Sinai campaign was followed by a period of relative tranquility on Israel's borders, and in the years following, there were indications of a more positive and realistic approach in certain sections of Arab opinion. Once again, however, these premature hopes proved to be an illusion. In the early sixties, a new Arab commando organization, *El Fatah,* was set up, and terrorist activity resumed. Syria in particular now took the lead in acts of belligerency against Israel, and from her fortified positions on the Golan Heights shelled Israel's settlements indiscriminately. No amount of retaliatory action by the Israel Army was able to convince the fanatical Syrians that they should desist. Time and again, serious warnings were issued by Israel's government, but to no avail.

Six-Day War

In May 1967, one of these warnings was exploited by the Soviet Government to report to the Syrian and Egyptian Governments the allegation that Israel was massing troops on the Syrian frontier in preparation for a general attack. Even though no less a personality than U.N. Secretary-General U Thant confirmed that the report was false, the damage was done. Nasser (whose prestige in the Arab world had fallen low), not wanting to be accused of "deserting" his brethren in their hour of need, moved his armor into the Sinai Peninsula and demanded the expulsion of the U.N. force, to which U Thant timidly acceded. Israel took precautionary measures but hoped that Nasser's latest threats were merely a bluff.

As the month of May progressed, however, it became increasingly clear that this was not so, and when Nasser closed the Straits of Tiran, war became inevitable. Israel, now fully mobilized, made every effort to settle the conflict by diplomatic means and called on the nations of the world to intervene. At the same time, she made it abundantly clear that she would not submit to a policy of slow strangulation. As in the past, the U.N. proved itself impotent, and the Arab radio and press drove the masses into a frenzy of bloodthirsty enthusiasm. Radio Cairo on May 30, 1967, issued the following statement: "Following the closing of the Gulf of Aqaba there are now two courses open to Israel — either of which is drenched in her own blood: either she will die of strangulation under the Arab military and economic siege, or else she will perish under the fire of the Arab forces encompassing her on the north, the south, and the east."

Israel decided neither to die of strangulation nor to perish under fire. On the morning of June 5, 1967, Israel's Air Force destroyed the combined Arab Air Forces on the ground in three hours, and there began one of the swiftest and most brilliant campaigns in military history. A last minute effort was made to avoid conflict with Jordan but convinced of the invincibility of Arab might, King Hussein unleashed his forces in an attempt to capture Jerusalem. Within six days, Israeli forces reached the Suez Canal, drove the Jordanians out of Judah and Samaria, and successfully stormed the Syrian fortifications on the Golan Heights. Jerusalem was re-united. Through the heroism and valor of its soldiers, over seven hundred of whom died in the combat, Israel was able to breathe freely again. From Mount Hermon in the north to the Suez Canal in the south, Arab military power lay shattered. This time, Israel made it plain that there would be no withdrawal without peace — peace arrived at by direct negotiations between the combatants. Israel's policy has always been that the Middle Eastern dispute must be settled by the people of the area themselves without outside interference.

Continuing Problem

Israel's leaders have repeatedly declared that Israeli representatives were ready to meet Egyptian, or any other Arab representatives in direct negotiations at any time, at any place, and without preconditions. The Arab reply, however, was formulated at a Summit Conference held at Khartoum in August 1967 — no peace with Israel, no negotiations with Israel, no recognition of Israel.

The Soviet Union not only immediately replaced the equipment lost in the Six-Day War, but also supplied Egypt with even more modern equipment, military advisers, and eventually pilots. When he again felt strong enough, Nasser openly declared a war of attrition against Israel and announced that the cease-fire was no longer in effect. At the same time, the Arab terror gangs waged indiscriminate war against Israel, her citizens, and even against her civilian airline, El Al.

Militarily, despite the almost daily loss of life, Israel not only held out but delivered counterblasts. Despite pressure from the Soviet Union, France, and even from her friends, Israel remained determined that nothing would move her — nothing, that is, except peace. Israel needs peace so that she may devote her energies and resources to the complete rehabilitation of the country, and to the economic, social, and cultural integration of her people into a creative, democratic, and progressive society. But she has always stressed that peace can only be real when it respects her security.

Israel maintains diplomatic and consular relations with over a hundred countries, and has given technical and other assistance to developing countries out of all proportion to her size and wealth. Thus she believes that the normalization of relations between her and her Arab neighbors would lead to an era of unprecedented prosperity for the people of the Middle East as a whole.

ISRAEL PHILHARMONIC ORCHES-TRA: Israel's foremost musical institution. Founded in 1936 as the Palestine Symphony Orchestra by the world-renowned violinist Bronislav Huberman, it was mainly composed, at first, of some of the finest refugee musicians from the Nazi-dominated countries. As a sign of his esteem and sympathy for the Jewish people, the great conductor Arturo Toscanini agreed to conduct the inaugural concert. Since then, the orchestra has grown in quality and has attained an international reputation. Its performance center is at the Frederic Mann Auditorium in Tel Aviv, but it gives concerts throughout the country and lately, the world. It has 36,000 subscribers — a world-record percentage of the population, and today over 40 percent of its

Israel Philharmonic Orchestra in Tel Aviv

104 members are Israeli-born or Israeli-trained. Many world-famous conductors and soloists have appeared with the Philharmonic, and the orchestra undertakes frequent tours abroad. In recent years, a further step forward was taken with the appointment of Zubin Mehta, the brilliant young conductor, as the orchestra's musical adviser.

ITALY: Jews settled in Rome as early as the 2nd century B.C.E., making it one of the oldest Jewish communities in Europe. From there they spread to the southern parts of the Roman Empire and along its many trade routes. The Roman-Jewish wars (66–70 C.E. and 132–135 C.E.) considerably increased this settlement. Thousands of Jewish captives were brought to Rome to be sold as slaves, but many subsequently gained their freedom. Despite occasional repression, the Jews suffered no great legal restrictions apart from the poll tax, known as the *Fiscus Judaicus,* paid to the temple of Jupiter in Rome. At this time there were some twelve different Jewish communities in Rome leading a rich Jewish cultural and religious life.

All this changed with the Christianization of the Roman Empire in the 4th century. Discriminatory measures adopted by the Christian church were vigorously applied. Nevertheless, the Jews were officially under the protection of the Popes and their policy, as expounded by Pope Gregory the Great (590–604),

was to humiliate the Jews, not destroy them. They were permitted to practice their faith, but little beyond this. The church followed this policy throughout the medieval period but it was not always understood by the masses who translated "humiliation" by massacres and pogroms. During the second half of the 13th century, various Italian city-states began to invite wealthy Jewish financiers to open "loan banks" for the benefit of the poor. Thanks to the activities of these loan bankers, a number of famous Jewish communities were established at Venice, Ancona, Padua, Ferrara, Verona, and other cities. During the Renaissance the condition of Jewish life was generally favorable, and a number of Popes pursued a liberal policy toward them. Jews played a distinct part in certain aspects of the Renaissance and made important contributions to philosophy, art, music, and the theater.

Throughout its history, Italy was an important center of Jewish culture and the home of many creative and scholarly Jews. The Catholic counter-reformation, however, brought in its train a drastic deterioration and the position of Italian Jews became worse than it had ever been before. In 1555, Pope Paul IV issued a bull (Papal declaration of policy) confining Jews to a ghetto, restricting their economic activities, excluding them from the professions and other work, and imposing the wearing of the badge of shame upon them. This policy was imitated all over the

The Vittorio Veneto synagogue, Israel Museum

country. The age of degradation of Italian Jewry continued until the close of the 18th century when the armies of Napoleon brought them emancipation. However, this was shortlived. With the fall of Napoleon, a severe reaction set in. Later, the growth of Italian unity spread a spirit of equality and liberation, and in 1870 when Rome became the capital of a united Italy, Jews participated in the general emancipation. In the years that followed, Italian Jewry enjoyed a larger measure of freedom and civil rights than any other Jewish community in Europe. They entered into the life of the country, occupying positions of the highest authority, including that of Prime Minister. Even with the rise of Mussolini and the establishment of a Fascist state, this position at first remained unchanged. After the alliance concluded between Mussolini and Hitler in 1938, however, an anti-Semitic policy was instituted although it never reached the violent proportions of German-occupied Europe. When Italy surrendered to the Allies in 1943 and the Germans occupied the northern part of the country, thousands of Italian Jews were sent to the death camps. The Jewish population of Italy today numbers some 35,000.

The Holy Ark of the Veneto-Veturio synagogue, Israel Museum

JABOTINSKY, VLADIMIR (Ze'ev; 1880–1940): Zionist leader, journalist, writer, and orator. One of the most controversial figures in the history of the Zionist movement, adored by his disciples and passionately hated by his opponents, Jabotinsky was born in Odessa, the great center of Jewish life on the Black Sea. His journalistic talents led to his appointment as Rome correspondent for various Odessa newspapers from 1898–1901. His Zionist activities began in 1903 when he helped organize a Jewish self-defense corps in Odessa in the face of a threatening pogrom. He was soon recognized as one of the advocates of Jewish minority rights, self-defense, and the revival of Hebrew. He was by now totally identified with the aims of political Zionism, and when World War I broke out in 1914 he advocated the recruiting of Jewish units to fight on the side of the British, whom he hoped would be the instrument for the realization of the Zionist ideal. He took part in the formation of the Zion Mule Corps which served at Gallipoli and was finally successful in persuading the British to raise three battalions, the first of which, the 38th Fusiliers, fought with Allenby in the campaign against the Turks in 1918. He himself enlisted, rising to the rank of lieutenant. After the war and the granting of the Palestine Mandate to Great Britain, Jabotinsky became disillusioned with the failure of the British to implement the Balfour Declaration, which to him meant unlimited Jewish immigration and the establishment of a Jewish state within the historic boundaries of the land of Israel. In 1920, in the face of Arab riots, he organized the first Jewish self-defense units in Jerusalem. He was arrested and sentenced by the British military tribunal to 15 years imprisonment. The outcry that ensued, however, was so great that he was soon pardoned and the conviction revoked. From 1920–23, he was a member of the Zionist Executive but resigned through lack of sympathy with Weizmann's policy, which he considered too pacifist and cautious. Accordingly, in 1925 he founded an opposition group later known as the Zionist Revisionists. This was followed by the establishment of a militant youth movement, *Berit Trumpeldor* or *Betar,* named after Joseph Trumpeldor. Jabotinsky was insistent on the need for Jewish military and police units and the immediate establishment of a Jewish state. With the rise of Nazism in Germany and the danger of extinction hanging over European Jewry this insistence was intensified. The official Zionist movement, however, still tried to co-operate with the British, believing that nothing could be done without their consent, and furthermore laid stress on a policy of gradual and careful colonization. In 1935, Jabotinsky and his followers seceded from the official Zionist Organization to found the dissident "New Zionist Organization." His policy was by now totally activist, leading to the formation of an underground para-military group, the *Irgun Zvai Leumi.* This group began to bring in illegal immigrants and to operate openly against the British. Jabotinsky died in 1940 while on a visit to the United States. In his last will and testament he requested that his remains be transferred to the Holy Land, but only by

Vladimir Jabotinsky

the express wish of the government of a sovereign Jewish state. The controversy generated by Jabotinsky's fiery views and policies prevented the fulfillment of this request when the state was first founded. With the passing of time, however, all segments of Jewry both in Israel and the Diaspora came to recognize Jabotinsky's contribution to the Zionist cause. Accordingly, in 1964, Israel's Prime Minister Levi Eshkol ordered the transfer of Jabotinsky's remains to a place of honor on Mt. Herzl in Jerusalem.

JEREMIAH: Biblical prophet of the 7th–5th centuries B.C.E. His prophecies are recorded in the book bearing his name which is the second of the three major Books of Prophets in the Bible. The call to be a prophet came to Jeremiah in the year 625 B.C.E., and his ministry extended through the reigns of the last kings of Judah. The period of Jeremiah's prophetic career up to 586 B.C.E. coincided with the

most fateful and tragic period in the history of Judah. He witnessed the decline and fall of the mighty Assyrian Empire at the hands of Babylon, the Babylonian defeat of Egypt, Judah's futile alliance with Egypt and resistance to Babylon, and the final destruction of the Temple and Judean State.

Like Moses before him, Jeremiah at first attempted to refuse the call issued to him by God: "Ah, Lord God! Behold, I do not know how to speak, for I am only a youth" (Ch. 1). God, however, overruled his objections, and having once accepted the inevitable implications of his mission, Jeremiah left the peace and quiet of Anathot, the village of his birth, three miles north of Jerusalem, and plunged into the task set for him. The period of religious reform carried out by King Josiah came to an end in 609 B.C.E. with the latter's untimely death in battle against the Egyptians. His sons did not continue in the same path and all the gains achieved during Josiah's reign were soon dissipated. Moreover, the refusal of King Jehoiakim to accept the hegemony of Babylonia, his insistence on remaining loyal to Egypt, made a clash with Jeremiah inevitable. Jeremiah was convinced that only by submitting to Babylon could Judah be saved. His prophecies of wrath and doom infuriated the authorities and on one occasion, Pashur, the Temple officer, struck him and put him in prison. Later he was put on trial for his life but was saved by some officers. In the year 605 B.C.E., the year of the Babylonian victory over Egypt, Jeremiah dictated all his prophecies to his secretary and loyal disciple, Baruch, son of Neriah. The prophecy of doom concerning Judah, unless it submitted to Babylon, so infuriated Jehoiakim that he had the entire manuscript burned and Jeremiah was forced to flee. After the deportation of the royal family and the nobility in 597 B.C.E., Jeremiah chose to remain in Jerusalem. To his dismay, King Zedekiah, on the advice of his captains, continued the anti-Babylonian policy of his predecessors. When rebellion again broke out, Jeremiah publicly performed numerous acts symbolizing the final inevitable fall of Jerusalem. His conduct enraged the masses who turned on him as a traitor. When he called for surrender and urged the soldiers to desert, he was imprisoned and thrown into a pit. Strangely enough the king continued to consult him, obviously hoping to hear words of encouragement. Finally the officers demanded his death as a public enemy and Zedekiah was forced publicly to agree, although secretly he had the prophet rescued from the pit. After the final destruction of the Temple in 586 B.C.E., the Babylonians freed Jeremiah, having learned of his opposition to the rebellion. Jeremiah urged the remnant of the population to live peacefully under Babylonian rule, preaching final redemption and the establishment of a new covenant with Israel. After the assassination of Gedaliah, the governor appointed by the Babylonians, panic ensued, and Jeremiah and Baruch were forced to accompany the fleeing survivors to Egypt. There, Jeremiah uttered his last prophecy against the idolatry of the Jews in Egypt. It is not known how and where he died. Jeremiah is the most tragic and pathetic of the prophets. He is in a continual state of conflict between his love for his people and country and his burning need to preach the truth as revealed to him by God. Gentle and compassionate by nature, his mission was distasteful to him in the extreme. Yet his first loyalty was to truth and the word of God, and for that he was prepared to undergo humiliation, imprisonment, and even face death. The book bearing his name contains fifty-two chapters. He has also been credited with the authorship of the books of Kings and Lamentations, according to rabbinic tradition.

JERICHO: One of the oldest towns in the world. Excavations uncovered remains of the first fortifications dating back to around 8000 B.C.E. It lies 820 feet (250 meters) below sea level, on the western bank of the southern Jordan Valley. It is, and was in ancient times, a favorite winter resort. Its climate and vegetation are tropical and today the area is surrounded by orange groves and banana plantations. In biblical times, Jericho was known as the "City of Palms," from the tracts of date palms that surrounded it. It was the first city to be captured by the invading tribes of Israel. The famous story of how "the walls came tumbling down" is recorded in the book of Joshua (6:1–26). Thereafter its ruins lay abandoned and desolate until the 9th century B.C.E. when the Israelite King Ahab had it rebuilt. Herod built himself a winter palace in Jericho, where he died. The Romans destroyed the city in 68 C.E. but in the 4th century C.E. Jericho was rebuilt at its present location, about a mile to the east of the ancient *tel.*

Monastery on Hill of Temptation, Jericho

After Israel's War of Independence, the population was greatly augmented by over 60,000 Arab refugees. With the approach of Israel's Army during the June 1967 Six-Day War, most of these refugees fled over the Jordan so that in late 1967 the population numbered only 6,800.

JERUSALEM (Yerushalayim): Capital of the State of Israel, the seat of its government and Supreme Court, and the location of the Supreme Religious Authority, the Chief Rabbinate. Jerusalem is one of the most ancient cities in the world. Archeological evidence suggests that it had its beginnings during the Early Bronze Age (3500–2000 B.C.E.), when the Canaanites first established themselves in the land. The name Jerusalem appears in ancient Egyptian, Akkadian, and other texts in various forms such as *Rushalimum* or *Urushalimum, Urusalim,* and *Ursalimmu.* The book of Genesis (Ch. 14, 18) relates that Melchizedek, King of Shalem, welcomed Abraham with bread and wine. Scholars generally feel that Shalem is none other than Jerusalem, and Melchizedek the priest-king ruler of a Canaanite city of that name at the time of the patriarchs. The origin of the name Jerusalem is not clear; it may be a compound of two elements, Yarah meaning to set up or to found, and the name of the Semitic God Salem.

Ancient Jerusalem was situated on two ridges circumscribed by two valleys, the Kidron valley on the east and the Hinnom valley on the west, so that the city could be attacked only from the north. The added factors of its being situated on the watershed between the Mediterranean and the Jordan and at the junction of main highways gave it important strategic advantages.

Before its conquest by the Israelites, Jerusalem was in the hands of the Jebusites and was known as "Jebus" or the "City of Jebus." David succeeded in capturing the city and made it his capital, partly because of its strategic position and partly because it was not identified with any of the powerful tribes. It now became known as the City of David. By transferring the ark of the Lord to Jerusalem he began the process of making it the spiritual center of the people of Israel, a process which his son Solomon completed by building there the

View of Jerusalem

first Temple. Jerusalem thus became the Holy City or the City of God, and so it has remained. After the split in the kingdom Jerusalem was the capital of the southern section, the Kingdom of Judah, and of the Davidic dynasty. Various attempts to capture and destroy it were made by the kings of the Northern Kingdom of Israel, and in 785 B.C.E. Joash made a breach in its wall. Prior to that, it had been plundered by the Egyptian Pharaoh Shishak. The Assyrian Empire, which destroyed the Northern Kingdom of Israel in the year 721 B.C.E., almost succeeded in taking Jerusalem twenty years later. Only a last minute miracle, a plague which broke out among the Assyrian forces, prevented a catastrophe. With the rise of Babylon Jerusalem's preeminence faded, and when King Zedekiah, despite the Prophet Jeremiah's objections, rebelled against Nebuchadnezzar, the latter captured the city and destroyed the First Temple in the year 586 B.C.E. By this time, Jerusalem had become the symbol of the Jewish faith. The exiles in Babylon, who never gave up hope of returning, gave expression to this faith in the words, "If I forget thee O Jerusalem, may my right hand forget its cunning . . . ."

Their hopes were rewarded in 538 B.C.E. when the Persian conqueror of Babylon, Cyrus, issued his famous proclamation allowing the exiles to return to their homeland. Temple worship was renewed in 519 B.C.E. In the ensuing centuries Jerusalem, like the rest of Judah, came successively under Persian and Seleucid rule, although it was autonomous in internal and spiritual matters. The attempt by the Syrian King Antiochus Epiphanes to enforce a hellenistic way of life on the population led to the revolt of the Maccabeans and the rededication of the Temple by Judah the Maccabee. Jewish rule was restored in Jerusalem by his brother Jonathan, and in the Hasmonean period Jerusalem again became the capital of a united land of Israel. But it was occupied by the Roman general Pompey in the year 63 B.C.E. and ruled by Herod, the Roman puppet, from 37 B.C.E. until his death in 4 B.C.E. Herod embarked on lavish building projects, including the renovation of the Temple on a vast scale (in recent years, extensive excavations have revealed something of the ambitious scope of Herodian Jerusalem). In the year 66 C.E., the Jewish population of the country revolted against the unbearable yoke of the Romans, but after a heroic resistance lasting three years and a bitter siege, Jerusalem fell. The Temple was burned by the Roman legionnaires under the future Emperor Titus on the ninth day of the Hebrew month of Av in the year 70 C.E., exactly six hundred and fifty-six years to the day from its destruction by Nebuchadnezzar. Once again, in the years 132–5, rebellion broke out, this time under the leadership of Bar Kokhba, and Jerusalem was even liberated for a time. The Romans reacted viciously and after stamping out all resistance the Emperor Hadrian ploughed the city, renamed it Aelia Capitolina, and forbade Jews to approach it under pain of death. With the acceptance of Christianity as the official religion of the Roman Empire by Constantine in the 4th century C.E., Jerusalem became a holy city for the new religion and was turned into a city of churches and monasteries.

With the rise of the Arab empire, Jerusalem became holy to the adherents of Islam as well. In the year 638 it was occupied by the Caliph Omar who set up a place of prayer on the Temple site, which was subsequently rebuilt in 691 as the Dome of the Rock. The second principal mosque El-Aqsa was built in the Temple area in the 8th century. The Arabs, acknowledging the sanctity of the city, called it *Al Makdas* (The Temple), or *El-Kuds Esh-Sharif* (The Venerable Sanctuary). For a period of almost five hundred years, Jerusalem was ruled by the caliphs until it became the main object of contention in the religious war between Islam and Christianity. The Crusaders captured it in 1099 and made it the capital of their domain in the land of Israel, which was known as the Kingdom of Jerusalem. The Crusaders also destroyed the Jewish community which had lived there under the Arabs. In 1187 the city was retaken by Saladin and subsequently remained in Moslem hands, with the exception of a few years in the 13th century. In the year 1517 it was captured by the Turks and held by them for four hundred years. Although restricted in number by the government, the Jewish community grew, reinforced by pious immigrants from many lands, especially after the expulsion from Spain in 1492.

In 1860 the first Jewish suburb, subsequently called *Yemin Moshe,* was built outside the walls of the Old City on the initiative of the English philanthropist Sir Moses Montefiore. Thus was New Jerusalem born. The new city developed rapidly and soon outgrew the old, with the Jewish population outnumbering the Arab. Initially the Jewish settlement was primarily religious in character, but soon the newcomers were active in all aspects of the city's development.

Turkish rule was brought to an end in 1917 by the British Army under General Allenby. Jerusalem became the military and civil headquarters of the British Mandatory authorities. It was the scene of Arab riots in 1922, 1929, and 1936–9, in which many Jews were killed. These riots, however, generally gave a new incentive to the Jewish pioneers, and development and consolidation went ahead. The United Nations partition decision of November 1947 provided for the internationalization of Jerusalem, but this scheme was brought to a speedy end by the attack of the Arab armies. The Old City fell to the Transjordanian Arab Legion; Jewish Jerusalem, whose 1948 population numbered some 80,000, was subjected to a terrible siege.

Despite being cut off from the rest of the country and being drastically short of food and munitions, the Jewish city held out heroically. The armistice agreement of 1949 recognized Jerusalem as a divided city with Jordan having control over the Old City and Israel over the New City, with a rigid frontier cutting the city in half. Jewish Jerusalem enjoyed a large influx of immigration; many and extensive new suburbs were built and the population more than doubled. At the same time it once again became the spiritual center of world Jewry. It housed the residence of the president, parliament *(Knesset),* the Supreme Court, the Chief Rabbinate, the Hebrew University, and the Israel Museum.

At the outbreak of the Six-Day War in 1967, despite Israel's efforts to avoid a confrontation with Jordan, King Hussein ordered his Arab legions to bombard the city as a preliminary to its attempted capture. The effort backfired, and as a result of the Israel Army's reaction the Old City was taken and the artificial division of Jerusalem brought to an end. On June 29, 1967, the Israel Government formally proclaimed the unification of the city. For the first time in 2,000 years, Jews had free access to their most sacred shrine, the Wailing or Western Wall, and the sanctity of all holy places sacred to all faiths was guaranteed. Today Jerusalem has a population of about 275,000 of whom 200,000 are Jews and 70,000 are non-Jews, mainly Moslems.

JEWISH AGENCY (FOR ISRAEL): The body set up during the British Mandate to represent the interests of the Jewish population in the land of Israel. A part of the World Zionist Organization from 1929 (the year in which the title "Jewish Agency" was formally adopted), its executive was initially comprised of both Zionists and prominent non-Zionists who nevertheless supported the development of a Jewish homeland. In time, the agency became a type of shadow cabinet of the Jewish population in the land and conducted the political, economic, and military struggle in the years preceding the establishment of the state. Most of Israel's future leaders received their early experience and training as members of the agency's various departments.

With the establishment of the State of Israel in May 1948, the agency automatically ceased to be the spokesman for the country's Jewish population. Its authority and power were now invested in the Government of Israel. It continues, however, as the body which coordinates all the assistance granted Israel by Jews throughout the world. The Jewish Agency organizes immigration, prepares for the absorption of the immigrants, looks after them during their initial stages of integration, and assists them in procuring employment and housing. It also plays an important role in education through Youth Aliyah which is affiliated to the agency. Outside Israel, it is responsible for the organization of aid to Israel, fosters Jewish education and culture, and grants vital support to Jewish youth movements. Working in close cooperation with the Government of Israel, the Jewish Agency has brought close to $1\frac{1}{2}$ million Jews to Israel since 1948.

JEWISH BRIGADE: Infantry force composed of Jewish soldiers, mainly Palestinian, which fought as part of the British Army in the later stages of World War II. At the outbreak of war Chaim Weizmann wrote to the British Prime Minister, Neville Chamberlain, offering the services of the Jewish Agency in enlisting Jewish soldiers for the British Army within the framework of an all-Jewish unit. The proposal, accepted in principle, was then deferred by the British who were unwilling to offend the Arabs. After much procrastination, the proposal was finally put into effect and in February 1945 the brigade went into action in Italy under the command of Brigadier

Jewish Brigade emblem in World War II

A. P. Benjamin. For the short period in which it fought, the brigade served with distinction and valor, losing forty-four men in action. Later, the brigade was stationed on the Italo-Austrian-Yugoslav border where it made contact with Jewish survivors of the Nazi concentration camps. The sight of the Jewish flag and at times even the mere rumor of the brigade's existence inspired many of these survivors to head for Italy and thence for the land of Israel. After the war, the growing tension between the Jews in Israel and the British authorities led to the disbanding of the brigade in February 1946. The experience gained by the Jewish soldiers, however, was of inestimable value when the Israel War of Independence broke out in 1948.

JEWISH LEGION: Jewish fighting unit which took part in the British campaign to oust the Turks from the land of Israel toward the end of World War I. The idea, which originated in Zionist circles in Europe and in the U.S.A., was actively pursued by the Zionist leaders Vladimir Jabotinsky and Joseph Trumpeldor. At first, however, the British only agreed to the formation of the Zion Mule Corps which, recruited mainly from Jewish refugees in Egypt, served in the ill-fated Gallipoli campaign of 1915–16. Not only was there

British opposition, but Jabotinsky also encountered opposition from British Zionist circles who feared that the existence of such a unit could affect the status of Jews in enemy countries. Finally, however, the opposition was overcome and three battalions with some 5,000 troops were formed. The 38th Battalion, under the command of Colonel J. H. Patterson, participated in the 1918 British offensive against the Turks. The legion was disbanded soon after the war.

JEWISH NATIONAL FUND (Keren Kayemet Le-Yisrael):

The body responsible for land development in Israel. Set up at the 5th Zionist Congress in 1901, its purpose was to acquire land in Israel which would remain the permanent property of the Jewish people. From the beginning of the 1920's, the J.N.F. began to undertake vast projects in afforestation, swamp drainage, roadbuilding, and the establishment of new settlements. It has reclaimed over two hundred thousand acres of land, planted close to 100 million trees, and built 1,300 miles of road in frontier regions and sparsely populated areas. Among its crowning achievements have been the opening up and drainage of the Jezreel Valley, the Plain of Hepher, the Plain of Zevulun, and the Huleh Basin. It has planted hundreds of forests, each named to honor a distinguished individual or group who has made a contribution to the building up of Israel. After the establishment of the state, the J.N.F. registered as an Israeli company. The traditional sign of the J.N.F., the blue collecting box, is present in many Jewish homes throughout the world.

J.N.F. at work on a new project

JOB, BOOK OF:

Third book of the third section of the Bible, *Ketuvim*. It takes its name from its central character, Job. The book of Job has been acknowledged as one of the great masterpieces not only of Hebrew but of world literature. Its theme is the age-old problem of why the righteous suffer and how to reconcile this suffering with the idea of a just and benevolent God. The book has forty-two chapters and may be divided into three parts. In the first two chapters, Job is introduced as a man of exemplary character whose righteousness and piety are unquestionable. He prospers and enjoys the benefits of those who serve God in truth. Then a member of God's heavenly council, Satan, casts doubt on Job's sincerity, claiming that were he to suffer and not prosper he would soon curse God. Accordingly, Satan is given permission to test Job's faith. Job is suddenly visited by a series of calamities which threaten to destroy him physically and mentally. Sudden hammerblows strike him, sweeping away Job's wealth and children until finally he himself is smitten with loathsome boils and reduced to the depths of despair. He nevertheless resists the temptation to curse God. Chapters 3–37 are taken up by a series of poetic dialogues between Job and his friends Eliphaz, Bildad, Zophar, and Elihu. For the most part, "Job's Comforters" maintain the traditional view that suffering is a consequence of sin and that his humiliating condition must have arisen as a result of his misconduct. Job cannot accept this proposition and insists that he is not conscious of having done wrong. In any case, his whole being cries out against a punishment that has no crime as its cause. Finally, God speaks to Job from a whirlwind, emphasizing the Lord's majestic greatness as compared with man's pettiness, his inability to understand God's ways. In Chapter 42, in an epilogue, Job is vindicated and his friends condemned. "They have not spoken of me the thing that is right," says God. Job's trial is ended and he is granted even greater contentment and prosperity than he had at the beginning.

The book of Job is one of the most difficult in the Bible and has presented Bible scholars with innumerable problems. Questions of authorship, language, and inner meaning remain unsolved. In rabbinic literature, suggestions of authorship and date range from Moses to the time of the Judges, the Babylonian exile, and the period of the Persian King Ahasuerus.

According to one sage, "Job never was and never existed, but is only a parable."

Modern scholarship tends to assign a non-Jewish origin to the book. This theory is upheld by the universal nature of the contents, the non-Jewish identity of the characters and the vast amount of Semitic words in the text. The legend of a pious man of that name must, however, have been ancient, for Job is mentioned together with two others, Daniel and Noah, in the 14th chapter of Ezekiel.

According to the Talmud, the High Priest read the book of Job on the eve of the Day of Atonement. Among Sephardim, it is customary to read it on the fast of the 9th of Av.

JOHANAN BEN ZAKKAI (1st century C.E.): Palestinian rabbi who lived at the time of the destruction of the Second Temple by the Romans. He was the pupil of Hillel and carried on his traditions. He was also one of the leading opponents of the Sadducees. Ben Zakkai emphasized the study of the Torah, and his main objective during the siege of Jerusalem, when the Romans seemed about to destroy the city and its Temple, was to insure that the great Jewish traditions of study and learning would survive. He therefore thought that war against Rome was a mistake. According to Talmudic legend, when he saw that the rebellion was doomed, he decided to escape from the beleaguered city. Unable to do so unnoticed, he got some of his pupils to announce that he had died, and they asked permission to carry his body for burial outside Jerusalem. They placed him in a coffin and, once outside Jerusalem, he made his way to the Roman general Vespasian and prophesied that before long he would become Emperor of Rome, which happened soon afterward. Vespasian asked Johanan ben Zakkai what he wished to receive from him and Johanan asked permission to found a house of study in Jabneh, a city near the sea coast. This modest request was readily granted by Vespasian.

It must have seemed a small thing to Vespasian but in fact it proved one of the momentous events in Jewish history, because under the direction of Johanan ben Zakkai, Judaism was able to survive the shock of the destruction of its religious center, the Temple. Jabneh was for a time the spiritual center of Judaism and the seat of the Sanhedrin. Johanan ben Zakkai was widely admired in his time and his work was continued by the great students who studied under him, of whom the best known was Rabbi Akiva.

JONAH: The fifth book of the Minor Prophets. A prophet by that name is mentioned in the second book of Kings as having lived during the reign of Jeroboam II, about the middle of the 8th century B.C.E. He was thus witness to the rising might and corruption of ancient Assyria. According to the story as narrated in the book of Jonah, he was sent by God to Nineveh, capital of Assyria, to warn the inhabitants of its impending destruction. Instead of proceeding on his mission, Jonah disobeys and sets out by boat from Jaffa for Tarshish. A violent storm blows up and he is thrown overboard by the superstitious sailors. A huge fish swallows him but after earnest prayer he is deposited on land unhurt. He goes on to carry out his divine mission, the Ninevites repent, and God forgives their sins and reprieves the city. Jonah is disappointed at his unexpected outcome but is rebuked by God, who teaches him that one must be tolerant even to one's cruel enemies.

The book of Jonah has unfortunately been misused and misunderstood, largely because of the fish episode. In fact, it conveys one of the most beautiful messages in the whole Bible — the creed of universalism. God accepts repentance not only from Jews but from gentiles as well who are also God's creatures and worthy of pardon if sincerely repentant. Furthermore, gentiles should not be denied God's care, love, and forgiveness.

Estimates of the date of authorship of the book of Jonah range from the 8th to the 4th centuries B.C.E. The book of Jonah is given a place of honor in the synagogue on the Day of Atonement when it is read as the prophetic portion of the afternoon service. This choice is based on the fact that repentance and forgiveness are the central themes of that day.

JOSEPH: The eleventh son of the Patriarch Jacob, born to his favorite wife Rachel. His story is related in the book of Genesis, Chapters 37–50. Jacob's obvious preference for him aroused the envy and hostility of his brothers. This jealousy increased with Joseph's arrogant behavior toward his brothers. He told tales to his father, and worse, he related to his brothers dreams of glory in which he unashamedly implied that they would one day pay him homage as their superior. At first, they plotted to kill him but instead sold him as a slave to merchants traveling to Egypt and then pretended to

their father that he had been devoured by a wild beast. In Egypt, Joseph underwent a series of trials and tribulations. At first he was in the service of Potiphar, the captain of the pharaoh's guard, who treated him kindly. But when he rejected the advances of Potiphar's wife, she falsely accused him of improper conduct and he was once again imprisoned. In prison, he correctly interpreted the dreams of his fellow prisoners, the royal butler, and the baker, so that when the pharaoh himself had unusual dreams and none of his advisers was able to interpret them, Joseph was called in. His prediction of seven years of plenty followed by seven years of famine proved correct. Joseph was elevated to the rank of Viceroy, second in power only to the pharaoh himself, and was given the authority to implement his economic policy. This resulted in Egypt's setting aside sufficient reserves of food for the years of famine. Joseph married an Egyptian woman, Asenath, who bore him two sons, Ephraim and Manasseh. When the famine came, Joseph's brothers went to Egypt seeking food. Joseph, after avenging himself by having them accused of spying, finally revealed his true identity. The dramatic encounter with his brothers was followed by the transfer of Jacob and his entire family to Egypt where they received land and grazing privileges in Goshen. Thus began the Israelite settlement in Egypt. Despite his rise to fame, Joseph did not forget his origins, and on his death at the age of 110 he left instructions to be buried in Israel.

JOSEPHUS, FLAVIUS: Historian, soldier, and politician who lived from approximately 37–100 C.E. His real name was Joseph ben Mattityahu Ha-Cohen, and he came from a prominent priestly family. In the year 64 C.E. he was sent to Rome where he remained for two years at the court of Nero. On returning to the Holy Land, he found the country seething with

Josephus before Vespasian *(medieval manuscript)*

rebellion and was given command of Galilee. He clashed with the extremist zealots, especially John of Giscala who seems to have suspected Josephus' loyalty. As it turned out, this suspicion was justified, for Josephus not only did not offer much resistance to the invading Roman forces under Vespasian but committed treachery by surrendering and then going over to the enemy. He adopted the name Flavius, the family name of Vespasian, and during the siege of Jerusalem, as a member of Titus' staff, he was employed to speak with the Jews and urge them to give up their hopeless struggle. With the fall of Jerusalem he lived in Rome and was an accepted member at the Roman court. Whether out of pangs of conscience or because he sincerely felt he was a patriot, his writings are staunchly pro-Jewish. In his day, he defended Judaism and Jews against attacks from various quarters. He wrote four works giving the history of the developments leading up to the war against Rome and of the war itself: 1) *The Jewish War;* 2) *The Antiquities of the Jews,* chronicling the history of the Jewish people from their beginning until the outbreak of the rebellion against Rome 3) *Autobiography;* and 4) *Against Apion* where he defends the Jews and Judaism against the attacks of the anti-Semitic Alexandrian writer, Apion. His writings are a main source of Jewish history of the first centuries B.C.E. and C.E., and particularly of the great rebellion from 66–70 C.E. His description of the various sects — the Pharisees, Sadducees, and the Essenes — have received added significance as a result of recent discoveries, notably the Dead Sea Scrolls. Although it has been alleged that he was unreliable, recent evidence — especially archeological — has confirmed much of the information previously known only from his writings.

JOSHUA (Yehoshua): The first book of the second division of the Bible, *Neviim* (Prophets). Its hero is the first great military commander in Jewish history and Moses' successor. His name was originally Hoshea but Moses prefixed to it the divine name *Yah*. His apprenticeship in leadership was served under Moses, and he commanded the children of Israel in their first military engagement against the Amalekites. Of the twelve spies sent by Moses to survey the land, only he and Caleb brought back an optimistic report, for which they were excluded from the punishment imposed on the rest of the people. He was thus Moses' natural successor, and Moses, before his death, laid his hands on Joshua, thus entrusting him with the task of leading the conquest of Canaan which he successfully carried out with the exception of the valley area and the coast.

The book of Joshua contains twenty-four chapters, and the contents may be divided into two parts: the story of the conquest (Ch. 1–12), and the details of the division of the land among the tribes (Ch. 13–24), including Joshua's farewell address and death.

According to Jewish tradition, the book was written by Joshua himself, with the obvious exception of the last few verses which tell of his death. Modern Bible scholars and critics have questioned this tradition. They are of the opinion that the book is not the work of one author but is composed of different documents and traditions which at a later date were combined into one.

See also: BIBLE, PROPHETS.

JUDAH, KINGDOM OF: Name given to the Southern Kingdom, comprising the tribes of Judah and Benjamin, which remained loyal to the Davidic dynasty when King Solomon's kingdom split in two after his death in the 10th century B.C.E. The secession of the ten northern tribes was followed by two generations of intermittent warfare between Judah and the Northern Kingdom, which took the name of Israel. The split had converted an empire into two second- or even third-rate powers. Judah was the weaker of the two in population, resources, and territory. This weakness was amply demonstrated in the fifth year of the reign of Solomon's son Rehoboam,

when Pharaoh Sheshak of Egypt devastated both the Southern and Northern Kingdoms with relatively no difficulty. The fighting between the two kingdoms dragged on for over half a century without reaching any conclusion. The strain on the manpower and economies of both countries must have led them to realize that further bloodshed would be suicidal. So after two generations the war ceased. Relations with the Northern Kingdom thereafter fluctuated. In the reign of King Jehoshaphat (875–851) there was close commercial and military cooperation with Ahab of Israel, while King Ahaz (735–720) was forced to appeal to the Assyrians for aid against the attacking Israeli-Aramean coalition. Judah was generally the more stable of the two kingdoms, the northern state being characterized by extreme internal instability. With one exception, the Davidic line was preserved peacefully from father to son in Judah, whereas the history of the Northern Kingdom is replete with palace revolutions, violence, and continual changes of government. Judah's population was also more homogeneous, and its relative geographical isolation protected it from the foreign influences which so often penetrated into the Northern Kingdom.

Monotheism was thus preserved more easily in the Southern Kingdom. This is not to say that heathenism was unknown in Judah. On the contrary, there were periods of spiritual deterioration and idolatrous worship as well, especially during the reign of Manasseh (692–638), whose ambition was to destroy all remnants of the monotheistic tradition. In Judah, however, there arose kings carrying out religious reformations whose aim was to restore the true worship of the one God. Two of these, Hezekiah and Josiah, are especially singled out by the Bible in this regard. To this must be added the influence of the prophetic movement, which was greatest in the south. In the end Judah became the victim of political forces stronger than herself, and of bad political leadership. When Ahaz appealed to the Assyrians for aid, Judah, in effect, became a vassal state of Assyria. She survived the destruction of the Northern Kingdom in 721 B.C.E., but was constantly involved, together with Assyria's other vassals in the area, in rebellion against that mighty empire. Against the advice of the prophet Isaiah, Hezekiah rebelled, and Jerusalem was saved only by a last minute miracle in which a plague broke out among the Assyrian soldiers. After the fall of Assyria, Babylon became the supreme power in the area. Once again the Judean leaders attempted to question her authority, and entered into an alliance with Egypt. The prophet Jeremiah, like Isaiah before him, regarded the Egyptians as unreliable and warned of the disastrous consequences that would follow. His words fell on deaf ears, and when Zedekiah, the last of Judah's kings, rebelled, the Babylonians destroyed Jerusalem and the First Temple in the year 586 B.C.E. The attempt to set up a Babylonian puppet state under Gedaliah ended in the latter's assassination in 582 B.C.E. Four hundred and fourteen years after the rise of King David, the Judean state ceased to exist, and while the exiles in Babylon were able to return after fifty years, except for the brief period of Hasmonean rule, Judah never succeeded in regaining her past grandeur.

JUDAH HA-LEVI (c. 1075—1141): Spanish-Jewish poet and religious thinker. He was born in Tudela and brought up in Toledo, then the capital of Christian Spain, where he received a broad religious and secular education. He studied medicine and practiced with great success in Toledo. Later he moved to Cordoba in Mohammedan Spain, but eventually he was seized with an irresistible longing for the Holy Land. Having completed his famous philosophical work, *The Kuzari*, he left his home, wife, daughter, and grandson to set out for the land of Israel. He visited Egypt, Tyre,

and Damascus and apparently died in Egypt before he even reached the Holy Land. However, there is a legend that he was murdered by an Arab horseman while gazing at Jerusalem and reciting one of his famous *Odes to Zion*.

Judah Ha-Levi is regarded as the greatest Hebrew poet of the Middle Ages. He began writing poetry at an early age and continued throughout his life. In general, his poetry can be divided into three classes: secular, religious, and national. From his secular poetry, one can discern that Ha-Levi's life was peaceful and serene for the most part, unmarred by disappointments or hardship. He sings of friendship, love, and wine, revealing a keen sense of beauty and a love of nature. His religious verse is marked by an intense and at times mystical love of God. His deep thirst for God knew no bounds, while even his sacred poems are imbued with a nationalistic spirit. Ha-Levi is the poet *par excellence* of the Jewish nation. The land of Israel is the focus of all his aspirations, for in exile the life of individuals and of the nation as a whole is incomplete. Judah Ha-Levi's ideas read like a modern Zionist manifesto. He sees the people of Israel as a spiritual superrace, whose mission is to be a "Light unto the Nations." But this mission can only be accomplished with the return to Zion and a spiritual redemption. The *Ode to Zion* is recited in most synagogues on the Fast of the 9th of Av. Many of his sacred poems found their way into the liturgy, especially in the Sephardi rite. In his poetic style, Ha-Levi applied the rhythmic and metrical conventions of Arabic poetry to classical Hebrew. As a thinker, Judah Ha-Levi exerted a strong influence on his own and subsequent generations. He was severely critical of the medieval school of Jewish philosophers who occupied themselves so busily with reconciling Judaism and reason. While, said Ha-Levi, there is nothing in the Bible that contradicts human reason, the Bible is, nevertheless, above reason; it is not rational but suprarational. God cannot be sought in philosophical speculation but in revelation. Ha-Levi stressed the concept of God as Lord and Ruler of history. Thus, God is known through His actions, manifested in Jewish history. In refuting the approach of the philosophical school of thought, Ha-Levi has no hesitation in using philosophical arguments himself. His ideas are expressed in his classic work *The Kuzari*, in which his religious philosophy is expounded in the form of a Platonic dialogue between a rabbi, a Christian, a Moslem scholar, and an Aristotelian philosopher. Their discussion takes place before the King of the Khazars who, after hearing the viewpoint of each, chooses to convert to Judaism in preference to the other faiths. *The Kuzari* is regarded as one of the classics of Judaism.

JUDAH HA-NASI (c. 135–c. 217): The Patriarch *(Nasi)* and undisputed leader of Palestinian Jewry during the critical period following the abortive Bar Kokhba rebellion and the end of Jewish independence. The son and successor of Simeon Ben Gamaliel, he was without rival among his contemporaries for learning and was often referred to simply as *Rabbi* (teacher *par excellence*). He was a rich man and had considerable influence with the Roman authorities, while his personal life was characterized by extreme sanctity and piety. For this he was also known as *Rabbenu Hakadosh*, our holy teacher. No one could have been better fitted for the major task for which Judah ha-Nasi earned eternal fame—the compilation of the *Mishnah*. Rabbis Akiva, Meir, and Nathan had all attempted to assemble the vast mass of oral tradition *(halakhot)*, but their compilations were divergent and not coordinated. Judah, it was said, had studied with every one of Rabbi Akiva's disciples and he had the cooperation of all contemporary scholars in bringing order into the Oral Law. For the first time, he assembled all the material according to subject matter, thereby establishing a code of laws which could guide students in their studies and teachers in rendering decisions in practical cases. After the Bible, the *Mishnah* became the basic textbook of Jewish law and thought. Judah ha-Nasi was the last of the *Tannaim*, the teachers of the *Mishnah*. His successors, the *Amoraim*, used his edition of the *Mishnah* as the basis for the further development of the Oral Law. From their deliberations the two Talmuds emerged.

Most of Judah ha-Nasi's active life was spent in Galilee, first at Bet Shearim, then at Sepphoris. He was buried in Bet Shearim, a fact which made the area the preferred resting place for thousands of Jews in later centuries. *See also:* TALMUD.

JUDAISM: To find a single definition of Judaism, with its 4,000 years of history and development, is a task which almost defies the imagination. Nevertheless, if one were pressed to give a definition of Judaism and its world outlook, one of the most inclusive descriptions would be "ethical monotheism." The concept of monotheism — the belief in one God — has a natural corollary in the belief in human brotherhood. If mankind has one father, then it follows that all human beings are brothers. Monotheism teaches the fundamental unity of the universe. Jewish ethics as contained in scriptures and elucidated in rabbinic literature teach the unity of mankind. *Shema Yisrael* — "Hear O Israel, The Lord our God, the Lord is one" — is the central religious statement of the Jewish faith. "Thou shalt love thy neighbor as thyself" is its practical outcome. Both are intricately interwoven and cannot be separated from one another. Judaism thus insists equally on the performance of one's obligations to God and to one's fellow human beings.

Until modern times, there was no Hebrew word for "Judaism" and the one coined, *Yahadut*, refers both to the religion and to the Jewish community. This is a significant duality, for the two are interdependent. From the time of the patriarch Abraham, Judaism has influenced and been influenced by external factors — no single definition has been found which is acceptable to all its adherents. Its horizons are wide enough, its vision so deep as to allow varied and even conflicting approaches. It is not correct to speak of Judaism as simply a religion, in terms of the synagogue and its ritual, the Sabbath and the festivals, and the various religious observances required of the individual. Judaism encompasses far more than mere ritual observances. It has aptly been described as "a way of life" or even a "civilization" of which religious ritual in the narrower sense of the word is only one — albeit important — part. The historian Josephus used the term "theocracy" to describe Judaism, explaining that this means "placing all sovereignty in the hands of God." In other words, God's rule encompasses every sphere of life. The word religion is derived from the Latin *religio* meaning "to bind" and if it is to be applied to Judaism, then it must be in the sense of a total binding of man to God. The purpose of Judaism, therefore, is to sanctify life and imbue every phase of human existence with a sense of holiness. Thus there is no radical differentiation between the secular and the holy, for even secular life is to be sanctified. Differences between secular and holy are merely a matter of degree; they are not qualitative or intrinsic. The legislation contained in the Bible and in later rabbinic literature such as the Talmud and the codes, covers not only what is usually included under the heading of "religion" (laws of prayer, Sabbaths, and festivals, etc.) but also civil and criminal law. Judaism is concerned with life in all its minute details. It is, therefore, as dynamic as life itself. The stress in Jewish thought is not so much on what a man

would think, but on what he must do. Unlike Christianity, Judaism never accepted that man's salvation can be achieved through faith alone. Faith is abstract, emotional, and other-worldly. Judaism is active, practical, and filled with action. In Jewish thought man is judged by his deed, his conduct, and his way of life. Not that Judaism minimizes faith, but faith must be implemented in everyday life. In Judaism, faith in God must become a living reality which is expressed in deeds and this, in Jewish terms, means observance of the commandments. The breadth of Judaism and its stress on action does not make the task of defining it any easier. Perhaps it is for this reason that attempts to formulate a coherent and systematic approach to Jewish theology have always failed. Perhaps it is simply too wide for any single definition. From the outset, Judaism has included a wide range of differing opinions and has allowed for various interpretations of its ideas, beliefs, and concepts. Thus in ancient rabbinical literature there were sages who opposed the study of mysticism and philosophy. Yet Judaism developed a rich literature and made worthy contributions to world thought in both mysticism and philosophy.

Judaism has always made provision, within certain confines, for differences of outlook and opinion. During the Middle Ages attempts were made to formulate a creed of Judaism with its own specific dogmas. The most famous of these attempts was that of Maimonides whose thirteen principles of faith were incorporated into the Jewish prayer book and are recited in some communities after the daily morning service. These thirteen principles were not universally accepted as the authoritative statement of Jewish belief. Two categories of Jewish thinkers opposed them: First, those who agreed with Maimonides as to the existence of dogmas in Judaism but who differed from him as to what those dogmas were, or disagreed about the number 13; and secondly, those who categorically denied that Judaism had dogmas. In view of this divergence of opinion among the most eminent Jewish authorities, Judaism could never be described as having a universally accepted creed or set of dogmas. It does, however, uphold certain basic principles which unite all groups and individuals within it.

The division in modern times into Orthodox, Conservative, and Reform groups, and the bitterness engendered by these divisions, had tended to blur the essential unity among believing Jews. In addition, there is no difference of opinion with regard to the ethical commandments regulating human relations. These are accepted by all groups within Judaism. The major split is the result of differing outlooks on ceremonial observances and rabbinic law. Throughout its history Judaism has maintained a delicate balance between tradition and progress, some groups stressing the former, others the latter.

To sum up, one may say that Judaism covers the widest possible range of human existence. It includes the Jewish religion in the narrow sense and the history, music, art, nationalism, language, philosophy, mysticism, folklore, and literature of the Jewish people in the largest sense. Thus it is clear that it cannot be defined. To try to limit Judaism within the bounds of a definition would inevitably do it an injustice. The reader is accordingly referred to the separate articles on Orthodox, Reform, and Conservative Judaism and to other articles in this book.

JUDGES, BOOK OF (Sepher Shophetim): Second book of the second division of the Bible, the Prophets *(Neviim)*. It follows immediately after the book of Joshua and continues the history of the struggles of the tribes of Israel to take possession of the land of Israel. The period of the Judges was one of adaptation, adjustment, and consolidation. It was also one of general insecurity and lack of unity among the tribes. The period is best described by the verse (21:25) "In those days, there was no king in Israel; every man did what was right in his own eyes." As a result of their contact with the local Canaanite population, the Israelites absorbed some of their idolatrous customs and practices. This, in turn, was followed by what was seen as God's punishment, generally in the form of oppression by one of the surrounding nations such as the Ammonites, Midianites, the Moabites, and Philistines. The people would then naturally regret their idolatrous conduct and would pray to God for deliverance. This would come in the form of a Judge who would lead a tribe, or a coalition of tribes, in battle against the oppressor and redeem the oppressed Israelites. The cycle described above then repeated itself. The Judges were not Judges in the conventional sense. They are rather to be understood as inspired leaders who, impelled to action by the spirit of God, arose in times of crisis. They were not similar or alike in character and they never led a united Israel into battle. What they had in common were personal qualities which convinced the people that God's spirit was upon them. They thereby served as a rallying force for a clan or clans in their fight against a foe. The book of Judges contains twenty-one chapters consisting of three well-defined portions: 1) an introduction presenting a view of the condition of the country at the time when the period of the Judges began (Ch. 1–2:5); 2) the history of the Judges (Ch. 2:6–16); 3) an appendix (Chs. 17–21) describing in detail two incidents of the period: the migration of part of the tribe of Dan and the crime of Gibeah resulting in the civil war between the tribe of Benjamin and the rest of Israel. There were altogether twelve Judges: six major ones — Othniel, Ehud, Barak (with Deborah), Gideon, Jephthah, and Samson; and six minor ones —

Shamgar, Tola, Jair, Ibzan, Elon, and Abdon. The period of the Judges ended with the appearance of the Prophet-Judge Samuel, who according to tradition is the author of the book of Judges.

JUDITH: Legendary Jewish heroine, whose story is related in the apocryphal book of Judith.

Judith and Her Maid *by Botticelli*

According to the story, the Assyrian king set out to "bring all the world under his empire." Naming the formidable Holofernes as his general, the king ordered him to destroy all the gods of the earth so that only he should be worshiped by its peoples. Holofernes and his army stormed through Cilicia, Mesopotamia, and the plains of Damascus. So awesome was his reputation that ambassadors surrendered their countries before Holofernes had even entered them. But when he invaded Judah and Samaria, the Jews of Bethulia offered resistance. The enemy surrounded the

town, cut off its water supply, and all seemed lost.

Seeing the seeming hopelessness of her people's situation, Judith made her way to Holofernes' headquarters and won his admiration and respect. Holofernes was very attracted to her and she easily gained his confidence. Entering his tent one night when he lay in drunken sleep, she took the sword from his side and used it to cut off his head. Then she escaped through the enemy's lines and safely delivered the severed head to her own besieged people. The discovery of Holofernes' headless body frightened the Assyrians so much that they fled, leaving much booty behind them. The Jews divided the spoils among themselves, Judith giving her share to the Temple.

Modern scholars doubt the historical truth of the Judith story, but it nevertheless inspired the imagination for centuries. The story of Judith's courage is a familiar theme in art, music, and drama.

JUSTICE: The basis of all biblical, rabbinical and subsequent Jewish legislation is the passion for justice, free, accessible and absolutely impartial — "Justice justice shalt thou follow, that thou mayest live, and inherit the land which the Lord thy God giveth thee" (Deut. 16–20).

The concept of justice as the foundation of society is inherent in the biblical exhortations to protect the interests of the underprivileged classes such as the poor, the orphan, and the widowed. "Let justice roll down as waters and righteousness as a mighty stream," is the clarion call of the prophet Amos. On the other hand, strict justice involves absolute fairness both to the rich and the poor. Not only must a judge not show favor to a rich litigant for fear of offending him, but he is also warned against giving an unjust judgment out of pity to the poor man. The command "not to respect persons" applies to rich and poor alike. Justice is one of the attributes of God given to the world upon creation. The divine name *Elohim*, the rabbis say, always refers to God as a judge, while the proper name of God, YHVH, stands for his quality of mercy. The world could not exist governed by rigid justice alone, say the rabbis; therefore, God judges His human children by justice tempered with mercy. Judges, too, are exhorted not to always reach their decision according to the strict letter of the law. Mercy and love, on the other hand, likewise cannot exist independently of justice. According to Judaism, there can be no love or mercy in a society based on discrimination and injustice. The prophet Micah sums up this idea when he says, "What doth the Lord require of thee but to do justly, to love mercy, and to walk humbly with thy God" (Ch. 6:8). Justice precedes mercy and is in fact an essential prerequisite for the latter. The idea of reward for the righteous and punishment for the wicked, so often stressed in the Bible and Talmud, is implicit in the concept of God as the judge of the world. This applies not only to individuals but to nations as well. The prophets castigated not only Israel, but other nations for their failure to be just with each other. As there is social justice, so there is international justice based on the respect for the national sovereignty and integrity of the various nations. Judaism has often been accused of being harsh and strict, and meting out severe penalties for violations of the law. Some Christian theologians have contrasted Judaism's "eye for an eye" attitude with Jesus of Nazareth's "turn the other cheek" humanistic approach. The comparison is a distortion of the truth for Judaism has always stressed love of neighbor (Lev. 19: 18) and the pursuit of peace. Where there is no justice and equality before the law, however, there can be no peace or love. Revolutions are born out of a sense of injustice and oppression. In rabbinic literature, Aaron is described as the supreme example of a lover of peace, but this love of peace led him to make the golden calf, thus shaking the very foundations of the Israelite society. Moses, on the other hand, is the prototype and protagonist of strict justice, in the view of the rabbis. Strict justice in Jewish law means that no person can be convicted of any crime unless there is one hundred percent proof of his guilt. Witnesses are made to undergo rigorous cross examination and no circumstantial evidence may be admitted even of the most convincing kind. No man is forced to be a witness against himself, nor will he be convicted as a result of his own confession. Capital punishment, while theoretically possible, was virtually eliminated. In fact, so rigid were the rules with regard to the death penalty that a court which sentenced only one person to death in seventy years was still regarded as a court of murderers.

KABBALAH (Receiving, that which is received, tradition): Term originally used to denote laws not contained in the five books of Moses but nevertheless sanctified by tradition. From the 13th century on, however, the *Kabbalah* became almost exclusively associated with Jewish mystical philosophy. Like most religions, Judaism has produced deep and probing thinkers who yearned to know more about the mysteries of life and God's nature than could be gained from a superficial reading of formal literature such as the Bible and the Talmud. Their thirst for God led them to search for hidden meanings in the words and phrases of the Bible in the hope of finding these mysteries revealed in the words of the scriptures. By the use of allegory and symbols, Bible passages, words, and stories are made to stand, not for their apparent meaning, or the story they seem to tell, but for something else of which the words are only symbols. Their true meanings are great supreme ideas and the delineation of past or future events.

During the Tannaitic period, mystical speculation of this kind is said to have been centered around the personality of the great sage Johanan ben Zakkai and his disciples. The ancient rabbis divided this mystical speculation into two main categories: 1) *Maaseh Bereshit* — the work of creation (based on Genesis 1 and 2), and 2) *Maaseh Merkavah* — the work of the Divine Chariot (based on Ezekiel 1) which is the greater mystery of the two and is concerned with the vision of Divine Majesty on its throne of glory. The vision into the truth was attained by the ascent of the soul to the heavenly spheres in a state of mystical ecstasy. This experience, known as "entering *Pardes*" (Paradise), was extremely dangerous both physically and mentally and was reserved for very special individuals only. The *Talmud* tells the story of four sages: Ben Azzai, Ben Zoma, Aher (Elisha ben Avuya) and Akiva, who entered *Pardes*. Ben Azzai looked and died. Ben Zoma looked and went mad. Aher became an apostate. Only Akiva entered in peace and came out in peace.

During the 8th and 9th centuries, Babylonia and Byzantium were centers of mystical speculation and produced a vast literature. It dealt mainly with the different *Hekhalot* (palaces or worlds) populated by angels and through which the mystic passes until he reaches the seventh palace where the divine glory is located. The vision of the divine is generally accompanied by trembling and a deep feeling of awe. The *Kedushah* prayer reflects the influence of this literature. Much importance is attached to the mysteries of the Bible and the letters of the Hebrew alphabet. This tradition was transmitted via Italy to Germany where in the 12th century the movement known as *Hasidei Ashkenaz* (the pious of Germany) thrived. The leading figure of the movement, Judah the Pious (who died in 1217), stressed modesty, otherworldliness, suppression of physical passions, and devotion through prayer. It was, however, in Spain that Jewish mysticism reached its decisive stage and developed in the form of the *Kabbalah*. The name *Kabbalah* was designed to impress upon people that this doctrine, no less than any other tradition, was received by the ancients and transmitted from generation to generation. For this reason perhaps, the classic work of the *Kabbalah*, the *Zohar* (Hebrew Splendor), which appeared in Spain at the end of the 13th century, was attributed by Kabbalists to the 2nd century Talmudic sage, Simeon bar Yohai. Modern scholarship, however, has shown that the main part of the *Zohar* was written toward the end of the 13th century by Moses de Leon, a Castilian Kabbalist who died in 1305. The *Zohar* teaches the doctrine of the ten spheres (*Sephirot*) through which God reveals Himself. God Himself, however, is *En-Soph*, infinite and beyond the grasp of the human mind which can only comprehend the *Sephirot*. The basic premise of the *Zohar* is that the material or lower world is the visible aspect of a higher spiritual world. Everything which is above has its counterpart below, and in the view of the Kabbalists, the upper world not only influences the lower world but vice versa. Man, who is the synthesis of both worlds, may, through the mystical interpretation of the *Torah*, influence the upper world and in a sense become the active partner of the Almighty.

The expulsion of the Jews from Spain in 1492 led to the establishment of Kabbalistic centers in the Turkish Empire. Chief among those was Safed in Upper Galilee. In the 16th century it became the capital of Jewish mysticism. Here such luminaries as Moses Cordovero and the famous Isaac Luria, known as *Ari*, flourished and added their own peculiar touch to already established doctrines. Luria's teachings belong to the "practical" (wonder-working) *Kabbalah* as distinguished from most of his predecessors who belonged to the "speculative" (theoretical) *Kabbalah*.

Luria, one of the most remarkable personalities in Jewish history, claimed that his doctrines were communicated to him by the prophet Elijah. Two of his doctrines influenced not only Kabbalistic thought but played an important role in the

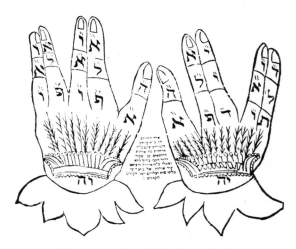

Illustration from Kabbalistic *book*

movement associated with the false Messiah, Shabbetai Tzevi. According to Luria, in the early stages of creation a cosmic catastrophe occurred in which sparks of the divine light fell into chaos. This is known as "the breaking of the vessels." Man's task is to restore the sparks to their proper place by a process known as *tikkun* (repair). Luria's esoteric and extraordinary ideas on pre-existence and the transmigration of souls were written down by his disciple Ḥayyim Vital.

The *Kabbalah* was undoubtedly influenced by various beliefs and doctrines drawn from both Jewish and non-Jewish sources. The rabbinic hesitance to allow free reign in the sphere of mystical speculation is understandable in the light of the fact that Shabbetai Tzevi's followers actually based their leader's apostasy on Luria's teachings. Thus, when Kabbalistic influences surfaced again in the 18th century in the form of *Hasidism*, a movement which extended mysticism to the masses instead of keeping it the privilege of a select few, voices were raised in warning against a possible new heresy. In modern times, the late Chief Rabbi of the Holy Land, Rabbi Avraham Yitzhak Ha-Kohen Kook (1865–1935), formulated a mysticism centered around the soul of the Jewish nation.

KADDISH: Prayer for the universal sanctification of God's name, whose central formula is "May His great name be blessed for ever and for all time." The prayer concludes with a petition for peace. The *Kaddish* is recited with slight variations during every prayer service. The half *Kaddish* is read by the reader at the end of a section of the service and he recites the full *Kaddish* after the *Amidah* prayer. The mourner's *Kaddish*, which is intended to express the mourner's faith in God and his resignation to his will, is said after the *"Aleinu"* prayer and after special psalms. For a parent or child, *Kaddish* is recited for a period of 11 months; for a wife, brother, or sister, for one month. It is also recited each year on the anniversary of a death. In Conservative and Reform congregations, female mourners also recite the *Kaddish*. A special *Kaddish* called *Kaddish Dirabbanan* is recited after study of the Talmud. It is the same as the full *Kaddish* except that the sentence beginning *Titkabel* is replaced by a prayer for the welfare of the rabbis and their pupils. The extended *Kaddish* (or *Kaddish* of Renewal) is recited at the graveside immediately after a burial, and it contains requests for the resurrection of the dead and for the rebuilding of the Temple. The *Kaddish* was already known during Second Temple times, and the language is almost entirely Aramaic. A quorum of ten male Jews *(minyan)* is necessary for the recital of the prayer.
See also: MINYAN, PRAYERS.

KARAITES: Jewish sect which arose around the year 750 C.E. Its founder was Anan ben David. The story goes that Anan, who was of noble descent, was next in line for the position of *Exilarch* (head of Babylonian Jewry) but due to his suspect religious views was refused the appointment. In retaliation he organized a separate religious sect which seceded from the main body of Judaism. While Anan's disappointment may have been the excuse he needed to justify his action, the matter undoubtedly went deeper, and reflects a deep-seated dissatisfaction with the authority of the rabbis, who regarded themselves as the sole interpreters of Jewish law. The oral law, too, had grown in immensity and had become for many far too burdensome. Anan's chief tenet was that no Jew need feel himself bound by the reasoning and conclusions of the rabbis. His thesis was "Search the Torah thoroughly," and like the Sadducees of old he accepted only the authority of the Scriptures, the written Torah. Paradoxically, he proceeded to do exactly what he claimed to be rebelling against; that is, he adopted rabbinic methods of interpretation of the Bible, together with his own explanations, when confronted with the problem of applying the Bible to everyday life, thus creating an oral law of his own. Furthermore, the second half of his thesis, "and do not lean on my opinion," while meant sincerely, led to the absurd situation in which his own disciples offered different interpretations from those of the founder of their sect. The result was division and dissension, which prevented the formation of a unified sect. The name *Karaites* (from *kara*, "a reader" of scripture), which came into being after Anan's time, was coined by Benjamin ben Moses Nahavendi, who was the first *Karaite* scholar to write in Hebrew. The rabbis avoided attacking the new sect until the advent of the great leader of Babylonian Jewry, Saadiah Gaon (died 942). The latter, in a series of devastating onslaughts, sought to exclude the *Karaites* from the Jewish community. The lines were now tightly drawn and those who identified with Saadiah in his defense of rabbinic authority and the oral tradition were called *Rabbanites*. The controversy, in fact gave the new movement an impetus previously lacking; for the need to provide an answer to a man of Saadiah's learning united the various factions and brought into the movement men of ability and scholarship. By the 10th century, the sect had acquired an unmistakable identity. with its own laws and literature. The 11th and 12th centuries witnessed the "Golden Age" of *Karaism* and during this time the movement spread to the land of Israel, to Egypt, and to Europe. Later the movement began to wane. This was partially because the *Rabbanites* were always able to produce leaders of greater scholarship and standing, such as Moses Maimonides, with whom the *Karaites* were unable to contend. Furthermore, it is highly doubtful whether their strict and literal interpretation of the Bible was calculated to bring them more adherents. For example, they prohibited the use of any light or fire on the Sabbath and were far stricter than the *Rabbanites* in matters of ritual cleanliness. They also rejected rabbinic "customs" such as *tephilin* and *mezuzah* and the festival of *Hanukkah*.

There was a minor revival among the Russian *Karaites* in the 19th century, but after the Second World War only a few thousand adherents remained in Russia and the Middle East. Most of the latter have emigrated to the State of Israel, where there were 10,000 *Karaites* with nine synagogues in 1969.

KETUBBAH (Writ): Jewish marriage document, introduced in the 1st century B.C.E. as a protection to wives in the event of becoming widowed or divorced. It specifies the obligations a bridegroom undertakes toward his bride and in rabbinic law is an essential condition of marriage. In addition to specific economic obligations, the bridegroom promises to honor his wife, work for her, maintain her, and honestly provide her with everything necessary for her comfort.

The *ketubbah,* which is signed by two male witnesses not related to the bride or the groom or each other, is read under the marriage canopy as part of the wedding ceremony. The *ketubbah* is written in Aramaic, the vernacular of the Jews of the land of Israel at the time the present text was composed. In some countries a short summary is read in the vernacular by the officiating rabbi. After the ceremony it is given to the bride for safekeeping as proof of her husband's obligations toward her.

Ketubbah *from Verona, 1655*

The document is sometimes artistically decorated. A number of *ketubbot* of great artistic interest are preserved in various museums. Reform Judaism has discarded the traditional *ketubbah* as irrelevant and in recent years Conservative Jews have introduced modifications in the traditional text.

KHAZARS: A tribe probably of Turkish origin which assumed control of the Steppe region, between the Caspian Sea and the Black Sea, at approximately the beginning of the 7th century. Their capital was Itil in the Volga delta, and at the height of their power, from the 8th–10th centuries, the Khazars extended their empire to the borders of Persia, the Byzantine Empire, the Dnieper and the Don. Khazaria lay

between two great world powers, Byzantium in the west and the Arabian Caliphate
in the south. It also straddled the main
international trade routes which brought
merchants from many lands, including
numerous Jews, to Khazaria. All three
faiths, Judaism, Christianity, and Islam,
were thus influential within Khazaria.
Judaism, however, was the only monotheistic religion not backed by a political
or military force, and this factor was
decisive in the conversion of the Khazars.
The desire to remain neutral in the struggle
between Christianity and Islam may have
been a factor leading the King Bulan and
many of the nobility to accept Judaism
which was politically neutral. Even before
the conversion, Jews were treated as
equals with all other elements of the
population. The political factors which
motivated the Khan to embrace Judaism
compelled him to maintain a tolerant
attitude toward the other faiths. The date
of the conversion has been variously
estimated by scholars as at the end of the
8th century or the middle of the 9th. The
population at large, however, does not
seem to have embraced Judaism to any
great extent, and the Jewish element
remained a minority. There were separate
courts for the members of the three faiths.
Furthermore, no specific Jewish cultural
life is known to have developed in Khazaria. At about the end of the 10th century,
the Khazars were defeated by the Russian
Prince Svyatoslav and Khazaria ceased to
exist. The Jewish settlement on the Caspian
shore disappeared.

The conversion of the Khazars kindled
the imagination of Jews throughout the
world and legends grew associating them
with the ten lost tribes. Judah Ha-Levi
made the competition between the three
faiths to convert the Khazars the central
theme of his work, *The Kuzari*.

KIDDUSH (Sanctification): Prayer recited
in the synagogue and the home on Sabbaths
and festivals. It officially proclaims the
holiness and sanctity of the day. It is said
over wine and is composed of two benedictions, one for the wine and one for the
Sabbath or festival. In the absence of wine
it may be recited over bread.

At home, the *Kiddush* is usually chanted
by the head of the family who, after drinking, gives all present a sip of the wine. In
some homes, however, it is customary for all
present, or for all males over bar-mitzvah
age, to say the *Kiddush* either in unison or
separately. The custom of reciting the *Kiddush* during services in the synagogue has
its origin in the period when wayfarers and
the poor were given their Sabbath or
festival meal on the synagogue premises.
On Passover eve, therefore, when it is
assumed that even the poorest have been
invited to the *seder*, the *Kiddush* is not
intoned in the synagogue.

The *Kiddush* is also said on Sabbaths
and festivals after the morning service.
This is known as *"Kiddusha Rabbah,"* the
Great *Kiddush*, but since it is not actually
the main *Kiddush* it may be recited over all
kinds of drink, not necessarily wine.

The origin of the *Kiddush* has been attributed to the men of the Great Assembly.

KNESSET (from the Hebrew verb "to
enter"): Israel's parliament. The present
Israeli Knesset has its origins in the *Va'ad
Leumi* (National Council of Palestine
Jewry), which represented the *Yishuv* under
the British Mandate. With the end of that
Mandate in sight, this group realized that
a new government would be needed and,
on March 1, 1948, it created the Provisional
Council of State to establish the instruments of such a government. On May 14
the Supreme Representation of the *Yishuv*
formed *Mo'etzet Ha'am* (People's Council),
which met during its first days in the
Tel Aviv Museum (the home of Mayor
Dizengoff). This body, in turn, became the
Provisional Council of State.

Chaim Weizmann was elected the first

Marriage ketubah *from Isfahan, Iran, Israel Museum*

president of the council, which governed until Feb. 10, 1949. Among its first acts were the drafting of a constitution and the repeal of the White Paper of 1939. By that repeal, the restrictions of Jewish immigration and land purchase were removed, opening the land of Israel once more to the Jews of all the world. Another of the acts of the council during its first month of existence was the establishment of a regular armed force: the Israel Defense Force. On July 8 a 13-member committee, composed of representatives of all the existing political parties, drafted a resolution calling for elections. With the elected representatives sworn in, the Knesset was born.

During the early years of the Knesset, Israel was faced with many crises, both foreign and internal. There was little time or money, therefore, to devote to the Knesset's actual meeting place. It moved from its first home in the Jewish Agency Building in Jerusalem to the Kessem Cinema and adjoining San Remo Hotel in Tel Aviv and back to other temporary quarters in Jerusalem. Finally, in 1966, it was able to move into its permanent home in west Jerusalem.

single chamber. Known as *haver* (comrade), each member must be 25 years old at the time of his election. Every Israeli citizen has the right to vote at the age of 18 and this right may not be revoked even in the case of a citizen convicted of a felony, or one who is mentally ill.

Elections take place every four years and are run on a system of proportional representation based on the total number of votes cast. Each party submits a list of candidates to the whole country and seats in the forthcoming Knesset are allocated according to the proportion of the total vote received by each party. The resulting government is invariably based on a coalition between a number of parties but unlike similar governments in Europe it may not be dissolved before its four-year term is ended. During election time parties are given free time on the national broadcasting system to present their platforms.

The official language of debate is Hebrew, although simultaneous translation into Arabic is available. Israel has no written constitution and there is nothing similar to the veto power of the American president. Nor is there any court with the

The Knesset, Jerusalem

Like the "Great Assembly," the first supreme legislative authority elected by the Jews during the Second Commonwealth, the Knesset has 120 members sitting as a

authority to declare a law passed by the Knesset unconstitutional. Bills are presented, sent to a committee for amendments, and finally debated and voted upon.

LADINO: Judeo-Spanish dialect, the Sephardi equivalent of the Judeo-German (Yiddish) dialect spoken by Ashkenazi Jews. It originated among the Jews of Spain and is based primarily on a medieval Castilian dialect combined with many Hebrew words and expressions as well as elements of other Spanish dialects, including Portuguese. After the expulsion of the Jews from Spain in 1492, the language was infused with other elements such as Turkish, drawn from the exiles' countries of residence. The first printed book in Ladino appeared in Constantinople in 1510, and henceforth a lively literature mainly religious in character, developed. The main center of Ladino before World War II was Salonica. It is still spoken among the Sephardim of the Mediterranean countries and in Israel and the Balkans. Ladino was originally written in Hebrew characters but in modern times the Latin alphabet has been used instead.

LAG BA'OMER: The 33rd day (*Lag* is composed of two Hebrew letters whose numerical value is 33) of the counting of the *Omer* (sheaf of barley). According to legend, a devastating plague broke out among the students of Rabbi Akiva during the Omer period, and ceased only on this date, which became known as the "scholars' feast." During the Crusades, thousands of Jews were massacred at this time of the year.

The whole period is therefore a period of semi-mourning in which no weddings are solemnized, and joy is kept to a minimum. These prohibitions are suspended, however, for one day — *Lag Ba'Omer*. According to tradition, *Lag Ba'Omer* also commemorates the death of Simeon Bar Yoḥai, the Talmudic sage and reputed author of the mystical *Zohar*. He is said to have escaped from the Romans with his son to the hills of Galilee, where he hid for thirteen years. According to legend, Elijah eventually appeared before them and told them that the Roman Emperor Hadrian had died, whereupon Simeon settled in Meron. He died on this date while transmitting his mystical teachings.

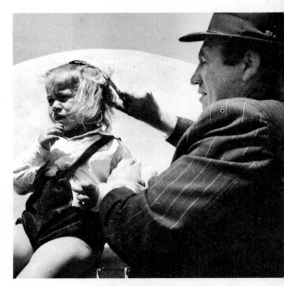

Lag Ba'Omer *haircut in Meron*

In Israel masses of people — especially Ḥasidim — make a pilgrimage on this day to the little village of Meron where Simeon Ben Yochai is reputed to be buried. The pilgrimage to his tomb is a joyous event accompanied by much singing and dancing while school children throughout the country light bonfires on this night.

See also: PASSOVER.

LAMED VAV (two Hebrew letters, the numerical value of which is 36): According to a statement by the talmudical sage Abbaye, "The World must contain not less than 36 *(Lamed Vav)* righteous men who are vouchsafed the sight of the Divine Presence." Accordingly, there arose the legend of the 36 righteous people who must live in each generation if the world is to survive. They are generally humble and unknown and their special spiritual gifts are not recognized. Numerous folk tales, legends, and stories have been woven around the legend of the *Lamed Vav*, the "secret saint."

LAMENTATIONS (Heb. *Eikha*): from the first word, also known as *Kinot* ("Dirges"): The third of the five scrolls or *Megillot* contained in the third and final section of the Bible: Writings *(Ketuvim)*. The book consists of five chapters, of which the first four deal with the calamity that befell the people of Judah and Jerusalem in the year 586 B.C.E. as a result of the siege and capture of Jerusalem by the Babylonians. The fifth chapter is a prayer for Israel's redemption. Traditionally the book is assigned to the prophet Jeremiah who warned of the impending destruction and had the agonizing experience of seeing his prophecy come true. The prevalent theme is that the destruction and desolation is the result of the sins of all the people, king, priests, prophets, and commoners alike. God's forgiveness and mercy will come only when the people repent. Even those scholars who do not accept Jeremiah's authorship agree that the vivid and pathetic descriptions contained in the book indicate that is was written either by an eye witness to the destruction or shortly after. The book of Lamentations is read in the synagogue in the evening and morning of the fast of the 9th of Av, which commemorates these tragic events.

LEVITES: Tribe descended from Levi, son of the patriarch Jacob. According to biblical tradition, they were deliberately chosen to perform specialized and sacred functions in place of the firstborn who by joining in the worship of the Golden Calf had forfeited that ancient privilege. Within the tribe, the family of Aaron was promised perpetual priesthood and his descendants were henceforth known as *Kohanim*. The other Levites were relegated to a subordinate status and restricted to the performance of secondary religious functions. These functions included the carrying of the Ark of the Covenant and the portable tabernacle during the wilderness period and, later on, the maintenance of the Temple and its sacred vessels. They also acted as Temple gatekeepers and played a vital role in the sacred service as musicians and singers. Being dedicated to the service of God, the Levites were not allotted a portion of their own when the land of Israel was divided among the tribes. They were instead spread out throughout the land, having forty-eight levitical cities set aside for them. This enabled them to perform religious and educational functions for the benefit of the people as a whole. They were supported by the "tithe" (the tenth part of all produce) which all the people were obliged to allow them; the Levites, in turn, had to present a tenth of their tithe to the priests. The destruction of the Temple meant the loss of their special position for the Levites, as for the priests. The only reminder of their former status lies in their being called second to the reading of the Torah in the synagogue, immediately after a priest.

They also pour water over the priest's hands before the latter gives the priestly benediction.

MACCABIAH: The Jewish "Olympic Games," first held in Czechoslovakia in 1929. This international sports festival for Jewish sportsmen takes place every four years under the auspices of the Maccabi World Union. Since 1932, with a break from 1935 to 1950, the games have been held in Israel.

MAGEN DAVID ("Shield of David"): The *Magen David* is composed of two superimposed equilateral triangles which form a six-pointed hexagonal star. It was adopted as a symbol by the first Zionist Congress in 1897 and is today recognized as a symbol of Judaism. It appears in synagogues, on ritual objects, and on seals of Jewish organizations. The star also represents the Red Magen David, Israel's equivalent of the Red Cross. During the Nazi era it was referred to by Hitler as a "badge of shame," and Jews were forced to wear it as a sign of identity.

The *Magen David* was not originally a Jewish symbol. It was used also by Egyptians, Hindus, Chinese, and Peruvians, and in the 9th century served as an Arab amulet. Although it is found occasionally among Jews from early times, it did not have any special Jewish connotation until comparatively recently. Its exact origin as a Jewish symbol is unknown.

The exact meaning of the shield is also unclear. The cabalists claimed that the two stars, one upright and the other inverted, represent the two worlds, visible and invisible. The linking of the two stars indicates the linking of the two worlds. Another possible explanation is that the shield represents the week. Each point, in this theory, represents a day, and the hexagon in the center, the Sabbath.

MANASSEH BEN ISRAEL (1604–1657): Dutch rabbi of Marrano parentage. He was brought to Amsterdam at an early age, and when only eighteen was appointed rabbi of the Neveh Shalom Congregation. Of a mystical turn of mind, he was renowned as a scholar in both Jewish and gentile circles. He was the founder of the Jewish printing press in Amsterdam and

The Maccabiah

Magen David *in Jewish seal*

was an acquaintance of the great Rembrandt who painted his portrait.

The rise to power of Oliver Cromwell and his Puritan movement in England brought greater religious toleration and gave rise to hopes that the Jews would again be readmitted to that country.

Accordingly, with encouragement from Jewish and non-Jewish associates and after prolonged negotiations, Manasseh Ben Israel went to London to negotiate for the formal readmission of Jews. He was cordially received by Cromwell himself and a conference was held at Whitehall. Despite the opinion of Cromwell's legal experts that there was no law excluding Jews from England, there was considerable opposition from merchants, theologians, and others. Cromwell decided not to take any official steps but from that time on the entry of Jews into England was unobtrusively accepted. Disappointed by the apparently inconclusive results of his journey, Manasseh Ben Israel returned to Holland, where he died shortly after. His mission had, however, prepared the way for the resettlement of Jews in England under much better conditions than even he had dared to hope for.

MARCUS, DAVID (1902–1948): David

"Mickey" Marcus is known for his distinguished service to America in World War II and to Israel in her War of Independence. His tombstone, the only one in the West Point Cemetery to mark the grave of a soldier killed fighting for a foreign flag, reads "Colonel David Marcus — A Soldier for All Humanity." Behind this simple epitaph is the story of one of the greatest and best-loved Jewish soldiers of modern times.

David Marcus first learned about fighting from his older brother on the Lower East Side of New York City, where Jews

David (Mickey) Marcus

were often the victims of harassment and sometimes of violent attack. As a boy he spent many hours working out in the local gymnasium to build his body, and word soon spread that this Jewish boy would not take such attacks passively.

After graduating from West Point he served with the U.S. Armed Forces in World War II, being awarded many honors, including the Distinguished Service Cross. He voluntarily participated in the D-Day invasion of Normandy Beach as one of only two parachutists who had had no previous training in parachute operations.

After the war, he returned to New York, to his wife and his law practice. But he was not to remain there for long. He soon realized that the principles for which he had fought as an American soldier were being threatened again, this time in Israel, which had just been declared a state.

David Marcus' contributions to that fight came from many sides. He arrived in Israel to find the fighting forces composed of dedicated but untrained units that had not learned to work together. He referred to these forces as fingers that needed to be knit together into a "striking fist." To do this, he wrote a 400-page military manual that became the basis of the officers' training. He also insisted that proper boots, clothing, and weapons were essential and played a crucial role in obtaining this equipment for his men.

However, he is perhaps best known for his campaign to free Jerusalem. As well as constantly attacking Latrun, the Jordanian-held key to the besieged city, he built the "Burma Road." This road, seen by engineers as "impossible," allowed food and supplies to reach Jerusalem, which before the road was completed could get these supplies only by mule, donkey, camel, and foot.

During the battle to save Jerusalem, David Marcus was made, at Ben-Gurion's request, a General of the Army of Israel — the first to hold that title since Judah Maccabee in 167 B.C.E. He was accidentally killed by an Israeli guard who mistook him for an enemy, the last casualty before the cease-fire. An Israeli housewife who had known him wrote to his wife, "Many could come, but he was the only one who came; and we will never forget."

The life of David Marcus did indeed "cast a giant shadow," and this was the phrase chosen by Ted Berkman as the title of his biography. The book has since been made into a movie of the same title.

MARRANOS: Derogatory Spanish term meaning "swine," applied in Spain and Portugal to the *Conversos* or "New Christians" — Jews who had accepted Christianity under pressure of persecution or through coercion but who secretly adhered to the Jewish faith or were suspected of doing so. The Hebrew term for Marranos is *Anusim* (forced converts), most correctly applied to those given no choice whatsoever, such as the Jews of Portugal who in 1497 were dragged by force to the baptismal font. The Spanish Marranos, who were offered the choice of baptism or death, are those who chose not to make the supreme sacrifice of martyrdom. In later generations, however, the rabbis were generally sympathetic toward their appalling dilemma and ruled that Marranos who had continued to observe Jewish customs in secret were not to be regarded as voluntary apostates, nor were those wishing to return officially to Judaism to be subjected to any discrimination.

The phenomenon of these New Christians — the first and only time in the history of the Jews that counsels of despair prevailed and large numbers accepted baptism as their only escape from a horrible death — arose out of the persecutions and violence against Jews throughout Spain in 1391. All through the ensuing century, the original number was reinforced by a constant flow of fresh converts. The group became numerous and prominent socially, economically and politically. Many continued in their former occupations while, with the religious barrier removed, many others reached leading positions in public life. Far from solving the "Jewish problem" for the Catholic Church, their conversion actually aggravated it, for they were suspected — often with reason — of secretly remaining loyal to their old religion. The old religious prejudice against the Jews, became antagonism toward the New Christians. They were attacked from the pulpit, and riots against them became commonplace. The Dominicans were especially zealous in their fanatical persecution of the Marranos and in 1480, under the influence of Tomas de Torquemada, the Inquisition was established in Spain.

The Inquisition was a Roman Catholic ecclesiastical body established in order to expose and eliminate "heresy." The earlier medieval Inquisition, set up under the control of the Dominican Order in the 13th century, had not been primarily concerned with Jews but had concentrated its attention rather on the heretical Albigenses in southern France. Its jurisdiction was strictly limited to members of the Christian Church, hence it was empowered to deal with the Marranos (but not with Jews who remained faithful to their religion). From the time of its establishment in Spain, its main purpose was to seek out renegade Marranos, although it also paid attention to ex-Moslems, Protestants, and others. After stamping out the secret Jews in Spain, it extended its activity to Portugal, whose Jews, forcibly converted in 1497, provided ample material for the inquisitors. The Inquisition was also extended to Spain and Portugal's overseas territories, its long arm reaching out to persecuted Marranos who had fled to South America.

The climax of the Inquisition's "inquiries" was the *auto-da-fe,* "act of faith," which ultimately became a great public spectacle. Here the sentences would be pronounced, ranging from flogging, banishment, and imprisonment to death by burning. At almost every *auto-da-fe*, Marranos were convicted of fidelity to Judaism. The Inquisition lasted for 350 years, for although its power had already begun to diminish in the 18th century, it was not finally abolished until 1834. It is estimated that from its establishment in 1480 up to the year 1808, over 30,000 Marranos

were sentenced by the Inquisition to be burned at the stake. The existence of the Marranos contributed in no small extent to the decision taken in 1492 by the Spanish monarchs, Ferdinand and Isabella, to expel the Jews from Spain. The Church's fanatics argued that it would be impossible to uproot the secret Jews from Spain while professing Jews remained to teach their brethren by precept and example the practices of their former faith.

Despite the many difficulties and prohibitions, numbers of Marranos managed to emigrate and reached various countries on both sides of the Mediterranean where they were able to practice their true faith freely. Later communities were established in the south of France, Amsterdam, and Hamburg. Marranos also settled in London, despite the general ban on Jews living in England. Manasseh Ben Israel's mission to London was made largely for the purpose of finding a place of refuge for Marrano refugees from the Inquisition. Fleeing Marranos set up the earliest Jewish communities in the West Indies and North America. In general, they made an important contribution to international commerce and literature, and produced many men of distinction in every intellectual field (e.g., Spinoza).

After the abolition of the Inquisition, it was thought that the Marranos of Spain and Portugal had disappeared. However, in 1920 it was discovered that there were a number of New Christians in northern Portugal who still maintained their individuality and some semblance of a now hardly recognizable Jewish tradition. A synagogue was established for them in Oporto and some of them returned to Judaism.

MARTYRS, MARTYRDOM: Those who sacrifice their lives rather than deny or disavow their faith. Such a sacrifice, even at the cost of life, is regarded in Jewish thought as the noblest and purest of acts. Jewish history is replete with countless examples of individuals and whole communities enduring torture and death rather than submitting to baptism or idolatry. The ideal of martyrdom goes back to the episode of the "binding" of Isaac in which Abraham was commanded to sacrifice his only son at God's command. Although the decree was rescinded at the last moment, Abraham's readiness to sacrifice his most precious possession on the altar of his faith inspired generations of martyrs for whom there were no last-minute reprieves. The first real acts of Jewish martyrdom occurred during the Maccabean revolt, when the Jews defied Antiochus Epiphanes' decree prohibiting the practice of Judaism. In the famous legend of Hannah and her seven sons narrated in the Second Book of Maccabees, Hannah says to her youngest child, "Go to Abraham, our Father, and tell him that I have bettered his instruction. He offered one child to God; I offered seven. He merely bound the sacrifice, I performed it." During the Hadrianic persecution, following the failure of the Bar Kokhba rebellion, Judaism was once again outlawed and numbers of saints and sages paid the supreme penalty rather than forego instructing their pupils in the Torah. The legend of the ten martyrs which is incorporated in the additional service of the Day of Atonement and in the elegies recited on the Ninth of Av graphically illustrates this episode. To die *Al Kiddush Hashem*, "for the sanctification of God's name," as the act of martyrdom is called in Hebrew, henceforth became an all-too-commonplace occurrence in Jewish history. During the massacres perpetrated by the Crusaders, whole communities committed suicide on the orders of their leaders rather than submit to baptism. One outstanding example was the destruction of the Jewish community of the city of York in 1190. Some communities began to keep memorial books (German *Memorbuch*) in which the names of martyrs who lost their lives were recorded, and a special prayer, recited to this day for "the holy congregations who laid down their lives for the sanctification of the Divine name," was introduced into the Sabbath service. During the vicious persecution of the Jewish communities of Spain in 1391 and thereafter, thousands of Jews chose life on any terms and for the first time in Jewish history submitted to baptism rather than face an agonizing death. These were the Marranos. At the same time there were others who, rather than profane the name of God, made the supreme sacrifice. Despite this major exception, Jews have generally followed the path of their ancestral faith, even when it demanded the laying down of life itself. It should not be imagined, however, that Judaism views martyrdom with relish. On the contrary, life and the duty to save life, known in Hebrew as *Pikkuaḥ Nefesh*, take precedence over all other considerations. The legal basis for the act of martyrdom was laid down at a famous rabbinic conference held at Lydda during the Hadrianic persecutions. The sages assembled there ruled that under duress, and in order to save his life, a Jew could violate all the commandments except for three cardinal sins: Idolatry *(avodah zarah)*, adultery or incest *(gillui arayot)*, and homicide *(shefikhat damim)*. Transgression of one of these three was considered the highest form of *ḥillul hashem*, the profanation of God's name. The above ruling was based on the Biblical verse, "Ye shall therefore keep my statutes and my ordinances which if a man shall do, he shall live by them. I am the Lord" (Lev. 18:5). To this verse, the rabbis add the following comment. "He shall live by them — the law was given to live by, not to die by." In times of severe religious persecution, however, the Jew was enjoined to observe every one of the lesser commandments if its observance constituted a public demonstration of religious loyalty, even if it cost him his life. The importance of preserving one's life is placed so high that some rabbinic authorities are of the opinion that he who suffers martyrdom when not legally obligated to do so has committed the unpardonable act of suicide. Rashi and Maimonides, on the other hand, exhorted the Jews of their day to have tolerance and understanding of those Jews who did not have the courage to sacrifice their lives in time of persecution. The concept of dying *Al Kiddush Hashem* is not only applicable to those who make the supreme sacrifice in times of religious persecution. The martyrdom suffered by the six million Jews of Europe at the hands of the Nazis, while not arising from a religious persecution but a racial one, is also considered a sanctification of God's name. Furthermore, all those who have laid down their lives in the struggle to establish and defend the State of Israel have sanctified God's name and brought honor to the people of Israel. Moreover, the way a Jew lives may bring either the sanctification of God's name or the opposite. To hallow God's name is one of the positive commandments of the Bible, and every member of the Jewish community is enjoined to do so by his life, and, if need be, by his death.

MASSADA: Fortress stronghold of the Jewish rebels during the Roman-Jewish war of 66–73 C.E. Archeological excavations carried out at the site in 1955–56 and, in particular, by Prof. Yigael Yadin in 1963–65 uncovered the fascinating remains of Herod's palace, evidence of the hardships of the Roman siege and also the oldest synagogue yet discovered in the land of Israel. Massada is situated on a lofty isolated rock in the Judean Desert, one mile west of the Dead Sea. It was originally fortified by the Maccabean king Alexander Yannai, and later Herod built himself a palace on the site. When the rebellion against Rome broke out in

The desert rock fortress of Massada

66 C.E., the rebel leader Eleazar ben Yair annihilated the Roman garrison and converted the mount into an almost impregnable fortress. Stores of food, water, and weapons were laid up against the impending siege. After the fall of Jerusalem in 70 C.E., the Romans turned their attention to Massada. Unable to take it by storm, they built a wall more than three miles long around the foot of the mountain, so that no one could come in or out and the defenders were totally cut off from the rest of the country. For three long years the Roman legions surrounded the fortress, constructing long dikes up which they laboriously hauled their great "siege engines," the battering rams and catapults which at last broke through the defenses. With the Roman soldiers at the very doors of the last stronghold, the Jewish defenders determined that rather than fall into the hands of the Romans they would commit mass suicide. Lots were drawn, by which ten men were chosen as executioners. Then, by a further lot, one of these was chosen to kill the other nine and then himself. Nine hundred and sixty men, women, and children thus met their deaths in heroic fashion and when the

victorious Romans broke in, the scene that met their eyes could give them little satisfaction.

Massada was the last Jewish stronghold to fall to the Romans in the war and its capture marked the final end of the rebellion and Jewish independence. The name "Massada," however, became a living reality in Jewish history, giving courage to Jewish freedom fighters, especially in modern times. The youth of Israel make regular trips and pilgrimages to the site, which has also become a major tourist attraction.

MEDICINE: Medical science has not only played an important role in Jewish thought but has always exercised a peculiar fascination for the individual Jew. In the ancient Near East, medical concepts as described in Egyptian and Babylonian texts were almost entirely magical and superstitious. Some of these ideas undoubtedly penetrated Israelite society, but as reflected in the Bible, Israelite attitudes to health and medicine were generally conditioned by the monotheistic outlook of the people. The source of life and health, as well as disease and death, is the one God. "I kill, and I make alive; I have wounded, and I heal" (Deut. 32:39). God is, in fact described as being the physician of His people (Ex. 25:26) and the medical healer or doctor is His intermediary. The obligation to resort to medical aid is derived by the rabbis from Exodus 21:18–19 where it is stated specifically that in the event of a fight between two men and subsequent injury to one of them, "He shall cause him to be thoroughly healed" — i.e., the party who caused the injury is obliged to pay the doctor's bill. In ancient Israelite society, the priests performed medical functions in those spheres which had a bearing on religious practice and belief, such as the laws of "uncleanliness" arising from contact with a dead body and, in particular, the dreaded disease of leprosy. In this connection, it is noteworthy that the principle of quarantining a person who had contracted a contagious disease was early accepted as an essential step in the prevention of an epidemic. Thus, a person suspected of having contracted leprosy was isolated for a period of time until the diagnosis became more certain; when it was confirmed, he was compelled to reside outside the camp (Lev. 13:45–46). During the Second Temple period, the existence of physicians had evidently become an established fact as evidenced from the exhortation delivered by the author of the book of Ecclesiasticus, Jeshua the son of Sira (180 B.C.E.) "Honor the physician according to thy need of him with the honor due unto him, because verily the Lord hath created him." There is a considerable literature in the Talmud devoted to medical matters and in certain spheres the rabbis demonstrated a sound knowledge of basic medical therapy. They understood the rudiments of surgery and even administered a "sleeping drug" — an anesthetic — during an operation. They also performed brain surgery and the amputation of limbs as well as being capable of treating simple fractures. Although anatomical knowledge was limited by the ban on human dissection as being contrary to Jewish law which forbids the desecration of a corpse, the rabbis' preoccupation with matters of ritual impurity and dietary laws led to their gaining a considerable insight into the subject. During the post-Talmudic period and especially after the rise of Christianity, Jewish activity in medical science diminished, as it did in most other spheres, due to the discriminatory measures imposed by the Church. With the Arab conquests, however, and in particular between the 10th and 12th centuries when Arab culture reached its zenith, Jewish physicians together with their Arab colleagues had a marked influence on the progress of medical science. Jews systematically translated Greek medical writings and a number of Jewish physicians attained prominence as medical advisers to some leading personalities of the times. Thus Shabbetai Donnolo, who made an important contribution to pharmacy, served as personal physician to the Governor of Calabria and to Church dignitaries. Ḥasdai Ibn Shaprut, a physician by profession, served as statesman at the courts of the caliphs at Cordova. The 12th century produced Moses Maimonides, who not only achieved fame and distinction as talmudist and philosopher but also as physician, serving the viceroy of Egypt.

In the Christian world, Jews were severely restricted. The Church placed great obstacles in the way of Jews wishing to practice medicine. In certain countries, laws were passed forbidding Christians from calling upon Jewish doctors. Ironically, however, many of the Popes themselves employed Jewish physicians. During the Renaissance period, the situation changed for the better and numerous Jews contributed to the medical literature and progress of the period. Most interesting of these was Amatus Lusitanus, the son of Marrano parents, who was appointed professor of medicine at the University of Ferrara and served as medical consultant to Pope Julius III. Italy was the only country in Europe where Jewish medical students were accepted freely, and for a long time, from the 12th–17th centuries, Jewish students from all over Europe flocked to the medical school of Padua.

It was only after the French Revolution and the beginning of emancipation in the 19th century that Jews were admitted to the Austrian and German universities. The results were not long in coming, for in many aspects of medical research and discoveries, Jews were in the forefront. In all branches of medicine — immunology, ophthalmology, and in particular in the pathological, bacteriological and biochemical laboratory, they achieved astounding success, and many received Nobel Prizes for their pioneering work. Some of the most important tests made in the pathological laboratory, such as the Widal test for typhoid, the Wasserman test for syphilis, and the Zondek-Ascheim test for pregnancy were discovered by Jews. The study of blood diseases received a new impetus from the work of Paul Ehrlich who discovered the drug Salvarsan. Ferdinand Cohn is universally recognized as the father of bacteriology. The accepted importance of psychological factors in the cause of certain diseases and indeed the development of the sciences of psychiatry and psychoanalysis themselves are the result of the pioneering work of Sigmund Freud, most of whose disciples were Jews. During the Nazi period, countless thousands of Jewish doctors and researchers met their deaths in the extermination camps, thus depriving Germany itself and the world as a whole of immeasurable talent. Many, however, were able to make their way to other countries, particularly the United States and Israel. In both countries they made a vital contribution to medical progress. In the United States, Jonas Salk developed the vaccine which gives immunity against poliomyelitis and Albert Sabin developed the orally administered anti-polio vaccine. Sabin later settled in Israel as President of the Weizmann Institute oi` Science. In England, Boris Chain was one of the discoverers of penicillin and Schneour Waxman discovered streptomycin.

In Israel there are various health services generally referred to as *Kupat Ḥolim* (Sick Fund). Doctors are trained at the Hadassah Medical School in Jerusalem and at the Tel Aviv University. Israel has played an important role in building up the health services of the new countries in Africa.

MEGILLAH (Scroll): Parchment scroll on which books were written in ancient times.

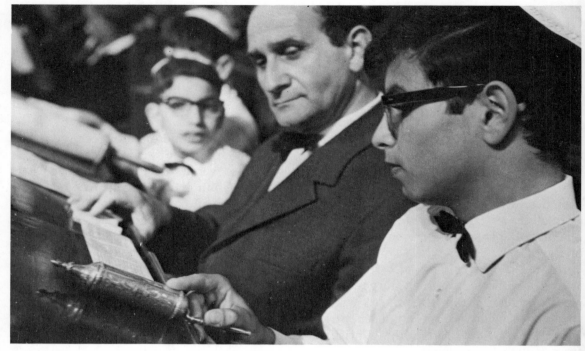

Reading the Megillah at Purim

The Scroll of the Pentateuch used for public reading in the synagogue, however, is now generally referred to not by the word *Megillah* but as *Sefer Torah*. The term *Megillah* is more specifically applied to the five books contained in the third section of the Bible, *Ketuvim*: the Song of Songs, Ruth, Lamentations, Ecclesiastes and, especially, the book of Esther.

MEIR (formerly Myerson), GOLDA (1898—): Israel statesman. Born in Kiev, Russia, she emigrated with her family to the U.S.A. in 1906, settling in Milwaukee. While studying to become a teacher, she became an ardent Zionist, taking an active part in the work of the Labor Zionist Movement. This culminated in her immigration to the land of Israel in 1921. From 1924 on, she held important posts, first in the *Histadrut* and then in the Jewish Agency. In the crucial period around the establishment of the State of Israel in 1948, she served as Ben-Gurion's secret emissary to Abdullah, King of

Golda Meir

Jordan, in an effort to persuade the latter to avoid hostilities with Israel. In this capacity she made a secret trip to Amman disguised as an Arab woman. In June 1948, she was appointed Israel's first representative in the Soviet Union where her presence inspired numbers of local Jews to demonstrate their pro-Israel sympathies, much to the displeasure of Soviet officials. In 1949, she returned to Israel where she became a member of the Knesset and then served as Minister of Labor in successive governments. In 1956, Golda Meir replaced Moshe Sharett as Foreign Minister. During her period in office, she initiated Israel's policy of collaboration with and technical assistance to many of the newly independent African States. From 1966 to 1968, she served as secretary of *Mapai* and then of the Israel Labor Party.

In 1969, she was chosen to succeed Levi Eshkol as Israel's Prime Minister.

MENDELE MOCHER SEPHORIM

(1836–1917): Pen name of Shalom Jacob Abramowitsch, Yiddish and Hebrew writer. By modern literary standards, he was the first Yiddish writer of importance and his services to its literature are inestimable. At the same time, he was also one of the pioneers of modern Hebrew literature and was regarded as the mentor of modern Hebrew writers. Abramowitsch was born in the town of Kapuli in White Russia. His father was a leading member of the community and he personally supervised the education of his son, which in addition to the customary instruction in Talmud included a thorough study of the Bible. He studied at the *Yeshivot* of Slutzk and Vilna, and after a period of wanderings throughout White Russia, Volhnyia, the Ukraine, and Podolia, he settled at Kamenetz-Podolsk. Here he came under the influence of the *Haskalah*, and became a firm believer in the Enlightenment movement, broadening his education to include secular studies. In 1858, he moved to Berdichev. At the beginning of his literary activity he wrote in Hebrew under his real name. Through his writing he aimed to bring enlightenment to his people, to improve their economic and social status, and alleviate the misery of the poorest. After ten years of writing in Hebrew, he realized that he was not reaching the mass of the people. So he turned to writing Yiddish and Abramowitsch became *Mendele Mocher Sephorim*, Mendele the bookseller. The traveling bookseller played an important role in the life of East European Jewry, bringing them knowledge and serving as a link between the widespread communities. Abramowitsch chose this symbolic character as his pen name and using a language and style which the poorest Jew could understand and the most intellectual still appreciate, he quickly widened his audience and became famous.

No other writer succeeded as did Mendele in depicting the life of East European Jews in all its aspects. He was more satirist than novelist and presented the ghetto in its entirety, without omitting a single type or trait.

Mendele regarded Zionism as just another manifestation of the Jewish propensity for daydreaming and impractical adventures. He accepted pogroms as an inevitable condition of Diaspora life which would be eliminated only by the slow progress of human civilization. However, the trends of the time did not altogether pass him by. Odessa was the center of the new growing Hebrew literary movement as well as of the movement of Jewish nationalism. Thus, in his third and last literary phase, he turned once again to writing in Hebrew.

Mendele's major works are: *The Wishing Ring, The Meat Tax, Fishke with the Crooked Legs, The Mare, The Travels of Benjamin, The Call-Up, Shem and Japheth in the Chariot*, and *Days of the Storm*.

MENDELSSOHN, MOSES (1729–1786):
Philosopher, Bible commentator translator, pioneer of the Enlightenment or *Haskalah* movement among Jews in Germany.

Mendelssohn was one of the key figures in the shaping of the modern period of Jewish history. He was also one of the leading personalities in the hard fight for Jewish emancipation. Born in the ghetto of Dessau, he received the rudiments of Jewish learning, philosophy, Bible, Hebrew language, and grammar from his father and later from his rabbi, David Frankel. At the age of fourteen, he followed Frankel to Berlin, broadening his knowledge further with the study of mathematics, Latin, French, and English. His friendship with the German poet and dramatist Gotthold Lessing enabled him to enter the intellectual circles of the day. Lessing, without Mendelssohn's knowledge, published the latter's "Philosophical Discourses," which made a great impression on the literary world. It was unusual, at the time, that a Jew should master the German language so completely, and even the king, Frederick II, made inquiries concerning this young Jew who wrote such beautiful German. In 1763, Mendelssohn won the prize of the Prussian Academy after competing with noted personalities like the philosopher Immanuel Kant, who won second prize. Mendelssohn was by now one of the most sought-after personalities, and his home became a meeting place for intellectuals, both Jews and non-Jews. Such was his standing that Frederick the Great granted him the status of a "privileged Jew," meaning that he was permitted to reside where he chose and could move freely from place to place.

Mendelssohn reached the pinnacle of his fame with the publication of his philosophical work *Phaedon*, dealing with the problem of the immortality of the soul. As a result of this work, he was generally referred to as the German Socrates. Many people visited Germany with the express purpose of seeing Mendelssohn, and famous non-Jewish scholars sought his guidance and advice. Normally, the exceptional rise to fame of a ghetto Jew could well have resulted in his assimilation and rejection of Judaism as the price of acceptance in gentile society. But not Mendelssohn. On the contrary, his position of distinction in contrast to the masses of impoverished and persecuted Jews made him feel uneasy. He was determined to dedicate his life and wield his influence for the improvement and emancipation of the Jews.

Mendelssohn, however, did not only make demands of the non-Jews. He believed fervently that the Jews could contribute toward their emancipation by freeing themselves from the shackles of ghettos. This could be achieved by studying western (in particular, German) culture and by broadening their intellectual horizons. Accordingly, Mendelssohn undertook to translate the Bible into German together with his own commentary. He hoped this would bring the Jewish people closer to the German language while in no way lessening their loyalty to Judaism. The Orthodox forces, however, objected to his translation and even attempted to have it banned. They feared that it was but the first step on the road to increasing Germanization and a loosening of the hold of the Talmud. Mendelssohn believed that there need be no contradiction between modernization and tradition. In his book *Jerusalem*, he states his religious philosophy. In accordance with the spirit of the age, Mendelssohn was a rationalist, that is, he believed in the supremacy of human reason. He regarded Judaism as the highest form of religion because it is, according to him, the religion of reason *par excellence*. The existence and unity of God, His providence, and the immortality of the soul are known to man by reason and are merely confirmed by Judaism.

Furthermore, Judaism is the most tolerant of all the religions. Unlike Christianity, it never sent missionaries to convert people of a different religion.

Mendelssohn was an observant Jew who believed that the practical commandments, the majority of which can be explained rationally, are of the utmost value in maintaining Jewish identity. Judaism is a religion of deeds and action, and its basic faith, ethics, and morality are given practical expression through the observance of the commandments. He believed that religion should, however, not be enforced by the power of law or excommunication. Judaism is compatible with the best of the modern world and its culture. Its practice therefore should be no obstacle to the granting of civil rights to the Jewish people. If, however, the price which Jews are expected to pay for emancipation is the sacrifice of their religion, they should rather forego emancipation.

When Mendelssohn died, he was mourned by Jew and gentile alike. The leading Prussian newspaper of the day declared him the pride and ornament of the country. Unfortunately he was misunderstood, sometimes inadvertently and at other times purposely, by both his disciples and his antagonists. Most of the exponents of the *Haskalah* movement stressed only Mendelssohn's admiration for German culture and his desire for the modernization of Judaism. Mendelssohn's own family (including his grandson, the famous composer) left Judaism for the most part and either embraced Christianity or became totally assimilated. The Orthodox regarded Mendelssohn as one of the founders of Reform Judaism which arose shortly after his death. From his views noted above and certainly from his conduct, this is a misjudgment to say the least.

MENORAH (candelabrum): Seven-branched candelabrum. The first *menorah* was made by Bezalel for the tabernacle in the wilderness. It was designed to provide perpetual light and its lamps were supplied daily with oil. A *menorah* was a central feature of both Temples. According to tradition, the *menorah* from the Second Temple was taken to Rome by Vespasian, carried in the triumph of Titus, and is supposed to be depicted in the carving in the Titus Arch. However, in recent years it has been shown that this was not the real *menorah*, for it is quite different in appearance from the real *menorah* illustrated in a crude but contemporary drawing unearthed in the Old City of Jerusalem.

In the 1st century C.E., the *menorah* was considered the main symbol of the Jews and was often carved or drawn on tombs and monuments.

Another candelabrum of great significance in Jewish life is the one used at *Ḥanukkah* for lighting the candles. This one, however, has eight candles. It developed late in Jewish history in imitation of the seven-branched *menorah*, and has been the subject of much artistic decoration.

The *menorah* was adopted as the official emblem of the State of Israel. Its official form is that of a seven-branched candelabrum between olive branches.

Menorah *engraving at Kfar Naḥum synagogue*

MERON: Settlement in lower Galilee. Meron is the traditional burial place of

Synagogue remains, Meron

Rabbi Simeon Bar Yoḥai and his son Eleazar. Bar Yoḥai, who lived in the 2nd century C.E., was forced to flee the Roman oppressors and according to legend he spent thirteen years living in a cave. During this time he is reputed to have written the *Zohar,* the standard work of the *Kabbala.* Sixteenth century *Kabbalists* from Safed made the festival of *Lag Ba'Omer* the occasion for a mass pilgrimage to Bar Yoḥai's tomb. The custom has survived until today, with thousands of Jews participating in the pilgrimage with singing and dancing. Among some Orthodox groups, the festival is made the occasion for their children's first haircut.

A religious settlement was established in 1949 at the foot of the nearby Mount Meron.

MESSIAH: The term Messiah (in Hebrew *Mashiaḥ,* from which the English is derived) means "the anointed." It was originally used to describe anyone entrusted with a divine mission, such as a king, a prophet, or a priest. Even the non-Jewish King Cyrus, who was chosen by God to conquer Babylon, is described in the Bible as the "anointed" (Isaiah 45:1). It was only after the Babylonian exile that there arose the idea of a divinely elected descendant of the house of David who would redeem Israel and bring about the ingathering of its exiles in their own land. This idea was associated with the concept of the "end of days," expressed in earlier prophecies by Isaiah and Micah. Thus there evolved the concept of the Messiah who would not only redeem Israel but would also usher in the Messianic Era, the epoch of universal peace in which "Nation shall not lift up Sword against Nation" and in which the sovereignty and oneness of Israel's God would be recognized by all. During the period preceding the destruction of the Second Temple and the intensification of Roman persecution, Messianic enthusiasm and speculation grew. The Pharisees generally regarded the Messiah as the ideal human being. No superhuman qualities were ascribed to him and he was not expected to perform miracles. In fact, the performance of such miracles was not considered by the rabbis as proof of Messiahship. Furthermore, the advent of the Messiah was not expected to change the nature of man or the course of nature. The only change to be expected was that God's unity and sovereignty would be acknowledged by all and that justice and equality would flourish. The rabbis expressed this principle in the maxim "There

Esther megillot *from the collection of the Israel Museum*

is no difference between the present time and the days of Messiah except for the yoke of Kingdoms," i.e., the restoration of Israel's independence. In other circles such as the Dead Sea Community, however, the Messianic concept was given a far more other-worldly emphasis. The stress was not on national redemption but on the advent of the Kingdom of God and the Day of Judgment. This Day of Judgment idea went much further than that expressed by the prophets who saw it as a day of judgment over the peoples who oppressed Israel, or over Israel itself. It came to mean a judgment of all men which only the righteous would escape. In some circles, a supernatural redeemer known as the "Son of Man" was awaited. Jesus of Nazareth and the early Christians were undoubtedly influenced by these groups in their development of a Messianic philosophy. Immediately preceding and following the destruction of the Temple, the belief was rife that the end of the world was imminent, and many who fought in the war against Rome were convinced that they were engaged in the final battle of God which would be followed by the Messianic Era. Judaism in general accepted the Pharisaic concept of the Messiah as an ideal human being, observing God's commandments and fighting for the political redemption of the people. When Bar Kokhba, who never made any Messianic claims, led the rebellion against Rome, Rabbi Akiva hastened to proclaim him the Messiah.

Maimonides restates the Pharisaic-rabbinic views and belief in the coming of the Messiah as the twelfth of his thirteen principles of faith. This Messianic belief was enshrined in the daily prayers and, through them, in the hearts of the people who in times of suffering and distress found consolation in the thought that their suffering might be only a prelude to a better future. They believed that what they were experiencing were, in the words of the rabbis, "the birth-pangs of the Messiah."

In modern times, the European-Jewish martyrs of the holocaust actually went to their deaths singing, "I believe with perfect faith in the coming of the Messiah, and though he tarry I daily hope for his coming."

The Messiah concept has also brought misfortune and disillusion. The suffering of the Jewish people has always made them yearn for the coming of the Messiah. In times of trial and stress, therefore, they have been psychologically ripe for the appearance of pretenders claiming to be the Messiah. From time to time these false Messiahs set the people agog, kindled their imagination, and awakened in them boundless enthusiasm. This could only be followed by an inevitable let-down and disillusion. The Legend of the Messiah, the son of Joseph, served to confuse the issue. According to this idea, there will arise a dynamic God-inspired leader who will lead the people in battle against their enemies and attempt to conquer the Holy Land. He himself will be killed, but immediately following his death the Messiah, Son of David, will appear and usher in the long-awaited Messianic Era. The history of false Messiahs is as old as the Messiah idea itself, the first claims being made in the stormy period before the destruction of the Temple, and the last in the Yemen as recently as 1889. Some claimed to be Messiah, the son of Joseph, others Messiah, the son of David; all of them created havoc and spiritual chaos. In the 5th century a pretender, Moses of Crete, was drowned with a large number of followers while attempting to pass through the sea to the mainland. The fall of the Byzantine and Persian Empires in the 7th century brought to the fore various Messianic aspirants. One of them, Abu Isa al-Isfahani, led his followers in battle against the Caliph and was killed. The First Crusade (1096) which inaugurated an era of unprecedented anti-Jewish outbreaks, led to a spate of Messianic pretenders. In 1147, the legendary and spectacular David Alroy appeared, proclaimed himself Messiah, staged a revolt against the Sultan, and promised his supporters that he would establish an independent kingdom in Jerusalem. The list of false Messiahs is long and the end result always the same — failure and disappointment. The most remarkable and famous of all the false Messiahs was Shabbetai Tzvi, to whom a special article is devoted. He set the whole Jewish world aflame and even great rabbis and scholars were among his enthusiastic supporters. His conversion to Islam created shockwaves throughout the Diaspora but even that did not disillusion some of his followers who continued to believe in him and even justify his actions.

The failure of Shabbetai Tzvi created a backlash against the Messianic concept. This was reinforced in the 18th and 19th centuries by the rise of the *Haskalah*, the Jewish rationalist movement, and then by the development of Reform Judaism which replaced the idea of a personal Messiah with the belief in the advent of a Messianic era of peace and goodwill among all mankind. Then, there would take place "the unity of all men as the children of God in the confession of the One and Sole God."

The burning desire of the Jewish people for redemption has not been dampened, and the Zionist Movement has been described by some as a secular form of Messianism. Even in certain Orthodox circles, the establishment of the State of Israel is regarded as the "Beginning of the Redemption."

MEXICO: Marranos accompanied the Spanish conquerors to Mexico in the 16th century, only to be followed soon after by the Spanish Inquisition, which sought them out and burned some of them at the stake. The first *auto da fe* in America took place in Mexico in 1574. In time, the Marranos became absorbed into the Mexican population. There exists to this day a small group calling themselves "Mexican Indian Jews" who claim to be descendants of the Marranos, although more probably they are descended from converted Indians. They look like Indians or *mestizos* and conduct services in Spanish but include a few prayers and benedictions in Hebrew.

The present Mexican-Jewish community became sizeable only after World War I when there was a large immigration from eastern Europe and a smaller one from Syria. Of the country's 30,000 Jews, the majority are of eastern European descent. The second largest element are *Sephardim* and there is a smaller number of German Jews. Most of the Jews live in Mexico City, earning their living in commerce, light industry, and in the professions. The community is a prosperous one and has played a large part in the industrial development of the country. There are separate *Ashkenazi* and *Sephardi* community organizations, but there is also an overall Jewish representative body, the Comité Central Israelita de Mexico. Mexican Jewry boasts of the best organized and most flourishing Jewish educational system in Latin America, attended by the great majority of Jewish children. There are Jewish day schools, *Yeshivot*, a teachers' seminary and ten Jewish newspapers and periodicals. Aside from a short period during the 1930's, Mexican Jewry has not suffered from anti-Semitism and enjoys full political and civic freedom.

MEZUZAH (Doorpost): A small roll of parchment on which a scribe has written the first two paragraphs of the *Shema* (Deut. 6:4–9, 11:13–21). The parchment is placed in a tube like case of wood or metal with a small opening in the back through which the word. *Shaddai* (Almighty), inscribed on the back of the scroll, can be seen. The case is then fixed to the upper part of the right doorpost of all living rooms in a Jewish dwelling. It is placed about a third of the way down from the top in a slanting position so that the upper part inclines toward the house or room. The writing of the scroll may only be undertaken by a qualified scribe, and is carried out with the same care as the writing of a Torah scroll. The purpose

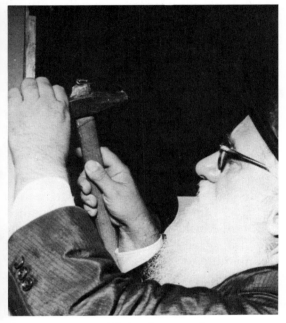

Affixing the mezuzah

of the *mezuzah* is to fulfill literally the biblical command contained in the first paragraph of the *Shema*: "And Thou shalt write them (the words of the Torah) upon the doorposts of thy house and upon the gates." The *mezuzah* has been regarded as a sort of good luck charm designed to ward off evil spirits. Whatever its origin, the *mezuzah* has become the distinctive mark of the Jewish home, and a continual reminder to the family of God's presence. Among extremely pious Jews it is customary to kiss the *mezuzah* or to touch it and kiss the finger with which it was touched, on entering or leaving the house.

MIKVEH ("Gathering," especially of water): Ritual bath used for the purification of objects or persons that have contracted some form of ritual impurity. In biblical times, it was used on recovery from leprosy, after menstruation, or after contact with a corpse. It was also used by the High Priest on the Day of Atonement. Although many of the rules of impurity no longer apply, the *mikveh* is still used in Orthodox circles, namely by women after childbirth and menstruation, by converts to Judaism, and by certain *Hasidim* and other pious Jews on the eve of Sabbath and festivals. In order to be fit for use, the *mikveh* must contain sufficient water to cover the body of an average-sized person and the source of the water must be a natural spring, rain, or water obtained from the melting of ice. Drawn water may be added only after the minimum requirement of approximately one hundred and eighty-five gallons of "living water" has been met.

MISHNAH (repetition, learning): A legal codification of the laws *(halachot)* that comprise the Oral Law. These *halachot* formed the body of learning taught in the rabbinical academies and learned off by heart. Throughout the generations, the *halachot* were preserved and added to without ever being written down, and inevitably divergences occurred between the *mishnot* of different rabbis and their schools.

At the time of the religious reconstruction that followed the destruction of the Second Temple, the need for a comprehensive, definitive *Mishnah* became overwhelming and the rabbis of the time (known as the *Tannaim*) began to undertake the task of compiling and editing the Oral Law. The first written *Mishnah* was the work of Rabbi Judah ha-Nasi (*Nasi* meaning president of the Sanhedrin), who collected the different existing *mishnot*, put them into systematic order according to subject and resolved the conflicts between different opinions.

The *Mishnah*, written in rabbinic Hebrew, is divided into six Orders *(sedarim)*, each one again divided into tractates *(masechtot)* which, in turn, are made up of chapters *(perakim)* and verses *(mishnayot)*.

The six Orders of the *Mishnah* include:
1) *Zeraim* (seeds), laws pertaining to agriculture, taxation, and charity.
2) *Moed* (festivals), laws pertaining to the Sabbath and the various festivals and holidays.
3) *Nashim* (women), laws pertaining to marriage and divorce and relations between husband and wife.
4) *Nezikim* (damages), laws pertaining to civil and criminal law.
5) *Kodeshim* (holy things), laws pertaining to sacrifices and services in the Temple.
6) *Taharot* (purification), laws pertaining to purity and impurity.

Subsequent discussion and expounding of the *Mishnah* by the rabbis is recorded in the *Gemarah* (interpretation or commentary on the *Mishnah*). Together, *Mishnah* and *Gemarah* comprise the Talmud.

MITZVAH (pl. Mitzvot): Meaning a precept or commandment of the Jewish religion and including the religious and moral obligations incumbent upon every Jew. Although the Torah (the 5 books of Moses) only mention 613 *mitzvot* directly (248 positive commandments and 365 negative), thousands of other *mitzvot* are included in both the Written and the Oral Law.

A *mitzvah* added by the rabbis of past generations must be observed as meticulously as one given directly by God.

The bar-mitzvah and bat-mitzvah ceremonies celebrated throughout the Jewish world when boys and girls reach the ages of 13 and 12 respectively, symbolize their having reached the age of personal liability when each person becomes responsible for his own observance of the *mitzvot* and avoidance of *averot* (sins).

The *mitzvot* encompassed in the Written and Oral Law together cover every facet of Jewish life, from the most commonplace acts to the sublime.

MONTEFIORE, SIR MOSES (1784–1885): One of the most prominent Jews of the 19th century. He was the best-known member of an English Sephardi family of Italian origin. As a stockbroker, he amassed a fortune and was able to retire from business at the age of forty. He devoted the rest of his life to philanthropy, with special stress on the plight of persecuted Jewish communities abroad and the welfare of the Jews in the Holy Land to which he paid seven visits, the last at the age of ninety. The first Jewish Quarter to be built outside the walls of Jerusalem was pioneered by Montefiore in 1855 and subsequently was named "Yemin Moshe." At the same time, he purchased land near Jaffa and financed the planting of citrons, but the experiment proved unsuccessful. He originated the idea of a Jewish chartered company for the development of the land of Israel. Montefiore achieved international prominence in 1840 when he undertook a mission to the Middle East on behalf of Jews in Damascus who had been accused of ritual murder. Together with a French Jewish philanthropist and statesman, Isaac Adolphe Cremieux (1796–1880), he succeeded in having the charges dropped and in obtaining a statement from the Sultan of Turkey condemning the ritual murder trial. Successively in Russia, Morocco, Rumania, and Italy, he intervened on behalf of oppressed Jewry, and was everywhere treated with the respect due to an official British representative, although he did not bear such a title. Montefiore was universally recognized as the leader of Anglo-Jewry, and served as President of the Board of Deputies of British Jews from 1838 to 1874. He was knighted by Queen Victoria.

MOSES: Prophet, law-giver, and architect of Jewish nationhood. The son of Amram and Jochebed of the tribe of Levi, his birth and youth have, as with many great leaders, been surrounded by a halo of legend and mystery.

According to the biblical story, his mother hid him at birth because of the Egyptian decree that all Hebrew male children were to be cast into the Nile. When she could no longer hide him, she placed him at the river's edge in a water-tight basket made from bulrushes. The Egyptian ruler's daughter saw the ark and had mercy on the infant. Moses' sister Miriam, who was conveniently posted near the scene, offered to have the infant nursed by a Hebrew woman (in this case, his own mother), and then returned to the princess for adoption.

Thus the future agent of Israel's deliverance grew up in the very court and atmosphere with which he was destined to clash. His story might well have ended

Moses with the Tablets of the Law, *by Lesser*

Finding of Moses *(18th cent.* Haggadah*)*

with his life at the court but for the prophetic sense of justice with which Moses was endowed, a sense of justice which led him to identify himself with his oppressed brethren. One day, seeing an Egyptian official strike a Hebrew slave, he intervened on the slave's behalf and killed the Egyptian. Quite obviously this action could not remain a secret, and Moses was forced to flee from Egypt to save his own life.

His deep sense of justice was not limited to his brethren only. When he arrived in Midian he defended the daughters of the Midianite priest Jethro against bullying shepherds, and thereby earned Jethro's gratitude. He married Jethro's daughter, Zippora, who bore him two sons, Gershom and Eliezer. He spent many years in Midian, and, while in the desert shepherding Jethro's flock, Moses' spirit matured. When Moses was eighty, God revealed himself to him in a burning bush that was not consumed and entrusted him with the mission of liberating his people from slavery. Moses at first demurred, claiming that he was not worthy of the task. Furthermore, he protested, a speech impediment prevented him from fulfilling the tasks of statesmanship. Only when God agreed to appoint his brother Aaron as his collaborator and spokesman before Pharaoh, did Moses reluctantly accept the divine mission. Together with Aaron, he embarked upon the campaign for the liberation of the Israelites. The task was not easy, for not only did they meet with intransigence on Pharaoh's part, they also had to overcome the opposition of the children of Israel themselves, whose will to fight had been weakened by years of slavery. The knowledge that they were the bearers of a divine mission, coupled with God's active intervention on behalf of his people in the shape of the ten devastating plagues in Egypt, helped them to overcome all obstacles. The Pharaoh who stubbornly refused to heed the clarion call, "Let my people go," was finally reduced to begging the children of Israel to leave. Despite a temporary change of heart on Pharaoh's part, the Exodus proceeded, and culminated in the miraculous crossing of the Red Sea (the Sea of Reeds).

The Exodus from Egypt, however, was only a stepping-stone on the way to the Promised Land. Moses' ambition was to make of his people a holy nation and a kingdom of priests. At Mount Sinai, God revealed Himself to the whole people and proclaimed the Ten Commandments; and Moses, in a solemn covenant, bound the people of Israel to God. Moses then ascended the mountain to receive the Tablets of the Law, and spent forty days in the presence of God who according to Jewish tradition also gave him the Oral Law. On descending, he found that the people, impatient with his absence, had made a golden calf to worship. In his anger, he smashed the tablets. The un-

enviable task of turning a horde of slaves into a Chosen People was a heavy burden. Their incessant complaints and murmurings drove Moses to fits of anger, some justified, others not. Throughout the years of wandering, he was confronted with the stubbornness of a "stiff-necked people" who at times even wished to return to Egypt. There were also acts of outright rebellion, as in the case of Korah and his followers. Like most leaders, Moses was the subject of malicious gossip, even on the part of his own brother and sister. When the people accepted the pessimistic report of the spies sent ahead to investigate the land of Canaan, Moses realized that the generation of the wilderness was not yet ready to conquer the land. Only a new generation, born in freedom, would be able to fulfill the mission of conquest. Despite Moses' disillusionment with the people, his sense of justice and mercy triumphed over his despair; and when God wished to destroy the people, Moses interceded on their behalf. Moses himself was not vouchsafed the privilege of leading the people into the Promised Land. He had sinned by striking the rock to bring out water instead of speaking to the rock as instructed by God. The punishment may well have been out of proportion to the deed, but God's decision was final and no amount of imploring by Moses could change it. He lived to see the conquest of Transjordan, and before his death appointed his loyal and carefully-groomed successor, Joshua, to lead the people. In his last public address, he summarized the events of the preceding forty years, blessed the people, and gave them guidance for their life in Canaan. He died at the age of 120, and the place of his burial was purposely kept unknown, so as to prevent pilgrimages to his grave and the consequent attachment of a cult to his person.

In Jewish tradition, Moses, though a mortal and fallible being, remains basically the "Servant of God." He is *Moshe Rabbenu*, Moses our Master, who made monotheism the property of the people as a whole. Whereas before his time it had been nurtured by the patriarchs, it was Moses who gave it form and substance. No biblical personality has been the subject of as many legends and commentaries as Moses. Moses was the greatest of the prophets who alone among men knew God "face to face." This belief was enshrined by the great medieval Jewish philosopher, Moses Maimonides, in his thirteen principles of faith, the seventh of which states, "I believe with perfect faith that the prophecy of Moses our teacher, peace be unto him, was true, and that he was the chief of the prophets, both of those that preceded and of those that followed."

MOSES BEN MAIMON, known as MAIMONIDES, or popularly by the initials of his name: RAMBAM (*Rabbenu Moshe Ben Maimon*); (1135–1204): Talmudist, philosopher and physician. Born in Cordoba, Spain, Maimonides spent his youth and received his initial Hebrew and secular education in the enlightened atmosphere of Moorish Spain. He was, in a way, the last product of the "Golden Age" of Spanish Jewry. When he was 13, Cordoba was captured by the Almohades, a fierce, intolerant, and fanatical sect who would not tolerate the slightest deviation from the Koran. Maimonides, together with his family, was forced to flee, first to Fez in Morocco, then in 1165 to the land of Israel. After a period of extreme hardships and severe suffering, he settled finally in Fostat (Old Cairo). Although he was yet to undergo much hardship and personal tragedy — including the drowning at sea of his younger brother and the loss of the family fortune — Maimonides had at last found a place conducive both to his studies and work, and a Jewish community worthy of his leadership. Here it was that he made his mark as a physician, eventually,

in 1170, being appointed physician to the ruler of Egypt. He was the author of many medical works and was one of the leading authorities on medicine in this time.

In view of the turbulent conditions of his life, it is remarkable that Maimonides managed to produce such a prolific spate of writing. Moreover, his versatility in so many different spheres of knowledge, each of which he conquered, reaching the level of a specialist, is astounding. Maimonides undoubtedly had the most comprehensive mind of medieval Jewry, and his range of scholarship was encyclopedic. It encompassed the Bible and the Talmud, mathematics, astronomy, ethics, philosophy, and medicine. His mark on Hebrew and world culture, however, was made by his three greatest and best-known works: the commentary on the *Mishnah*, concluded in 1168; the *Mishneh Torah*, completed in 1180; and the great philosophical work *Guide of the Perplexed (Moreh Nevukhim)*, completed in 1190.

The commentary on the *Mishnah* helped to bring this work to the level of the people. It states its legal decisions in addition to its beliefs and doctrines, clearly and precisely. It was indeed a pioneering work. By virtue of this commentary, Maimonides has been aptly described as the great popularizer of the *Mishnah*. This work, however, was but a prelude to his great rabbinic work known as *Mishneh Torah* (The Second Torah) or *Yad ha-Ḥazakah* (The Mighty Hand). This was the only one of his works written in Hebrew. All his other works were written in Arabic because he wanted his ideas and thoughts to reach Jews who were no longer able to understand Hebrew. The *Mishneh Torah* is a complete codification and summary of biblical and rabbinic law, religion, and ethics. It arranges the mass of Jewish law contained in the "sea of the Talmud" in an orderly fashion. Only a man widely acquainted with Talmudic law, possessing an exceptionally keen and analytical mind, could have undertaken such a task. The code, which Maimonides divided into fourteen books, revolutionized rabbinic learning.

The *Guide of the Perplexed,* the third and last of Maimonides' major works, is an outline of the writer's philosophy of Judaism. Maimonides' purpose was literally to help those who had studied both Judaism and philosophy and were perplexed by what seemed to be contradictions between the two. Maimonides, who greatly admired the great Greek philosopher Aristotle, proceeds analytically to solve the problems that worried thinking Jews in his time. In only one major point does he disagree with Aristotle and that is over the latter's concept of the eternity of the universe. Maimonides takes the traditional Jewish standpoint that the world was created by God. He develops a completely spiritual concept of God and regards as heretical the attempt to depict the Almighty in physical terms. All such references in the Bible, he claims, are metaphors, descriptive accounts designed to bring God closer to the masses of people who find it difficult to comprehend the idea of a purely spiritual deity.

With the appearance of the *Guide,* Maimonides became universally famous. It became a standard theological reference and text book. Great Christian scholars such as Albertus Magnus (1193–1280), Thomas Aquinas (1225–1274), and Roger Bacon (1214–1294) studied the *Guide* and adopted many of its biblical interpretations. Maimonides had his opponents and critics. The *Mishneh Torah* and the *Guide* provoked a furor and criticism in certain circles. One of his greatest critics was Rabbi Abraham ben David of Posquieres (1125–1198), whose critical comments on the *Mishneh Torah* appear in the printed edition of the code.

Exception was taken to the fact that Maimonides did not mention his Talmudic sources when giving a legal decision, and that he seemed to regard the code as a replacement for the Talmud. After the appearance of the *Guide,* controversy once again broke out. Maimonides was accused of sacrificing Judaism to philosophy and of excessive rationalization. After his death the Jewish world was divided into two camps, pro- and anti-Maimonides. The controversy lasted a century and was accompanied by bitter recrimination, threats of excommunication, and even by attempts to burn Maimonides' works. The controversy ended only in 1305. With the passing of time, however, Maimonides' greatness and authority were accepted by all. His versatility enables him to mean something to everyone. In Orthodox circles, stress is laid on Maimonides as a rabbinic scholar who upheld the authenticity of Jewish tradition. To other more rationalist groups, he is the philosopher of Judaism *par excellence.* He is one of those rare figures whose influence seems to increase with the passing of time. It is no wonder that the proverb comparing him to the Biblical Moses ("From Moses unto Moses there was none like Moses") became widespread. After his death, his body was brought to the land of Israel and he is buried in Tiberias where his tomb attracts many pilgrims.

See also: THIRTEEN PRINCIPLES OF FAITH, GOD.

MOSES BEN NAHMAN, also known as NAHMANIDES or by the popular abbreviation RAMBAN, from the initials of his name, *Rabbenu* Moshe Ben Nahman (1194–1270): Talmudic scholar and Bible commentator. Nahmanides was rabbi of the important Spanish community of Gerona (in Aragon), but his unrivaled Talmudic and biblical scholarship made him the recognized spiritual leader of Spanish Jewry as a whole. His commentary on the Bible became highly popular and his mystical approach struck responsive chords for many generations.

Naḥmanides' great spiritual stature came to the fore when he represented the Jewish community in the public disputation with the apostate Pablo Christiani, held in the presence of the king in Barcelona in 1263 (see DISPUTATIONS). Although he had been promised that he would not be harmed, the humiliating defeat administered to Pablo Christiani was a blow to the Church's pride and Naḥmanides was accused of blasphemy. As a result, he was forced to leave Spain, and after a period in Castile and southern France he went to the land of Israel, settling in Acre in 1267.

Naḥmanides had stressed the importance of the settlement of the land of Israel, regarding it as one of the positive precepts of the Bible, and he was distressed at the desolation and poverty he found there.

He accordingly devoted all his energy to the rebuilding of the Acre Jewish Community, and it was there that he wrote his famous Bible commentary.

MOURNING: From the outset, Judaism recognized as legitimate the human need to express grief at the loss of a near relative. Mourning was regarded as an obligation honoring the deceased as well as an emotional outlet for the bereaved. The earliest mention of mourning in the Bible is in connection with Sarah's death and the steps taken by Abraham to honor her memory (Gen. 23:2). The Bible also mentions the various periods of mourning observed on the death of personalities such as Jacob, Moses, and Saul. Mourning customs practiced in the ancient Near East, such as rending the garments and covering the head with ashes and wearing sackcloth, were also adopted by the people of Israel. However, other customary demonstrations of unbridled grief such as cutting the flesh or tearing out the hair were prohibited. Mourning customs were also practiced in times of national tragedy.

As finally crystallized, the laws of mourning begin with an initial period of intense grief which gradually lessens in intensity over the course of a year. These laws apply to seven blood relatives: a mother, father, brother, sister, son, daughter, and spouse. They take effect after the burial. Prior to that, the mourner is referred to as an *Onen* and as such may not eat meat or drink wine, and is occupied with the approaching funeral. On returning from the funeral the first meal, consisting of hard boiled eggs, is provided by friends. This meal is referred to as *Seudat Havraah*. The first seven days complete the most intense period of mourning, commonly referred to as *Shivah* (i.e., "seven"). During this period, the mourner is forbidden to shave or cut his hair, to bathe, to use make-up, to leave his home, to study *Torah* (with the exception of the laws of mourning and the books of Job and Lamentations), and for the first three days he should not greet another person. Services are held in the house of mourning and it is customary to comfort the mourner with the formula, "May the Almighty comfort you together with all those who mourn for Zion and Jerusalem." In some communities, it is customary to wish the mourner "long life." On the Sabbath, the mourner attends synagogue and is publicly greeted by the rabbi. The seven-day period is followed by and included in the *Sheloshim*, the thirty days of strict but less intense mourning. Since it is forbidden to mourn on a festival, the advent of a festival terminates the *Shivah* or the *Sheloshim*, as the case may be. If the death occurs during the course of a festival, the mourning period begins only after its conclusion. In the case of the death of a parent, mourning is observed for eleven months. During this period, the *Kaddish* is recited at all services by the mourner and indulgence in festivities and excessive joy is prohibited. For other relatives, the period of mourning ends officially after *Sheloshim*. Each year, on the anniversary of the death (the *Yahrzeit*), the *Kaddish* is recited and amusement avoided.

It is also customary to light a memorial lamp in memory of the deceased throughout the initial seven-day period and on the anniversary of the death.

MUSIC, JEWISH: Unfortunately, very little is known about the musical forms of ancient Israel. The Bible mentions musical instruments which were later used in the service of the temple such as the harp, lyre, shepherd flute, trumpet, cymbals, and others. A comparison with ancient Egyptian paintings and inscriptions reveals the strong influence of ancient oriental musical instruments and forms, particularly Egyptian, on Israelite culture. The only instrument mentioned in the Bible which can be regarded as typically Israelite, is the *shofar* or ram's horn, which has more cultic than musical value.

After the children of Israel crossed the Red Sea, Moses' sister Miriam led the women of Israel in song and dance to the accompaniment of musical instruments. King David was a skilled player on the lyre and became the symbol of Jewish love of music. According to the Bible, he organized the musical framework for the Temple service, including a choir of Levites and an orchestra. It was through the psalms and the Temple service at Jerusalem that Jewish music entered the orbit of western civilization. Christian sacred music to this day is composed mainly of the psalms, and the words "Hallelujah," "Amen," and "Selah" are included in the texts of thousands of liturgical compositions. Even the various forms of psalm-singing have remained virtually unchanged. These are: 1) The solo-psalm sung by one person alone (Ps. 3–5), 2) The response psalm in which the congregation answers the soloist (Ps. 48, 100, 118), 3) The Antiphon in which two groups chant alternately (Ps. 136, 148), and 4) The refrain psalm in which a single refrain repeated over and over again is interjected into the singing of the soloist (Ps. 135:1–3). After the destruction of the Second Temple, the rabbis forbade the use of instrumental music as a sign of mourning. Prayers and scriptures were now sung or recited to a traditional melody. The preservation of the Jewish musical tradition became largely the task of the *Ḥazzan* or Cantor. The institution of the *Ḥazzan* is old. Originally, he was a communal official who performed numerous functions ranging from teaching the young to technical and administrative tasks. Services were led by a layman known as the *Shaliaḥ Tzibbur* — Emissary of the Congregation. In the course of time, however, as general knowledge of Hebrew declined and numerous hymns *(Piyyutim)* were added to the prayer service (many composed by *Ḥazzanim* themselves), the institution became professionalized. The *Ḥazzan* was expected to be a man of deep piety, of mature age, with a pleasant voice, and preferably married. Gradually, however, the stress was laid on the quality of his voice. It was largely due to the *Ḥazzanim* that in the period between 400 and 1000 C.E. the music of the synagogue attained an organic unity. One of the great leaders of Babylonian Jewry in the 8th century, R. Yehudai Gaon, himself a musician and *Ḥazzan*, codified and arranged the musical tradition of the Babylonian synagogues and sponsored the institution of professional *Ḥazzanim*. During the same period, what is regarded by scholars as the first attempt at musical notation was perfected by Jewish scholars known as the *Masoretes*. They instituted signs known as *teamim* to indicate the correct reading and chanting of the Scriptures. These signs, which at best may be described as semi-musical devices, served both grammatical and musical purposes and ensured the correct and unified chanting of scriptures. Jewish chants and cantillation made a major indirect contribution to the music of the Western world. The Gregorian chant, the authentic music of the Catholic Church, is of Jewish origin according to most authorities. In fact, it is possible to state that until the 9th century, the Church borrowed from the synagogue. Then the relationship gradually reversed itself and at the time of the Renaissance and later, Jewry was heavily indebted to the Church for many of its melodies.

The early Middle Ages saw a general retreat into itself by Jewry, in all spheres including music. This was imposed partly from without and partly from within. The Church, which was by now the central authority in musical development, excluded Jews from its discoveries and developments. Conversely, rabbinic authorities, fearful of harmful effects of church and other non-Jewish music on the spiritual life of the Jews, opposed the adoption of non-Jewish tunes into the synagogue repertoire. Thus when church music developed intricate polyphonic and contrapuntal systems, Jewish music remained a thin melodic line without part-singing and harmony.

However, secular music did invade the synagogue and toward the end of the Middle Ages, non-Jewish folk tunes were adopted even in the synagogue, despite the opposition of various rabbinic authorities. At the same time, the differences between Ashkenazi and Sephardi liturgy and the forms of chanting the Scriptures became crystallized. The Ashkenazim were generally more influenced by European music while the oriental Sephardim adopted Arab musical forms. Each group thus developed a poetic and musical style of its own.

The Renaissance, and in particular Italy, its center, once again brought Jews into contact with Western civilization and culture, including its music. The Italian Salomone Rossi (1565–1628) was the first Jewish composer of stature. He served as choirmaster at the Mantua Synagogue and was director of music at the Court of Mantua. He enjoyed the friendship of the great Italian master Monteverdi with whom he collaborated. He introduced modern musical forms, including harmony, into the synagogue and when this aroused queries and opposition, the famous Rabbi Leone de Modena, together with other rabbis, signed an official opinion to the effect that choral art music is not prohibited in the synagogue. Rabbi de Modena, himself a musician, founded the first artistic choir in synagogal history and urged Rossi to write special compositions for the synagogue. From his time on, Jewish composers and musicians have shared in the development of Western music, although for the most part there is very little of Jewish tradition to be recognized in their work. Most of the famous musicians of Jewish birth or origin who have contributed so greatly to Western music since the 18th century have been influenced and motivated by contemporary musical developments without regard to their Jewish heritage, even when writing music based on Jewish themes. Thus Meyerbeer (1791–1864), Mendelssohn (1809–1847), Offenbach (1819–1880), and Mahler (1860–1911) show no particular "Jewish line" in their music. Mendelssohn and Mahler were in fact totally estranged from Judaism. This process of "modernization" which began with the Renaissance continued into the 18th and 19th centuries when classical musical forms permeated the liturgy of the synagogue. *Ḥazzanim* began to study musical composition and harmony. Under the influence of Reform Judaism an attempt was made to beautify the synagogue service through the introduction, for the first time since the destruction of the Temple, of instrumental music and compositions reflecting the spirit of the times. Orthodox rabbinic authorities attempted to halt this process but it nevertheless grew, and under the influence of such eminent cantors and musicians as Solomon Sulzer (1804–1891), Samuel Naumbourg (1816–1880), and Louis Lewandowski (1823–1894), choral music in classical form was slowly adopted by all synagogues, Orthodox included. It is to

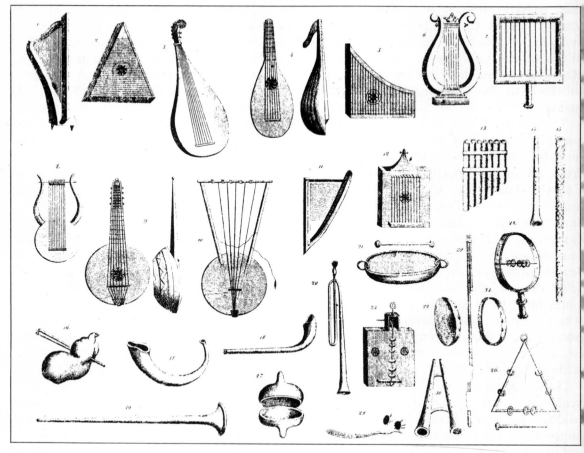

Ancient musical instruments played by Jews

their credit, however, that they maintained the basic traditional melodies, not sacrificing Jewish characteristics to artistic form. Their compositions have therefore remained the basis of the synagogue repertoire of all three Jewish religious streams, Orthodox, Conservative, and Reform. During the 19th and 20th centuries, there was a spate of outstanding cantors and musicians who attempted to maintain the synthesis between traditional Jewish melodies and modern musical forms. Some of these cantors achieved fame in non-Jewish circles as well as in the synagogue, Joseph Rosenblatt, Mordechai Hershman, Moshe Kussevitsky, and Leib Glantz being among the best known.

The Hasidic movement made its own unique contribution to Jewish music. The Hasidim from the outset attached great importance to music as a means of communion with God. Numerous wordless hymns called *Niggunim* composed by the Hasidic rabbis have come down to us. They reflect the various moods of the human being, ranging from the meditative to the joyful. Common to them all is the mood of ecstasy in which according to their beliefs the sick were healed, the insane led back to sanity, and sinners forgiven, all through the power of music. Hasidic music was greatly influenced by oriental and gypsy music, and is used both during prayer and at celebrations. The Hasidic congregation does not employ either a choir or a professional cantor. The congregation participates communally in the singing of the prayers. Hasidic music has undergone a renaissance in recent years in the State of Israel.

It is still too early to judge the effect and influence of the Jewish National movement on Jewish music, although the vast influx of Jews from the Yemen and other Arabic speaking lands, and the Balkans, has given rise to a trend toward orientalization. Modern Jewish composers are obviously more influenced by Jewish themes than in the past. This is evident from the works of Ernest Bloch (1880–1959), Leonard Bernstein (1918–), and numerous young Israeli composers.

NAḤMAN OF BRATZLAV: Ḥasidic leader, great-grandson of the founder of the movement, Baal Shem Tov. Naḥman was not a man of deep learning. He was, however, imbued with an enthusiastic and deeply emotional religious feeling. It is these aspects of Ḥasidic belief that he stressed, especially in prayer. He composed a number of prayers in Yiddish, believing that his followers should be enabled to express their devotion to God in the language they best understood. He was critical of other Ḥasidic leaders and regarded himself as the only true interpreter of the Baal Shem Tov's teachings. He visited the land of Israel in 1798, studying the *Kabbalah* at Tiberias. Naḥman of Bratzlav raised the status of the *Tzaddik* to that of a mediator between man and God. The duty of the Ḥasidim was not only to obey him, but to be as near him as possible in order to share his spirituality. He taught his followers through the medium of stories and parables which he composed. Unlike other Ḥasidic leaders, no Bratzlav dynasty was established after his death. He told his followers that he would still be with them even after death, thus there was no need to appoint a successor. The followers of his teachings used to visit his grave annually. Today a number of Bratzlav synagogues are still maintained in Israel and elsewhere.

NATIONAL JEWISH WELFARE BOARD: The National Jewish Welfare Board, founded in 1917, is the central organization of Jewish Community Centers. Through the centers and the Young Men's and Young Women's Hebrew Associations it offers summer camps, and its many lectures, social events, and organized sports activities continue throughout the year. Through the Jewish Book Council, the National Jewish Music Council, and JWB Lecture Bureau, it also offers many opportunities to the adult community. When the JWB merged in 1921 with the YMH and Kindred Associations, it was authorized by the United States Government to provide religious, welfare, and recreational services for Jewish members of the armed forces, a function it continues to perform.

Although the more than 350 centers affiliated with the JWB are in the United States and Canada, the organization is also concerned with world Jewry and many programs of Jewish culture throughout the world are presented each year. Recently, these programs have shown special concern for Jews in the Soviet Union.

Another recent development has been an increasing awareness of America's growing urban problems, and today many centers are involved in urban rehabilitation projects. This, the JWB explains, is a "valid expression of Jewish commitment and values," and it continues to seek new outlets to apply such values to concrete activities.

NAZARETH: Town in lower Galilee, Israel. It is first mentioned in the New Testament as the childhood home of Jesus. In Jewish sources it appears only from the 7th century C.E., although during the first centuries of the Christian era it was inhabited mainly by Jews. The Crusaders made it the capital of Galilee until destruction by the Moslems in 1263. Under the

British, Nazareth was the center of the administrative headquarters of Galilee. It was captured by the Israel Army on July 16, 1948.

Nazareth is Israel's largest Arab center with a population of 32,000, most of whom are Catholic or Greek Orthodox, with a

cultivated area of the Negev. In the northern Negev, the low, undulating terrain is cultivable if irrigated, while the valleys and hills of the central Negev can be cultivated with special techniques. The southern Negev forms typical eroded "badlands" and the rift valley depression known

View of Nazareth

Mountains near Eilat

Moselm minority. Because of its sacred significance to Christians, Nazareth is a major center of pilgrimage. It contains one of the most holy shrines of the Christian world, the Church of the Annunciation, built over the grotto where according to Christian tradition, the angel Gabriel appeared before Mary to announce the birth of Jesus. A church was built on the site in the 4th century. The present imposing cathedral was dedicated in 1969.

On the slopes overlooking the old city, a new town, Upper Nazareth, has been built which houses mainly recent Jewish immigrants.

NEGEV ("dry land"): Area of southern Israel which, following the United Nations 1947 partition resolution and Israel's War of Independence, constituted sixty per cent of the total area of the country. Despite its arid climate and barren appearance today, archeological evidence has proved that much of the Negev was settled and cultivated in ancient times. Today Israel's modern pioneers are again increasing the

as the Aravah can also be made to "blossom."

Israel's connections with the Negev go back to the days of the patriarchs. Abraham and Isaac both lived there and passed through it at different times of their lives. Then, as now, the Negev was the most sparsely populated part of the country. The spies whom Moses sent to report on the land went up first to the Negev and then on to Hebron. The Bible (Deut. 8:11) speaks of the "land whose stones are iron and out of whose hills thou mayest dig copper" (wrongly translated in most versions as "brass").

The strategic and economic importance of the Negev's vast deposits of copper, iron ore, and other raw materials was appreciated by King David, who by conquering the Edomites established Israel's hegemony over the area. His son Solomon mined copper in the southern Negev and had it smelted, as the American archeologist Nelson Glueck has shown, in the ancient furnaces of Ezion Geber. From the southern outlet to the Red Sea, Solomon sent ships to trade with Africa and southern Arabia.

After the division of the kingdom, the Edomites were again able to take control of the southern area from a weakened Judah, although periodically kings of Judah, like Uzziah, were successful in reasserting their supremacy. After the fall of Jerusalem, the Negev was occupied by the Nabateans, evidence of whose agricultural techniques can be seen and is indeed being copied today. Henceforth, the history of the Negev is one of fluctuations between decline and occasional bursts of prosperity, as in the late Roman and Byzantine period. With the Arab conquest in the 7th century, the settlements began to wither away and the Negev became a desert peopled only by Bedouins until the 20th century. During World War I, the British conquered the area from the Turks and the Negev became part of Mandatory Palestine. In the late 1930's and 1940's, a number of successful settlements were established in the Negev. One resident of these settlements, Israel's first Prime Minister David ben Gurion, made the development and resettlement of the Negev one of the prime goals of his life, stressing its vital importance for a country the size of Israel. During the War of Independence, the Egyptians attempted the conquest of the Negev, but after initial advances they were frustrated by the resolute resistance of the isolated Jewish settlements. In a campaign launched in October 1948 that lasted until the following March, the Israel Army drove the Egyptians out of the Negev (with the exception of the Gaza Strip) and reached Eilat. Exploitation of this outlet to the Red Sea, however, was prevented by the Egyptian blockade of the Straits of Tiran until Israel conquered Sharm el Sheikh in October 1956. That conquest was repeated in June 1967.

Since the establishment of the State of Israel, the Negev has once again begun to flourish. Settlements, cities, and develop-ment towns have brought an influx of population to the area. The provision of sufficient water, which is so vital in this area, has been assured by the Israel water carrier system which brings the water of the Sea of Galilee to the arid expanses of the Negev.

NEHEMIAH: Jewish governor of Jerusalem, appointed by the Persian king Artaxerxes. Together with Ezra, he played a vital role in reorganizing and reestablishing the life of the Jewish exiles returned from Babylon. The biblical book that bears his name tells of Nehemiah's life as the cup-bearer to the Persian king and of the work he did from the time he obtained the king's permission to go to help the returned exiles up to the occasion of his second visit.

There are 13 chapters in the book. Chapters 1–8 contain his memoirs, written in the first person; and Chapters 8–13 overlap the history recorded in the book of Ezra. According to the traditional account, Nehemiah collaborated with Ezra in his policies of strict religious reform leading to a reorganization of temple services, dissolution of mixed marriages, strict observance of the Sabbath, and the binding of the people to the Law in a solemn covenant. He also presided over the rebuilding of the walls of Jerusalem in the teeth of strong Samaritan opposition. The books of Ezra and Nehemiah were originally regarded as one unit and, together with the book of Chronicles, were considered of common authorship. Their place is at the end of the third section of the Bible, *Ketuvim.*

NEW MOON (Rosh Ḥodesh): The first day of the Hebrew month. In ancient times, this day assumed a festive character. The Bible (Num. 28:11–15) prescribed a special sacrifice for the occasion and a feast was held in honor of the day. Like the Sabbath, it was a day of rest (Amos 8:5) and was considered a propitious time to visit the prophet. King Saul invited guests to dine with him at the New Moon, and the meal had a certain religious character. During the Second Temple period, considerable importance was attached to the proclamation of the New Moon by the Sanhedrin, for the observance of the festivals and fasts in their appointed times depended on its correct determination.

The New Moon was only proclaimed as *mekuddash* (sanctified) after reliable evidence had been received from witnesses claiming to have seen the new moon who were thoroughly interrogated by the Sanhedrin. This interrogation took place on the 30th day of the month, and if the witnesses' testimony was accepted, that day was proclaimed *Rosh Ḥodesh* and the previous month had only twenty-nine days. If their testimony was not accepted, or if there were witnesses, the following day was proclaimed *Rosh Ḥodesh* and the preceding month had thirty days.

Messengers were then despatched throughout the land of Israel and to the neighboring countries informing the Jewish communities of the correct date of *Rosh Ḥodesh* so that they could observe the festivals that fell in the course of the month on the correct date. Because of distance, however, the messengers sometimes took a few weeks to reach their destination and the far-flung Jewish communities were usually in doubt as to the number of days in the previous month. To make sure that they were observing the month's festivals on the right day, Jewish communities outside the land of Israel began keeping two although only one is prescribed in the Bible. Around the year 360 C.E., the Jewish calendar was permanently and astronomically determined by the sage Hillel II so that the above procedure became superfluous. Nevertheless, the custom persisted in the Diaspora of celebrating holidays for two days instead of one, with the exception of the Day of Atonement. In modern times,

Reform Judaism has discarded the two-day observance.

The original festive character of *Rosh Ḥodesh* has disappeared, but the day is still commemorated in the synagogue by the recitation of special psalms (the *half-Hallel*), the additional *(Musaph)* service, and the special reading of the Torah. Fasting and mourning are forbidden on *Rosh Ḥodesh,* and the supplicatory prayer, *Taḥanun,* is omitted. On the Sabbath preceding the New Moon, a special prayer is recited and the date of the New Moon is announced. This is a relic of the ancient custom described above, when before the fixing of the calendar the New Moon was established on the evidence of eye-witnesses.

NEW YEAR FOR TREES (Rosh Ha-Shana La-Illanot; also **Tu Be-Shevat** i.e., 15th day of the month of *Shevat*): Hebrew Arbor day. Originally, this day had no religious significance. The sage Hillel regarded it as the date from which the age of a tree should be reckoned for purposes of assessing fruit tithes. The day marks the end of the rainy season in Israel, when the new sap starts to rise in the trees. In the 16th and 17th centuries, the Kabbalists of Safed sampled fifteen kinds of fruit on this day and, under their influence, a special ceremonial developed. In the State of Israel, the 15th of *Shevat* is celebrated by the planting of trees by schoolchildren.

NILI (Initials of the Hebrew phrase, "The Eternal of Israel will not lie," I Sam. 15:29): Palestinian Jewish underground organization which cooperated with and spied for the British against the Turks during World War I. It was established by Aaron Aaronson and Avshalom Feinberg, who believed that a British victory was essential for the realization of the Zionist ideal. Aaronson was a well-known agronomist and was chief agricultural adviser to the Turkish commander Jemal Pasha.

Some members of the Nili *group*

In 1911, he had founded the agricultural experimental station at Athlit and during the war it was from this spot that messages were flashed to British warships off the coast. Invaluable information concerning Turkish troop movements and strategy was thus passed on, enabling the allies to plan accordingly. The Turks, however, finally broke the ring and arrested many of its members including Aaron's sister, Sarah. She was subjected to severe humiliation and torture and rather than divulge any of the Nili secrets, she committed suicide. Aaron was able to make his way to Cairo where he served as an adviser to General Allenby. Although the activity of the Nili group was opposed by certain sections of the official Jewish leadership because of its supposedly dangerous implications for the Jewish community, the Nili spies can be seen in retrospect as having played an invaluable role in the struggle for Jewish nationhood and their activity constitutes a noble and heroic episode.

NOAH: Biblical figure, hero of the story of the flood (Gen. 6). Noah's generation, the tenth after Adam, reached a peak of wickedness and because of their evil ways, God determined to destroy all living things on earth by a flood. But Noah was a just and righteous man, "blameless in his generation," and he accordingly was saved with his family. At God's command he built an ark for himself, his family, and specimens of all living species who were thereby preserved. After the flood, Noah offered up a sacrifice and God entered into a covenant with him, setting the rainbow in the sky as a pledge that never again would there be a repetition of such a catastrophe.

Noah thus became the second father of mankind. From his three sons, sprang the first seventy people from whom all humanity was derived. Noah planted a vineyard and got drunk with its wine. His son Ham insulted him, while Shem and Japheth sought to protect him. In his anger at what had happened, Noah cursed Ham, predicting that his descendants would be slaves to the descendants of Shem and Japheth.

Much has been written about the biblical story of the flood and its resemblance to similar flood stories which were prevalent in the ancient Near East, particularly the parallel version in the Babylonian Epic of Gilgamesh. The biblical story is markedly similar to ancient Mesopotamian legend, but a comparison of the two only emphasizes the unique grandeur of Israel's God-idea. Whereas the Mesopotamian myth tells of warring gods and wanton destruction, and of a hero, Utnapishtim, who survives the flood by divine favor and is then made "immortal like the gods," the Israelite version gives this pagan tale a moral and ethical content, freeing it from all unseemly elements. Unlike its Babylonian counterpart, the Hebrew deluge is a proclamation of the eternal truth that the basis of human society is justice, and that any society devoid of justice deserves to perish and is inevitably doomed to destruction.

NORTH AFRICA: Jews have lived in what are now Morocco, Algeria, Tunisia, and Libya ever since the days of the Second Temple. It is quite possible that Jews played a part in the colonization of Carthage, which was founded by the Phoenicians, a people with whom the Jews had cordial relations. From Roman times, there is clear evidence of wide Jewish settlement throughout this area. Some Berber tribes are said to have converted to Judaism and the *Daggatun*, a people living in the Sahara region of Morocco, observe Jewish rites and claim to be of Jewish origin. With the Christianization of the Roman Empire, the position of Jews deteriorated drastically, and under the Byzantine rulers there was a spate of synagogue-burning. After the Moslem invasion in the 7th century, there was a general revival throughout the area although in some cases Jews fought against the invaders. The North African Jewish communities kept in constant touch with the Babylonian *Geonim* and their spiritual life was strongly influenced by the legal decisions taken in the Babylonian academies. Some North African centers, however, developed academies of their own, the most famous being those of Fez in Morocco and Kairouan in Tunisia. They played a major role as a link between the declining center of Babylonia and the rising new center in Spain.

In the 12th century, the area was conquered by the fanatical Moslem sect, the Almohades, who compelled all non-Moslems to convert. For over a hundred years the persecution and reaction lasted, compelling many Jews to seek refuge in other countries, particularly Egypt. In due course the Almohades lost their power and North African Jewish life returned to normal. After the massacres in Spain in 1391 and the explusion of the Jews one hundred years later, many Spanish refugees made their way to North Africa. With their superior culture and different mode of life, the newcomers often found themselves at odds with the native-born Jews and separate communities were established by the two groups. In time the differences disappeared and the two communities merged, becoming almost totally Arabicized in language, customs, and social habits. Unlike other areas of Moslem rule, the anti-Moslem code was strictly enforced in North Africa, particularly in Morocco. Jews lived in a ghetto known as the *Mellah*. They had to wear special clothing, pay heavy taxes, and were, subject to periodic outbreaks of violence. Individual Jews did achieve prominence from time to time, but the climate was one of intolerance and humiliation.

European colonization in the 19th century brought a measure of relief and emancipation. Under French rule, French citizenship was granted to those Jews who wanted it, and most availed themselves of the opportunity. But this did not lessen the friction between them and their non-Jewish neighbors. At the end of the 19th century, however, the position of the Jews improved and they continued to play an important role in the commercial life of their host countries. In Morocco they were active in the development of the international ports of Tangiers and of Casablanca. Casablanca became the largest center of Jewish settlement in North Africa, with a highly developed Jewish school system. However, conditions for the majority of the Jews remained miserable, confined as they were to the overcrowded *Mellah*, living in abject poverty.

The defeat of France and her surrender to Nazi Germany in 1940 put the North African Jews in danger of physical extinction. The puppet Vichy regime had a thorough-going anti-Semitic policy and revoked the privilege of French citizenship previously enjoyed by the Jews. Earlier, in Libya, the Italian Fascist regime had introduced discriminatory measures against Jews. When the German Army occupied North Africa from 1941–43, there were outbreaks of anti-Semitic violence throughout the area, and only the Allied defeat of the German armies saved North African Jewry from the fate of their brethren in Nazi-occupied Europe.

After World War II, conditions for Jews were restored to normal but relations between Jews and their Moslem neighbors deteriorated. This process was further aggravated by the rise of Jewish and Arab nationalism and the national movements in North Africa. All the North African states identified themselves with the Arabs and supported them in their avowed purpose of destroying the state of Israel, and the position of the local Jews in many of these countries became untenable. Most Moroccan Jews emigrated to Israel and today there are less than 50,000 remaining in the country, the majority living in Casablanca. After 1948, over 30,000 Jews left Libya for Israel and the remainder were forced to leave after the June 1967 Six-Day War. Tunisia, the most moderate of the Moslem states supporting the Arab cause, had a Jewish population of 67,000 in 1959. Ten years later, it had dropped to 10,000 as a result of a mass Jewish emigration to France. A similar process took place in Algeria, which was granted independence in 1962, when most of its 120,000 Jews moved to France. In 1948, there were some three-quarters of a million Jews in North Africa (including Egypt). By 1970, less than a tenth of this historic community was left.

ORT (initials of Russian *Obtscheswo Remeslenovo Truda,* i.e. Society for the Encouragement of Handicraft): International Jewish organization for the development of skills, handicrafts, and agriculture, founded in Russia in 1880. It established a network of vocational schools throughout Russia and after World War I, when its headquarters were transferred to Berlin, it extended its program throughout central and eastern Europe. In 1933, the head office was transferred to Paris and Ort schools were set up in South America, Canada, and Australia.

During and after World War II, Ort directed its activities to the training of Jewish refugees and displaced persons. It also began to establish schools in Israel and North Africa. Ort — whose headquarters are now in Geneva — has an annual budget of over fifteen million dollars, and its program embraces twenty-three countries and 50,000 students. In Israel alone, in 1968, it ran over 250 schools and courses in forty towns, and trained more than 35,000 pupils.

ORTHODOX JUDAISM: One of the three religious streams within Judaism, the other two being Conservative and Reform. The word "orthodox" was applied only in modern times. Prior to the 19th century, Judaism was monolithic and there was no need to qualify it. More recently, the term has been used to distinguish the traditional trend of Judaism from the modern variations of Reform Judaism, and subsequently Conservative

At an Ort School, Tel Aviv

Judaism. Orthodox Judaism itself cannot be spoken of as a homogeneous unit, for it is composed of many religious groupings, widely diversified in their outlook. Within Orthodoxy, conflicts on matters of belief and practice have arisen such as the dispute between Ḥasidim and *Mitnagdim* in the 18th and 19th centuries, and between anti-Zionists and Zionists in the 20th century. Religious custom varies, for example, between Ashkenazim and Sephardim and even within each grouping. Nonetheless, there are certain accepted basic principles within Orthodoxy which render the differences secondary and draw a distinct line between it and the other religious streams. All Orthodox Jews are united in their belief in the revelation at Mount Sinai, as described in the Bible. This principle of *Torah Min Hashamayim* involves the belief that the whole of Jewish law, the Written Law as contained in the five books of Moses and the basic Oral Law as contained in the *Mishnah*, were handed down to Moses on Mount Sinai. Orthodoxy rejects the idea of a progressive revelation which is basic to Reform Judaism. The law or Torah is eternally binding and may not be tampered with. The concept of evolution in religious thought and practice is alien to

Orthodox Judaism. The regulations governing the daily life and conduct of the Jew should not, and need not, be "modernized" — certainly not changed. God's central law, as transmitted from generation to generation, took into consideration all future possibilities. Thus, a rabbi deciding a matter of Jewish law in the 20th century is not creating anything new because his decision must be based on the Jewish law, the *Shulḥan Arukh*, which is based on the Talmud, which goes back to the oral tradition handed to Moses on Mount Sinai. Despite this, there is a certain amount of flexibility within the framework of Jewish law which has resulted in differences of approach and even in sharp splits. Thus, in the 19th century there arose in Germany, under the leadership of Samson Raphael Hirsch, the school of *Torah im Derekh Eretz*, the study of the Torah together with the acquisition of secular knowledge. Hirsch, who was one of the leading opponents of Reform, believed that by acquiring a secular education the Orthodox Jew would be even better equipped to defend traditional Judaism. In the *Yeshivot* of eastern Europe, a secular education was frowned upon and even forbidden. There was opposition to innovation in speech and dress.

The rise of the Zionist movement brought a further split in the ranks of Orthodoxy. The more extreme *Agudas Yisrael* opposed any attempt to bring about a man-made redemption of the Jewish people before the arrival of the Messiah, while the *Mizrachi* and its youth movement, *Bene Akiva*, played a vital role both in the land of Israel and outside, in the establishment of a Jewish homeland. After the establishment of the state, however, the more extremist opposition modified considerably and *Agudas Yisrael* even participated in various coalition governments. In the United States, Orthodox Judaism, dominated at first by eastern European-trained, Yiddish-speak-

Orthodox Jews in Jerusalem

ing rabbis, began to develop its own American-orientated institutions. The Yeshiva University, with its student body of over 6,000, its faculties covering a broad spectrum of secular and religious studies, its R. Isaac Elḥanan Theological Seminary and Albert Einstein College of Medicine, has come to be regarded as the symbol of American Orthodoxy. The Rabbinical Council of America, founded in 1923, is the Rabbinical Association of Ordained Orthodox Rabbis occupying pulpits in the U.S., Canada, and elsewhere in North America. Its members come from all recognized Orthodox theological seminaries in the United States. This organization frequently comes into conflict with the older, more conservative eastern European-orientated Union of Orthodox Rabbis of the United States and Canada, established in 1902. Throughout the Western world, the modern Orthodox rabbi is generally expected to possess an academic degree in addition to his rabbinic qualifications. This modern-type Orthodoxy is referred to as Neo- or Enlightened Orthodoxy as distinct from the earlier ghetto-type Orthodoxy. For all this, Orthodoxy will reject any practice, custom, or change which cannot be justified within the framework of Jewish law. Thus, the mixed pew, the use of an organ in the synagogue on Sabbaths and Festivals, and other innovations which involve the violation of a principle of Jewish law are rejected out-of-hand by Orthodoxy. In Israel, the modern type of Orthodoxy is represented by the National Religious Party and especially by its kibbutz wing and youth movement, *Bene Akiva*. The eastern European "old" Orthodoxy is widely prevalent in the *Yeshivot* and the *Agudas Yisrael* party. Although some leaders have begun to adopt a slightly more tolerant attitude toward the other two major groups within Judaism, they still rigidly refuse to recognize the marriages, divorces, and conversions of rabbis who do not accept the authority of traditional Jewish law. This includes both Reform and Conservative rabbis. In the Diaspora, where the civil marriage and divorce is binding on all religious groups, the problem, while serious, can nevertheless be overcome. In Israel, however, where the Orthodox rabbinate has exclusive jurisdiction in matters of marriage, divorce, and personal status — no civil marriage being possible — this refusal by the rabbinate to recognize civil marriage and divorce has, in recent years, been the subject of much controversy and debate.

PALMAḤ (abbr. of Hebrew *Pelugot Maḥatz* "shock companies"): Military shock troops attached to the *Haganah,* the main Jewish underground organization before the declaration of the State of Israel. The *Palmaḥ* was established by the *Haganah* high command in 1941, in the face of the deteriorating military situation in the Middle East and the threat of an invasion of the Holy Land by the Nazis. After the Nazi threat subsided, however, the *Palmaḥ* was increasingly used in the struggle for Jewish independence and in the fight against the immigration restrictions imposed by the British authorities. Accordingly, it played a vital role in the task of illegal immigration, and from time to time carried out military operations against the British. Under its first commander, Yitzḥak Sadeh, the *Palmaḥ* numbered only a few hundred men, but under Yigal Allon, from 1943–48, it grew into a force of 5500. Its members were handpicked and came mainly from the *kibbutzim*, dividing their time between farming and military training. When the 1948 war broke out and the newly independent State of Israel was invaded by her neighbors, the *Palmaḥ*, which constituted the best-trained force available at the time, was divided into four small brigades and spread throughout the country. Due to the intense pressure exerted by the invading Arabs and the lack of sufficient manpower and equipment, it was often necessary to transfer *Palmaḥ* units from one sector to another at maximum speed in order to bolster the defense. The members of the *Palmaḥ* thus bore a disproportionate role in the fighting, as witnessed by their heavy casualties — over 1,000 falling in action. Their heroism and attacking spirit, however, became legendary and played a vital role in the war's successful outcome. The decision to disband the *Palmaḥ* was taken by Israel's first prime minister, David Ben-Gurion, who felt that with the establishment of the state, all independent military and paramilitary units should be united within the framework of the Defense Forces of Israel. The decision led to much controversy at the time, but was justified by later events.

Aluf *Yitzḥak Sadeh*

PARACHUTISTS (in World War II): Young men and women from the land of Israel who were parachuted into Nazi-occupied Europe during World War II. Their task was to gather information for the Allied armies, to organize resistance, and, at the same time, to make contact with Jewish communities in the hope of organizing rescue operations. The group's organizer, Enzo Sereni, one of the founders of *kibbutz* Givat Brenner, was dropped in northern Italy, captured, and shot. Another parachutist, Hannah Szenes, was dropped into Yugoslavia, from whence she made her way to Hungary, the land of her birth. She was caught and brutally tortured by the Germans, but through all her agony she refused to divulge any information that could endanger her friends of the parachutists' operations. She was sentenced to death by the German military court and shot. In 1948, her remains were transferred to the State of Israel and re-interred with those of other parachutists on Mount Herzl in Jerusalem.

Only twenty-three when she died, Hannah Szenes was a poet and after her death a number of her poems were published. The best-known begins, "Happy is the Match that kindled a Flame." Besides Hannah Szenes and Enzo Sereni, five other parachutists met their deaths in this operation.

PASSOVER (Pesaḥ): Jewish festival celebrated for eight days (seven in Israel) from the 15th of *Nisan*. Its significance may be determined from the different names by which the festival is known. The "Festival of our Freedom" is at the very root of Passover. It commemorates the Exodus from Egypt and the miraculous redemption of the children of Israel from bondage. Passover marks the beginning of Jewish nationhood. *Ḥag Ha-Matzot*, the Festival of Unleavened Bread, refers to the state of oppression in which the children of Israel found themselves in Egypt; the matzot are the bread of affliction. It also refers to the haste with which the Israelites were finally driven out of Egypt, without sufficient time for the dough to rise, an indispensable element in the baking of bread. The name *Pesaḥ*, or Passover, by which the festival is most commonly known, is associated with the paschal lamb which in Egypt was slaughtered on the

14th day of *Nisan*. The door posts of all Israelite homes were sprinkled with the blood of the lamb, and the Angel of Death was therefore able to "pass over" these homes as he smote the first born of the Egyptians. The final name for the festival is *Ḥag ha-Aviv*, the Festival of Spring. This name is given to Passover because the month of *Nisan* is described in the Bible as the month of *Abib*, when the fresh young ears of barley begin to ripen. Passover, like *Shavuot* and *Succot*, is also an agricultural festival. All the above aspects of the festival are represented in its celebration. Passover was enshrined in Jewish history at its inception as the Festival of Freedom. *Nisan*, the month of freedom, became the first month of the year. Over and over again, the Bible admonishes the people of Israel never to forget that they were slaves in the land of Egypt. The Exodus is the central event in ancient Jewish history, and its message has inspired freedom fighters and oppressed people throughout the world.

It is as the Festival of Unleavened Bread that Passover is best known. For the duration of the festival, it is strictly forbidden to eat leaven, known as *ḥametz*, or even to have it in one's possession. On the eve of the festival, all leaven is cleared from the home, and Passover is generally a time for a thorough spring cleaning in most Jewish homes. Utensils which have been used for *ḥametz* are put away and replaced by new ones or by such as have been kept exclusively for Passover. Some vessels used during the year may be used for Passover after having undergone the process known as *kashering*. The baking of the *matzot* is thoroughly supervised so as to ensure that no moisture comes into contact with it to cause fermentation.

In Temple times, the paschal lamb was slaughtered on the eve of the festival and eaten on the first night. All who were prevented from performing their duty on the 14th of *Nisan* were allowed to offer the

Seder services on Passover

sacrifice one month later on the 14th of *Iyar*. This day was therefore called the Second Passover (Numbers 9:9–14).

The agricultural aspect of the festival found its expression in Temple times by the bringing of the *Omer*. The *Omer* was the first sheaf cut during the barley harvest, and it was offered in the Temple as a sacrifice on the second day of Passover. Forty-nine days were then counted until the festival of *Shavuot*, thus giving to this period the name *Sefirat Haomer*, the counting of the *Omer*. After Temple times, the *Omer* could no longer be offered up, but the counting of the days at nightfall continued to be strictly observed.

Passover is basically a family festival, and the Bible specifically directs the father to relate to his son the wonderful events that occurred. Hence the name *Haggadah* (narration) for the book read in the home on Passover eve. The Passover *Haggadah* is a running commentary on Jewish history up to the bondage in Egypt, the story of the ten plagues, and the redemption. It is in the form of the father's answer to the son's question, "Why is this night different from all other nights?" The answers are embellished with rabbinic legends and vivid descriptions. The *Hagga-*

dah is designed to stimulate the child's interest, to bring him to identify himself with his nation's history. It explains the distinguishing foods of the evening and all the important aspects of the Passover celebration. It is accompanied by a festive meal, the drinking of four cups of wine, and the recitation of the *Hallel* (Praise) psalms. This ritual in its entirety is known as the *Seder*, meaning order, and the *Haggadah* had approximated its present form already by the close of the Talmudic period. Later additions were popular folk songs such as *Addir Hu* and *Ḥad Gadya* with which the *Seder* is terminated. The book of the *Haggadah* has been one of the chief objects of Jewish ritual art. The *Seder* night has throughout history been a source of joy and inspiration to a persecuted and down-trodden people. It gave them hope and confidence that they too would be redeemed from bondage. It was also a time of terror for from the 12th century on the "blood libel," the accusation of using human blood in the celebration of Passover, was leveled against the Jew by fanatics. That libel has been responsible for a number of brutal massacres. It was on the eve of Passover, 1190, that the Jews of York, surrounded by a murderous mob, decided to commit suicide rather than fall into the hands of their persecutors.

In the synagogue, Passover is commemorated by the usual special readings from the five books of Moses and the Prophets, accompanied by the reading of the *Hallel* and the *Musaph* (additional) service for festivals. Because the rainy period in Israel ends early in *Nisan*, a prayer for dew, *Tephilat Tal*, is offered during the *Musaph* service.

In Ashkenazi communities, the "Song of Songs" is read on the intermediate Sabbath.

See also: LAG BA-OMER.

PATRIARCHS (Avot): Name given by Jewish tradition to the three founding fathers of the people of Israel: Abraham, Isaac, and Jacob, whose life stories are told in the book of Genesis, chapters twelve to fifty. Until recently, Bible scholars and critics viewed the early traditions of Israel with a skeptical eye. The worth of the patriarchal stories as sources of information concerning Israel's early history was regarded by many of them as minimal if not nil. Abraham, Isaac, and Jacob were seen as ancestors of clans, or even as mythological figures, and not infrequently their existence was denied. Since the Bible, it was held, was written hundreds of years after the events described in the book of Genesis, and the stories came down to the author by oral tradition, their historicity was, to say the least, extremely doubtful.

Research into the ancient Middle East as well as archeological excavations carried out during the past hundred years has brought a drastic revision of the above theories. The world in which the patriarchs moved has been revealed to the modern eye in an unbelievable manner. Places mentioned in the Bible such as Ur

Abraham's tomb at Maarat Hamachpelah, Hebron

of the Chaldees and Haran have been rediscovered through the precise methods of modern archeological science. Tens of thousands of texts contemporaneous with the period of Israel's origins have been deciphered and analyzed. Incidents and customs mentioned in the patriarchal stories, which for centuries puzzled the most talented Bible commentators, now appear easily understandable and meaningful in the context of ancient Mesopotamian civilization. Particularly revealing are the Mari texts of the 18th century B.C.E. and the Nuzi texts of the 15th century B.C.E. The former are of extraordinary interest to the reader of the Bible for they contain biblical names like Benjamin and David. Haran in upper Mesopotamia, Abraham's hometown, was an Amorite settlement in this period, and it is striking that towns in the area had names that in the Bible are given to Abraham's relatives: Peleg, Serug, Nahor, Terah, Haran. The Nuzi texts contain laws and customs which are especially illuminating. At Nuzi, for example, childless couples would adopt a son who would serve them as long as they lived and inherit from them on their death. This would explain Abraham's fear that his servant Eliezer would inherit from him. Again, as Sarah gave her slave Hagar to Abraham, so at Nuzi certain marriage contracts obliged the wife, if childless, to provide her husband with a substitute. The puzzling story of Rachel's theft of her father's idols *(teraphim)* is explicable in the light of Nuzi custom, according to which a man's possession of the household idols insured his leadership of the family and his claim on the family inheritance. One can therefore understand Laban's outburst, "Why hast thou stolen my gods?" The list is almost endless and the conclusion inevitable. The stories of the patriarchs, far from belonging to a later age, fit almost perfectly into the larger context of Mesopotamian civilization between the years 2,000 and 1,500 B.C.E. One must still proceed cautiously because no evidence has as yet been found in external sources which proves the existence of the patriarchs, nor have any specific references to the events recalled in the Bible been found. Furthermore, it must be remembered that even according to Jewish tradition, the stories were not finally committed to writing until the time of Moses and must have undergone various changes and perhaps even distortions in the process of oral transmission. The finds of archeology, however, have without doubt shown that the background and way of life of the patriarchs as described in the book of Genesis are deeply rooted in history. Abraham, Isaac, and Jacob stand in the truest sense at the beginning of Israel's history and faith. Any attempt to place their existence at a later date or to relegate them to the sphere of mythology has to face the findings of modern science.

As to the personalities and characters of the patriarchs, these are depicted in the relevant chapters of the book of Genesis. Abraham is the founder of the faith in one God, of monotheism, and of the Hebrew people. His unconditional obedience to the word of God characterizes his every move and thought. Thus, at the command of God he leaves his ancestral home for the unknown land promised to him and his descendants as an inheritance. This faith in and obedience to God manifests itself in his everyday life and for this faith he is even prepared to sacrifice his son Isaac. Abraham is a man of peace and attempts at all times to establish good neighborly relations with the Canaanites with whom he comes into contact. Rather than fight with his nephew Lot, he suggests a peaceful parting of the ways. This peaceful disposition is shattered, however, when he hears of Lot's being taken prisoner of war, and he hastily mobilizes what forces there are at his disposal in order to rescue his nephew. Being imbued with a deep sense of justice, he pleads with God to spare the evil cities of Sodom and Gomorrah for the sake of the righteous people living in them. His compassion goes out to his son Ishmael and his mother Hagar who are driven out at Sarah's bidding; the biblical text makes it quite clear that he disapproves. Abraham appears in the Bible as a model of hospitality and as a true lover of mankind. Abraham's life is one prolonged test and his character is not merely that of a respected old sheikh, but the tragic and peaceful figure of a wise and good man who lives in God, accepts Him, and strives with Him, and in the end achieves a certain measure of perfect happiness.

Abraham lived a full life and the Bible, in relating his story, concludes "and Abraham expired, and died in a good old age, an old man, and full of years, and was gathered unto his people."

In contrast to the positive, dynamic, and epoch-making Abraham, Isaac, his successor, is almost totally passive. As if to stress this, the Bible devotes only one chapter exclusively to Isaac — Genesis 26. The other chapters dealing with his life are told within the framework of the stories of Abraham, his father, and Jacob, his son.

He is no great innovator; neither does his personality reveal any startling traits worthy of comment. On the contrary, his relations with his wife Rebekkah and his twin sons, Jacob and Esau, reveal a lack of understanding and a tendency to be impressed by superficial things, such as Esau's talent for hunting.

Isaac, unlike his father, does not shape circumstances, but seems rather to be shaped by them. Nevertheless there is a certain greatness in Isaac. This lies in his carrying on the religious tradition started by Abraham. He inherits the true belief in God and loyally transmits it to the next generation. There is a virtue in his passivity, for after Abraham's religious revolution, there was need for a period of consolidation in order that the new faith should be firmly established. Isaac provided this period.

Jacob once again offers the reader of the Bible a positive and forceful personality. There has been a tendency of late among Bible commentators to judge Jacob negatively, as a result of his deceitful behavior toward his brother Esau and his father Isaac. Both incidents, they say, in which Jacob first tricks Esau into selling his birthright and then by a cheap impersonation takes away his blessing, stamp him as a master of intrigue and conspiracy. One of the hallmarks of the biblical narrative is that it does not attempt to portray its heroes as saints. The ideal human being is one who despite his closeness to God remains human. There is no sinless being in Jewish history. This applies to Abraham, Isaac, and Jacob as well. The Bible makes this point clear by following the story of Jacob's ruse in stealing Esau's blessing with the story of Laban's successful misleading of Jacob. Instead of granting him his daughter Rachel whom he loved, Laban replaces her with Leah, thus forcing Jacob to work an additional seven years for the hand of his younger daughter. He who deceives others will in turn be deceived, is the point made. Jacob's life is one continuous struggle to assert himself. When he finally succeeds in evading Laban's clutches, he is confronted with the potentially tragic reunion with Esau. With the latter hurdle overcome, he finally arrives in Canaan longing for peace and tranquility. Such is not to be his lot, for now family problems raise their head. First the tragic episode of his only daughter, Dinah, who is violated by the inhabitants of Shechem, then the ghastly retaliation by his sons Simeon and Levi, which Jacob never forgave. Like his father Isaac, he too discriminated among his sons, thereby bringing about the tragedy of Joseph. For all this, Jacob represents a further development in Israel's history. From him came the twelve tribes who are destined to conquer the Holy Land. Jacob wrestles with God in the form of an angel and in the final event is victorious.

The covenant between God and Abraham, and God and Isaac, is renewed with Jacob. His name is changed by the angel of God to Israel, and the children of the patriarchs are thereafter called Israelites. Despite his life of strife, suffering, and anguish, Jacob dies a happy man, having once again seen his beloved son Joseph. His death brings to an end the period of the patriarchs.

Rabbinic tradition has embellished the lives of the patriarchs with countless legends and anecdotes; as the founding fathers of the nation, they are remembered with affection and admiration. The concept of *Zekhut Avot* (the Merits of The Fathers) which emphasizes that the pious deeds of parents and ancestors secure blessings for their descendants too is in rabbinic literature, particularly connected with the patriarchs. The *Amidah* prayer, recited at every service, begins with the words "Blessed art thou O lord our God and God of our fathers, God of Abraham, God of Isaac, and God of Jacob. Who rememberest the pious deeds of the patriarchs and in love will bring a redeemer to their children's children for Thy name's sake." Because of Abraham's unique position as founder of the faith, the blessing ends with the words, "Blessed art thou O Lord, the shield of Abraham."

Rabbinic tradition also claims that the morning prayer was instituted by Abraham, the afternoon prayer by Isaac, and the evening prayer by Jacob.

PERETZ, ISAAC LEIB (1852–1915): Yiddish writer. Born in the city of Zamosc in Poland, he was raised in a Ḥasidic environment. Zamosc was also a center of the *Haskalah* movement, and Peretz received a secular as well as a religious education. He studied law and settled in Warsaw, becoming an official of the Jewish com-

munity. Although his first literary efforts
were in Polish and Hebrew, he later turned
to Yiddish, this being the language of the
people he wished to reach, and strove to
raise it to the status of a high literary
medium. Peretz was deeply influenced by
the shattering events which broke upon the
Jews of eastern Europe from the middle
of the 19th century on. He sympathized
with the suffering masses and also with
the revolutionary spirit raging in Russia.
When a movement developed to proclaim
Yiddish the national language of the mass
of the Jewish people, Peretz was made its
leader, against his will. He became the
recognized leader of the Yiddishist movement, and was close to the Jewish Socialist
Party, the Bund. Peretz was a man of many
contradictions, and it is misleading to
generalize about his opinions. His variegat-
ed tendencies are clearly manifested in
his writings. He wrote poems, short
stories, dramas, allegories, and satires,
but no novels. He is at once amusing and
pathetic, clear and mystical, outspoken and
symbolic. Despite his sympathy with the
mass of the people, he feared their attaining
power. For all his strong patronage of
Yiddish, he believed that Hebrew was the
Jewish national language and that Yiddish
was only a folk tongue. Yet he ridiculed
the idea of reviving Hebrew and was
opposed to Zionism, regarding its aims as
narrow-minded and impractical. Above
everything, however, was Peretz' love for
the Jewish people and sympathy for their
plight. Peretz portrayed individuals. His
heroes and heroines are simple people who,
although not always understanding why
they suffer, are nevertheless convinced
that there is a reason and meaning in it.
Peretz rewards their faith. He was able to
see, even in the misery of the Jews, a
spiritual inner beauty which lay beneath
the mass of ugliness and chaos. Peretz was
deeply sympathetic toward the Hasidic
movement, which he regarded as a genuine
attempt to endow religion with a sense of

beauty. Thus he depicted its world, with
its customs and legends, in inspired, often
moving themes and motifs in his stories.
Among his better known works are *Bontzie
Shvaig* and *Hasidic Tales*. Much of his
work has been translated into English and
other languages.

PERSIA (IRAN): The Jewish association
with Persia dates from the period when the
Persian King Cyrus conquered Babylon
and became ruler over the Jews living in
exile there (see the article on Babylon).
Subsequently, in the early years of the
Second Temple period, Judah was for a
long time (about which little is known)
subject to Persia. In Persia proper there
was a large Jewish settlement from the
5th–4th centuries B.C.E. The biblical book
of Esther speaks of Jews living in all the
one hundred and twenty-seven provinces of
the Persian Empire and being particularly
influential in the capital, Susa (Shushan).
During the first centuries of the common
era, first under Parthian rule and then
under Persian rule, particularly under the
Sassanid dynasty, Jewish life was vigorous
and rich in cultural and religious attain-
ments. In the 5th and 6th centuries, however, the situation of the Jews deteriorated
as a result of the dominating influence of
the intolerant Zoroastrian religion. The
Arab conquest of 641–2 brought a more
tolerant attitude, and Jewish life flourished.
The over-all leader of the community, the
Exilarch, was a revered figure in non-Jewish
as well as Jewish circles, and the spiritual
leaders, the *Geonim*, extended their influence throughout the Jewish world. Disputes,
however, between the Exilarch and the
Geonim often led to internal friction and
a consequent weakening of the community.
Less friendly, sometimes hostile rulers were
quick to exploit such developments to the
detriment of the Jewish community. The
dissident Karaite movement gained a strong
foothold in Persia during the 18th century,
the more so as its leadership was made up

of Persian personalities. In the 12th century, there were large Jewish communities in Ispahan, Shiraz, Susa, Holwan, and Hamadan. The rise of the false Messiah, David Alroy, in the first half of the 12th century, was a temporary cause of great anxiety to Persian Jews. The Mongol conquest of Persia in the 13th century led to a new upsurge of Jewish cultural activity. The Mongols regarded all men as brothers and did not differentiate between believers and non-believers, Christians, Jews, or pagans. This change in the religious attitude brought a considerable improvement in the status of non-Moslems, i.e., Jews and Christians. Under the Mongols, therefore, Persian Jews reached the zenith of their creativity. They became court officials, court physicians, court astronomers, and even viziers of the great Mongol Persian Empire. Sa'ad Ad-Daula rose from being court physician to the highest possible political office, that of vizier or prime minister. Under such conditions, the Jews were able to cultivate their own Jewish heritage and succeeded in developing a Judeo-Persian culture of their own, including Bible translations and research. This "golden age" came to an end with the re-establishment of Persian independence under the Safavid Dynasty (1502–1736), which regarded non-believers as ritually unclean. They proceeded to persecute and humiliate the country's Jews. All manner of restrictions were introduced including the wearing of a special Jew's hat, and there were periods of enforced conversions of Jewish communities throughout Persia, bringing them to the brink of destruction. Persian Jews were treated worse than anywhere else in the Moslem world. The Safavids were overthrown by the Afghan dynasty which, with the exception of the short reign of Nadir Shah (1736–1747), brought little change for the better to the Jews. The last-named ruler, however, was tolerant toward all religions and actually wanted to create a universal religion, a synthesis of all the existing ones. He settled Jews in the holy city of Meshed, despite the opposition of the fanatical *Shi'a* clergy. When he was murdered in 1747, the Jews not only lost their protector but were exposed to a vicious reaction on the part of the *Shi'a* clergy. In the 19th century, under the Qajar dynasty (1796–1925), Persian Jewry was among the most depressed of the world's Jewish communities, living under medieval conditions of persecution and intolerance. The theory of the ritual uncleanness of the Jew persisted and the imposition of heavy taxes, the Jewish badge, and a host of repressive measures led to the virtual disintegration of Persian Jewry, its cultural life sinking to its lowest ebb. Furthermore, the activities of Christian missionaries and the influence of the new Bahai movement made great inroads into the ranks of Jewry. In 1839, the entire community of Meshed was forcibly converted to Islam. They were given the name *Jedid Al-Islam* ("New Moslems"). They, like the Marranos, however, while outwardly paying homage to their new faith, continued to observe Jewish customs in secret. During the course of the 19th century, diplomatic representations on behalf of the country's Jews were made by a number of European powers. These secured, at best, only temporary alleviations. That Persian Jewry did not succumb entirely in the face of all the above dangers is due to a number of factors. First, the establishment of Jewish schools in the main cities of Persia by the French Jewish organization, the *Alliance Israelite Universelle*; second, the growth of a more liberal spirit; thirdly, closer contact with the Persian-speaking colony of Jerusalem and with the reviving Jewish life in the land of Israel. The Balfour Declaration brought a new awakening among the Jews of Persia also and today they enjoy political equality, although the socio-economic status of many of them has not much improved. Between 1948 and 1966, 53,000 Jews left

Persia for Israel, leaving a Jewish population of approximately 80,000. Iran — the modern name for Persia — has not joined the fanatical anti-Israel stand taken by most other Moslem states. It maintains certain links with the State of Israel, particularly in trade, and Israeli experts have contributed to the country's development.

PHARISEES AND SADDUCEES: Two of the largest sects in Israel during the two centuries prior to the destruction of the Second Temple in the year 70 C.E. The origin of both names is uncertain although many and varied hypotheses have been offered. The Hebrew for Pharisees is *Perushim* meaning those who withdraw or separate themselves; the name would therefore be related to the Pharisaic mode of life which dictated a strict separation from all impurity and unclean foods. Although the Pharisees were integrally bound up religiously with the common people, they continued the tradition of the scribes and the men of the Great Assembly, believing in the authority of the oral tradition, which they developed further. They believed in the doctrine of immortality, the non-literal interpretation of Biblical laws such as "an eye for an eye, and a tooth for a tooth" which they interpreted to teach the principle of monetary compensation, and they introduced popular education. They guided the development of the synagogue alongside the Temple and were responsible for establishing the synagogue ritual, most of which has remained the same since their days. No greater injustice was ever done to them than their dogmatic stigmatization as hypocrites in the book of Matthew, an attitude still prevalent in Christian circles today. The Talmud itself condemned self-righteous Pharisees, aware that sanctimonious prigs and deceivers occasionally attached themselves to the movement. Such charlatans, however, are no indication of Pharisaic

teaching in general, which was sincere, pious, and devoted to the people who by and large were loyal to the sect.

The word Sadducee is thought to be derived from Zadok, Solomon's High Priest. Their members were drawn mainly from priestly, aristocratic, and military circles. Despite their being in the minority, they had great influence with the later Hasmonean kings, and for a period of time exercised total power in the state. They rejected the doctrine of immortality and interpreted the Bible literally and strictly. They denied the authority of the oral tradition and consequently rejected new laws and innovations which the Pharisees introduced in response to historical necessity. The Temple and its hierarchy was sacrosanct in their eyes, and any attempt to modify its influence was powerfully resisted by them.

It was obvious that the two groups could not live together in peace. Their opposing religious and political philosophies, reinforced by their economic and social differences, led to tension, frictions, and in the later stages of the Hasmonean dynasty erupted into all-out civil war.

With the destruction of the Temple in the year 70 C.E. and the resultant loss of political independence, the Sadducees lost their *raison d'etre* and disappeared. Only Pharisaism fully recovered from the profound shock of the events of the years 66–70 C.E. and was developed by the rabbis into the normative tradition of Judaism.

See also: ESSENES, HASMONEANS.

POLAND: There is evidence of a Jewish settlement in Poland as early as the 9th century. Very little is known of this settlement or where it originated whether in the south or the west. Polish Jewish history proper begins from the middle of the 13th century. The continuous persecution of Jews in western Europe, particularly in medieval Germany beginning with the Crusades, caused a stream of Jewish refugees to flow eastward. Concurrently, Poland, which had been devastated by the Tartar invasions, was badly in need of new settlers to rebuild the destroyed areas and colonize hitherto unsettled regions. The Polish nobility encouraged foreigners, in particular Germans, to immigrate. In the wake of the Germans came the German Jews. King Boleslav V granted the Jews liberal charters of self-government in 1264 as they helped him build cities and found industry and commerce. In 1320, the Polish provinces were united under Casimir the Great (1333–1370), also known as the Charlemagne of Poland, and the liberal charter for Jews was renewed. It was not long, however, before anti-Semitism began to develop. German immigrant traders brought their own local brand of Jew-hatred with them, and the Catholic church and local urban population, or burghers, were alarmed at the extension of Jewish influence and economic power. The stand-ard accusations of ritual murder and host desecration were soon leveled against Jews, and the first pogroms broke out around the middle of the 15th century. A number of the privileges and much of the protection previously granted were rescinded. In 1496. what amounted to a ghetto was established in Cracow, and in the course of the next century, in other cities.

The position and status of the Jews were actually part of a greater internal struggle taking place in Poland. The burghers, supported by the Church, were opposed to increased centralization. They regarded the Jews as competitors and used their monopoly of city governments to bar Jewish economic activity. The princes and kings on the other hand, in their desire to increase their revenues and to colonize and develop the land, utilized the Jews and often employed them as agents and tax farmers. The nobility was for free enter-prise and opposed the monopolistic pri-vileges of the urban guilds. They tried to break the economic hold of the towns and did not hesitate to use the Jewish merchant and tax farmer to do so. The Jews, however, were not opposed to the urban guild monopolies in themselves, but were forced to undermine them because of their dis-crimination against Jews. It was an alliance of necessity, the Jews serving the nobility because of their need to survive and the nobility using Jews to break the monopoly of their urban rivals. Stronger kings such as Sigismund I and II were not intimidated by the clergy and continued to give the Jews their protection. Stephen Bathory (1576–86) confirmed Jewish privileges and sharply attacked blood libel accusations. The campaign against the Jews, however, continued to gather force so that they were forced to settle on the estates of the nobility as managers, or in the small towns and villages where they were often inn-keepers. The vicious circle described above kindled the hatred of the peasants against the Jews whom they regarded as the agents of the oppressors, the nobles. Throughout all this, immigration of Jews to Poland had increased. During the course of the 16th century, Poland became the greatest center of rabbinic learning and attracted scholars and students from western Europe. Poland during this period consisted of four provinces: Great Poland, Minor Poland, Podolia, and Galicia. In 1580 the Jewish communities of these four provinces estab-lished an autonomous central organization called The Council of Four Lands. This council was the unquestioned overall governing body of Polish Jewry, both in internal matters and vis-à-vis the state. It lasted until 1764. The Jewish population grew from an estimated 30,000 at the end of the 15th century to hundreds of thou-sands of the eve of the great massacres of 1648. In 1648, Greek Orthodox Cossacks under their chieftain, Bogdan Chmielnicki, rebelled against their Polish Catholic over-lords. They vented their rage against the priesthood, the German traders, the nobil-ity, and the Jews whom they regarded as puppets of the nobility, used by them to oppress the peasants. The Polish peasants gleefully joined in the massacre, especially since the dreaded and victorious Cossacks promised them they would be spared. It is estimated that about 100,000 Jews lost their lives and hundreds of communities were destroyed. The 1648 outbreak caused havoc throughout the Jewish world and gave rise to much messianic speculation. No sooner was the Cossack invasion ended than Russia and Sweden invaded Poland. Again the Jews were victims, both at the hands of the invaders and of the Poles who accused them of treason and collaborating with the Swedes, possibly because the latter treated the Jews more kindly. The Jewish communities never fully recovered from the 1648 tragedy despite occasional efforts on the part of local rulers to alleviate their lot and rehabilitate them. Anti-Semitism was by now ingrained, part of the very warp and woof of Poland, with every effort aimed at toleration frustrated by the general anti-Jewish atmosphere. Moreover, Poland as a state was on the verge of total disintegration. Attacked on all sides by greedy neighbors and beset by internal problems which could not be solved, the central authority collapsed. Parallel to this, the central autonomous bodies of the Jewish community also began to deteriorate and lose their moral hold over the people. For the first time, charges of corruption and exploitation were leveled against Jewish communal leaders by the people themselves. During the 18th century, Poland was invaded by Russia, then there was civil war. Finally, Russia, Austria, and Prussia partitioned the country, leaving only a small and weak rump state. The Jews of the province of Posen now became part of German-Jewish history, those of Galicia entering the orbit of the Austro-Hungarian Empire, and those of the eastern provinces bestowing an unwanted Jewish population on Czarist Russia. In what remained of Poland, Jewish history continued on the same plane. The brief improvement in the condition of the Jews initiated by Napoleon in 1807 was followed a year later by reaction. Despite active Jewish participation in Poland's struggle for independence from Russia, and an attempt on the part of the Jewish upper class to assimilate even to the extent of petitioning the authorities for better treatment than that accorded other Jews, anti-Semitism remained strong. The revolutionary movement of 1863 proclaimed equal rights for Jews but by this time the majority of the Jewish population no longer trusted Polish promises and their support for the movement was lukewarm. At the end of the 19th century, an active anti-Semitic movement supported by press and clergy launched a vicious campaign against the Jews culminating in a pogrom in Warsaw in 1881. Zionism and other ideological movements now began to influence Polish Jewry and a mass immigration to western Europe and the United States began. While Jews occupied positions of influence in foreign trade and all branches of finance, the mutual suspicion and hostility between them and their non-Jewish neighbors was heightened and the Polish nationalists imposed an economic boycott on them. Under the terms of the Versailles Peace Treaty after World War I, the newly independent Poland agreed to grant minority rights to its Jews. This agreement was never fully adhered to although the Jews exercised political rights and elected Jewish members to the Polish Parliament. Anti-Jewish propaganda increased and determined efforts were made to hamper Jewish economic activity. A movement to boycott Jewish businesses was started and the tax burden was made heavier.

By 1938 over 300,000 Jews were unemployed. It is to the credit of Polish Jewry that despite all the above, a high level of religious and cultural activity was maintained. Indeed for centuries Poland was one of the great flourishing centers of

Jewish culture. In large towns and in the small *stettl*, the Jews pursued their own individual way of life, generally with little impact from their non-Jewish neighbors. Many of the greatest Jewish scholars lived and taught in Poland, which was famous for its talmudic academies and other cultural institutions. It was a great center of many aspects of Jewish expression including Ḥasidism, Zionism, and Yiddish culture.

What Polish anti-Semitism could not do, the Nazis accomplished. After occupying Poland in September 1939, they established ghettoes in the major cities with the purpose of assembling all Jews together prior to despatching them to the extermination camps. (*see* HOLOCAUST).

Poland's 3,000,000 Jews underwent wholesale martyrdom and few survived. After the war, thousands of Jews returned to Poland and attempted to pick up the tattered threads of Jewish life. Initially, the Communist regime was opposed to anti-Semitism but its efforts to uproot it proved futile. The Gomulka regime decided therefore in 1956 that the best solution of the Jewish problem lay in emigration, and thousands of Polish Jews thus arrived in Israel. The ingrained anti-Semitism, combined with Poland's adherence to the Soviet line in the Middle Eastern crisis, brought about a vicious anti-Semitic campaign after the Six-Day War of June 1967. Loyal Jewish Communists were dismissed from all positions of influence in the life of the country, and a further emigration followed as a result. Thus one of the most famous and creative Jewish communities has virtually ceased to exist.

See also: WARSAW, WARSAW GHETTO

PORTUGAL: Jews settled in Portugal while it was still under Arab rule. With the establishment of the Christian state, the Jews continued to live in tranquility. Alfonso III reorganized the Jewish community, putting a Chief Rabbi *(Arrabi Mor)* at its head. During the civil war of

1373, the Jewish quarter of Lisbon was sacked by Castilian troops, but Portuguese Jewry was not affected by the wave of massacres that swept its neighbor Spain in 1391 and the ensuing years. When the Jews of Spain were expelled in 1492, it was natural for the exiles to turn to Portugal as a main haven of refuge. It was estimated that 120,000 Jews, two-thirds of the exiles, made their way across the Portuguese frontier. King John II was prepared to admit such a vast mass of immigrants only if they helped fill his coffers. With the exception of six hundred wealthy families,

Former Jewish quarter in Lisbon

each of whom paid one hundred ducats, the rest were admitted on payment of a poll tax and for only eight months. Those who remained after the time limit were to be made royal slaves. The king then made departure impossible by delaying the movements of ships, thereby ensuring that very few of the refugees were able to leave. In addition, a plague then ravaging the country hit the undernourished Jewish refugees harder than anyone else. They were, in short, unwelcome. Even the native Portuguese Jews were uneasy about the mass immigration. When Don Emanuel ascended the throne in 1496, the conditions of the immigrants improved. The new king began his reign by releasing Jews from bondage. He wanted, however, to marry the daughter of Ferdinand and Isabella of Spain. The princess agreed on condition that he would rid the country of all infidels. Accordingly, Emanuel signed an edict of expulsion in October 1496. He later changed his mind and had the whole community forcibly baptized. This mass conversion filled the country with vast numbers of insincere new Christians, and instead of solving Portugal's Jewish problem it perpetuated it in the form of the Marranos. To solve the problem, the Inquisition was introduced with all its succeeding horrors. Those Jews who succeeded in escaping its wrath established "Portuguese" congregations in London, Amsterdam, Hamburg, and New York in the 16th–17th centuries. During the Napoleonic Wars, a community was once again established in Lisbon by British Jews from Gibraltar. Complete freedom of worship, however, was only granted after the revolution of 1910. There were still Marranos, however, especially in the remote provinces, and in 1925 a movement was started to help them return to Judaism.

Aside from Marranos, whose numbers cannot be ascertained, Portugal has only a handful of Jews living mostly in Lisbon.

PRAYER BOOK (Siddur): Book containing the full text of the prayers recited by a Jew both in the synagogue and in the home. In ancient times prayers were not written down, but prayer in itself is as old as Israel. The scriptural narrative is interspersed with prayer — individual prayers as well as ritual prayers such as the priestly blessing in Numbers 6:22. Organized prayer was sufficiently established by the time of Isaiah to have drifted into conventionality and thereby aroused the indignation of the prophet (Isaiah 1:15). The basic outline of

Jewish prayer has not changed since the days of the Temple, where the *Shema* and the Ten Commandments were recited daily. After the Babylonian exile, the men of the Great Assembly laid down the lines on which all Jewish and congregational prayer has been conducted ever since. They made the blessing *(berakha)* the unit of Jewish prayer; each blessing begins with the six Hebrew words for "Blessed art Thou, O Lord our God, King of the Universe." To the *Shema,* they added the *Shemoneh Esrei*, also known as the *Amidah*, and they introduced worship into the home by instituting the *Kiddush* and *Havdalah* for the incoming and outgoing of Sabbaths and festivals. In the generation after the destruction of the Second Temple by the Romans, the synagogue service was in essentials identical with the service as known today. The Talmudic age (200–500) added several prayers of genius to the liturgy, notably those of the great Babylonian teacher Rav. The spiritual leaders of Babylonian Jewry, the *Geonim*, sanctioned various enlargements of the service, and in the 9th century, the first written prayer book was produced by Amram Gaon. This process continued in the ensuing centuries, but most of the editions are to this day mainly based on that first prayer book. In the course of time, there arose two main streams of liturgical tradition, the Sephardi based on the Babylonian rite, and the Ashkenazi based on the Palestinian. Within both groups there developed further divergences, but these are mainly with regard to minor prayers, supplications, and poems to be recited on special occasions. In all rites, the basic prayers are practically the same. The prayer book follows closely the routine of the sacrificial cult in the Temple. First come the daily services, then the Sabbath and festival services in order of their appearance in the Jewish year. Since the full liturgy for festivals is too extensive to be included in one volume, special books of prayers for the various festivals called

Maḥzorim were instituted. The remaining contents of the prayer book deals with the liturgy to be followed on all possible occasions and encompasses life's events in their entirety. Some prayer books include the whole book of Psalms, the Passover *Haggadah*, and some laws and customs. The contents of the *siddur* in non-obligatory matters however, are subject to custom, and this often differs from country to country. The first printed prayer book was the Ashkenazi *siddur* in 1490 and from that time on the prayer book became widespread and its use by every worshiper a matter of course. In modern times, the Reform, Conservative and Reconstructionist movements have produced their own prayer books in accordance with their religious philosophy. The Reform prayer book includes prayers in the vernacular, and various other modifications such as the omission of prayers for the restoration of the sacrificial cult. The Sephardic term for a prayer book is a *tephlla*.

PRIESTS AND PRIESTHOOD (Kohen, Kehunnah):

The priesthood was established in Israel after the Exodus from Egypt. In the time of the patriarchs, there was no official priesthood, and acts of public worship such as the offering of sacrifices were performed by the head of the family. This privilege was inherited by the first-born son. According to tradition, the first-born served as the priesthood until the completion of the tabernacle, Israel's first house of worship. As a punishment for their participation in the sin of the golden calf, they were replaced by the Levites who, during that tragic episode, remained staunchly loyal to God. The tribe of Levi was henceforth dedicated to the service of God while the male descendants of Aaron were granted the hereditary privileges and obligations of the priestly office. These obligations consisted of responsibility for the sacred service including the sacrificial cult, the supervision of hygienic purity, and,

to some extent, teaching and administering the law. The priests were strictly enjoined to observe ritual purity and were expected to uphold a higher standard of holiness than the rest of the people. Accordingly, they were forbidden to come into contact with a dead body except in the case of the seven immediate relatives (father, mother, brother, sister, son, daughter, and spouse). Furthermore, a priest was forbidden to marry a divorcee, a prostitute, a proselyte, or the offspring of such an illegal priestly marriage. In addition to the above, the High Priest was not permitted to marry a widow, nor was he permitted to come into contact with a corpse even of one of the seven immediate relatives. Being dedicated to the service of God, the priests, and indeed the whole tribe of Levi, were not granted an inheritance in the land of Israel as were the other tribes. In return for their service, they were granted certain gifts and privileges which ensured their livelihood. The priest's privileges, some twenty-four in number, included certain parts of the sacrifices offered and the *Terumah*, or Heave-Offering, which all Israelites were obligated to set aside from their produce. Even the Levites, who depended for their support on the tithe, had to give one-tenth of what *they* received to the priest. According to the Bible (Num. 6:23–27) the priestly descendants of Aaron were also obligated to bless the people. This ancient blessing has remained part of the synagogue liturgy to this day. The Levites, who for the most part performed secondary functions, resented the unique privilege conferred as a hereditary right on the family of Aaron. This resentment came to the fore in the rebellion of Korah (Numbers 16).

During the reign of King David, a radical reorganization of the priesthood was carried out, the priestly tribe being divided into twenty-four sections or watches, each of which took it in turns to officiate in the Temple for a week at a time. The hereditary priesthood was entrusted to the family of Zadok, a descendant of Eleazar, the son of Aaron. This arrangement continued until the time of the Hasmoneans. During the First Temple period, the priesthood, which was generally loyal to the house of David, became firmly entrenched and institutionalized. This inevitably led to a certain amount of corruption which the prophets were quick to condemn. Moreover, the existence of local sanctuaries throughout the land, particularly in the Northern Kingdom of Israel where priests not of the tribe of Levi were appointed, led to a weakening of the priesthood and its power. Under the kings Hezekiah and Josiah, however, all worship was centralized in the Temple at Jerusalem, and most local sanctuaries were destroyed. This strengthened the influence and status of the priests.

At the beginning of the Second Temple period, after the Babylonian Exile, the High Priest was regarded by the Persian authorities as the head of the nation. There were at this time more priests than Levites so that part of the Levitical tithes were diverted to the pockets of the priests. With the conquests of Alexander the Great and the spread of Hellenism, the priesthood tended toward assimilation and the acceptance of Greek culture. This was one of the factors leading to the rebellion of the zealously religious priestly family, the Hasmoneans. Furthermore, the rise of a lay class of scholars, rabbis, and teachers distinct from the priesthood, undermined the latter's influence. The priests joined with the aristocracy and the military and formed the Sadducee Party while the masses followed the Pharisees led by the great rabbinic sages. Under the Hasmoneans, the priesthood and leadership of the nation were combined, the eight heads of this dynasty, from Jonathan to Antigonus, being both High Priest and head of state. In the last chaotic days of the Second Temple, the High Priesthood became completely discredited, the office becoming a prize in the troubled politics of the period. For example, Jason was dismissed when Menelaus who was not even of the tribe of Levi made a higher bid for the appointment. Under Herod, the office of High Priest was at the disposal of the sovereign. He could appoint and dismiss nominees at his own caprice. Between 37 B.C. and 70 C.E. (the year of the destruction of the Second Temple), there were no less than twenty-eight High Priests chosen from several priestly families.

With the destruction of the Temple, the priesthood lost its meaning and the foundation of its existence. Its memory was kept alive by the practice of calling anyone of a priestly family first to the reading of the scriptures and by the bestowing of the priestly blessing in the framework of the synagogue service. The priest also performs the ceremony of the redemption of the first-born and may not marry a divorcee or convert or become ritually impure through contact with the dead.

Reform Judaism regards the priesthood as a relic of the past with no religious significance for the present. It has accordingly abolished all regulations, privileges, prohibitions, and restrictions relating to priestly families (Kohanim).

PROPHETS AND PROPHECY: In the Greek translation of the Bible, the Septuagint, the Hebrew word *Navi* is rendered by the Greek *Prophetes*, signifying one who "tells forth" a divinely inspired message. The etymology of the word *Navi* is uncertain. Some scholars derive it from an Arabic root meaning "to proclaim" or "to announce." Many modern authorities, however, connect it with an ancient Akkadian word meaning "to call." *Navi*, then, would imply one who is called to perform a divine mission. In the first book of Samuel (Ch. 9:9), we are told that "He who is now called a prophet was once called a seer." The Hebrew words *Ro'eh* or *Ḥozeh* both mean one who sees or knows (what is hidden from the eyes of ordinary men) and the above-quoted line is of value in the study of the prophetic office in Israel. There is evidence to suggest that the prophetic institution was prevalent in ancient Near-Eastern countries even prior to the rise of the people of Israel. This prophet, however, was more in the nature of the *Ro'eh*, a fortune teller or soothsayer corresponding more or less to the Arab dervish. He functioned through trances and ecstatic spells, and his prophecy was often accompanied by the inflicting of wounds or cuts on the body. While it is evident from the Bible that this type of diviner and soothsayer also functioned in ancient Israelite society during the earlier period of the Judges and the Monarchy, prophecy in Israel for the most part developed in a unique direction gradually throwing off all resemblances to its Semitic counterpart. The Bible describes different types of prophets. Moses is regarded as the chief of all the prophets. This is stated specifically in the book of Deuteronomy and was included among the thirteen principles of faith of Moses Maimonides. Moses spoke to God "face to face," while the rest of the prophets were given God's message through the medium of a dream, a trance, or a state of ecstasy. Moses the prophet was also a great lawgiver and judge. Samuel resembled Moses in that he fulfilled the double function of prophet and judge. During the early period of the monarchy, there were prophets attached to the king's court so that he could consult them on religious and political matters. In the very nature of things, these prophets, depending for their livelihood on the king, would tend to prophesy what the king wanted to hear. Even at this early stage, however, there arose prophets who regarded the proclamation of the truth as more important than their own popularity. Nathan, King David's court prophet, did not hesitate to express his moral condemnation of David's conduct in the "Bathsheba Affair." This image of the prophet as the man of truth regardless of the consequences is embodied in the personality of Elijah, the fearless defender of monotheism and ethical values at a time when idolatrous worship and moral degradation threatened to destroy the Kingdom of Israel.

The heyday of prophecy in ancient Israel lasted for a period of approximately three hundred years, from the middle of the 8th century B.C.E. to the early Second Temple period. This period is characterized by the appearance, in rapid succession, of a line of prophets commencing with Amos and Hosea and concluding with the last of the prophets, Malachi. These prophets are generally referred to as the "literary" prophets for they were the first whose prophecies were committed to writing. They are also sometimes called the "classical" prophets. Their writings are contained in the latter part of the second division of the Bible, *Neviim*, in the books of Isaiah, Jeremiah, Ezekiel, and the twelve minor prophets.

What manner of men were the prophets? Allowing for individual differences in personality, in style, in content, and in outlook, it is nevertheless possible to lay down certain basic principles common to the outlook, behavior, and religious and ethical philosophy of most of them. First and foremost, the prophet is the mouthpiece of God. He does not speak in his own name but prefaces his speeches and proclamations with the phrase "Thus saith the Lord!" He is an instrument — at times an unwilling one — of God, and whether he likes it or not, he must speak out. As God's emissary, he is the passionate defender of monotheism and conversely, the uncompromising denouncer of idolatry. Second, the prophet is a critic of the social order. He is the inveterate enemy of evil in all its manifestations; in particular, he pours out his wrath on those who exploit and persecute the underprivileged. No one is spared from the prophet's lashing tongue no matter how important his station in life. Kings, priests, and the masses of the people, all alike, are subjected to the scathing criticism of the prophet. When the Kingdom of Israel was at the zenith of its power and material prosperity during the reign of Jeroboam II (786–746 B.C.E.) the prophet Amos appeared to denounce the smugness, luxury, and self-satisfaction of the wealthy classes, the corruption of the judges, and the affliction of the poorer classes. When Judah, in alliance with Egypt, planned to rebel against Babylon, Jeremiah forecast the hopelessness of all resistance and the inevitability of the coming destruction. Both Amos and Jeremiah were denounced as demagogic agitators and traitors. Jeremiah was imprisoned and accused of treason. Yet they continued to proclaim their messages regardless of the consequences. And therein lies the great difference between the true prophets and those labeled false prophets. The latter were "professional prophets," that is, they received payment for prophesying. Quite naturally, therefore, they prophesied what the people who paid them wanted to hear. When Jeremiah prophesied defeat, the false prophets proclaimed unashamedly that victory was at hand. The false prophets tended to band together in groups, while true prophets, for the most part, led solitary existences. False prophets engaged in acts of frenzy to work themselves up artificially to their "divine" inspiration. The true prophet retains his consciousness and self-control under revelation. The true prophets were critics of the religious establishment. They denounced the priests for the mechanical performance of ritual and for personal corruption. They were not, as has been mistakenly assumed, opposed to ritual and the sacrificial system as such. They were opposed to the belief that religion was exclusively a matter of priesthood and temple. They insisted that

sacrifice must be accompanied by justice and correct ethical conduct. Religion, in the world-outlook of the prophets, includes both ritual and ethics. They regarded worship which is preceded or followed by evil action as an absurd hypocrisy.

A special word must be said about the general notion of the prophet as a predictor of the future. The prophet was not a fortune-teller. He envisaged the future on the basis of past experience, and more important, from the standpoint of divine will. He was also a political analyst, able to detect and predict the shifting trends in world politics. As foretellers, the prophets were not always successful and there are a number of prophecies recorded in the Bible which did not come to pass. To quote a distinguished non-Jewish scholar, "The prophets were not gifted in the art of reading the details of the future to any greater extent than experts along these lines elsewhere in the world. Insofar as they did indicate the general direction of human progress, it was due to the fact that they were better qualified students of the present than others."

The prophet has unjustifiably been accused of sternness and undue pessimism. The tragic conditions of their times, and the corruption and injustice surrounding them undoubtedly influenced their outlook. Nevertheless, their long-term forecast for humanity was optimistic. For despite the impending doom and destruction, they foresaw a time when God's people would return to their land and when humanity in general would live in peace and harmony. Furthermore they were imbued with a deep love of their people, and their prophecies of doom afforded them no pleasure whatsoever. On the contrary, the realization of their prediction, especially of national disaster, did not give them satisfaction or fill them with an "I told you so" attitude. Behind the prophet's stern warnings were love and compassion for mankind. He

Purim Adloyada in the streets of Tel Aviv

began with a message of doom, but ends with a message of hope and comfort. His message is not confined to Israel, but God's mercy extends to all mankind. Moreover, he teaches that true repentance may avert the evil decree, for God does not desire the death of the sinner but his repentance and his conversion to the path of righteousness. *(For individual prophets see separate entries.)*

PROVERBS: Second book of the third division of the Bible, *Ketuvim* (the writings). It belongs, together with the book of Ecclesiastes and Job, to what is known as "wisdom literature." This literature was widespread in the Orient in general. Its purpose was to provide maxims for the moral conduct of everyday life. In fact, some of the "words of the wise" in Chapter 22 closely resemble the ancient Egyptian proverbs of Amenhotep. The book contains thirty-one chapters, generally optimistic in tone, in which man is exhorted to carry out the dictates of wisdom for his own good. Wisdom is interpreted as getting the best out of life, and immoral and foolish behavior as a denial of the real joy of living. The tone of the Proverbs is universal, and while the word "Israel" does not occur once, the word *adam* (man) is used thirty-three times. Its teachings are applicable to all men and all times. The basis of the wisdom offered, however, is Jewish, since wisdom is defined as the fear of the Lord. The Proverbs, furthermore, deal with every phase of human relationships.

The opening sentence of the book assigns the Proverbs to King Solomon. While it is true that he is reported to have uttered three thousand Proverbs (I Kings, 5:12), there is unmistakable evidence in the book itself that it is not one continuous work written by one author. The Talmud states that "Hezekiah and his colleagues wrote *Isaiah, Proverbs,* the *Song of Songs,* and *Ecclesiastes.*" ("Wrote," in the above context, means compiled or edited.)

The most logical assumption is that the Proverbs, while originating in the days of Solomon, were further edited in the days of King Hezekiah, and received their final form after the Babylonian exile, during the period of the men of the Great Assembly.

PSALMS (Tehillim): First book of the 3rd section of the Bible, *Ketuvim* (the writings). The word "psalm" is derived from the Greek *Psalmas* meaning a stringed instrument, and is the word used in the Greek translation of the Bible, the Septuagint, for the Hebrew *Mizmor*, found in the heading of fifty-seven psalms. In rabbinical literature, the designation of the book is *Sefer Tehillim*, "the Book of Praises," and this name has passed into traditional usage among Jews. The book contains 150 sacred poems with an inner subdivision into five books, beginning respectively with Psalms 1, 42, 78, 90, and 107. In content, the psalms may be divided into three distinct groups: 1) Psalms of supplication relating to national disaster or individual entreaty; 2) Psalms of glorification relating to national and individual thanksgiving and praise, praise of the Torah, of Jerusalem, and the "Royal Psalms"; 3) Psalms of an instructive character dealing with right belief, action, and historic lessons.

In rabbinic tradition, the authorship of the psalms is assigned to King David. "Moses gave Israel the five books of the Torah and correspondingly David gave them the five books of the Psalms." This statement created the impression that according to Jewish teaching, the whole of the book of Psalms was written by David. However, elsewhere in the Talmud it is asserted: "David wrote the Book of Psalms, including in it the work of the elders, namely, Adam, Melchizedek, Abraham, Moses, Hanan, Yeduthan, Asaph, and the three sons of Korah." In other words, it was recognized by the rabbis of old that the book was a collection of psalms by different authors. The great medieval commentators, Rashi, Ibn Ezra, and Kimḥi also rejected the belief that the book, as it exists, was completed in the reign of the exiles from Babylon. Recent investigations into the religious poetry of the ancient Near East, however, tend to confirm the essential antiquity of the psalms, which in parts show a striking similarity to ancient Egyptian, Babylonian, and Canaanite hymns.

The singing of hymns by a choir of Levites and the assembly of worshippers to the accompaniment of string and wind instruments was an essential feature of the Temple service, and many of the psalms have introductory words with specific instructions to the musicians, for example, La-Menatzeaḥ, "to the chief musician."

However, the psalms are not treasured for the musical or poetic significance alone. Nor is the question of authorship relevant to their message. Their lofty conception of man and God, their ethical content, and their power to soothe and comfort, have made them one of the most cherished cultural and religious possessions of mankind, equally precious to both synagogue and church.

PURIM (Lots): Festival celebrated on the 14th of *Adar*, commemorating the deliverance of the Jews of Persia from the destruction plotted by Haman, minister of the King Ahasuerus. The story is told in the book of Esther, which relates how lots *(purim)* were cast to select a day for the annihilation of the Jewish community and how the king decreed that this should be done on the 13th day of the month of *Adar*. With the help and guidance of Mordecai, her uncle, the king's beautiful Jewish wife Esther intervened and the intended day of destruction was turned into a day of salvation. Haman was hung on the gallows he had had set up for Mordecai and the Jews were given free rein to wreak vengeance on their enemies. This they did on the 13th, celebrating their deliverance on the next day. In some places,

such as the capital Susa (Shushan), fighting continued on the 14th, so that the redemption could only be celebrated on the 15th. The tradition thus arose that cities which were walled at the time of Joshua, for instance Jerusalem, should celebrate the festival on the 15th of *Adar*, as was done in Susa.

Purim is the most joyous day in the Jewish calendar. In the synagogue, the major part of the service consists of reading the book of Esther from a specially prepared, handwritten parchment scroll known as *Megillat Esther*. The reading is preceded by a special benediction, and both men and women must listen to the *Megillah* recited both in the evening and the morning. It is the custom during the reading to greet every mention of the name of Haman with a din of rattles and shouts of disapproval. The *Al Hanisim* prayer which contains an account of the Purim story is inserted in the *Amidah* and in the grace after meals. In the morning service, there is a special reading from the Bible of the defeat of the Amalekites by the children of Israel. The reading is based on the tradition that Haman was a descendant of the Amalekite king, Agag. Another feature of the Purim celebration is the banquet which has become a traditional occasion for merrymaking. The rabbis display more latitude on Purim

Adloyada *in Tel Aviv*

than on any other occasion, even permitting wine drinking until the celebrants can no longer distinguish between "Cursed be Haman" and "Blessed be Mordecai." According to Jewish law, Purim is also the occasion for the sending of gifts *(Mishloah Manot)* to friends and the giving of charity to the poor. In the Middle Ages, it was customary to stage comic plays known as *Purim-Spiel*, in which Haman is the villain and Mordecai and Esther the heroes. It was accompanied by masquerading, dancing, and parties for children. The Purim festival thus became a sort of Jewish carnival.

In a leap year, Purim is celebrated on the 14th of the second month of *Adar*. The same date in the first *Adar* is referred to as *Purim Katan*, the minor Purim. While this day is not celebrated, the supplicatory prayer *(Tahanun)* is omitted, and fasting and funeral eulogies are prohibited.

The Purim *characters (17th cent.* Megillah*)*

RABBI ("My Master"): Title bestowed upon Jewish religious authorities and teachers. It was first used during the Mishnaic period as a mode of address for sages renowned for their learning and erudition. Gradually, however, the title was limited to ordained members of the Sanhedrin qualified to give decisions on Jewish law. The act of Ordination *(Semikhah)* could only be performed in the land of Israel. Babylonian scholars therefore were addressed as *Rav*. Although the ancient ceremony of Ordination was abolished in the 4th century, it was nevertheless felt necessary by rabbinic leaders to impose certain basic qualifications on candidates for the title *Rabbi*. There was thus introduced, particularly among Ashkenazi Jewry, a limited form of Ordination known as *Hattarat Horaah* — the permission to give decisions in matters of Jewish law. This ordination was obtained in writing after the candidate had undergone a thorough examination in the Talmud and codes of Jewish law conducted by an institution of higher Jewish learning such as a *Yeshiva* or by an individual rabbi renowned for his scholarship. This system has by and large remained in force until the present time. The academic demands made upon the candidate, however, vary according to the character of the three main groups (Orthodox, Conservative and Reform) within Judaism and the rabbinic institutions maintained by them. Most modern rabbinical institutions, Orthodox included, demand that the rabbinic student attain a secular degree in addition to or as part of his rabbinic studies. In more extremist circles, however, the *Yeshiva*

is still run on the pattern of its eastern European predecessor, with instruction being given in Yiddish and secular studies frowned upon. The functions, status, and authority of the rabbi have undergone a basic change in modern times. Until the late Middle Ages, the rabbi received no financial remuneration, and in order to support himself and his family had to have a private occupation. This was in accordance with Talmudic law which states that it is forbidden to derive any benefit or income from the Torah. After the expulsion of the Jews from Spain in 1492, however, many rabbis were unable to find a suitable occupation in their new environment, while at the same time the need grew for full-time rabbis to minister to the needs of the exiles. Generally speaking, the rabbis' duties were limited to the educational and religious spheres. He was often the head of the local court *(Bet Din)* which in certain cases was given wide powers by the non-Jewish authorities. He was also responsible for the running of the local *Yeshivah* and for the supervision of the dietary laws and ritual slaughter. He worked within the framework of the autonomous Jewish community, and while being invested with prestige and power was nevertheless subject to the lay leadership. Preaching was not one of his primary functions, and was usually limited to two special addresses delivered on the Sabbath preceding the festival of Passover, *Shabbat Hagadol*, and on the Sabbath between *Rosh Hashanah* and the Day of Atonement, *Shabbat Shuvah*. Preaching, as such, was the task of a specially appointed official called the *maggid*. The stress on the educational aspect of the rabbi's work may be discerned from the fact that in Mediterranean communities, he was referred to as *marbitz Torah*, "the spreader of Torah."

In modern times, the stress has shifted from the educational to the spiritual sphere. In common with his colleagues of other faiths, the rabbi has become a spiritual leader whose duties cover the wide spectrum of problems raised by modern living. He is a social and marriage counselor, he visits the sick, comforts the bereaved, and attempts to alleviate suffering in general. He participates in interfaith activities, and his image vis-à-vis the non-Jewish community is considered vital to both communities. Accordingly, his public speaking and preaching must be on the highest level. His educational activities for young people and adults, while considered part of his duties, are not, as in the past, the main part of his work. The above duties may in fact be carried out by someone who does not possess a full rabbinic diploma. In the British Commonwealth, such an official is referred to as a "Minister." The institution of a chief Rabbinate is not common to all Jewries and in the United States and Canada is unknown. During the course of the ages, Chief Rabbis were from time to time appointed by the secular authorities to act as intermediaries between them and the Jewish community. Such appointees were usually, in effect, glorified tax collectors. On the other hand, some rabbis achieved the distinction of being voluntarily accepted by the Jewish community as Chief Rabbi because of their undisputed learning and piety. In the British Commonwealth, the Chief Rabbinate is considered an integral part of the internal structure of the Jewish community. In the State of Israel, there are two Chief Rabbis, one Ashkenazi, the other Sephardi, for the country as a whole and for each large city. This system was introduced by the British in 1920.

RABIN, YITZHAK (1922–): Israeli soldier and diplomat. In June 1967, when the outnumbered Israel Army defeated the Arab Armies in the Six-Day War, Yitzhak Rabin was the Chief of Staff responsible for the brilliant strategy that won the war. Rabin was born in Israel of parents who immigrated from the U.S. As a professional soldier, he rose through the ranks, fighting in World War II, in Israel's 1948 War of Independence, and in the 1956 Sinai campaign. In 1964 he was made Chief of Staff of the Israel Army.

In 1967, shortly after the Six-Day War, when Rabin received an honorary doctorate from the Hebrew University, he said: "Our *sabra* youth . . . were exalted when they heard of the paratroopers who conquered the Western Wall. . . . These weeping soldiers had a direct confrontation with Jewish history. Our warriors prevailed not by their weapons but by their sense of mission. This army, which I had the privilege of commanding, came from the people and returns to the people."

Yitzhak Rabin left the army at the end of 1967 when he was appointed Israel's Ambassador to the United States.

Yitzhak Rabin

RASHI (Abbreviation of Rabbi Shelomo Yitzhaki, or Rabbi Solomon son of Isaac; 1040–1105): Scholar whose commentaries on the Bible and Talmud are regarded to this day as the basis for the study of these basic works of Judaism. Very little is known of his life, and Rashi has been the subject of many legends. He studied in Germany in the academies at Mainz and Worms but at the age of twenty-five returned to his hometown, Troyes, in France, where he organized his own academy. Rashi's commentaries on the Bible and Talmud are characterized by a simple style and by the clear manner in which he explains the most intricate problems. Unlike the *Tosaphists*, the school of commentators founded by his son-in-law and by his grandson, Rashi does not enter into complicated hair-splitting discussions and often anticipates in a carefully worded phrase the questions raised and the answers given at length by the *Tosaphists*. In his commentary on the Bible, Rashi made extensive use of rabbinic legends and *Midrash* when he felt that they contributed to the understanding of the text. Despite his greatness as a commentator, he would at times rather say "I cannot explain this," than give a forced interpretation. Scattered among Rashi's commentaries are some 10,000 French words, and thus his writings also provide a valuable source for the study of old French language and pronunciation. Throughout the centuries, young Jewish boys were initiated into their higher studies by the intensive study of the Bible with Rashi's commentary.

READING, MARQUESS OF (Rufus Daniel Isaacs, 1860–1935): British statesman. An outstanding lawyer, he entered Parliament as a Liberal and was the first Jew to hold the appointments of Solicitor General (1910), Attorney General (1910), and Lord Chief Justice (1913). He became British Ambassador to the United States in 1918, Viceroy of India in 1921, and Foreign Secretary in 1931. He was created a peer in 1916 and Marquess in 1926 — again the only British Jew to have received this honor. His wife Eva was president of the British section of the World Jewish Congress.

REFORM JUDAISM (also known as Progressive Judaism): A religious movement, one of the three mainstreams into which Judaism is divided today (the other two being Orthodox and Conservative.)

It originated in Germany, as a direct result of the gathering movement of emancipation for the Jews in the late 18th and early 19th centuries. The breakdown of the ghetto and the established institutions of Jewish life came suddenly and without sufficient preparation. After centuries of oppression and isolation, the dream of a free Jewry in a free enlightened state enjoying equality of rights and obligations no longer seemed remote or farfetched. Judaism and its ancient tradi-

Title page of Rashi's *commentary (1720)*

tions seemed outdated to many. Moreover, the practice of its tenets and commandments was an impediment to Jewish emancipation, for indeed, many non-Jews opposed granting equal rights to Jews on the grounds that their separate ways of life made them unassimilable. Furthermore, this was the age of science, and Judaism, together with other religions, found itself confronted with discoveries and theories that at first glance seemed to contradict the Bible. Many young Jews entering universities found themselves unable and eventually unwilling to attempt to reconcile Judaism with scientific knowledge. These winds of change blew with a fury that threatened to engulf the whole of western and central European Jewry. Many were those who chose the path of apostasy, baptism, and in other cases complete alienation from Judaism. Reform arose out of and in response to the situation described above.

Hebrew Union College Synagogue, Jerusalem

One of the first pioneers of German Reform was Israel Jacobson (1763–1828). He introduced changes in the ritual and sought to beautify the services. Prayers were shortened, instrumental music was introduced, selected portions of the prayers were read in the vernacular, and the sermon was made a regular feature of the service. A disciple of Moses Mendelssohn, he did not intend to break or tamper with the basic fundamentals of Judaism, but rather to eliminate what he considered obsolete. His was more of an external reform than anything else. It started a trend, however, that was to become a landslide. Abraham Geiger (1810–1874) has been described as the real founder of Reform Judaism in the theological sense. For him, a break with Orthodoxy was inevitable. Geiger was a profound scholar whose intellect could cope with all the attacks that were bound to come. He enunciated two principles which have remained basic to Reform Judaism. First, that Judaism is progressive and not static, that it is the result of a slow development, an evolution, and not something transmitted in one miraculous moment. Revelation is a continuing process which occurs to great sages and saints of every generation, and they have as much authority and right to pronounce decisions on matters of faith as the sages of old. The second principle followed from the first. If Judaism is a developing process, then it must be studied critically and in accordance with the knowledge available to each age. The learning in the synagogue must therefore be characterized by free investigation and the objective search for truth. These ideas led to radical conclusions, namely, that if truth is not static but progressive, then the authority of the Bible and the ancient codes of law may be challenged. Moreover, Geiger and other Reform leaders believed that if Jews were to play a part as equal citizens in their countries of adoption, it would be necessary to eliminate all the ideas and prayers that were obstacles to this aim. The universal aspect of Judaism and Jewry as a "Light unto the Nations" should be stressed whereas a Jewish nationalistic movement could prevent the Jews from fulfilling that universal mission. All the above led early Reform to the adoption of extreme attitudes toward Jewish traditions and observances. Ceremonies, commandments, and customs no longer considered meaningful were either modified or cut out altogether. References to the re-establishment of the Jewish state or the Temple were removed from the prayer book. The belief in the coming of the Messianic Age in which the ideals of universal peace and good will would be realized were substituted. It must be stressed, however, that early Reform was not only concerned with change but also with preservation. The threat of wholesale apostasy and the abandonment of Judaism, it was genuinely believed, could only be met by the modification, and if necessary, changes in Judaism so as to make it more meaningful to Jews who wished to live modern lives and at the same time remain faithful to the ancient reservoir of Judaism. With the growth of opposition to Reform on the part of the defenders of Jewish tradition, subsequently called Orthodox, Reform became even more extremist in its policy of change. It was, however, in the United States that Reform Judaism developed to its full stature. Men such as Samuel Hirsch (1815–1889), David Einhorn (1809–1879), and Isaac Mayer Wise (1819–1900) laid the foundations for what was to become a vigorous and large religious movement. Above all, it was Wise who gave to Reform its religious institutions — The Union of American Hebrew Congregations in 1873, The Hebrew Union College in 1875, and The Central Conference of American Rabbis in 1889. The first gave Reform its congregational framework; the second a training center for rabbis in the spirit of Reform Judaism; and the third

gave Reform its rabbinical association. Reform Judaism, true to its principles of progressive revelation, has not remained static. Early Reform, as was noted above, often adopted extreme positions either out of conviction or in response to the extremism of its opponents. Thus, in the United States, a conference of Reform rabbis held at Pittsburgh in 1885 adopted a program subsequently known as the Pittsburgh Platform which was extremist in character. This program, however, it must be noted, was never considered binding in the sense of dogma. Although Reform rabbis, in general, were opposed to Zionism, there were among its leaders those who supported the Zionist movement from the outset. Among these were such influential Reform rabbis as Stephen S. Wise and Bernard Felsenthal. While it is true that the Central Conference of American Rabbis originally opposed the Balfour Declaration, the opposition became less and less with the passage of time, and in the 1930's the process was reversed. The majority of Reform rabbis then adopted a pro-Zionist stand. Reform leaders played an important role in the struggle preceding the establishment of the State of Israel with Abba Hillel Silver exercising a crucial influence on the thinking of top American leaders. In recent years, the bonds between Israel and Reform have been further strengthened with the holding of Reform rabbinic conferences in Israel, the establishment of a branch of the Hebrew Union College in Jerusalem, and the founding of several Reform congregations throughout the country. Parallel to Reform's modification of its outlook on Zionism, there has been a reappraisal of its attitude to Jewish tradition and ritual. Many Reform leaders felt that Reform, like most revolutionary movements, had gone too far. Since the 1930s, there has been an increasing tendency to reintroduce traditional ceremonies and observances as well as the study and use of the Hebrew language, and

Blowing the shofar at the Western Wall

this trend is continuing today. But Reform Judaism is still faithful to its basic principles: total equality between men and women and the abolition of the partition separating the sexes in the family pew in the synagogue are essential features of all Reform congregations. The Union of American Hebrew Congregations is comprised of over 650 congregations with a membership of over a million. The Central Conference of American Rabbis has a membership of over 1,000, most of whom are graduates of the Hebrew Union College — Jewish Institute of Religion. Reform Judaism has spread to almost all free countries with Jewish communities. It is organized on a worldwide basis through the World Union for Progressive Judaism, founded in London in 1926.

RELIGIOUS SERVICES: There are three daily statutory services held in the synagogue or said by the individual unable to attend communal services. They are *Shaharit, Minhah,* and *Maariv.*

SHAHARIT, which means the dawn prayer, should be recited before the first quarter of the day has passed. It corresponds to the dawn sacrifice *(tamid)* offered each day in the temple and according to rabbinic tradition was instituted by the patriarch Abraham. It is the most extensive of the daily prayers and consists of the following sections:

1) Preliminary blessings of thanks and praise originally intended to be spoken by the individual at home on rising. They are called *Birkot Ha-Shahar;*

2) *Pesukei D'Zimra* — passages of song. These are psalms, scriptural verses, and doxologies (responses of adoration);

3) The *Shema* and its benedictions;

4) The *Amidah* (standing), also known as *Shemoneh Esreh* (eighteen [blessings]);

5) Supplications known as *Tahanun;*

6) Conclusion, consisting of Psalms 145 and 20, the *Aleinu* prayer, and the mourners' *Kaddish.*

The *Shema* and the *Amidah* constitute the morning service proper, and their recital may be traced back to Temple times. On Mondays and Thursdays, there is a short reading from the five books of Moses after supplicatory prayers. This custom has been attributed to Ezra and the men of the Great Assembly. Mondays and Thursdays were market days in ancient times, and the opportunity was therefore taken of reading from the Bible to those people who came into the city from outlying areas where it was not always read. On these days, the supplicatory prayers are also lengthened.

MINHAH. The second statutory daily prayer is *Minhah,* which means offering. It corresponds to the daily evening sacrifice in the Temple, which in practice was offered several hours before sunset. It may therefore be recited any time during the afternoon until sunset. It opens with Psalm 145 *(Ashrei)* and is followed by the *Amidah* said silently by each worshipper and then repeated by the reader. The *Shema* is omitted in the *Minhah* service since its reading is based on the Biblical words "when thou liest down and when thou risest up," in other words, at night and in the morning.

The *Amidah* is followed by *Tahanun, Aleinu,* and the mourners' *Kaddish.* In some congregations, the *Minhah* service is held late in the afternoon and followed immediately by the evening service, *Maariv.* According to rabbinic tradition, *Minhah* was instituted by the patriarch Isaac. It is also associated with the contest of the prophet Elijah and the prophets of Baal on Mt. Carmel where it is said (I Kings 18: 36) "And it came to pass at the time of the offering of the *Minhah* that Elijah the prophet came near and said Lord God of Abraham, Isaac, and Jacob, let it be known this day that Thou art God in Israel."

MAARIV, or evening service, derives its name from one of the opening words of its first prayer, but is also called *Arevit.* Since it has no corresponding sacrifice as do

Shaḥarit and *Minḥah,* the rabbis differed as to whether it was obligatory or optional. Those who are of the first opinion claim that the *Maariv* was instituted as a replacement for the burning of certain parts of the animals as sacrifices. Despite the fact that in Jewish practice it acquired the nature of an obligatory prayer, deference to the second opinion was shown by not repeating the *Amidah.* The *Maariv* consists of the *Shema* and its benedictions, the *Amidah, Aleinu,* and mourners' *Kaddish.* The *Maariv* can be recited at any time between nightfall and midnight. If as is the custom in certain congregations *Maariv* follows immediately after *Minḥah* close to nightfall, the *Shema* must be recited once again so as to ensure the fulfillment of the Command "when thou liest down," which means at night. Rabbinic tradition ascribes the institution of *Maariv* to the patriarch Jacob.

MUSAPH. On Sabbaths, festivals, new moons and the intermediate days of festivals, an additional service known as *Musaph* is added and usually said immediately after *Shaḥarit* and the Bible-reading although it may be recited later. It corresponds to the additional sacrifice offered in the Temple on these days. It consists of the *Amidah* and its repetition, and concludes with the singing of hymns such as *Ein K'eloheinu, Aleinu,* and the mourners' *Kaddish.* The intermediate benediction of the *Amidah* speaks of the special significance of the day, mentions the sacrifices offered in the Temple on that day, and includes a prayer for redemption and the rebuilding of the Temple.

NEILAH. On the Day of Atonement only, a fifth service is added, the closing service of the day called *Neilah.* It is recited with particular solemnity, as it offers the last opportunity to the worshipper of confessing his sins before the gates of heaven are closed. It opens with Psalm 145 and is followed by the *Amidah* and its repetition. Since the ark is open throughout *Neilah,* it is said standing. It terminates with the congregational proclamation of the 1st verse of the *Shema,* "Blessed be the name of the glory of His Kingdom for ever and ever," repeated three times and "The Lord is God," said seven times. The *shofar* is then sounded and with this the fast ends.

When prayer took the place of sacrifice, the synagogue service was drawn up on the lines of the sacrificial Temple routine and this pattern, as outlined above, remains basically the same throughout the year. Various occasions effected additions to and omissions from the order of service. Thus the supplicatory prayer, *Taḥanun,* is omitted on special occasions such as the eve of a festival or during the whole month of *Nisan,* the month of liberation. *Hallel* (Psalms 113–118 and Psalm 136) is added after the *Shaḥarit Amidah* on festivals and their intermediate days, but not on *Rosh Ha-shana.* At *Minḥah* on Sabbaths and fast days there is a short reading from the books of Moses while the *Maariv* on festivals is embellished with special poems known as *Piyyutim.* These, however, are not recited in all rites. The *Musaph* and *Shaḥarit* of *Rosh Ha-shanah* and the Day of Atonement are the longest prayers of the year, being embellished with petitions, blessings, and confessions in accordance with the significance of the day.

See also: AMIDAH.

ROSH HA-SHANAH: The beginning of the year, commonly referred to as New Year, a festival occurring on the first two days of the Hebrew month of *Tishri.* It ushers in the most solemn period of the Jewish year, the ten days of penitence, and culminates in the Day of Atonement on the 10th day of the month. The 1st of *Tishri* is designated in the Bible as *Zikhron Teruah,* a memorial of the sounding of the *shofar* (ram's horn) and *Yom Teruah,* a day of sounding the *shofar.* The name *Rosh Ha-Shanah* is mentioned in the *Mishnah,* which enumerates four different dates in the Jewish calendar as being the New Year for specific purposes: *Nisan* 1st for counting months; *Tishri* 1st for the agricultural year; *Elul* 1st for cattle; and *Shevat* 15th, the New Year for Trees. In the liturgy, two further names are used: *Yom Hadin*, the day of judgment, and *Yom Hazikaron*, memorial day. According to the rabbis, *Rosh Ha-Shanah* commemorates the creation of the universe, and on this day the Almighty sits in judgment on His creatures. In the words of the *Mishnah*, "On *Rosh Ha-Shanah*, all that come into the world pass before Him like flocks of sheep." The observance of *Rosh Ha-Shanah* is centered around the synagogue services and the accent is on prayer and repentance. The call to repentance is already issued during the month of *Elul* preceding *Rosh Ha-Shanah* when each morning, at the end of the *Shaḥarit* service, the *shofar* is sounded to prepare the people for the coming holy days. While the *shofar* was sounded in ancient times on various occasions such as the proclaiming of the jubilee year or the appointing of a king, it is now almost entirely confined to use in the synagogue during the high festival period. Many interpretations have been given for the significance of the sounding of the *shofar* on the high festivals, chief among which are the following:

1) Since *Rosh Ha-Shanah* is the anniversary of the creation, the *shofar*-tones are equivalent to the sounds of jubilation attendant on the proclamation of God as King of the Universe;

2) The ram's horn reminds us of the ram offered instead of Isaac as a sacrifice, and of Abraham's unconditional obedience to the word of God (see Genesis 22);

3) The *shofar* is also reminiscent of the revelation at Mt. Sinai which was accompanied by its sounding;

4) The *shofar* awakens us from our spiritual slumber, urges us to repent and not to waste our lives in the pursuit of material things which are only temporary and fleeting.

The sounding of the *shofar* has largely determined the character of the liturgy of *Rosh Ha-Shanah*, and in particular the *Musaph* (Additional) service which on this day is characterized by its length and solemnity. It is divided into three sections, each with an introduction and concluding paragraph. They are: 1) *Malkhuyyot*, which describes the sovereignty of God; 2) *Zikhronot*, which speaks of God's remembrance of His creatures; and 3) *Shopharot* which is related to the sounding of the *shofar*.

Each section consists of ten scriptural verses related to the above-mentioned concepts and the *shofar* is sounded at the end of each section according to a fixed pattern. (There are minor differences between the Ashkenazi and Sephardi rites.) The *shofar* is also sounded before the *Musaph* service after the reading of the Torah. *Rosh Ha-Shanah* is the only festival which is observed for two days in the land of Israel; if one of the two days falls on the Sabbath, the *shofar* is not sounded. Despite the stress on the synagogue and its ritual, *Rosh Ha-Shanah* is not entirely without home ceremonies. Thus it is customary on the first night to eat apples dipped in honey while reciting a prayer for a good and sweet year. On the second night, one partakes of new fruit for the first time in order to be able to say the *She-Heḥeyanu* blessing (recited when tasting a fruit for the first time in a year).

In the late Middle Ages, the custom began of going to the banks of a river, the seashore, or any body of water, to recite *Tashlikh*. This consists of scriptural verses concerning repentance and the forgiveness of sin, based on the words of the prophet Micah, "and thou wilt cast (Hebr: *tashlikh*) all their sins into the depths of the sea" (Micah 7:19). In this way, all sins are symbolically cast off. If the first day of *Rosh Ha-Shanah* falls on a Sabbath, the ceremony is performed on the second day.

Rosh Ha-Shanah does not commemorate

a specific event in Jewish history, and in the prayers the accent is on man, not the Jewish people. *Rosh Ha-Shanah* thus bears a universal message, a message of yearning for the establishment of God's sovereignty over the entire world and for the day "that all works may revere Thee and all creatures prostrate themselves before Thee, that they may all form a single band to do Thy will with a perfect heart."

ROTHSCHILD FAMILY: European Jewish family of bankers, financiers, and philanthropists. The name is derived from the emblem — a red shield — on the family house in Frankfort-on-Main. The family's fortune was founded by Mayer Amschel Rothschild (1743–1812), who became adviser and financial agent to the richest prince on the continent — William IX of Hesse-Cassel. In skillfully guiding the financial affairs of his master and patron, Mayer himself became enormously wealthy and entered commerce and banking. His five sons established business houses in England, France, Austria, Naples, and Frankfort. The various branches of the Rothschild family maintained close ties with each other and cooperated in the many and varied business projects in which the family engaged.

In addition to finances, their activities embraced mining, railways, and oil. Much of the development of Europe during the 19th century depended on their encouragement. In the first half of the 19th century, Count Apponyi, the Austrian Ambassador to Paris, was not exaggerating when he claimed that the influence of the Paris Rothschilds exceeded that of any great European power. In England, the Rothschilds financed Britain's dramatic acquisition of the Suez Canal shares, and Rothschild capital directly and indirectly played a vital role in the development of the American railroad system and American industry. In the main, the Rothschilds maintained strong Jewish sympathies which

Baron Edmond de Rothschild

were expressed in assistance to the early settlers in the land of Israel and to oppressed Jewry throughout the world. In addition, the English and Austrian houses refused financial assistance to the Czarist Government in Russia because of the latter's persecution of Jews.

Despite this deep Jewish loyalty, the philanthropic activities of the Rothschilds were never restricted by race or religion and their assistance was granted to all worthy causes, regardless of the recipient's origin or nationality. A number of the family's members attained prominence in science, the arts, and in sports. The Naples house broke up after the dissolution of the Kingdom of Naples and Sicily; the Frankfort branch dispersed at the beginning of the 20th century; and the Vienna firm ceased to exist when the Nazis conquered Austria in 1938. In England and France, however, the Rothschilds continued to exert a powerful influence in finance and politics and served as leaders of the local Jewish communities.

In England, Lionel Rothschild (1808–1879) helped to finance the Crimean War and provided the funds for the purchase of the Suez Canal shares. He was the acknowledged leader of Anglo-Jewry, and was the first Jew to be admitted to Parliament. His son Nathaniel (1840–1915) was the first Jew to enter the House of Lords. The London firm is now headed by the descendants of Leopold Rothschild (1845–1917), who was a brother of Nathaniel.

The Paris branch of the Rothschild firm was founded in 1817 by James, the 5th son of Mayer Amschel. The most prominent of his sons was Edmond (1845–1934), commonly referred to as the Baron Edmond de Rothschild. It was Edmond who came to the rescue of the early settlers in the land of Israel, who because of little agricultural know-how and an absence of financial backing were on the verge of collapse. Edmond assisted them and for the remainder of his life made the development of Jewish agricultural settlements in Israel one of his principal concerns, investing millions of francs in this work. He visited the land of Israel five times, and was the first Honorary President of the Jewish Agency. The village of Binyamina is named after him, his Hebrew name being Binyamin. In 1954, the remains of Edmond and his wife Adelaide were taken from Paris and reinterred in the beautiful Rothschild gardens at Zikhron Yaacov. His son James (1878–1957) was educated in England, sat in the British Parliament as a Liberal, and achieved distinction as a sportsman. In his will, he left a large sum of money for the construction of Israel's new Parliament *(Knesset)* building.

RUMANIA: There is evidence of Jewish settlement in what is now Rumania as early as the Roman period, when the territory was known as Dacia. Very little is known about this settlement and it is only from the 14th century on that it is possible to speak of Rumanian Jewish history. In that century, and in subsequent years, Jews came in large numbers to the principalities of Moldavia and Wallachia into which the area was divided, most of them coming from Poland. During the 17th century, the Jews of Moldavia suffered both from the Cossack uprising against Poland and from the antagonism of the Orthodox church. In the various Russo-Turkish Wars, fought in the late 18th and early 19th centuries, the Jews suffered from both sides. However, despite the wars, the Jewish population grew through the settlement of large numbers of Polish Jews in the country. The movement toward Jewish emancipation was gaining ground throughout Europe at this period, but the Rumanians, like the Poles and the Russians, fought every effort to secure equality for their Jewish minority. Discriminatory legislation was introduced and violent anti-Jewish outbreaks were regular occurrences. There were cases of the forcible baptism of Jewish children and ritual murder charges against Jews. In the mid-19th century, anti-Semitism became part of internal Rumanian policy, and a period of expulsions and barbarities followed that shocked the world and brought strong protests from the United States government. At the Congress of Berlin in 1878, when Rumania was granted complete independence, she was forced to promise to grant equality to all citizens. Nevertheless, through various subterfuges and stratagems, she succeeded in avoiding the fulfillment of her obligations under the 1878 treaty. She even managed to ignore or defy protests and interventions by Germany, Austria, Britain, and the United States. As a result of the continued persecution, 70,000 Jews left Rumania between 1898 and 1904, mostly for the United States. After World War I, Rumania again signed specific provisions for equality, but once again evaded her responsibilities. In 1937, the National Christian Party of Octavian Goga came to power and pursued a vigorous anti-Semitic policy. Laws based on the pattern of the Nazi Nuremberg Laws were introduced and numerous pogroms took place. During World War II, half of Rumania's 800,000 Jews were exterminated by the Nazis and their Rumanian collaborators.

Since the end of World War II and the advent to power of the Communist regime, Rumania's Jewish policy has been somewhat ambivalent. From 1948–52, Jews were permitted to emigrate to Israel, and 125,000 of Rumania's 400,000 Jews did so. In 1952, emigration was stopped, and Rumania's policy toward her Jews hardened. In the late 1950s, emigration resumed and many of the remaining Jews departed. When Rumania began to assert her independence of the Soviet Union, her attitude toward the Jews and toward Israel relaxed considerably. After the June 1967 Six-Day War, Rumania was the only country of the East European Communist bloc which did not break off diplomatic relations with Israel, and cultural and economic relations between the two countries were even intensified.

Rumania's Jews, numbering approximately 115,000, were by then enjoying what was probably the most peaceful era in Rumanian Jewish history.

RUSSIA: There is evidence to suggest that the first settlement of Jews within what are now the boundaries of the Soviet Union took place as early as the 2nd century B.C.E. During the Roman period, organized Jewish communities existed on the shores of the Black Sea and the Sea of Azov. At the beginning of the 7th century, with the establishment of the Khazar State (see Khazars) the Jews spread eastward to the shores of the Caspian Sea. By the 11th century, Kiev, which had become the main political and cultural center of the southeastern Russian principalities, had a substantial Jewish community which played an important role in foreign trade. The cultural level of Russian Jewry at that stage was not high, and those Jews requiring higher rabbinic learning attended western *Yeshivot*. The Tartar invasion of the 13th century destroyed all trace of Jewish settlements and nothing further is heard of Jews on Russian territory until the 15th century when they made their appearance as merchants and physicians. A number of prominent Russians adopted Judaism and this conversionist activity even penetrated Moscow court circles, arousing the wrath of the Russian Orthodox Church and of Ivan the Terrible. The latter had three hundred Jews drowned, and, when this failed, banished all Jews from Russian territory. Terrible massacres were perpetrated in 1648 by cossack hordes led by Bogdan Chmielnicki. One of the ironies of Russia's relationship with the Jews is that as much as she tried to rid herself of them, she acquired them in ever-increasing numbers. Thus in 1655, with the annexation of parts of Lithuania, more Jews came under Russian rule, and the work of banishment began all over again. Peter the Great, in 1721, also acquired vast numbers of Jewish subjects through the conquest of Swedish territories along the Baltic coast. In 1762, Catherine the Great expelled all Jews and made Russia "off limits" to them. Ten years later, there were more Jews in Russia than in all Europe combined. This resulted from the dismemberment of the Polish Kingdom by Prussia, Austria, and Russia, and its partition in three stages from 1772 to 1795. A new "Jewish Problem" was created in all three countries, with Russia now being responsible for the bulk of east European Jews. Through the partitions, she acquired an additional one million Jewish subjects. The solution attempted was to limit Jewish residence to the newly-acquired territories on Russia's western border. Thus there came into existence the Pale of Settlement, consisting of the former Polish territories with the addition of certain other regions. Jews were forbidden to live in the interior

Russian cities. The czarist policy toward the Jews was a mixture of contradictions and pipe dreams. Essentially, however, its purpose was to make life as hard as possible for them. Occasional moves toward increasing Jewish rights were always countered by reactionary and even more restrictive measures. Thus, while by a law of 1804 Russian schools and universities were opened to the Jews, they were driven from the villages where most of them made their living, and difficulties were placed in the way of the Jewish merchants. While aiming at the absorption of the Jews and their possible abandonment of Judaism, the law by its discriminatory nature contributed to their further separation. In 1827, Nicholas I introduced compulsory military service for Jews. In any other country, this might well have been considered a privilege. In Russia, however, the motivation was Christianization of the young. Anyone from the age of twelve to twenty-five was eligible and the term of service was at least twenty-five years. The unwillingness of the Jews to yield to such enslavement led to forcible enlistment of Jewish children. The government made this the responsibility of local Jewish communal leaders. A system of kidnapping was practiced in which children were seized on the streets by government officials, often never to be seen again.

Alexander II (1855–1881) embarked on a general system of reforms in which the Jews were included. A number of anti-Jewish restrictions were lifted. Certain selected groups of "useful" Jews were permitted to settle in the interior of Russia. At the same time, however, efforts were made to eliminate Jewish exclusiveness by abolishing the *Ḥeder*, and by a law stipulating that teachers and rabbis must be graduates of one of the government-sponsored rabbinical academies. Jewish resistance achieved the abolition of these measures. By this time Russian Jewry had become a major center of Jewish culture

Russian immigrants arriving in Israel

and religion. There were hundreds of *Yeshivot*; Russian Jewry played an important role in the foundations of Zionism and in the revival of Hebrew as a modern language. Many of them, moreover, joined forces with the various social revolutionary groups within Russia whose members had begun to plot the overthrow of the czarist regime in the belief that only thus would the hard lot of Russia's people be alleviated. Jews could hardly be expected to disagree with the above conclusion, especially since their situation continued to deteriorate. When Alexander III ascended the throne in 1881, Russian Jewry was the victim of a wave of government-inspired pogroms which swept the country and affected more than one hundred localities. These were followed by the restrictive laws of May 1882. These pogroms were repeated with the foreknowledge of the government on still larger scales in 1903 and 1905. During this period began the mass exodus of Jews from Russia to the United States and western Europe.

Under the last of the czars, Nicholas (1894–1917), the repression increased, some Russian statesmen not even bothering to conceal their hostile intentions. Thus the infamous procurator of the Holy Synod, Constantin Pobedonostsev, defined the object of imperial policy as the emigration of one third of Russian Jewry, another third to become Christian, and the final third to perish. The premature revolution of 1905 with which thousands of Jews were identified and which was brutally crushed, was utilized by the authorities to incite the masses against the Jews. Jews were also accused of helping the enemy during the Russo-Japanese War and it was at this time that the infamous forgery, *The Protocols of the Elders of Zion* (see ANTI-SEMITISM) appeared. During the First World War, the Jewish population, still living mainly on Russia's western borders, was caught between the conflicting armies and suffered great loss and privation. They also experienced persecution at the hands of cossack forces. Thousands were deported to the remote interior of Russia.

The 1917 Revolution brought emancipation to the Jews of Russia — at least in theory. Lenin was sharply opposed to anti-Semitism, and in July 1918 he outlawed it as a counter revolutionary crime. The constitution of the Soviet Union formally prohibits anti-Semitism, and some of the Soviet Union's most prominent early leaders such as Trotsky, Zinoviev, and Kameneff were Jews. Despite this, the Communist party's policy has been one long chain of contradictions vis-à-vis Jews, and in many respects the Bolshevik Revolution has resulted in unfavorable developments. The opposition to religion in any form made the position of traditional Judaism well-nigh untenable. Added to this, Communism has an intrinsic antagonism to Zionism. The equality of all citizens envisaged by Soviet leaders was at the price of all meaningful Jewish identity. Religious education and the teaching of the Hebrew language were discouraged and Zionism was persecuted. A special section of the Communist party known as Yevsekztia was set up and exercised full control of Jewish affairs until 1930 when it was disbanded. It outdid everything else in its fanaticism. Hundreds of synagogues were closed and turned into workemen's clubs, and a campaign was instituted against religious ob-

servances. The study of Hebrew, except as a foreign language, was forbidden. The desire of Jews for minority rights was pandered to by creating, in theory at least, an autonomous Jewish state in Biro-Bidjan in eastern Asia. Nothing substantial came of the plan. Yiddish, however, was recognized and literary journals in that language permitted. During the great purges of the 1930s, many Jewish Communists, among them Stalin's closest associates, were liquidated. When the Nazis attacked the Soviet Union in June 1941, over 3,500,000 Russian Jewish subjects in eastern Poland, the Baltic States, western Russia, Bukovina, and Bessarabia were in immediate danger. Over 2,000,000 were exterminated. Over 400,000 Jews served in the Soviet armed forces including many distinguished generals. For a brief period after the war, the Soviet Union's attitude to Zionism was modified and Russia was one of the major supporters of the creation of a Jewish state. Indeed, it was one of the first to recognize Israel and even grant it much-needed military assistance. This policy did not last long, however, and in the early 50s the Soviet Union began to support the Arab cause. At the same time, anti-Semitism, which had never completely died in Russia, began to raise its head. Leading Yiddish writers were arrested and shot. Toward the end of Stalin's life, a lurid story about a "Jewish doctor's conspiracy" against the state seemed to be the prelude to a new persecution of Jews and their speedy elimination from all positions of influence. After Stalin's death, those who survived were released and the anti-Jewish stance of the state was toned down somewhat. But basically the situation did not improve. After the June 1967 Six-Day War, the Soviet Union adopted a totally pro-Arab policy, replacing Egypt's military losses and supplying military advisers and additional military equipment to that country. At this time, a rekindling of Jewish and Zionist aspirations took hold of large sections of Soviet Jewry, despite the years of constant propaganda and the dangers involved in identifying with Israel. Petitions by individuals and groups to be allowed to leave Russia and emigrate to Israel accelerated and became commonplace. The Jews in Russia are forbidden to develop their own culture. Unlike every other Russian minority, they are not allowed to run their own schools, to have their own daily newspaper, or (with a few exceptions) to publish books in their own language. The constant anti-Israel campaign has anti-Jewish undertones. But despite everything, there is evidence that much of Soviet Jewry has maintained its identity with the Jewish people and its aspirations. In 1971, the Jewish population was officially estimated at 2,151,000. The number, however, may be considerably higher.

RUTH: Second of the five *Megillot* (scrolls) which form part of the third section of the Bible, *Ketuvim*. The story, set in the days of the Judges, has as its heroine the Moabite woman Ruth.

Elimelech of Bethlehem in Judah leaves the famine-stricken land of Israel with Naomi, his wife, and two sons. They settle in Moab, where the sons marry Moabite women, Orpah and Ruth. Elimelech and his sons are stricken with disease and die, and Naomi decides to return to her home in Bethlehem. The two daughters-in-law want to accompany her, but she persuades Orpah to remain in Moab. Ruth, however, refuses to leave her mother-in-law. In some of the most poignant words between two women in literature, she declares: "Whither thou goest, I will go, and where thou lodgest, I will lodge; thy people shall be my people and thy God my God." They return to Bethlehem, where Ruth must work to keep herself and her mother-in-law. While gleaning in the fields, she catches the eye of Boaz, the landowner, a relative of Elimelech's, who after learning who she is, marries her. Their son Obed becomes the grandfather of David.

According to rabbinic tradition, Samuel the prophet was the author of Ruth, but Bible critics are more of the opinion that the book was written after the Babylonian exile. The book demonstrates that a sincere proselyte, Ruth, a Moabitess, can obtain a high and honored position among the people of Israel, even becoming an ancestor of the great King David.

The book of Ruth is read in the synagogue on the festival of *Shavuot*.

The **SABBATH:** The seventh day of the week, observed as a day of rest, on which no work is permitted. Of all the holy days in the Hebrew calendar, the Sabbath is second in importance only to the Day of Atonement (the Sabbath of Sabbaths). The command to observe the Sabbath is repeated many times throughout the Bible and appears as the fourth of the Ten Commandments. The Ten Commandments, which are repeated in the Bible (Exodus 20 and Deuteronomy 5), give two basic reasons for the observance of the Sabbath: the first religious, and the second national. God created the universe in six days and on the seventh He ceased to work *(Shabbat)*; therefore, resting on the Sabbath is a sign that we recognize God as the creator of all things. The second reason for keeping the Sabbath is in commemoration of the Exodus from Egypt. God gave freedom to a group of slaves and made them into an independent people. The Sabbath, thus, is the symbol of human freedom, of the right of every man to be free. This does not apply only to Jews; even servants and domestic animals are entitled to their rest. The idea that everyone needs periodic rest is so much a part of our civilization that it is now taken for granted. Yet the Romans and the Greeks mocked the idea and accused the Jews of being lazy and superstitious. The Jewish Sabbath, however, is not only a day for physical rest and recreation. It is a day of spiritual activity and refreshment. The observance of the Sabbath was considered so important by the leaders of the people that they surrounded it with all sorts of restrictions and prohibitions. The Bible says that it is forbidden to work on the Sabbath but it does not specifically define "work." A few examples are given such as gathering sticks, lighting a fire, traveling beyond a certain distance, and conducting one's business. In time, the list grew until the rabbis listed thirty-nine principal kinds of work, plus other acts, which are forbidden because they could lead to the desecration of the Sabbath.

Despite all these restrictions, the Sabbath was never considered a sad day. The exact opposite is true. The Sabbath laws were regarded as a means of freeing a person from his daily worries and material cares. The atmosphere was one of joy. The prophet Isaiah tells the people to call the Sabbath "a delight" *(Oneg)*, a day of spiritual and physical pleasure. It is considered a *mitzvah*, a positive command, and a praiseworthy action to eat, drink, and be joyful on the Sabbath. Throughout Jewish history, even the poorest families scrimped and saved during the week so that there should be sufficient to eat on the Sabbath. In the darkest days of exile and persecutions, the Sabbath candles brought a light into each Jewish home which no amount of suffering could snuff out. Far from being a burden, the Sabbath was something to look forward to, a precious gift given by God to his people. The Sabbath was compared to a bride and Israel to the bridegroom going out to meet his beloved. This is the theme of the famous *Lekha Dodi* prayer recited in all synagogues on Sabbath eve. Both the prayers in the synagogues and the festivities in the Jewish home are dominated by joy and happiness.

In the home, the Sabbath is inaugurated by the mistress of the house lighting her candles and her husband reciting the *Kiddush* (sanctification) prayer over wine. The *Kiddush* is also recited by the cantor in the synagogue. This latter custom is a survival of the ancient way of providing for the poor and the stranger. In ancient times, food and accommodation were given to the poor in rooms next to the synagogue, and it was for these people that the reader recited the *Kiddush* before they began the evening meal. Sabbath morning is one of the occasions when the additional service *(Musaph)* is recited. It is considered a *mitzvah* to eat three meals on the Sabbath. In between courses, special songs known as *Zemirot* are sung. The last meal, the *Seudah Shelishit*, is accompanied by prolonged singing and usually lasts until the appearance of three stars, signaling the end of the Sabbath. The evening service is then recited, followed by *Havdalah*, a prayer with which Jews formally bid farewell to the Sabbath. In many communities the custom persists of partaking of a fourth meal after the Sabbath. This meal is known as *Melaveh Malka* ("escorting the bride"), and is celebrated with singing and even dancing. Sadness is forbidden on the Sabbath day. When any of the fast days (except the Day of Atonement) happens to fall on Sabbath, the fasting is put off *(nidheh)* till the next day or observed (as in the case of the Fast of Esther) on the previous Thursday.

The Sabbath was given to man for his enjoyment and for his own benefit. Even the strictest Sabbath laws fall away when human life is endangered. The principle of *Pikkuah Nefesh* (the saving of life) overrides all the commandments concerning Sabbath observance. This principle not only applies to the individual but to the nation as a whole. During the Maccabean war the decision was taken to fight back if attacked on the Sabbath, although offensive operations were avoided, and this has remained the law.

During the months of *Adar* and *Nisan* before Passover, there are four Sabbaths on which additional sections are read from the Bible. The first is *Shabbat Shekalim*, on which the law concerning the half-shekel contribution is read (Exodus 30:11-16). The second *Shabbat Zakhor* falls on the Sabbath before Purim. It is so called because the special part read begins with the word *Zakhor*, "Remember what Amalek did unto thee." The connection between this portion and the festival of Purim lies in the fact that Haman, the villain of the Purim story, is believed to have been a descendant of Agag, King of Amalek. The third Sabbath, *Shabbat Parah*, the Sabbath on which the law concerning the sacrifice of the red heifer is read (Numbers 12:4) is the Sabbath after Purim (or, when *Adar* 15 or 16 falls on Saturday, the second Sabbath after Purim). The fourth Sabbath is *Shabbat Ha-Hodesh*, the Sabbath before the 1st of *Nisan* (or on the 1st of *Nisan* if it falls on a Saturday), and the portion read (Exodus 12:1-20) fixes *Nisan* as the first month and deals with the laws of Passover. In addition to these four Sabbaths, the Sabbath before Passover is known as *Shabbat Ha-Gadol*, the great Sabbath; the Sabbath on which the song of the Red Sea (Exodus 15) is read is known as *Shabbat Shirah*; the Sabbath after the fast of the Ninth of *Av* is called *Shabbat Nahamu*, the Sabbath of comfort (after the words of the prophet Isaiah "Comfort ye my people" which are read on that day); and the Sabbath between *Rosh Ha-Shanah* and the Day of Atonement is known as *Shabbat Shuvah*, the Sabbath of repentance, after the words of the prophet Hosea read on that day, "Return O Israel."

In modern times, the question of Sabbath observance has given rise to much debate and sometimes bitter argument. The Reform movement claims that changing conditions have made many of the Sabbath laws outdated, while those who still adhere to Jewish tradition reply that although the Sabbath was given for man's benefit, he has no right to change God's law which is eternal. In the State of Israel too, the question has led to much controversy. Thus far a form of compromise has been reached in which the Sabbath is observed publicly and officially. The Sabbath is an official holiday, and public transport does not run in most places. Places of entertainment and business are closed but the individual is more or less free to observe the day in the manner he thinks fit.

SAFED (Tzefat): A town in upper Galilee situated in a glorious mountain area, its highest point being 3,150 feet (about 950 meters) above sea level, the most elevated inhabited spot in Israel.

Safed is mentioned in the Talmud as one of the places where bonfires were lit to signal the coming of the new month and the New Year. The Crusaders built fortifications on its heights during the 12th century. In Jewish history, however, Safed assumes importance only in the 16th century, when it became the center of rabbinic and kabbalistic learning, chiefly the latter. After the expulsion of the Jews from Spain, a major center of Jewish learning was established in Safed by pious and learned rabbis. The Jewish mystical philosophy known as *Kabbalah* flourished here. Its pure air was regarded as ideal for spiritual reflection. Doubtless its proximity to Meron, the traditional burial place of the sage Simeon Bar Yoḥai, reputed author of the kabbalistic classic, the *Zohar*, was an added attraction. It was in Safed that famous rabbis and sages such as Moses Cordovero, Joseph Karo, and Isaac Luria lived and died. The last-named, better known by the title Ari *(Adonenu — our master, Rabbi Isaac)* was the prime exponent of Jewish mysticism. It was here, too, that Joseph Karo wrote his famous code of law, the *Shulḥan Arukh*.

The first printing press in the land of

Old quarter in Safed

Israel and in all western Asia was installed in Safed and, in 1578, its first Hebrew book was printed there.

The "golden age" of Safed was followed by a period of sharp decline, due to Bedouin attacks, the bad administration of the Turks, epidemics, and earthquakes. The earthquake of 1738 claimed four thousand victims, mainly Jews, and the town was demolished.

In 1948, Safed was inhabited by twelve thousand Arabs and about 1,700 Jews, mostly elderly people. The Arabs dominated all the strategic positions on Mount Canaan, including the police station, and the only military force available to the Jews was a group of 120 young men who had crossed through the Arab lines under cover of darkness. These few defenders succeeded in assaulting the Arab positions, and in the panic that ensued the Arab population fled en masse. Safed's present population is 13,100. Owing to its crisp air and splendid panorama it has become a popular summer resort. As mystics were attracted to Safed in the Middle Ages, so today it has become a source of inspiration to artists, and many of Israel's leading painters and sculptors spend their summers in its artists' colony.

SAMARIA (Shomron): Capital of the Northern Kingdom of Israel, built on a tall, ideally defensible hill by King Omri (reigned 876–869 B.C.E.) and completed by his son Ahab (reigned 869–850 B.C.E.) The site was situated some seven miles northwest of Shechem (Nablus), and archeological excavations have shown that its fortifications were unequalled in ancient Israel for their excellent workmanship. The luxury and corruption of Samaria were often the subject of rebuke by the prophets. In the year 721 B.C.E. Samaria fell to the Assyrians who, in accordance with their policy of exchange of populations, deported the inhabitants and resettled the city with a hodgepodge of different peoples. These intermingled with the remaining Israelites who had escaped deportation and adopted a form of Judaism, strictly monotheistic, based only on the five books of Moses. They refused to recognize the authority of the prophets, except Moses. These heterogeneous people were known as Samaritans (the Talmud called them *Kutim*, i.e., Cutheans, Cutha being one of their places of origin). They call themselves *Benei Yisrael* or *Shamerim* (observant ones). When the exiles from the Kingdom of Judah returned from Babylon in the 6th century B.C.E., the Samaritans offered to assist in the rebuilding of the Temple. The offer was rejected, and the Jewish leadership, especially in the time of Ezra and Nehemiah, prohibited intermarriage with this sect whose form of worship was in their eyes tainted with heathenism. The ensuing friction, often violent, between the two groups severely hindered the returnees' program of rebuilding.

In the 4th century B.C.E., the Samaritans, with the permission of Alexander the Great, built a rival temple on Mount Gerizim, the sanctity of which is a cardinal principle of their faith. This temple was destroyed by the Hasmonean king, John Hyrcanus, but rebuilt by the Romans. Herod renamed the site Sebate, which is the Greek for Augusta in honor of the Roman Emperor Augustus Caesar. The city flourished in Roman times, as evidenced by the impressive ruins which remain. The second Samaritan temple was destroyed by the Emperor Zeno in the year 486 C.E.; and in 529 C.E., after Justinian issued a decree against the Samaritans, their autonomous existence practically ceased. In the 14th century, the sect experienced a certain spiritual revival, but since then has gradually declined. Not being considered "People of the Book," their history under Moslem rule has been one of persecution. The Samaritan Bible consists of the five books of Moses, and only this is recognized by them as Holy Scripture. The text, despite alterations and emendations, is ancient.

In 1965, there were 250 Samaritans in Nablus (Shechem) and 150 in Holon. Their synagogue with the ancient Bible is at Mount Gerizim where they still hold their annual Passover sacrifice.

Ruins in Samaria

SAMBATYON: Legendary river beyond which the ten lost tribes are said to dwell. According to the legend, the river is made up of sand and rubble flowing with such force that it could crush a mountain. It was this torrential flow that prevented the ten tribes from returning. The river rested on the Sabbath day but on this day Jewish law prohibits traveling. According to another account, however, the Sambatyon is static for six days of the week and flows only on the seventh day. The legend had already gained currency in Talmudic times and is mentioned by Rabbi Akiva in his discussion with the Roman general, Tineius Rufus, as proof of the divinity of the Sabbath regulations. It is also mentioned by Josephus and the Roman historian, Pliny. During the Middle Ages, the legend cropped up periodically in connection with the search for the ten lost tribes. The 9th century traveler, Eldad ha-Dani, however, claimed that only the "Sons of Moses" dwelt beyond the Sambatyon. The false Messiah, Shabbetai Tzevi, intended journeying to the Sambatyon in order to marry Moses' daughter and then lead the ten tribes back to the land of Israel.

SAMSON: The last of the judges. His story is related in the book of Judges, Chapters 13–16. A Nazirite from birth, Samson is said to have possessed abnormal and even supernatural strength. At a time

Samson and the Lion

when the tribes of Israel were under Philistine domination, Samson, utilizing his amazing strength, conducted a one-man guerrilla campaign against the enemy, inflicting heavy losses upon them. His weakness for women, however, enabled the beautiful Delilah to entice him into telling her the secret of his strength, which was his long hair. While he was sleeping, she had his hair cut off, rendering him helpless and unable to resist. The Philistines imprisoned and tortured him. They blinded him and made him turn the prison mill. As a final act of mockery, they displayed him before the laughing crowds in the Temple of Dagon. Praying to God to grant him strength just once more, Samson grabbed hold of the temple pillars, pulled them apart and brought the building crashing down, killing the enitre assembly, himself among them.

SAMUEL: Israelite judge and Prophet whose name was given to the third book of the second division of the Bible (the Prophets — *Neviim*). The book, originally a single unit, was divided into two (I Samuel and II Samuel) in the first Greek translation of the Bible, the Septuagint, and that division was subsequently adopted by the printed editions of the Bible. The book of Samuel deals mainly with the lives of three people — Samuel, Saul, and David, and historically it covers the time from the end of the period of the Judges to the last days of David. Samuel's name was given to the book since his personality dominates the first part of the book, and it was he who appointed both kings: Saul and David.

Samuel presided over a critical phase in Israelite history, the transition from a tribal confederation to a monarchy. When he was a lad, his mother, Hannah, consecrated him to the service of God in the sanctuary at Shiloh under the tutorship of Eli, the High Priest. Following the destruction of Shiloh and the capture of the ark by the Philistines, it was the leadership and statesmanship of Samuel that kept the people from becoming completely demoralized. He was accepted as a prophet-judge by the people; he lived in Ramah but visited the sacred towns of Bethel, Gilgal, and Mizpeh in order to act as judge. He is said to have founded schools of prophets in which men were trained to act as the religious leaders of the people. In his old age, Samuel was approached by the people and asked to set up a monarchy in Israel. To Samuel, who regarded the request both as a rebellion against God and his own leadership, this was a bitter blow. He was, however, sufficiently "big" to realize that only a strong centralized government would be able to deal with the Philistine menace which threatened Israel's very existence, and so reluctantly he acceded to the popular demand.

It was Saul's fate to be entrusted with the task of being the first king of Israel, of unifying the country and defeating the Philistines. To his credit he did not attempt to foist too strong a central government on a people not yet prepared for it. He conducted himself with humility, and his court was by no means extravagant. He succeeded in defeating the Philistines and in laying the foundation of the future united kingdom. He was, however, the victim of forces beyond his control. Had he succeeded to an already established regime, he might have made a great king. He was just not strong enough for the task of creating a new kingdom. The tension and final break with Samuel depressed him, and the rise of the young David filled him with a jealousy which became an obsession, leading to numerous efforts to kill David. Mentally ill and deeply disappointed, he met his death in battle against the Philistines.

The third main character of the book of Samuel is David, whose life story is told from chapter sixteen of the first book to the end of the second book.

The book of Samuel is written in beautiful prose and gives an authentic picture of the rural life and religious traditions of ancient Israel. Its authorship, like that of most books of the Bible, has been the subject of much debate. According to the Talmud, Samuel himself wrote the first part of the book, while the remainder was written by the prophets Nathan and Gad. The generally accepted view is that the book was written at a later date after the division of the kingdom, but the sources used by the author are almost certainly contemporaneous with the events described.

SAMUEL, HERBERT LOUIS, VISCOUNT (1870–1963): British statesman and philosopher. Samuel entered Parliament in 1902 and subsequently became the first professing Jew ever to serve in a British cabinet. He held various offices in the Liberal Government of 1905–1916 and again in the National Government, 1931–32. He was chairman of the Royal Commission on the Coal Industry and from 1931–35 was leader of the Liberal Party in the House of Commons. He played a significant role in assisting the negotiations leading up to the Balfour Declaration in 1917, and in 1920, under the British Mandate, was appointed first High Commissioner for Palestine. Despite his strong Zionist convictions, he to some extent antagonized the Zionist leadership because of his fairness and impartiality toward the Arab population. During the 1930s, he devoted himself to the rescue of Jewish victims of Nazism and to the rehabilitation of Jewish refugees.

He wrote a number of important works on philosophy and was president of the Royal Institute of Philosophy from 1931–1956.

SANHEDRIN (Council, Court): Supreme Court and legislative body in the land of Israel during the later Second Temple period. Detailed information on the activity of the Sanhedrin is unfortunately scanty. According to the Talmud, there were two Sanhedrins, the Great Sanhedrin comprising seventy-one members who met in the Temple chamber known as the Hall of Hewn Stone, and a lesser Sanhedrin of twenty-three members. There were lesser Sanhedrins both in Jerusalem and throughout the country. At the head of the Great Sanhedrin were two sages, the one acting as *Nasi* or president and the second as *Av Bet Din,* head of the court. Although the lesser Sanhedrin was also competent to try capital cases, the Great Sanhedrin acted in fact as the Supreme Court of Appeal on all disputed points of law or religious practice. It was responsible for the appointment of judges, for the proclamation of the New Moon and of a leap year, and was qualified to try national figures such as the High Priest or the king. Also, as the need arose it had authority to pass new decrees and ordinances in matters of Jewish law. From the writings of Josephus and the New Testament, it would seem that the Sanhedrin also functioned as a political court. This has led some scholars to postulate the existence of a political Sanhedrin side by side with a religious Sanhedrin. There is, however, no convincing evidence to back up this assumption. For a great part of its existence, the Sanhedrin was the scene of a vicious power struggle between the Pharisees and Sadducees. The Maccabean ruler John Hyrcanus broke with the Pharisees as did his successor, Alexander Yannai, who purged them from the Sanhedrin. After the latter's death, however, Queen Salome Alexander restored the Pharisees to their former position of pre-eminence. From the time of the Roman occupation until the destruction of the Second Temple in 70 C.E., the authority of the Sanhedrin was limited to religious matters only. After the destruction, the Sanhedrin passed from one center to another until, at the beginning

Traditional tombs of the Senhedrin, Jerusalem

of the 5th century C.E., it ceased to exist. Throughout the ages, there was talk of reconstituting the Sanhedrin from time to time. The idea has been raised again since the establishment of the State of Israel with its complicated religious problems. The proposal, however, appears impracticable.

SCHECHTER, SOLOMON (1847–1915): Scholar, theologian, and architect of Conservative Judaism. Schechter was born in Rumania and studied in Vienna and Berlin, where he came to the attention of the Anglo-Jewish scholar and religious reformer, Claude G. Montefiore, who in 1882 invited Schechter to England. In 1890 he was appointed lecturer in rabbinics at Cambridge University and in 1899 became Professor of Hebrew at University College, London. He had by now attained international fame, in particular through his journey in 1896 to Cairo, where he gathered thousands of medieval Hebrew manuscripts in the *Genizah* (storeroom) of the ancient synagogue. This find was of major importance for rabbinic scholarship and medieval Jewish history and literature. The quantity is so vast that 75 years later much of it has still not been examined. In 1901, Schechter was appointed President of the Jewish Theological Seminary in New York, and under his guidance this institution became one of the central pillars of Jewish scholarship in America. In 1913, he established the United Synagogue, Conservative Judaism's synagogal body and its main institution. While being far from fanatical in his religious views, Schechter was nevertheless a firm believer in "historical" and traditional Judaism and as such, was an outspoken opponent of the Reform movement. He developed the concept of catholic Israel by which he meant Israel in its all-embracing entirety. Only catholic Israel could make decisions regarding changes in Jewish law and practice. He did not, however, define this concept in detail and did not provide any criteria deciding which group or groups formed part of catholic Israel. Schechter was from the outset, an ardent supporter of Zionist aims and aspirations, and guided the Conservative movement in this direction although he fervently believed that the rebirth of Israel's national consciousness and the revival of Judaism were inseparable. Schechter published numerous essays on Jewish history and rabbinic theology, the most popular of which are his three-volume *Studies in Judaism*.

SEMITES AND SEMITIC LANGUAGES:
Nations which, according to the Bible, derived from Noah's son Shem are Semites. They include the Babylonians, Arameans, Assyrians, Phoenicians, Hebrews, and Arabs. While there is no such thing as a Semitic race, there are several linguistic and cultural traits common to various Semitic peoples. Modern archeology has contributed substantially to the understanding of ancient Semitic languages and their influence on biblical Hebrew. In the light of this research, many previously inexplicable biblical words and verses are now understandable. Scholars are of the opinion that, at one time, a common proto-Semitic language existed, from which all subsequent Semitic languages developed. Accordingly, the study of the grammar and

language forms of Semitic languages affords a better understanding of the origin of Hebrew grammar and Hebrew forms.

Semitic languages may be briefly categorised as follows:
1) East Semitic — This consists of Akkadian and the related Babylonian-Assyrian dialects.
2) Northwest Semitic, comprising the ancient Amorite tongue and the recently-discovered, highly important Ugaritic.
3) Canaanite, including Hebrew, Phoenician, Punic (the language of Carthage), and Moabite.
4) The Aramaic dialects, which are all North Semitic and of which there are many — e.g., biblical Aramaic, Palestinian Jewish Aramaic, Babylonian Jewish Aramaic, and Samaritan.
5) South Semitic, comprising North and South Arabian dialects, ancient and modern, and Amharic (spoken Ethiopian). Egyptian, with its successor, Coptic, is also considered a Semitic language.

The connection between Hebrew, Aramaic, and Arabic was established by scholars as early as the 10th century, and this connection has been consistently upheld and systemized by modern authorities. Hebrew, as indicated above, belongs to the Canaanite branch of Semitic languages. It is the language of the books of the Bible (with the exception of parts of the books of Daniel and Ezra, which are in Aramaic). In the course of its long history, it has undergone various modifications but its essential structure remains the same.

See: HEBREW LANGUAGE.

SEPHARAD, SEPHARDIM:
Hebrew for Spain and Spaniards. The term *Sephardi* was applied to the Jews of Spain and their descendants after the expulsion of Spanish Jewry in 1492. They settled all along the coast of North Africa, in Italy,

Egypt, the land of Israel, in the Balkans, and in the central provinces of the Turkish Empire where large Jewish centers were established in Salonica and Constantinople. Later on, the Marranos established communities in England, Holland, France, and the United States which, while numerically small, had a political and economic influence out of all proportion to their numbers. Today, all oriental Jews, including any who cannot be defined as Ashkenazim, are labeled Sephardi (see ASHKENAZIM).

The differences between Sephardim and Ashkenazim result from centuries-long differences in conditioning. They have been attributed by most scholars to three basic causes: anthropological, religious, and environmental.

The anthropological theory holds that when the Second Temple was destroyed in 70 C.E., the emigration of the Jewish population of the land of Israel took two directions. Jews from the northern part of the country went mainly to the north; those from the south went westward. The former intermingled with various racial types: mongoloid, alpine, and northern elements to form the Ashkenazi type, while the latter, by a similar mixture of oriental and Mediterranean racial elements, became Sephardim. Like all racial theories, it is difficult to determine how far this view is justified and it has been vehemently opposed by the upholders of the purity of the Jewish race. The influence of external conditions upon the life of man should be neither minimized nor exaggerated.

The second theory explains the differences between the two groups as the continuation of the different traditions adhered to in ancient times by the Palestinian and Babylonian schools. From the time of the Babylonian exile and after, there developed great differences between the Jews of Babylon and those of Palestine in — among other things — ritual, customs, marriage laws, and in the pronunciation of Hebrew. Spanish Jewry, linked to Babylon

From a Sephardi burial ceremony (18th cent.)

through North Africa, continued the Babylonian tradition and came under the influence of the Babylonian *Geonim* during the period of Mohammedan rule. The Jews of France and Germany on the other hand came under the influence of Palestine by way of Italy. Thus many of the differences between the two oriental Jewries were transplanted to Europe. It must be noted, however, that there are cases in which the Sephardim adopted Palestinian usage and the Ashkenazim that of Babylon.

The third theory stresses the environmental factor and the different social and political conditions in which Ashkenazim and Sephardim lived. The Franco-German communities lived in a Christian society and despite the restrictions imposed upon them were not completely cut off from their gentile neighbors, especially in the economic sphere. Their thinking, habits, and even general way of life were accordingly influenced by the outside environment. No less a scholar than Rabbi Judah the Pious (Regensburg, 12th century) makes the following statement: "The usage of the Jews is in accordance with that of the non-Jews. If the non-Jews of a certain town are moral, the Jews born there will be so as well." Likewise, the Sephardim who lived for the most part under Mohammedan rule were influenced no less than their Ashkenazi brethren by the outside environment. The golden age of Spanish Jewry runs parallel to the golden age of the Moslem Empire, and it was in Spain that Jewish interest in broader knowledge of philosophy, mathematics, and medicine was sparked by the Moslem pursuit of higher learning. Ashkenazi Jewry during the same period concentrated in the main on the narrower sphere of Talmudic learning, the outside environment being not only hostile but also limited in its cultural achievements.

Ladino, the language still spoken by many of the Sephardim of the Mediterranean countries is based on the Castilian speech of the Middle Ages.

While the Sephardim (Spanish exiles) became the "aristocrats" of the new communities in the Western world, in Islamic countries they tended to be dragged down to the general stagnation which affected the Jewish communities there. With the modern exodus of Jews from North Africa to France and especially to Israel (where the Sephardim constitute almost half the population), the cultural gap which had developed over the years between sections of Sephardi and Ashkenazi Jewry is now being bridged. Sephardim constitute 17 percent of the world Jewish population.

SHABBETAI TZEVI (1625–1676): False Messiah, whose claim to Messiahship in the year 1665 led to one of the greatest upheavals in Jewish life. While Shabbetai Tzevi seems to have regarded himself as the Messiah even before the above-mentioned date, no one seems to have taken him seriously, not even his closest friends. His peculiar behavior and his practice of pronouncing the proper name of God had, it is true, aroused the ire of numbers of rabbis, and wherever he went, his mystical enthusiasm caused an uproar and frequently led to his expulsion from the community. The distance between this and an organized messianic movement, however, is vast.

Professor Gershom Scholem, one of the foremost authorities on the subject, has shown that Shabbetai Tzevi's association with Nathan of Gaza (1644–1680) was the decisive factor in what subsequently transpired. Shabbetai Tzevi went to consult Nathan of Gaza as a patient would a doctor — more specifically, a doctor of the soul. For Shabbetai Tzevi alternated between bouts of depression and fits of ecstatic exaltation and in this state of exaltation tended to commit acts which are contrary to Jewish law. Nathan of Gaza, instead of curing the patient, dispelled all Shabbetai Tzevi's doubts as to his Messiahship and urged him to proclaim himself the Messiah. Nathan, who had first met Shabbetai Tzevi in Jerusalem in 1662, had by his own evidence received a prophetic vision in which he had seen the figure of Shabbetai Tzevi. He thus became the brains behind the movement.

It has been suggested that the destitute state of Jewry after the vicious Chmielnicki persecutions of 1648 prepared the ground for the appearance of an enthusiast with messianic pretensions, and that the yearning of the Jewish masses for redemption from their trials and tribulations rendered Shabbetai Tzevi's and Nathan of Gaza's task easier than would normally have been the case. Whatever the reasons, Shabbetai Tzevi's proclamation was greeted with enthusiasm throughout the Jewish world. Very large numbers of people were swept on a tide of emotion and some actually sold all their belongings in preparation for the coming of the Messiah who would lead them to freedom. In 1666 Shabbetai Tzevi went to Constantinople in order to claim his kingdom from the Sultan. He was arrested and finally confronted with a choice between Islam or death, chose the former. His apostasy led to confusion, shame and disillusionment. Such was the blind faith of his followers, however, that they preferred to see in his conversion a symbolic action. Exploiting the teachings of Isaac Luria (see KABBALAH), the Sabbatian movement claimed that Shabbetai Tzevi had descended into the pit of sin in order to restore the sparks of divine light caused by the "breaking of the vessels," thus bringing about the eventual state of *Tikkun* (repair) which was the mission of the Messiah.

This concept of the holy sinner brought further catastrophe when developed into the Frankist movement founded in Poland by Jacob Frank (1726–1791), who turned sin into an ideal, leading to the eventual baptism of all his followers.

SHARETT (formerly Shertok), **MOSHE** (1894–1965): Israel statesman. Born in Russia, Sharett emigrated in 1906 to the land of Israel where he became active in Zionist-Socialist circles. In 1933 he was appointed head of the Jewish Agency's political department and played a major role in the struggle against Britain's discriminatory immigration policies from 1936. In 1946, he was arrested together with numerous other Zionist leaders and detained at Latrun. Sharett led the Jewish Agency delegation at the sessions of the United Nations which culminated in the decision to establish a Jewish State, and, when the State of Israel was proclaimed, he was appointed its first Foreign Minister. From 1953–1955 he succeeded Ben-Gurion as Prime Minister when the latter retired. On Ben-Gurion's return to active politics, Sharett once again served as Foreign Minister, but in 1956 he resigned after differences of opinion with Ben-Gurion over Israel's foreign policies. Sharett generally took a more moderate line than Ben-Gurion. From 1961, as chairman of the Jewish Agency, he made numerous trips abroad on behalf of Zionist causes.

SHAVUOT: Festival celebrated on the 6th day of the Hebrew month of *Sivan* (6th and 7th outside Israel). It occurs exactly seven weeks after the first day of Passover, hence the name *Shavuot* (weeks) and the Greek name *Pentecost,* which means "fiftieth," that is, the fiftieth day from the beginning of the counting of the *Omer* (sheaf cut in the barley harvest). The rabbis speak of *Shavuot* as the "concluding festival" to Passover, since it comes at the end of the counting of the *Omer* which began with Passover. In the *Mishnah,* the festival is referred to as *Atzeret,* meaning "termination" or "conclusion." *Shavuot* is also known as *Ḥag Ha-Katzir,* the festival of the wheat harvest, and *Yom Ha-Bikkurim,* the day of first fruits. In biblical times, *Shavuot* was, in the main, a harvest festival. On the fiftieth day after the bringing of the *Omer,* the start of the wheat harvest was celebrated by a thanksgiving offering of two loaves made from the new crop. In addition to this, the first fruits of the field were brought by the farmer to the Temple in Jerusalem on *Shavuot* as a token of gratitude for the Almighty's bounty.

In post-biblical literature, the festival is referred to as *Zeman Mattan Torateinu* — "the Season of the Giving of our Torah," and with the passage of time its celebration became almost exclusively associated with the revelation on Mt. Sinai and the giving of the Ten Commandments. The exact date of the revelation is not expressly mentioned in the Bible but is calculated by the rabbis to have taken place on the 6th of *Sivan.* Accordingly, the solemn reading of the Ten Commandments in the synagogue constitutes the central part of the *Shavuot* service. The reading of the Torah is enriched by the recitation of *Akdamot,* rhymed hymns of glory to God, in Aramaic. In some communities it is customary to spend the night of *Shavuot* in the reading and study of selections from the Scriptures, as well as rabbinic and mystical literature. A special book of service for this purpose is known as *Tikkun Leil Shavuot.* It is also customary to eat only dairy foods, symbolic of the Torah which is likened to milk and honey. For a long time, it was also the practice to initiate the Jewish child into the study of the Hebrew language and the Jewish religion on *Shavuot,* the festival of the giving of the Torah.

In many communities the book of Ruth is read, and this has a threefold purpose. First, it mentions the barley and wheat harvests. Second, its heroine, a Moabite woman, became a loyal convert to Judaism by accepting the Torah; and third, because of the legend that Ruth's grandchild, David, was born and died on *Shavuot.*

In the Diaspora, the agricultural aspect of the festival was neglected, for obvious practical reasons, except for the nostalgic custom of decorating the synagogue with plants and flowers on this day. With the return of the Jewish people to the land of Israel, this aspect is once again stressed by the holding of "first fruits" ceremonies throughout the land, especially in the schools and on the *kibbutzim.*

SHAZAR (RUBASHOV), SHNEOUR ZALMAN

(1890 —), Third President of Israel and a veteran Zionist leader. Zalman Shazar was born in Russia to a family who adhered to the *Ḥabad* branch of *Ḥasidism.* Shazar was a Zionist from his early youth. He worked in Vilna in the editorial office of a Yiddish newspaper which propagated the ideas of Labor Zionism. During World War I, as a student in Germany, he was one of the founders of the Labor Zionist Movement there. In 1924, Shazar decided to settle in the land of Israel. There he was active in the Labor Movement and edited its newspaper, *Davar.* He was Minister of Education and Culture in the first elected government of the State of Israel, and later directed the education program of the Jewish Agency. After the death of President Ben Zvi in 1963, Shazar was elected President of Israel. Shazar is an excellent speaker in several languages, a writer and educator, publicist and editor, and a socialist leader of the first rank.

President Zalman Shazar

SHEMA YISRAEL: One of the most important sections of the Jewish liturgy, so-called after its opening words: "Hear O Israel, the Lord our God, the Lord is One." It consists of three biblical paragraphs: 1) Deuteronomy 6: 4–9, which teaches the unity of God, the love of God, the command to instruct one's children in the commandments, the precept of *tephillin* and the fixing of the *mezuzah* on the doorpost and city gate; 2) Deuteronomy 11: 13–21, which contains the promise of reward for obedience to God's law and threatens punishment for its violation; and 3) Numbers 15: 37–41, which contains the law of wearing fringes *(tzizit).*

The custom of reciting the *Shema (Keriat Shema)* was part of the Temple service and was taken over by the synagogue. The rabbis based its recitation twice daily on the words in the first paragraph, "And thou shalt speak of them ... when thou liest down and when thou risest up."

Shema Yisrael *on settlement foundation stone, 1825*

The importance of the *Shema* in the rabbinic consciousness may be judged from the fact that the whole Mishnah opens with the question, "From what hour is the evening *Shema* to be read?"

Though not strictly a prayer, the *Shema* is an integral part of the morning and evening services. In the morning, it should be recited before the first quarter of the day has passed; and in the evening, before midnight, although if this is impossible, it may be read any time during the night. Its recitation is preceded and followed by benedictions, three in the morning, four in the evening. In addition to this, the first paragraph is said by the individual before retiring at night, and the first verse chanted when the Torah Scrolls are taken out of the ark, as part of the *Kedusha* of *Musaph,* and at the conclusion of the *Neilah* service on the Day of Atonement. Over the ages, the *Shema,* especially the first verse proclaiming the unity of God, became a sort of Jewish "confession of faith." During every persecution and massacre, from the time of the Crusades to the holocaust in our day, *Shema Yisrael* has been the last sound on the lips of the victims. It is one of the first prayers learnt by a Jewish child, and it is uttered by a Jew on his deathbed.

SHOLEM ALEICHEM (1859–1916): Pen name of Shalom Rabinowitch, regarded as the greatest of Yiddish humorists. Born in the Ukraine, he had a happy childhood, followed by a more difficult adolescence and early manhood. After becoming a tutor in the home of a Jewish landowner whose daughter he subsequently married, things began to improve for him. After the death of his father-in-law, he conducted a successful business for a time but later moved to Kiev where he indulged in all kinds of speculation, primarily in the stock exchange. These adventures ended in bankruptcy in 1890 and he moved to Odessa. There, together with the two other great Yiddish writers, Mendele Mocher Seforim and I. L. Peretz, Sholem Aleichem created a wealth of Yiddish literature.

In the early stages of his career, Sholem Aleichem was undoubtedly influenced by Mendele. In fact he regarded himself as his literary grandchild, referring to Mendele as *Der Zeide* ("the grandfather"). He, like his mentor, described the world of the Jews of eastern Europe in broad and human terms. He depicted a later period than that of Mendele, a more secular world in which the modern age had penetrated the ghetto. Sholem Aleichem writes as part of the world and life he describes. He does not try to educate or to moralize, although of course his stories do much of both. His aim was to make people laugh, to bring a moment's pleasure into a drab and miserable existence. With masterful touches he conveys the wry, latent sense of humor of the ghetto Jew, his capacity for laughing at his own trials and tribulations and his inherent optimism in spite of the cruel political, economic, and social conditions in which he generally lived.

Sholem Aleichem's originality came to the fore in his stories about Kasrilevke, a town of poor but cheerful Jews. One of the happy-go-lucky heroes of these stories is Menahem Mendel, who laughs at Jews — including himself — for their persistence in improbable undertakings doomed to failure. Tevye the Dairyman, the naive yet philosophical laborer, also appears in the sketches with his unshakable affirmation of life and the Jewish faith. The Tevye stories were later dramatized and in recent years have reached a wide public through the musical version, "Fiddler on the Roof."

In 1906, Sholem Aleichem visited the United States, stopping off at the large Jewish centers of Europe on the way. He immediately began writing about the new Jewish life on the American continent. After returning to Russia, he contracted tuberculosis and left for Italy. At the outbreak of World War I he returned to the United States, where he spent his last years.

Sholem Aleichem has remained the most popular of the great Yiddish writers of his time and his writings, in translation, are still widely enjoyed in many countries, including the U.S.A. and the U.S.S.R.

SHULHAN ARUKH ("Prepared Table"): Standard code of Jewish law compiled by Joseph Karo (1488–1575) and published in 1565. The attempt to arrange the great mass of Jewish law and practice as contained in the Talmud had been made before, notably by Maimonides (1135–1204) and Jacob ben Asher (c. 1270–1343). The latter's code, called *Sepher ha-Turim* (Book of the Rows — an allusion to the four rows of stones set in the breastplate of the High Priest), was considered insufficient by Karo because of its brevity and omission of sources. He therefore wrote his great work *Bet Yoseph,* which he intended to be his code. The *Shulhan Arukh* was written as a digest of the *Bet Yoseph,* intended for use as a study manual for younger students before they embarked upon his larger work. It achieved such success, however, that it was not long before it became the major code. In deciding on matters of Jewish law, Karo relied almost exclusively on Sephardi rabbinic authorities and Sephardi practice. Ashkenazi Jews, therefore, did not accept the code until Moses Isserles (c. 1525–1572) wrote his additional comments and glosses, adding Ashkenazi customs. The *Shulhan Arukh,* with Isserles' additions, became the standard authority for Orthodox Jews throughout the world and has remained so until today.

Karo followed the arrangement of the *Sepher ha-Turim* and divided the *Shulhan Arukh* into four parts: 1) *Orah Hayyim* — laws affecting the Jew's daily life, his prayers and festivals; 2) *Yoreh Deah* — dealing with dietary laws, laws of mourning, ritual laws, etc; 3) *Even Ha-Ezer* — laws of marriage, divorce, and personal status; and 4) *Hoshen Mishpat* — the laws that bear on civil life and the dispensation of justice in all its phases under Diaspora conditions.

SIEFF, ISRAEL, LORD (1889–1972): Born in Manchester, he was a collaborator of Chaim Weizmann and Secretary of the Zionist Commission to Palestine in 1918; in 1934 he founded the Daniel Sieff Research Institute at Rehovot. President of the chain store Marks and Spencer since 1967, he was one of Israel's most vigorous and dedicated supporters.

SINAI: Desert peninsula linking the continents of Africa and Asia. Triangular in shape, it is almost completely surrounded by water — the Mediterranean in the north and two branches of the Red Sea, the Gulf of Suez and the Gulf of Eilat in the south. Because of its unique geographical situation, Sinai has always occupied an important place in world history. In times of peace, it served as an important trade route for caravans making their way to and from Africa and Asia. In times of war, the sounds of armies on the move broke the stillness of the desert.

In modern times, the Sinai Peninsula assumed even greater strategic importance as a result of the building of the Suez Canal. In 1917, the British Army crossed the desert in order to conquer the Holy Land from the Turks, thereby securing the Canal which by then was one of the most important links of the British Empire.

Bedouin farm at Wadi Firan in central Sinai

In Jewish history, however, Sinai has a deep spiritual significance. It was here that God appeared to Moses in the vision of the burning bush and promised to redeem His people from Egyptian bondage. Later on, the Ten Commandments were given to the people in the revelation at Mount Sinai. The exact location of this site has been the subject of much conjecture and to this day remains undetermined. Traditionally, however, the Monastery of St. Catherine is supposed to have been built on the site. In modern Jewish history, Sinai has once again played an important role. Three times in twenty years it was penetrated or conquered by the Israel Army. In 1948, the invading Egyptians were repulsed and pursued into the desert by the Israel Army which withdrew under pressure from Britain. In 1956, the Sinai campaign culminated in the conquest of the area almost as far as the banks of the Suez Canal. Once again Israel's forces were compelled to withdraw, this time under pressure from the United States, Russia, and the United Nations. The withdrawal was carried out on the understanding that peace and quiet would follow. This was the case for the next ten years. Then in June 1967 the Egyptians once again massed their armies in Sinai, threatening Israel with extinction. Once again, the Israeli Army reacted and history repeated itself. This time, Israel's forces reached the canal.

The origin of the name Sinai is unknown although it has been associated with the ancient Babylonian moon god, *Sin*. Jewish tradition associated it with the burning bush which in Hebrew is *Sneh*.

SOLOMON: (reigned 961–922 B.C.E.): Third king of Israel, son of David and Bathsheba. Solomon inherited an empire from his father and throughout his reign, except for minor troubles in Edom and Syria, he was generally successful in maintaining it intact. No external enemy of major proportions threatened his realm, and he was thus able to devote himself to the task of consolidation. This does not mean that he neglected Israel's defenses. On the contrary, he fortified key cities and developed the chariot forces of his army — a fact attested to by the archeological excavations at Megiddo, Taanach, Eglon, and Gezer. Solomon's reign was one of industrial and economic progress, depicted in the Bible as a golden age in which "Judah and Israel were many, as the sand which is by the sea in multitude, eating and drinking and making merry." His policy of foreign alliances, cemented by ties of marriage, brought much benefit to the state. Especially close were his ties with the Phoenician kingdom of Tyre, an alliance already effected by David. This brought great economic benefits to the Israelite state. The Phoenicians supplied hardwood for Solomon's building projects and sent technical experts to assist in the building of the Temple. Phoenician sailors, the best in the world at the time, also manned a fleet which Solomon built in order to develop trade with Africa. One of Solomon's most important achievements, which is not mentioned in the Bible at all, was his development of the copper mines in the southern Negev (Aravah).

Solomon's great lifework, however, was undoubtedly the building of the First

Temple in Jerusalem. Begun in the fourth year of Solomon's reign, it was completed seven years later and dedicated with great pomp and ceremony, Solomon himself presiding. It is no wonder that Solomon's reputation for wisdom and understanding reached distant countries. The Bible attributes the visit of the Queen of Sheba (a kingdom in what is now the Yemen) to her desire to meet the famous Solomon in person. It is more likely, however, that her visit was connected with matters of trade and commerce, especially in view of Solomon's southward trade expansion.

At the same time, however, in internal matters Solomon exhibited an amazing shortsightedness which hastened the disintegration of the kingdom.

During his reign, the process of centralization started by David was completed. The northern tribes resented their loss of identity and self-rule. Solomon divided the kingdom into special administrative districts for purposes of taxation. This taxation grew increasingly severe as his commitments and building projects expanded. The costs outran his income, and the people bore the burden of payment. The Bible, too, accuses Solomon of corruption in his old age, but assigns this to the influence of his foreign wives.

The words spoken to his son and successor, Rehoboam, by the leaders of the ten northern tribes: "Thy father made our yoke grievous, now therefore make thou the grievous service of thy father and his heavy yoke lighter, and we will serve thee," give a clear indication of how the people felt toward Solomon. On Solomon's death, the whole national structure collapsed and Israel was split into two petty, relatively unimportant states.

Jewish tradition has stressed the wisdom of King Solomon and has assigned to him the authorship of the biblical books Proverbs, Ecclesiastes, and the Song of Songs.

SONG OF SONGS (Shir ha-Shirim, also known as the Song of Solomon or Canticles): The first of the five scrolls or *Megillot* contained in the third section of the Bible, *Ketuvim* (writings). Its eight chapters comprise love poems written in dialogue form, in which the lovers express their feelings of bliss, yearning, and exaltation in passionate, uninhibited, even erotic, phrases.

The contents have been variously interpreted, some scholars finding in the book no more than a collection of very beautiful love poems with many parallels in ancient (and modern) literature, some of which may even have been composed at or about the time of King Solomon.

Because of their secular and erotic nature, many of the rabbis refused to regard the book as sacred and were reluctant to include it in the Bible. Only at the Synod of Yavneh, at the end of the first century C.E., was the decision taken to include it on the grounds, first, that traditionally the

Song of Songs (from a Passover Maḥzor*)*

author of the book was supposed to be King Solomon and, second, because it was interpreted as an allegory of the love of God, the bridegroom, for his bride, Israel.

However, the verses reveal so open a delight in human love that the allegorical interpretation imposes quite a strain on credulity. Another theory gives the poems a dramatic theme: the love of King Solomon for a country girl, Shulamit. A similar theory provides for three principal characters: Solomon, the maiden, and her shepherd lover. The poems tell how the maiden is taken from her home in the country and brought to the king's palace, but Solomon is unable to win her love. Even promises of honor and glory do not tempt her, for she has already pledged her heart to her young shepherd. In the end she is permitted to return to her home and is reunited with her lover.

During the Middle Ages a mystical note was added to the allegorical interpretation, the bridegroom being God and the bride, the human soul.

Whatever view is accepted, the Song of Songs remains among the most beautiful love poetry ever written. Because of its springlike atmosphere, the book is read in the synagogue, according to the Ashkenazi rite, during the spring festival of Passover. Sephardim read it on Friday afternoons in preparation for the Sabbath, traditionally regarded as the Bride of Israel. They also read it on *Seder* night.

SOUTH AFRICA: Although Jews were connected with South Africa from the very earliest period of its colonization, it was only in the middle of the 19th century that organized Jewish life began to take shape. The establishment of the first congregation in Cape Town in 1841 led to a similar process in other centers. Several of the early Jewish settlers contributed to the economic and industrial development of the country: Nathaniel Isaacs explored the then unknown Zulu country, now the

Synagogue in Pretoria

province of Natal, and his *Travels in Eastern Africa* was the first textbook on the geography and ethnography of that province. The Solomon family, which subsequently left Judaism, gave to South Africa the great liberal leader in the Cape colony, Saul Solomon, whose son became a Chief Justice. The persecution of Jews in Russia and the discovery of gold and diamonds in South Africa toward the end of the 19th century combined to attract many Jews to South Africa. Jewish names such as Barnett Barnato, Alfred Beit, Sir Lionel Phillips, Isaac Lewis, and others figure prominently in the development of the diamond and gold industries. With the establishment of Johannesburg as the center of the gold industry, the Jewish community there grew into the largest in the country, with Cape Town next in size.

After World War I, a large influx of Lithuanian Jews gave a new impetus to the community and, during the 1930s, numbers of German-Jewish refugees were able to settle in South Africa. Although at that time restrictions limiting Jewish immigration were introduced, officially and legally, there has never been an organized anti-Semitic movement in South Africa.

From its earliest period, South Africa extended to Jews equal citizenship rights, and Jews have been able to progress reasonably well in all spheres, including Parliament. During the 1930s, however, the Nationalist Party exhibited anti-Semitic tendencies, and no Jew was eligible for membership in that party. After coming to power, however, the Nationalist Party did all in its power to prevent further recurrences of anti-Jewish feeling, and Jews today may join the party, as indeed many have done.

The South African Jewish community is one of the best organized in the world. In civil matters, it is represented by the South African Jewish Board of Deputies whose main task is to act as a watchdog over Jewish civil liberties, but which also plays a part in educational and other activities. The board has enunciated the point of view that race relations in South Africa are a political matter and in politics there is no specific Jewish point of view, Jews like other citizens being free to vote for whom they see fit.

Zionism has strong roots in South Africa among non-Jews as well as Jews. Successive South African statesmen since the Boer leader Jan Christian Smuts have all supported Zionist endeavor. Dr. D. F. Malan was the first foreign head of state to go to Israel (albeit on a private visit). Since Israel has voted consistently against apartheid at the U.N., relations with the South African government have often been strained and South African Jewry placed in a difficult position vis-à-vis supporters of apartheid in the country.

Nevertheless, there has been no diminution in their support for Israel and their financial contribution to Israel is the largest per person, in the world. A steady flow of immigration continues to reach Israel from that country, so that the South African community in Israel numbers some five and a half thousand.

In education, South African Jewry has made rapid strides in the last twenty years, with the establishment of Hebrew day schools throughout the country and the first *Yeshiva* in Johannesburg.

In religious tendencies, the community is divided into Orthodox and Reform, with the former in the majority. There is a Chief Rabbi over the Transvaal, the Orange Free State, and Natal, and a separate Chief Rabbi for the Cape Province.

The Jewish population of the Republic of South Africa is 115,000.

SPAIN: Conclusive evidence for Jewish settlement in Spain dates back to the 1st century C.E. Inscriptions from the Roman period have been discovered. When the Barbarian tribe, the Visigoths, first conquered Spain from the Romans, the Jews were treated favorably. In the year 589, however, the Visigoths embraced the Roman Catholic faith and there followed a wholesale persecution of the Jews. Under King Sinebut and his fanatical successors, Judaism was prohibited and its adherents given the choice of baptism or banishment. This period of persecution lasted one hundred years and was brought to a close by the Moslem conquest of 711 C.E. Spanish Jews generally welcomed the invaders. Under the Caliphate of the West, which had its capital at Cordoba, they grew both in influence and in numbers. The period from about the year 900 to the middle of the following century has been justly described as the Golden Age of Spanish Jewry. In all spheres of life Jews advanced rapidly, side by side with their Moslem neighbors. They cultivated the arts and sciences as well as theology and philosophy, and produced a glittering array of prominent figures. The first outstanding figure in Spanish Jewish life was Ḥasdai Ibn Shaprut (c. 915–970), who was physician and diplomatic adviser to the Caliph Abd er-Rahman II. After him, Samuel Ibn Nagdela (993–1063), poet and talmudist, became Grand Vizier to the King of

Granada. Jewish cultural activity embraced all spheres: talmudics, mathematics, philosophy, astronomy, poetry, and medicine. Moslem rule was enlightened, and the incidence of anti-Jewish discrimination was almost negligible. The Golden Age was brought to an end in 1146 when a fanatical sect known as the Almohades, who had previously overrun northwestern Africa and brought disaster on the Jewish settlements there, conquered Spain. They refused to tolerate divergent religious beliefs, and Jews were compelled either to accept Islam or to flee. As a result, the center of the Jewish settlement shifted to the Christian-ruled states of Castile, Aragon, and Catalonia. These kingdoms were tolerant, at first, and welcomed the Jews, finding them useful as diplomats, financiers, and agricultural colonists. Under Alfonso VI of Castile (1072–1109) and his grandson Alfonso VII (1126–1157), the Jews reached the height of their influence, producing a series of eminent statesmen and philosophers as well as great religious scholars and leaders. They enjoyed a high degree of autonomy and were allowed to maintain their own courts, in some cases even empowered to inflict capital punishment.

From the beginning of the 13th century, however, the situation deteriorated. The Crusades introduced an increasingly intolerant spirit into Christianity, and with the gradual elimination of Moslem influence throughout Spain, this intolerant spirit began to spread. Anti-Jewish regulations by the various church councils were introduced, and a vicious anti-Jewish propaganda campaign was vigorously followed, particularly by the Dominican monks. In an attempt to bring about the mass conversion of the Jews, a new tactic was adopted — public disputation (*see* DISPUTATION) in which Jewish leaders were forced to defend Judaism against the attacks of Christian representatives who were usually apostate Jews. There were sporadic outbreaks of violence, which

assumed serious proportions in areas where the central authority was weak. In the late 14th century, the Dominican monk Ferrand Martinez took the lead in anti-Jewish activity, and his inflammatory preaching resulted in an unprecedented outbreak of violence in the year 1391. The outbreak started at Seville but soon spread like wildfire throughout the country. Jews were given the choice of baptism or death. Many chose the latter, but for the first time in Jewish history there were also thousands of Jews who accepted baptism in order to escape death. These converted Jews constituted the New Christians or Marranos (*see* MARRANOS), who henceforth presented Spain with a major problem. These secret Jews utilized their equality as legal Christians to make progress socially and economically. They aroused the jealousy and ire of their Christian "brethren" who suspected, not without cause, the sincerity of their fidelity to the church and resented their acquisition of wealth and influence. It was to solve the Marrano problem that the Inquisition was introduced in Spain in 1478. As for those Jews who remained faithful to their heritage, they never recovered from the events of 1391. The growth of Spanish nationalism coupled with the incitement of prominent church leaders such as Vicente Ferrer, led to further outbreaks of intolerance and suppression. The presence of Jews faithful to Judaism was, in the opinion of Ferrer and others, a bad influence on the converted Jews, who seeing their brethren unmolested were encouraged to practice their religion in secret. These zealous churchmen accordingly began to press for the mass expulsion of Jews as the only solution to the problem. Even the power and influence of such Jews as the tax-farmers Abraham Seneor and Meir Melamed and the royal court's financial adviser Don Isaac Abravanel were unable to avert the decree. The Edict of Expulsion was issued by the Catholic monarchs Ferdinand and Isabella on

March 30, 1492 and took effect four months later. The expulsion, which is regarded as one of the greatest tragedies of Jewish history, is estimated to have involved about 150,000 persons in all, the majority of whom found refuge in North Africa and the Turkish Empire. Many went to Portugal where they also met a tragic fate. Spain remained free of all Jews, with the exception of the Marranos, until recent times. The expulsion edict was officially revoked in 1931. During World War II, many refugees from Nazi Europe found refuge in Spain. In 1967, a law granting Jews freedom of religion was passed and in 1968 a synagogue was formally dedicated in Madrid. Jews, however, have not immigrated to Spain in large numbers and the community numbers approximately. 7,000, most of whom reside in Barcelona and Madrid.

SPINOZA, BENEDICT (BARUCH)

(1632–1677): Dutch philosopher of Marrano parentage. His father and grandfather escaped from the Inquisition in Portugal to Amsterdam, where they became leaders of the Jewish community. Although Spinoza received a traditional Jewish education, his philosophical views were opposed to some of the basic principles of Judaism. In July 1656, he was summoned before the Amsterdam Bet Din, and when he refused to retract his views he was excommunicated. Consequently he left Amsterdam, spending his time in various Dutch cities in the company of Christian friends and pupils, earning a modest living as a lens polisher. Spinoza wrote two major works: *Theologico-Political Treatise* and *Ethics*. Because of possible hostile reaction, however, he published the former anonymously and the *Ethics* appeared only after his death. Spinoza's religious, ethical, and political views were indeed radical, at least for the times in which he lived. He advocated a thoroughgoing pantheism, rejecting the accepted idea of a God who is transcendent and above nature. In his view, God is nature and nature is God. Furthermore, Spinoza adopted a critical attitude toward the Bible and was in many respects the forerunner of modern Bible criticism. He pointed to certain contradictions in the scriptures and promulgated the theory that the law was given not in the time of Moses but in that of Ezra the Scribe. Spinoza was opposed to religious coercion and the rule of the church, advocating religious tolerance and the separation of church and state. Freedom of thought is an essential precondition for the development of the intellect, and the latter enables man to conquer his emotions, thus leading him to the highest virtue and happiness, the "intellectual love of God." Spinoza's philosophy was at first denounced as being materialistic, naturalistic, and atheistic. Subsequently, however, his thought greatly influenced the development of Western philosophy. A number of Jewish scholars have attempted to reconcile Spinoza's philosophical system with Judaism, but while he was acquainted with and even influenced by the medieval Jewish philosophers to a certain extent, his contribution is to be sought in the development of philosophy in general rather than in the sphere of Judaism.

SUKKOT

SUKKOT (Tabernacles): Festival commencing on the 15th day of the Hebrew month of *Tishri* and lasting seven days. The name is derived from the verse in Leviticus (Ch. 23:42–43) "Ye shall dwell in Sukkot seven days . . . that your generation may know that I made the children of Israel to dwell in Sukkot when I brought them out of the land of Egypt." In the Talmud there is a debate as to whether the verse should be taken literally to indicate that the children of Israel actually dwelt in *Sukkot* during their wanderings or whether the *Sukkot* mentioned are symbolic of the clouds of glory with which the Almighty protected them.

Whatever the answer, the *Sukkah* is a reminder of the divine providence which surrounded the Israelites during all the years of wandering and trial in the wilderness.

The *Sukkah* must be a frail temporary dwelling in which all meals are taken during the festival and in which, climate permitting, one should also sleep. As laid down by the rabbis, the *Sukkah* must be at least 10 but not more than 20 cubits (1 cubit = between 17–21 inches) in height; there must be more shade than sunlight; and, above all, it must be open to the stars. Only thus can one identify with the circumstances in which the children of Israel found themselves.

Sukkot is also known as *Ḥag Ha-Asiph* (the Festival of the Ingathering), and in ancient times it was an important agricultural celebration and a time for rejoicing. "And you shall take, on the first day, the fruit of goodly trees, branches of palm trees and boughs of leafy trees and willows of the brook; and you shall rejoice before the Lord your God seven days" (Leviticus 23:40). This command-ment refers to the "four species" consisting of the *lulav* (the palm branch), *hadasim* (three myrtle branches), *aravot* (two branches of the willow), and the *etrog* (citron). On each day of the festival, with the exception of the Sabbath, the *lulav* is taken up during the recitation of the *Hallel* and is waved in every direction, symbolizing God's sovereignty over all the world. Every day, after the *Amidah* of the additional service, circuits are made around the synagogue with the *lulav* and *etrog* while the reader and congregation chant special prayers beginning with the word *Hoshana* (Save us). On the seventh day, seven circuits are made, accompanied by the recital of many *Hoshana* prayers. This day thus came to be called *Hoshana Rabbah* (the Great Hoshana). During the Middle Ages, the seventh day increased in importance and acquired a solemn signi-ficance. It came to be looked upon as a continuation of the Day of Atonement, affording sinners a last chance, so to speak, of repenting. The *Hoshana Rabba* service concludes with the beating of a bundle of willow branches, the worshiper

Israeli children decorating the sukkah

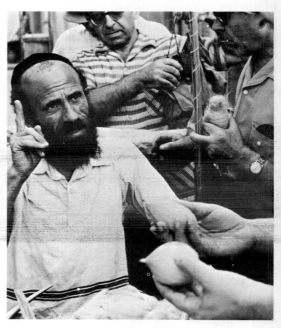

Choosing the etrog

thereby symbolically casting off his remaining sins. In the main, however, the atmosphere of *Sukkot* is a happy one, as testified to by another of its names, *Zeman Simhatenu* — the Season of our Rejoicing. In the Bible and the Talmud, the festival is also known simply as *Hag* (Festival).

In Temple times, the joyful ceremonial of the festival reached its climax with the ceremony known as *Simhat Bet Ha-Shoevah* (The Joy of the Water-Drawing), which consisted of a festive procession to and from the spring that supplied the water for the libations in the sanctuary. The ceremony was accompanied by singing and dancing, and the *Mishnah* says that "He who has never witnessed the rejoicing at the ceremony of water-drawing has never seen real joy in his life."

The eighth day is called *Shemini Atzeret* (the Eighth Day of Solemn Assembly), and with it the cycle of *Tishri* festivals is brought to an end. It is considered as a separate festival in certain respects, notably in that meals are not eaten in the *Sukkah*, and the *lulav* and *etrog* do not figure in the service for that day. In other respects, however, it is regarded as a continuation of *Sukkot* and in the liturgy is still referred to as *Zeman Simhatenu* (the Season of our Rejoicing). It is characterized in the synagogue by the special prayer for rain said during the *Amidah* of the additional service, and, in some communities, by the reading of the book of Ecclesiastes. In the Diaspora, where the biblical festivals are extended to two days, the second day of *Shemini Atzeret* is celebrated as *Simhat Torah* (The Rejoicing of the Law). In Israel, the day of *Shemini Atzeret* is also *Simhat Torah*. The latter is a comparatively recent celebration, for it is not mentioned either in the Bible or the Talmud. It seems to have developed gradually during the Middle Ages, and its basis is the completion on that day of the annual reading of the Torah, and its immediate recommencement from the first chapter of Genesis "in order that

Satan shall have no opportunity of accusing the Jews of having finished with the Torah." The custom arose of taking all the scrolls of the Torah from the ark, and of making seven circuits known as *Hakkaphot* around the synagogue. It also became customary to call an unlimited number of worshipers to the reading of the Torah, and of calling children en masse. The greatest honor that can be bestowed on *Simhat Torah* is to be either *Hatan Torah* (Bridegroom of the Torah), and be called to the reading of the last section of Deuteronomy, or *Hatan Bereshit* (Bridegroom of Genesis), and be called to open the reading of the Torah.

Simhat Torah has, together with Purim, come to be one of the most joyful occasions in the Jewish calendar.

SYNAGOGUE (from the Greek for "assembly," **Bet Knesset**): Most important religious institution in Jewish life; after the destruction of the Temple, a place of public prayer and frequently a communal center. Services held daily, on Sabbaths, festivals, and special occasions such as weddings, days of memorial, and Israel's Day of Independence, serve to ensure the participation of Jews in some form of divine service during the course of the year.

The origin of the synagogue is shrouded in mystery. The predominant view is that it had its beginnings during the Babylonian exile. Deprived of their Temple, the people used to gather from time to time in the presence of one of their leaders, such as the prophet Ezekiel, in order to hear the word of God and perhaps to recite some of the ancient psalms with which they were familiar. From these small beginnings the synagogue developed, and when the exiles returned to the land of Israel they brought with them this new institution.

Others are of the opinion that the synagogue came into existence only after the time of Ezra and Nehemiah. A third body of opinion traces the synagogue's origin even further back, to before the

The synagogue at Mikveh Yisrael

Babylonian exile. When the King of Judah, Josiah, abolished the local high places and sanctuaries, people who lived far away from Jerusalem were left without a means of spiritual expression. The thrice-annual pilgrimage to the Temple was not sufficient to satisfy their spiritual thirst, and thus there arose throughout the country local institutions for prayer. Most scholars tend to accept the first viewpoint.

During the period of the Second Temple, there were synagogues throughout the land of Israel. The oldest one so far discovered is in the desert fortress of Masada. By the 1st century C.E. the synagogue was already an ancient institution. The Great Synagogue of Alexandria was famed throughout the world in Roman times, and excavations carried out at various places in Syria and Israel have revealed a number of beautiful decorations. The synagogue was generally situated on high ground, in accordance with the Talmudic ruling that it should be the highest building in the town. However, the Christian Church

later did all in its power to prohibit the building of synagogues and insisted that they be lower than churches. With time, the synagogue became the focal point of Jewish life and everything was centered around it. This idea of the Jewish communal center with the synagogue as its pivot has been revived in modern times, especially in the U.S. In ancient times, the synagogue was governed by an *archisynagogus,* other officers, and the *hazzan,* who in addition to his other duties was responsible for the general upkeep of the synagogue. Later on, the officers were the *gabbai* (warden), the *hazzan* (now strictly limited to the recitation of the prayers), and the *shamash* (responsible for order and cleanliness).

Synagogue architecture has varied from place to place and has always been influenced by general architectural style. But one thing is constant — the ark was placed against the wall facing Jerusalem, and it was in this direction that the congregation faced to pray. Originally the ark was portable and was brought into the synagogue only for services, but eventually it was placed there permanently.

Controversy arose in the 19th century when the Reform movement decided to abolish the partition *(mehitzah)* between men and women. This partition — either in the form of a women's gallery or a separate section — goes back to the days of the Temple, where there was a separate section for women *(ezrat nashim)*. Reform Judaism, stressing the importance of family prayer and making the equality of women one of its major tenets, abolished this custom. It also moved the reader's platform *(bimah)* from the center to the eastern wall, in front of the ark containing the scrolls of the Torah.

In eastern Europe, in particular, the synagogue was often only a small prayer-room *(stiebel),* often combined with study facilities *(bet midrash)*.

In modern times, the trend has been

toward grandiose and luxurious Jewish communal centers (often designed by leading architects) supplying all the cultural needs of the community of which the synagogue (which many Reform Jews call a temple) is but a part.

See also: RABBI, TEMPLE.

SZOLD, HENRIETTA (1860–1945): Zionist leader, founder of Hadassah and leader of Youth Aliyah. She was born in Baltimore, U.S.A. and inspired by her father, Rabbi Benjamin Szold, to pursue Jewish studies. She was the first woman to study at the Jewish Theological Seminary in New York. For 24 years, from 1892–1916, she was Secretary of the Jewish Publication Society of America. In 1912, she founded Hadassah, the women's Zionist organization of America, and after World War I supervised the organization of health services in Israel. In 1927, she was appointed a member of the Zionist Executive, with responsibility for education and health. After the rise of Nazism, she devoted herself almost entirely to the work of Youth Aliyah, which under her leadership rescued thousands of Jewish children from Europe and brought them to youth villages and settlements in Israel. Her name became an almost legendary symbol for thousands of young people who, thanks to her energy,

Henrietta Szold

leadership, and devotion, were able to find a new life for themselves. Her humanitarian ideals were not only confined to Jewish spheres, but expressed themselves in the attempt to foster ties of friendship between Arabs and Jews.

TABERNACLE: The people of Israel's first house of worship, set up in the wilderness of Sinai in accordance with God's instructions (Exodus 26–7). It was a portable tent called in Hebrew *Ohel Mo'ed,* the Tent of Meeting. It was here that God spoke to Moses "face to face" (Ex. 33:11). Whoever wished to consult the Almighty went to the tent where Moses interceded between him and God. It was also called the *Mishkan* — the Dwelling or Abode of God. The Tabernacle, which was built through donations contributed by the people, was rectangular in shape and was covered with bands of fine woven material sewn together and embroidered with figures of cherubim. The whole construction was covered with the skins of rams, dyed red, and then by very light leather hides. The frame was constructed of acacia wood overlaid with gold. The most important part of the Tabernacle was the Holy of Holies which contained the Ark of the Covenant, the seven-branched candelabrum and the table of shewbread. It was separated from the rest of the Tabernacle by a veil. Throughout the wanderings of the Children of Israel, the Tabernacle was carried from place to place by the Levites and in the time of Joshua, was set up at Shiloh.

TALLIT: A rectangular piece of cloth with a fringe at each of its four corners worn by males as a prayer shawl. The purpose of the fringes, also known as *tzitzit,* is explained in the Bible: "That ye may look upon it and remember all the commandments of the Lord and do them ... and be holy unto the Lord your God" (Num. 15:39–40).

The *tallit* is wrapped around the head and shoulders after the recitation of a special benediction and before putting on the *tephillin.* It is worn at all morning and additional services, but on the fast of the 9th of *Av,* it is put on at the afternoon instead of at the morning service. On the Day of Atonement, it is worn at all services, including the evening service. At regular afternoon and evening services, however, it is only worn by the reader or cantor. The *tallit* should preferably be made of wool with woolen fringes attached. Other fabrics, however, may be used as long as the fringes are made of the same fabric. In many communities silk is used, but linen should be avoided. In some Orthodox circles, the *tallit* is worn only by married men. It is also referred to as the *tallit gadol* (large tallit) to distinguish it from the *tallit katan* (small tallit) or *arba kanphot* ("four corners") which is the *tzitzit* worn perpetually by observant Jews under the outer garment during waking hours. The latter was introduced during the Middle Ages when four-cornered garments were no longer worn and persecution made it advisable for Jews not to exhibit their fringed garments. The wearing of the *tallit gadol* was thus limited to worship only. When it is put on, the blessing is recited: "Blessed art Thou O God who hast commanded us to wrap ourselves in the *tallit.*"

TALMUD: Comprehensive term for Jewish tradition transmitted orally from generation to generation until finally committed to writing.

According to Jewish tradition, when Moses received the Torah from God on

Mount Sinai, he received with it an oral explanation. This explanation was not written but handed on from generation to generation until finally committed to writing centuries later. The belief in the antiquity of the oral tradition was later formulated as the first teaching of the "Ethics of the Fathers." "Moses received the *Torah* on Sinai and handed it down to Joshua; Joshua to the Elders; the Elders to the prophets; and the prophets handed it down to the men of the Great Assembly." The assumption of an oral explanation to the Torah is a logical one, for there are numerous laws and regulations in the five books of Moses that are not clearly phrased or explained. For example, while the Torah prohibits work on the Sabbath, it does not define what constitutes "work." If the Torah were to become the law of the land, it would have to be interpreted so as to cover all the possibilities of everyday life. In fact, the writings of the prophets contain numerous laws which are not mentioned in the five books of Moses and which nevertheless seem to have been accepted in their day as normal practice. This would therefore point to the existence of some form of oral tradition *(Torah she-be-al-peh)* distinct from and parallel to the written tradition *(Torah she-be-ktav)*.

Historically speaking, however, it was the Babylonian exile which gave this development its real impetus. A nation deprived of its land and Temple had to find ways and means of ensuring its spiritual survival. These were found. Most scholars agree that it was in Babylon that the synagogue developed not only as a house of worship but also as a *bet knesset,* a house of assembly. Here, under the guidance of men such as the prophet Ezekiel, the exiles would assemble to pray, to reminisce and, undoubtedly, to read those portions of the Scriptures which were in their possession. In Babylon, there also grew up a class of teachers known as *sopherim* (scribes), not in the sense of writers but as "men of

letters." Foremost among these was Ezra. They not only read the Torah but interpreted and explained it. Their guiding philosophy was Torah as a way of life. The book of Ezra (Ch. 7:10) relates that "Ezra had set his heart to seek the Torah of God, and to do it, and to teach in Israel statutes and judgments." The word "to seek" in the Hebrew text is *dorash* and the method known as *Midrash* was used to interpret the Torah. By it, every word and even letter of the Torah is meaningful. Being of divine origin, it cannot contain anything superfluous. When Ezra came to the land of Israel from Babylon he founded, according to tradition, a school of teachers known as the men of the Great Assembly. They continued and developed even further the methods of interpretation in their zeal to implant the Torah as the everyday law of the people. So the oral tradition grew. The Great Assembly ceased to exist either in the middle or at the end of the 3rd century B.C.E. It was followed, however, by the Sanhedrin which was responsible for the affairs of the community in Judea. The names of five famous *zugot* or pairs who served as president and vice president respectively of this body have come down to us. The last of these were Hillel and Shammai. Both of these sages founded schools which differed vastly from each other in their interpretation of the law. The Talmud records over three hundred points of disagreement between them, but, in the end, the teaching of Hillel prevailed. Hillel also made a major contribution to the development of the Oral Law by establishing seven methods by which the text of the Bible may be interpreted. His arrangement, however, was still preserved only orally.

The question as to why the traditions were not written down has bothered many scholars, and no real answer has yet been found. It may be assumed, however, that the rabbis wished to maintain that freedom of interpretation and debate which a written code tends to stultify.

A page from a Talmud *manuscript*

The purpose of the oral tradition was to enable the Torah to be a way of life and, where necessary, to be adjusted to new circumstances by interpretation of the text. Committing the tradition to writing would perhaps have prevented it from achieving this purpose. Furthermore, it must be remembered that in the ancient Orient, memory was more highly developed, and learning was acquired not so much from books as from the lips of teachers. The fact is, however, that it was a principle not to commit the oral tradition to writing and, conversely, not to teach the written law orally.

After Hillel, subsequent sages such as Rabbi Akiva and Rabbi Meir made their own unique contribution to the process of development. Rabbi Ishmael extended Hillel's seven methods of interpretation to thirteen, and these subsequently became thirty-two. Akiva may be described as the real architect of the plan of the *Mishnah,* and his disciples, especially Rabbi Meir, continued along the lines marked out by him.

It was, however, Rabbi Judah, "the Prince," born in the year 135 C.E., three years after Akiva's death, who finally decided that regardless of previous principles the time had come to codify the oral tradition. His title, *Ha-Nasi* (the Prince), was based on the circumstance that until his death in 219 C.E. he occupied the office of patriarch; in other words, he was the officially recognized leader of his community. He realized that the mass of oral tradition had grown so large as a result of centuries of development that it was in danger of being forgotten. He thus set out to arrange it in an orderly fashion. The result of his labors was the *Mishnah.* The word is derived from the Hebrew *shanah,* meaning to repeat or to teach, and indicates oral tradition or what is learned by repetition. It is arranged in six orders, *Shishah Sedarim,* hence the abbreviated term *Shas.* Each order consists of a number of tractates known as *Massekhtot,* and each tractate is divided into chapters and paragraphs. There are 63 tractates and 524 chapters in all. The six orders are: 1) *Zeraim* (seeds), dealing mainly with the agricultural laws; 2) *Mo'ed* (appointed times), dealing with the laws of festivals and fasts; 3) *Nashim* (women), chiefly on marriage and divorce; 4) *Nezikin* (damages), dealing with civil and criminal law; 5) *Kodashim* (sanctities), which is primarily concerned with the Temple service; and 6) *Tehorot* (purities), dealing with the laws of ritual purity and impurity.

The language of the *Mishnah* is Hebrew, but it contains words borrowed from Greek and Latin and shows a marked Aramaic influence. The teachers quoted in the *Mishnah* are known as *tannaim.* Judah the Prince did not succeed in gathering all the material, and other collections of Tannaitic teaching have come down to us. Chief among these are the

Tosephta (supplement), and *Baraita,* meaning in Aramaic "that which is external" — in other words, material not incorporated in the *Mishnah.* No sooner was the *Mishnah* completed than it became the subject of intensive study in the academies of the land of Israel and of Babylonia. The scholars of the post-Tannaitic period did to the *Mishnah* what the *tannaim* had done to the Bible. If the *Mishnah* is a commentary and interpretation of the Bible, so the *Gemara* which followed is a commentary and interpretation of the *Mishnah.* It was analyzed, discussed, and debated, so that once again an oral tradition developed, this time based on the *Mishnah.* The Palestinian and Babylonian academies conducted their research independently, for by this time Babylon was rapidly developing as the main center of Jewish learning. The two great scholars, Rav and Samuel, laid the foundation of Babylonian Jewish scholarship, while in the land of Israel the most distinguished teacher was Johanan bar Nappaḥa, the head of the Academy of Tiberias. Thus in both centers the process of analyzing the *Mishnah* went on at one and the same time. The post-Mishnaic rabbis were named *amoraim* (speakers, expounders) and the fruit of their work is called the *Gemara* (Aramaic for completion), because it completes the *Mishnah.* The *Mishnah* and the *Gemara* regarded as a single unit are what we call the Talmud, meaning teaching. The tradition of the schools of the land of Israel was finalized at the end of the 5th century C.E., and that of the Babylonian schools about a hundred years later. Hence the terms Palestinian Talmud and Babylonian Talmud. Both Talmuds have essentially the same *Mishnah* but differ with respect to the size and content of their *Gemara* and the form in which the *Gemara* is arranged. The Palestinian Talmud covers 39 tractates of *Gemara,* and the Babylonian 37, but the Babylonian

Gemara is seven to eight times the size of the other. Even in language there is a difference, the Palestinian Talmud being composed in western Aramaic and the Babylonian in eastern Aramaic.

The subject matter of the Talmud may be divided into two main categories, *Halakhah* and *Aggadah.* The former is the legalistic code, the way of life which the sages wished the people to follow. The latter consists of legends, anecdotes, parables, and such subjects as astrological speculation, cures for various diseases, and almost anything that people talk about. A legalistic discussion may suddenly be interrupted by a flight into the world of fantasy and imagination. The discussions are disorderly — to keep to the point was not one of the principles of the Talmudic sages. The *Sea of the Talmud* is the best description given to date of the contents of this vast literary production, the fruits of approximately 800 years of discussion and learning. Of the two Talmuds, the Babylonian is considered more authoritative, perhaps because that community was more numerous after the destruction of the Temple and attracted men of superior intellect to those of the Palestinian academies.

Obviously, the vastness of the work gave rise to the inclusion of many irrelevent and even offensive passages. In the main, however, the Talmud is the product of sincere, scholarly, and wise men whose sole purpose was to ensure the continued existence of the Jewish people, even though they were deprived of their political independence. It is no exaggeration therefore to state that the study and analysis of the Talmud by countless generations of Jews contributed more than any other factor to the spiritual survival of the nation, and to the fact that illiteracy has always been a non-existent problem for the Jewish people. It is no wonder then that the enemies of the Jews throughout the ages saw in the Talmud the root of all evil, causing Jewish stubbornness in the face of their missionary activity. More than once the Talmud was burned publicly as a sign of the church's displeasure with and frustration at its hold over the Jewish people.

TECHNION, HAIFA (Israel Institute of Technology): Israel's oldest institution of higher learning, established in 1912 at the initiative of German Jews and with the financial backing of philanthropist Jacob Schiff of New York and the Wissotsky estate of Moscow. At first there was a question whether the teaching language should be Hebrew or German, but eventually it was decided that it should be Hebrew.

The Technion trains engineers, technologists, scientists, and architects. In 1948 there were 778 students; in 1969 there were 4,000 undergraduates studying for B.Sc. degrees and 1,700 working for M.Sc. or D.Sc. degrees as well as 1,650 in the junior technical college, 2,625 in the school for senior technicians, and 11,350 in extension courses. The teaching staff exceeds 1,000. In 1954, work was begun on a new 300-acre campus on Mt. Carmel called Technion City. Today, almost all the faculties and departments are located here. The following are the faculties and departments: Civil Engineering, Chemical Engineering, Materials Engineering, Electrical Engineering, Agricultural Engineering, Aeronautical Engineering, Industrial and Management Engineering, Architecture and Town Planning, Mathematics, Physics, Chemistry, Mechanics, Nuclear Science, Food and Biotechnology as well as teacher training. Over 70 percent of the engineers and applied scientists practicing in Israel today are graduates of the Technion.

TEL AVIV (Hill of Spring): Largest city in Israel, containing about one seventh of the country's population (385,000). Tel Aviv was founded in 1908 by a group of Jews calling themselves *Aḥuzat Bayit* (House Holding), who wished to leave the unsanitary and primitive conditions of Jaffa. With the aid of the Jewish National Fund, they purchased land on the sand dunes north of Jaffa and set about building a "European-style" settlement. They called the new quarter Tel Aviv, which is the title of the Hebrew translation of Theodor Herzl's novel, *Altneuland*. A settlement of that name existed in ancient Babylon, and many of the Judean exiles lived there (Ezekiel 3:15). One of the first buildings erected was the Herzlia Secondary School, which is to this day one of Israel's leading educational institutions. It was demolished in 1959 and rebuilt on new premises in north Tel Aviv. On its original site, Tel Aviv's first skyscraper, the *Migdal Shalom* (Tower of Peace), was erected.

During World War I, the Turks expelled all of Tel Aviv's residents, but under the British Mandate the city developed rapidly. In 1921 it was separated from Jaffa and recognized as a separate municipality. Arab riots in Jaffa and a steady immigration served to ensure its continued growth.

In 1947–48, heavy fighting broke out between Jewish Tel Aviv and Arab Jaffa and on the eve of the establishment of the state, Jaffa surrendered, most of its residents having fled. It was resettled with new immigrants and in 1949 the two cities were amalgamated under the name Tel Aviv — Jaffa. Jaffa has subsequently become the center of much of Tel Aviv's night life and also houses an artists' colony. Tel Aviv has grown into a thriving metropolis with all the problems of city life. Its main thoroughfare, Dizengoff Street, named after the city's first mayor, is lined with sidewalk cafés which are jammed with people at all hours of the day and night. Traffic congestion and frayed tempers are commonplace occurrences, as in most large cities.

Tel Aviv is also a cultural center housing,

View of Tel Aviv

among other organizations, the *Habimah* Theater and the Israel Philharmonic Orchestra, both with elegant, modern halls.

The art museum which was bequeathed by the first mayor, Meir Dizengoff, is also used for chamber music concerts. It was in this museum that Ben-Gurion proclaimed the establishment of the State of Israel.

The headquarters of Israel's trade union movement (the *Histadrut*), as well as the Defense Ministry are in Tel Aviv as are many luxury hotels.

Tel Aviv University is situated in one of the newer sections of Tel Aviv, Ramat Aviv, and has 12,000 students and an academic staff of over 1,500. While Jerusalem is the capital of Israel and its government center, Tel Aviv is the leading city both for business and for cultural activities.

TEMPLE (Bet ha-Mikdash): The central house of worship in Jerusalem during the 1st and 2nd Jewish commonwealths. The first temple was built by King Solomon on the traditional site of Mt. Moriah, where the binding of Isaac had taken place. The idea, however, was first conceived by Solomon's father, David, who in transferring the Ark to Jerusalem, intended to erect an edifice to house it, thereby making Jerusalem the religious center of Israel. David was not granted his wish since he was a warrior and had shed blood. The privilege was given to his son, Solomon, whose name in Hebrew signifies peace. The building of the Temple occupied Solomon from the fourth to the eleventh year of his reign. It was built by a Phoenician architect contracted through Hiram, King of Tyre. The timber was brought from the Lebanon and the stone was quarried near Jerusalem. The bulk of the labor force was conscripted from the Israelite population but the skilled workers were for the most part Phoenician. A detailed description of the Temple is given in I Kings 6–7, and a further summary in II Chronicles 3–4. In view of the important role played by the Phoenician specialists, it is quite understandable that the Temple was constructed according to a pattern then current in the land of Israel and Syria.

The Temple was a long building, rectangular in shape and facing east. The interior consisted of three distinct sections: 1) a vestibule, ten cubits long, called the *Ulam,* 2) the main hall of the sanctuary, forty cubits long, referred to as the *Heikhal,* and 3) the *Devir,* twenty cubits long, known as the Holy of Holies. The last was a dark windowless inner sanctum containing the Ark of the Covenant. The Temple was surrounded on the outside by a three-story building erected against the walls of the *Devir* and the *Heikhal.* It was divided into cells and rooms for the storing of sacred vessels and treasure. The Temple served a twofold purpose: to shelter the Ark of the Lord which symbolized God's covenant with the people of Israel, and to serve as

Reconstruction of Second Temple courtyard

a meeting place for the people for sacrifice and prayer. To the east of the Temple was a large altar used for sacrificial purposes. It has been suggested that this is identical with the rock in the Mosque of Omar, also known as the Dome of the Rock, which was built on the Temple mount in the 8th century. The Temple of Solomon was the central pivot of the nation's spiritual life. The religious services, conducted to the accompaniment of choral and instrumental music, were indeed impressive, and on the three pilgrimage festivals (Passover, Pentecost, and Tabernacles) Jerusalem and the Temple area were thronged with thousands of pilgrims from all over the country.

During its almost four-hundred-year existence, Solomon's Temple was part of the flux and change in the kingdom of Judah's spiritual and political fortunes. There were times when it was violated and its sanctity profaned by foreign and local rulers. The worst desecration was reached during the reign of King Manasseh. Possibly under Assyrian influence, this king introduced idolatrous statues and other forms of worship into the Temple. He erected altars to false gods and an idol of Asherah. The prophets, who revered the Temple, were from time to time called upon to condemn the evil practices, the hypocrisy,

and the mechanical performance of the ritual perpetrated by a corrupt priesthood. On the other hand, there were also pious and devout kings such as Hezekiah and Josiah who carried out far-reaching religious reforms to purify the Temple worship and remove all vestiges of idolatry from the Temple and the land. The standard of religious purity maintained in the Temple mirrored the religious life of the nation as a whole. The Temple also symbolized Judah's political independence and sovereignty and with its destruction by King Nebuchadnezzar of Babylon in the year 586 B.C.E. Judean independence came to an end and the Babylonian exile commenced.

In the year 538 B.C.E., King Cyrus of Persia, the conqueror of Babylon, authorized the exiled Jews to return to Jerusalem and to rebuild their Temple there at the expense of the royal exchequer. He also returned to them the gold and silver furnishings which Nebuchadnezzar had carried off as booty. The first exiles to return set up an altar on the site of the old one, and laid the foundations of the Second Temple. Due to Samaritan obstruction and a degree of apathy on the part of the returnees, the work was interrupted. It was resumed again in 520 B.C.E. and completed in 515 B.C.E. The Second Temple, for the most part, followed the plan of the former Temple. During the persecutions begun by Antiochus Epiphanes the Temple was looted. In the year 167 B.C.E., a statue of Zeus was set up on the altar. The Temple services were interrupted for three years and were only resumed in the year 165 B.C.E. when Judah the Maccabee conquered Jerusalem and rededicated the Temple, an event still commemorated in the observance of the Ḥanukkah celebration. When the Roman general Pompey took Jerusalem in the year 63 B.C.E., he desecrated the Temple by entering the Holy of Holies but he respected the Sanctuary and did not touch the treasury. In approximately 20–19 B.C.E., in the 18th year of his reign, Herod began to rebuild the Temple. He added numerous beautiful buildings and offices. Additional courtyards were added which on the pilgrimage festivals were packed to capacity. Included among these was the chamber of hewn stone which was the seat of the supreme legislative body, the Sanhedrin. Herod's Temple, according to all accounts, was a glorious edifice. At the same time, however, the spiritual level deteriorated because for the first time the High Priesthood ceased to be a hereditary office. Priests were appointed and dismissed at the whim of the Roman rulers and of Herod himself, and the appointment was often granted for political reasons or on the payment of substantial sums of money. The Temple nevertheless remained the national and spiritual symbol of the people of Israel, and when it was destroyed by the Roman general Titus in the year 70 C.E., the nation was enveloped in mourning.

The Temple remained at the center of Israel's hopes and yearnings. The belief in its restoration and the renewal of the sacrificial rite have formed an integral part of Jewish liturgy and ceremonial. There is hardly an occasion in Jewish life in which the Temple is not mentioned. The daily prayers, the grace after meals, and the wedding ceremony all contain elements which commemorate the Temple or specific supplications for its rebuilding. On the Day of Atonement, the *Musaph* service is embroidered with a lengthy description of the *Avodah,* the service in the Temple on that day when the High Priest entered the Holy of Holies, the only occasion during the year on which he was permitted to do so. Reform Jews, however, have omitted all references to the restoration of the Temple service from the prayer book. In their view, the synagogue has long since replaced the Temple, and perhaps for that reason, the early reformers instituted the use of the word "temple" for the house of worship, instead of "synagogue."

The only remaining part of the Temple, the Western or Wailing Wall, has been a place of pilgrimage for pious Jews throughout the ages, in particular on the fast of the ninth of *Av* which commemorates the destruction. It is only since the June 1967 Six-Day War, however, that unhindered free access to the wall has been available to Jews. Shortly thereafter, excavations began immediately adjacent to the ancient walls of the Temple enclosure, and many finds have been made connected with the Temple and demonstrating its imposing grandeur as rebuilt by Herod.

TEN COMMANDMENTS (also known by the Greek term *Decalogue*): Ten principles of ethical and religious conduct formulated by God during Moses' revelation on Mount Sinai. Containing only one hundred and twenty Hebrew words in all, the Ten Commandments have exercised more profound influence on the moral and social life of humanity than any other group of laws. They are regarded by Jews and Christians alike as the fundamental pillars of their faith. The Decalogue covers the whole range of religious and moral life and lays down the guidelines in the relationship between man and God and man and man. A somewhat artificial

Moses receiving Commandments, 16th c. tapestry

division can be made between the first five and last five commandments. The first five commandments deal with laws relating to man's duties toward God, and the other five regulate man's conduct toward his neighbor. The fifth commandment, "Honor thy Father and thy Mother," according to the above, is considered a duty toward God who in rabbinic tradition is the partner of the parents in creating a child. The Ten Commandments are given twice in the Bible with slight variations, once in Exodus 20:2–14, and the second time in Deut. 5:6–18. The main difference between the two versions is found in the fourth commandment which deals with the observance of the Sabbath. In Exodus, the reason given for the observance of the Sabbath is that God rested on the seventh day of creation, while in Deuteronomy the reason invoked is the deliverance from Egyptian bondage. According to the Bible, the commandments were inscribed by God on two tablets of stone which were broken by Moses in his anger on seeing the people worshiping the golden calf. When Moses reascended the mountain and God forgave the people, he was given a second set of tablets, which were afterward placed in the Ark, hence the name Ark of Testimony or Ark of The Covenant.

In Temple times, the Ten Commandments formed an integral part of the religious service, being recited daily just before the *Shema*. The practice was abolished by the rabbis because of the existence of certain sects who claimed that the Decalogue was more important than other sections of the Bible, contrary to rabbinic belief which affirms that the whole Torah and not only the Decalogue was given on Mount Sinai. Despite this, the rabbis continued to regard the Ten Commandments as the basis of Judaism, claiming that the tablets on which they were written were prepared on the eve of creation, antedating humanity and therefore independent of time or place. Furthermore,

they said, the divine voice divided itself into the seventy languages spoken on earth so that all men might understand its message.

When the Ten Commandments are read in the synagogue, the congregation rises and the commandments are intoned by the reader to a special solemn tune. The festival of *Shavuot,* according to tradition, commemorates the revelation at Mount Sinai, and the solemn reading of the Decalogue constitutes the highlight of the religious service on that day.

TEN PLAGUES: Ten devastating blows inflicted by God on the Egyptian Pharaoh, his people, and his country, in order to secure the release of the Israelites. The plagues are vividly described in the book of Exodus (7:14–12:30), and form a symmetrical, patterned scheme. The first nine plagues consist of three series of three each: 1) blood, frogs, lice; 2) fleas (possibly the tsetse fly), murrain, boils; 3) hail, locusts, darkness. In each series, the first plague is announced to Pharaoh on the brink of the Nile, the second is proclaimed by Moses at the palace, and the third is sent without warning. There is a regular repetition of the moment when Pharaoh begs Moses to remove the scourge and offers to release the Israelites in return. Once the plague has been removed, however, the Pharaoh again hardens his heart and refuses to fulfill his promise. The climax is reached with the tenth and final plague, the death of every Egyptian firstborn child. The Pharaoh now not only agrees to the departure of the Israelites, but actually orders them to leave without delay.

A number of scholars have pointed out that far from being supernatural phenomena, the plagues were miraculously intensified forms of diseases and other natural events liable to occur in Egypt at different times of the year. Whether the emphasis is placed on the natural or supernatural interpretation, the Bible is concerned with a primarily moral message, i.e., that tyranny and oppression cannot forever flaunt the laws of justice and morality. Freedom will triumph in the end, whatever the hardships involved.

The recitation of the story of the ten plagues is the central part of the *Haggadah* narrative read in the home at the *Seder* celebration on the eve of Passover. As each plague is mentioned, a drop of wine is poured out, in memory of the Egyptians who died. Although enemies of Israel, they too were God's creatures.

TEPHILLIN: Phylacteries worn by male Jews over the age of 13 at the daily morning service, with the exception of Sabbaths, festivals, and the fast of the 9th of *Av,* when they are worn at the afternoon service. It has been suggested that the word is connected with the Hebrew *Tefilla,* "prayer," thus signifying something used during worship.

The Biblical basis for the command to put on *tephillin* is the verse contained in the *Shema* (Deut. 6:8) "And thou shalt bind them for a sign upon thine hand, and they shall be for frontlets between thine eyes." Accordingly, the *tephillin* consist of two black leather boxes attached to leather straps. One is bound ("laid") on the left upper arm against the heart and wound a number of times around the forearm, hand, and two fingers. The other is placed on the front part of the head above the center of the forehead. The hand *tephillin* are put on first, followed by the head *tephillin.* Appropriate benedictions are recited as each is put on. At the conclusion of the service, when the *tephillin* are removed, the order is reversed and no benedictions are said. Within the leather boxes are four sections of the Bible written by a scribe on parchment. They are: 1) Exodus 13:1–10, containing the passage concerning the dedication of the firstborn; 2) Exodus 13: 11–16, describing the redemption from Egypt; 3) Deut. 6:4–9 containing the

Bar Mitzvah *boys laying on tephillin at Massada*

Shema; and 4) Deut. 11:13–21, the second paragraph of the *Shema* dealing with reward and punishment. In the hand *tephillin,* all these sections are written on one piece of parchment whereas in the head *tephillin* the sections are written on separate pieces of parchment and placed in four different compartments. The exact order of the text on the four parchments was the subject of debate among the rabbis, a point further illustrated by the differing examples from before the destruction of the Second Temple, found in the Dead Sea caves. This debate was renewed in the 12th century between Rashi and his grandson, Rabbenu Tam. Although Rashi's views were accepted, some Jews put on two sets of *tephillin* corresponding to the two traditions.

Since the *tephillin* are put on as a "sign" of God's covenant with Israel, they are not worn on Sabbaths or festivals since these days are themselves signs of God's covenant with Israel. Custom varies as to whether they must be put on during the intermediate days of festivals. In Israel they are not worn on those days. The purpose of the *tephillin* is to direct man's thoughts and emotions to the service of God. In the words of Maimonides, "as long as the *tephillin* are on the head and on the arm of a man, he is modest and God-fearing; he will not be attracted by hilarity or idle talk, and will have no evil thoughts, but will devote all his thoughts to truth and righteousness."

In modern times, the Reform movement discarded putting on *tephillin*. Some Reform leaders maintain they are relics of paganistic practice and superstition.

THEATER, JEWS IN: Jews have been associated with the theater since the earliest times. During the Roman period some rabbis denounced the theater as a source of immorality. Later, Jews played a part in the rise of modern drama, especially in Italy where there was an all-Jewish dramatic company which performed in the town of Mantua. As early as the 13th century, troupes of Jewish entertainers and actors performed at weddings and other joyous celebrations. During this period, the Purim play began to be an essential feature of that festival's celebration. Such plays were performed both by local and by traveling troupes and had a variety of plots based on the Purim story, the story of Joseph and his brothers, and the binding of Isaac. From the 18th century onward, Jews played a vital role in the development of the modern theater as playwrights, actors, producers, managers, and critics.

A professional Jewish theater was established when Abraham Goldfaden founded the first Yiddish theatrical company in

Habima Theater, Tel Aviv

Rumania in 1876. Goldfaden served as actor, producer, and playwright. The company performed throughout Europe and finally settled in the United States. Before World War I, numerous Yiddish theaters were performing throughout the world, the Yiddish Theater of Warsaw, headed by Esther Rachel Kaminski, being particularly well-known. In the United States, Maurice Schwartz founded a Jewish Art Theater in New York in 1918. He produced more than one hundred and fifty plays by noted Jewish authors, plus the international classics in Yiddish translation. In the Soviet Union, the Yiddish theater was of a high professional standard, but it declined rapidly after World War II as the Stalin regime's campaign against Jewish culture and religion progressed. The Nazi destruction of European Jewry sounded the death knell of many Jewish cultural institutions in eastern Europe, including the theater. In Poland, however, the Yiddish theater again flourished after the war under the guidance of the famous actress Ida Kaminska. She left Poland, however, during the anti-Semitic campaign of 1968, and today the only remaining Yiddish theater is in Rumania. The modern Hebrew theater *Habimah* was founded in Moscow in 1917, under the inspiration of Stanislavsky. Among its famous early productions was An-Ski's *The Dibbuk*. Because of opposition from the Communist regime, the theater's subsidy was abolished and in 1926 the *Habimah* troupe left Russia. After a series of performances in Europe and the United States they made their home in Tel Aviv, Israel. Their present repertoire includes original Israeli and Jewish works and Hebrew translations of both classics and modern plays. Since 1958, *Habimah* has been the Israeli National Theater. In addition, there are numerous other companies in Israel, large and small, professional and amateur.

In modern times, Jews have made outstanding contributions to the theater and show business generally. Eminent Jewish playwrights include Elmer Rice, George Kaufmann, Lillian Hellman, Clifford Odets, Arthur Miller, Harold Pinter, Lionel Bart, Arnold Wesker, Bernard Kops, Peter Shaffer, Wolf Mankowitz, and Dannie Abse.

THIRTEEN PRINCIPLES OF FAITH: The customary designation for Maimonides' formulation of what he considered the basic dogmas of Judaism. Judaism developed without official dogmas; as a result, no one formulation of Jewish belief has attained universal recognition and acceptance by all sections of Jewry. Maimonides' thirteen principles, however, have proved the most popular formulation and have found their way into the prayer book in two versions: a prose version in which each principle is introduced with the phrase, "I believe with perfect faith...," recited after the daily morning service, and a poetic version in the form of the well-known hymn, *Yigdal*. The principles, originally expounded by Maimonides in his commentary on the *Mishnah,* are as follows: 1) God's Existence; 2) His Unity; 3) His Spirituality; 4) His Eternity; 5) Belief that He alone must be worshiped; 6) Belief in the Prophets; 7) Belief in Moses as the Chief of the Prophets; 8) Belief in the Divinity of the Torah; 9) The Torah is eternal and unchangeable; 10) God's Omniscience; 11) Reward and Punishment; 12) Belief in the coming of the Messiah; 13) The Resurrection of the Dead.

However, despite their popularity. Maimonides' formulation was never accepted as binding or universally authoritative, and was indeed even opposed by several thinkers on various grounds, including opposition to the very concept of a formal creed for Judaism.

TIBERIAS (Teveriya): Galilee town on the western shore of Lake Kinneret. Founded about 18 C.E. by King Herod Antipas, the city was named after the Roman Emperor Tiberius. After the destruction of the Temple, Tiberias became a major seat of Jewish learning, and it was here that both the *Mishnah* and the Palestinian Talmud were completed. It was also a main center of the activity of the Masoretes, the originators of the written Hebrew vowel system, which they inserted in the Hebrew script of the Bible. Under Arab rule, Tiberias was an important center, but, as a consequence of the battles fought in the area between Crusaders and Moslems in the 12th century, it was destroyed. With the beginning of Turkish rule in about 1560, the Sultan Suleiman the Magnificent granted Tiberias to a Jew, Joseph Nasi, but his attempts to reestablish the city as a Jewish center were unsuccessful. Much later, with the rise of the Zionist movement and the establishment of many Jewish settlements in the area, Tiberias grew both in population and in importance. The present population is about 24,000. Many tourists and visitors are attracted to Tiberias, which because of its hot climate is an ideal winter resort. The hot springs south of the city are an added source of attraction to people suffering from rheumatism, gout, and some nervous disorders.

According to tradition, the graves of many of Israel's famous sages lie in Tiberias, including those of Rabbi Johanan ben Zakkai, Rabbi Akiva, Rabbi Meir, and the medieval philosopher and scholar, Moses Maimonides.

TORAH, READING OF THE:

The public reading from the five books of Moses during divine service on Sabbaths, festivals, fast days, new moons, and ordinary Mondays and Thursdays. According to the Talmud the practice is an ancient one dating back to Moses, who instituted the reading on Sabbaths, festivals and the new moon. Later, Ezra the Scribe expanded the custom to include Mondays, Thursdays, and the Sabbath afternoon service. The public recitation of sections of the Scriptures in the synagogue was designed to implant God's law in the hearts of the people. For this reason, the occasions for the readings were those days on which the masses were free from work and on market days such as Mondays and Thursdays when they would assemble in the towns. The form and content of this reading has undergone development and change since ancient times. At first the portions to be read were not definitively marked out. Gradually, two different customs arose: one Palestinian, the other Babylonian. In the land of Israel, it was customary to complete the Pentateuchal reading in a three-year cycle, while in Babylon the reading was completed annually. The Babylonian custom was eventually adopted by all Jewry including that of the land of Israel. The Pentateuch is therefore divided into fifty-four sections known as *Parashot* or *Sidrot,* one to be read each week. However, since Jewish years seldom contain fifty-four Sabbaths, and since when festivals coincide with the Sabbath the usual portion is replaced by a special reading related to the festival concerned, two portions were combined on certain Sabbaths in order to complete the annual cycle. This cycle commences with the reading of the beginning of the book of Genesis on the Sabbath after *Simḥat Torah,* and is concluded on the following *Simḥat Torah* with the end of Deuteronomy. Each Sabbath of the year is named after its portion. The name is derived from the

Scribe at work on the Torah

first important word or phrase contained in the reading. On Sabbath afternoons, as well as on Monday and Thursday mornings, the first section of the following Sabbath's portion is read. Originally, it was customary for each person "called up" to the Torah to read his own portion. However, in order not to shame those who could not read the difficult text, a specially trained reader, known as a *Baal Koreh,* was gradually introduced for the purpose. The reading had to be performed meticulously and in accordance with the signs and accents contained in the written text.

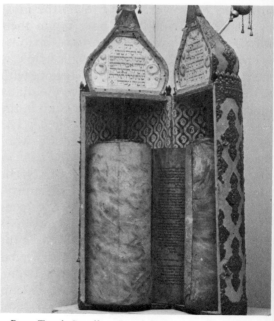

Rare Torah Scroll at Bezalel Museum, Jerusalem

The worshiper honored with an *Aliyah* merely recites the benedictions preceding and following the reading. In Yemenite congregations, the original custom of each person reading his own portion still prevails.

The reading of the Torah requires the presence of ten males over the age of bar mitzvah, known as a *minyan*. The number of persons "called up" to the reading of the Torah varies. On Mondays, Thursdays, fast days, Hanukkah, Purim, and on Sabbath afternoons, three people are so honored. Four are "called up" on the intermediate days of festivals and on the new moon, five on festivals, six on the Day of Atonement, and seven on Sabbaths. On Sabbaths, festivals, and fast days, an extra portion known as *Maphtir* is added. This consists of a repetition of the last verses of the reading, or, as in the case of festivals, of a special reading connected with the festival. The congregant "called up" for *Maphtir* then goes on to recite a reading taken from the prophetical books of the Bible, the *Haphtarah*. When a bar mitzvah is celebrated this honor is usually reserved for the bar mitzvah boy. The order of those called to the reading of the Torah is as follows. If a *cohen,* a person of priestly descent, is present, he is called first. The second to be called must be a Levite, and the others are chosen from the remainder of the congregation. The act of being "called up" is known as *Aliyah.* An *Aliyah* is considered to be an honor, especially the third person called up *(Shelishi)* and *Maphtir.* There are certain occasions when it is considered obligatory to be called to the reading of the Torah. The most important of these days are: the one on which a male Jew celebrates his bar mitzvah; the Sabbath preceding his marriage; the anniversaries of the death of his parents; and the Sabbath following a recovery from illness or escape from danger. The reading of the Torah in its traditional form has been abolished by some Reform congregations and considerably shortened

in others. In some Conservative congregations there is a trend toward the reintroduction of the ancient three-year cycle mentioned above.

The scroll from which the reading is conducted is known as a *Sepher Torah,* and it is Judaism's most venerated ritual object. It is written by a specially trained scribe on parchment made from the leather of a "clean" animal.

Originally, only a reed-pen was employed for the purpose, but later quill-pens were also permitted. The scribe or *Sopher* must be a pious Jew, and intense concentration is demanded of him during the writing of the scroll. In the event of a mistake, the scribe can erase a letter unless the error occurs while writing the divine name. If three mistakes are discovered in a Torah scroll, it is considered blemished and may not be used. A *Sepher Torah* which is either worn out or blemished may not be destroyed. It is placed in a special storeroom (*see* GENIZAH) or is ceremoniously buried. There is no punctuation, vocalization, accentuation, or verse division in the written scroll. Sections are indicated either by leaving the rest of the line blank or by leaving a space in a line. The former is known as *Petuḥah,* an open section, and the latter, *Setumah,* a closed section.

It is considered a *Mitzvah,* a meritorious deed, to participate in the writing of a Torah scroll. The men of the community are given the honor of writing the final letters, while the women sew the stitches on the last leaf of parchment. The presentation and consecration of a new scroll is considered an occasion for communal celebration and the holding of a special feast *(Seudat Mitzvah).*

In oriental and some Sephardi communities, the scroll is enclosed in a wooden or metal case known as a *Tik*. This is sometimes very splendid, excluding the need for other ornaments. Among *Ashkenazim,* the scroll is attached to two rods or staves each bearing silver finials known as *Rimmonim* and a silver crown called *Keter Torah*. After the reading, the scroll is raised and displayed before the entire congregation. It is then tied with a sash and covered by a decorated satin or silk mantle called a *Mappah*. Outside, a breastplate is suspended together with a pointer *(yad)* which the reader uses to indicate his place in the scroll during the reading. Being the Jewish religion's most venerated object, the *Sepher Torah* is treated with reverence and awe. It is housed in the Ark, and when the latter is opened, the congregation rises. When the scroll is carried from the Ark to the reading desk, it is customary to kiss the mantle, and if a scroll is accidentally dropped, those present are obligated to fast. In the event of danger to the synagogue, the scrolls must be the first things rescued.

TRUMPELDOR, JOSEPH (1880–1920): Soldier and Zionist leader. As a volunteer soldier in the Russian army, Trumpeldor took part in the Russo-Japanese War (1904–5), losing an arm in the battle for Port Arthur. He achieved the distinction of being made the first Jewish officer in the Russian Army. Trumpeldor settled in the land of Israel in 1912. During World War I, in exile in Egypt, he worked with Jabotinsky to establish a Jewish fighting unit. Their efforts resulted in the establishment of the Zion Mule Corps which participated in the Gallipoli campaign. In 1917, he returned to Russia to organize pioneer youth for agricultural settlement in Israel. From his efforts emerged the *He-Ḥalutz* movement. Returning to the land of Israel with one of the pioneer groups, he organized volunteers to protect Jewish settlements exposed to Arab attack. He was killed defending Tel Ḥai in Upper Galilee with a handful of comrades against a horde of attacking Bedouins. The building in which he fell became an object of pilgrimage and a monument was erected nearby in his memory.

Trumpeldor memorial at Tel Hai

Trumpeldor's last words, "It is good to die for our land" have served to inspire Jewish youth throughout the world. The youth movement of the *Ḥerut* party (formerly Revisionist Movement), *Betar,* is called after him, the name being an abbreviation of the words *Brit Trumpeldor*.

TSCHERNIKHOVSKI, SHAUL (1875–1943): Modern Hebrew poet, regarded, like Bialik, as a national poet of Israel.

Tschernikhovski was not as deeply rooted as Bialik in Jewish tradition, the European yeshiva, and Jewish life in the Russian Pale of Settlement. He was born in a small country village in the Crimea, in which friendly relations existed between the Jews and the local peasants. His childhood memories were very different from those of most other Hebrew poets. While not extensive, his Jewish education enabled him to study the Bible, from which he developed a devotion to the Hebrew language. From the outset, although Russian was his mother tongue, he wrote in Hebrew.

Torah mantle, breastplate, and finials from Italy, Israel Museum

Tschernikhovski lived in two worlds, one Jewish, the other non-Jewish. He studied medicine in Heidelberg, Germany, and during World War I served as a medical officer in the Russian Army. After the war he settled in Berlin and in 1930 emigrated to the land of Israel. This background explains the philosophy he expressed in his poems, sonnets, essays, and stories. His concept of nature was not in accord with the Jewish view which places God above nature. Tschernikhovski's view was pantheistic, i.e., he identified God with nature itself. This love for and identification with nature was supplemented by a love of life and pleasure. Life to Tschernikhovski is the Supreme Good and must be enjoyed to the full. Thus his poems contain little tragedy or tears; they are imbued with hope and joy. As he admired nature, so he admired strength and beauty. In his poem

Shaul Tschernikhovski

"Before the Statue of Apollo," he sings of Apollo, the god of life and joy. At other times, he sings odes to life as symbolized by the pagan gods, for instance his poem "Ashtarte and Bel." In his national and Jewish songs, Tschernikhovski exhibits an intense patriotic spirit. The Jewish fate disturbed him as it did Bialik. However, he was not prepared to weep and wail over it. In his poem *Ḥarbi* ("My Sword"), he calls for a sword with which to avenge the age-old sufferings of his brethren. Tschernikhovski is also filled with rage at his people's weakness and impotence. He sees Jewish tradition as somewhat to blame for this, because it has contributed to the physical weakening of the Jew. The poet looks back with pride to the days of Joshua, the conqueror of Canaan, and to the Maccabees.

There is, in Tschernikhovski's writing, a yearning for revenge, an adoration of heroism. His secular, paganistic, anti-traditional approach evoked much protest from religious circles but it had a strong emotional appeal to Jewish youth especially in the land of Israel. Like Bialik, Tschernikhovski was responsible for important innovations in the content and form of Hebrew poetry.

TURKEY: From very early times, Jews settled in regions that subsequently became the Ottoman Empire. The first settlement in Turkey proper dates to 1326, when permission was granted for the building of a synagogue at Brusa, then the capital. The period of Turkish conquest and establishment of the Ottoman Empire in the 15th and 16th centuries brought masses of Jews under Turkish rule. The change from Christian to Ottoman rule was, with some exceptions, for the better. This was especially so in Turkey itself which, after the expulsion of the Jews from Spain in 1492, became a major Jewish center. The Turks were a people of warrior-farmers for whom city life held no attraction. Commerce and trade were left to the non-Moslem elements of the population, and since the loyalty of the Christian minority was suspect, the Jews presented a reliable and industrious alternative. Thus, after 1492, the Turkish Sultans opened the gates of the Ottoman Empire to the exiles from Spain, and later on to those from Portugal who were fleeing the Inquisition. These immigrants brought with them skills often lacking among the Turks themselves, such as medical knowledge, handicrafts, the woolen industry, metalworking, glassmaking, firearms manufacture, and the import-export trade. Subject to payment of a poll tax, required of all infidels under the Moslem code, the Jews were favorably treated. They settled in every Turkish city, particularly Constantinople and Salonica. Salonica became a great center of Jewish learning and culture, and with its 30,000 Jews was probably the greatest Jewish community of the period. With the Turkish conquest of Egypt and the land of Israel in 1517, a similar rule was extended to these territories. It was not uncommon for Jews to achieve high prominence as political and economic advisers to the Sultans. An outstanding example was the case of the Portuguese Jew, Joao Miguez, who on his arrival in Constantinople in 1554 adopted the name Joseph Nasi. Suleiman the Magnificent appointed Nasi one of his chief advisers and entrusted him with Tiberias and its environs, as the nucleus of an autonomous Jewish settlement (an experiment which ended in failure). This active pro-Jewish policy was continued under Suleiman's successor, Selim II, but after Selim's death the position of the Jews began to deteriorate and restrictions began to be

imposed on them. Nevertheless, the general condition of the Jews in the Turkish Empire was relatively stable. Even the pseudo-Messianic fervor engendered by the false Messiah, Shabbetai Tzevi, and his followers who aimed to depose the Sultan, did not lead to the expected anti-Jewish reaction on a large scale. The movement did, however, drastically weaken the spiritual and moral fiber of Turkish Jewry and it never recovered. By the 18th century, the status of the Turkish community had deteriorated drastically, materially and spiritually. The decline of the Ottoman Empire in the 19th century brought parts of its Jewish population under the aegis of other authorities, the changes being generally for the worse. This process culminated in the defeat of Turkey in World War I and the destruction of the Ottoman Empire.

The nationalist revolution of Kemel Ataturk and his followers led to the reconstitution of Turkey on nationalist lines and an exchange of population with Greece. Most of the minority groups, with the exception of the Jews, disappeared. This did not strengthen the position of the Jews, who were no longer a favored minority. However, under the Treaty of Lausanne (1923), the Jews of Turkey were given a special status with certain guaranteed rights. Many Jews, however, preferred to be treated as Turkish citizens and assimilated into Turkish life. As a result, the spiritual and cultural level of the old days of Turkish Jewry finally disappeared. After 1948, 37,000 Jews immigrated to Israel, leaving a Jewish population of approximately 40,000, most of whom are centered in Istanbul.

UNITED JEWISH APPEAL: Organization created to coordinate fund-raising in the United States.

The UJA was formed in 1939, uniting the fund raising of the United Palestine Appeal, the American Joint Distribution Committee, and the National Refugee Service. It was originally created to deal with the suffering of Jews in Europe.

Abba Hillel Silver and Jonah B. Wise headed the first campaign, which was designed both to raise funds and to educate Jews on their responsibility to world Jewry and familiarize them with the problems faced by Jews outside America. From this first campaign until 1957, over one billion dollars were raised, more than 90 percent of this income being from federations.

When Israel became an independent state in 1948 the UJA contributed to the Jewish Agency. By 1962 its donations to the agency had helped to settle over 2 and a half million Jewish refugees.

Today the UJA provides community services such as speakers and supports Jewish education through the Israel Education Fund established in 1964 to build schools and provide scholarships, equipment, facilities, and teacher training programs. It is also active in other educational projects, health, agricultural settlements, and housing. While it does not operate these services directly, it helps other organizations who do.

In 1968 the UJA raised 71.1 million dollars, not including additional funds raised for the Jewish Educational Fund and the Israel Emergency Fund created to aid Israel's recovery from the Six-Day War.

UNITED NATIONS, JEWS AND: The very idea of an international organization for the maintenance of peace and international cooperation has its roots in Jewish thought. It was, after all, the prophet Isaiah who foresaw the day when "They shall beat their swords into plowshares and their spears into pruning hooks; nation shall not lift up sword against nation, neither shall they learn war any more" (Isaiah 2:4). The United Nations and its ill-fated predecessor, the League of Nations, were, it seemed to many, the fulfillment of Isaiah's vision and the bearer of good tidings for humanity in general and the Jewish people in particular. When the League of Nations was established after World War I, it undertook as part of its obligations the protection of religious, racial, and national minorities, the system of international mandates, and the assistance of refugees. The Mandate for Palestine, in which the Balfour Declaration was included, was handed over to Great Britain, while certain east European countries in which Jews were persecuted, such as Poland and Rumania, were forced, at least theoretically, to accept obligations to respect the minority rights of their Jewish populations. Despite its good intentions, the league soon proved impotent in the face of violations, both of international relations in general and of the rights of Jews in particular. Poland disregarded her minority obligations and Britain, in the face of increasing Arab pressure, was slow and even loath to implement the Balfour Declaration. With the rise of Hitler, the problem of Jewish persecution and refugees occupied the conscience of the world, but

UN meeting – decision to partition Palestine

little was done about it. The league was unable to do more than protest; it appointed a High Commissioner for refugees, but practically nothing was achieved. With the outbreak of World War II, it ceased to exist. The United Nations organization emerged from the shattered ruins left by World War II. It had as its purpose the achievement of "international cooperation in solving international problems of an economic, social, cultural, or humanitarian character, and in promoting and encouraging respect for human rights and for fundamental freedoms for all without distinction as to race, sex, language or religion." These lofty principles were soon to be put to the test.

In 1947, Britain, no longer able to control the situation in the land of Israel, decided to relinquish the mandate and brought the question before the United Nations. A special United Nations Committee on Palestine was set up, composed of distinguished statesmen and jurists from eleven member states. U.N.S.C.O.P. recommended the partition of the country into independent Jewish and Arab states, linked in an economic union. On November 29, 1947, the General Assembly passed the historic

decision by more than the required two-thirds majority. This was one of the rare occasions in which both the East, led by the Soviet Union, and the West, led by the U.S., voted together. Despite this, when the newly born state was invaded by the armies of seven Arab nations, the U.N. was powerless to come to its assistance, although the invasion was verbally denounced by the representatives of both the U.S. and the Soviet Union. It was only the bravery of the people of Israel who stood alone that saved the infant state from being strangled at birth. The U.N. provided the mediators who negotiated the various cease-fires and subsequent armistice agreements. A truce supervisory organization was set up with headquarters in Jerusalem. Israel was formally admitted to the United Nations on May 11, 1949.

In the ensuing years, the U.N. did an about-face and Israel was often the victim of a peculiar double standard of morality. The Soviet Union and its satellites, disappointed in Israel's lack of support, became increasingly pro-Arab, while the West, fearful of its oil interests in the Arab world, tried to maintain its relationships with the Arab countries through concessions to them. Israel became a stepchild in this East-West competition for Arab friendship. Her position was further complicated as the U.N. expanded. New member states, many of whom were either part of the Soviet bloc or sympathetic toward it, or staunchly anti-West, succumbed to Soviet and Arab propaganda depicting Israel as a tool of Western imperialism and colonialism. The campaigns of terror and boycott conducted by the Arabs against Israel were often passed over in silence at the U.N. while any Israel retaliation was condemned as "agression." Within the General Assembly, Israel has been discriminated against because of Arab pressure, and she has never served on the Security Council, while Arab countries continually do so. Her representatives have also been denied election to other U.N. bodies. The signature of Arab countries on armistice agreements and their U.N. Charter commitments not to attack a fellow member of the U.N. did not prevent the Arab States from incessantly threatening the existence and sovereignty of Israel. Thus, although the Security Council Resolution of September 1951 called upon Egypt to guarantee Israel freedom of navigation through the Suez Canal, nothing came of the resolution. A similar one in 1953 was vetoed by the Soviet Union. When Israel, in order to break the Arab blockade and terminate the destructive activities of Arab terror gangs, launched the Sinai campaign in October 1956, both the U.S. and the Soviet Union mobilized world opinion to demand Israel's immediate withdrawal of her troops. Under severe pressure, Israel complied, but only on the understanding that armed incursions into Israeli territory would cease and that there would be no attempt to hinder navigation through the Straits of Tiran. A special United Nations Expeditionary Force was placed between the belligerents. The impotence of the U.N. became clearly apparent when, in May 1967, at the demand of Egypt, United Nations Secretary General U Thant unilaterally withdrew the U.N. Force. This enabled Egyptian armor to enter Sinai and hastened the outbreak of hostilities. The Six-Day War of June 1967 brought the Middle East question to the forefront of the U.N.'s agenda, and there it has remained ever since, with Israel constantly having to fight back against hostile groupings in the Assembly which frequently constitute a majority against her.

Despite Israel's disillusion with the U.N., she continues to participate in various United Nations Agencies such as Unesco — The United Nations Educational, Scientific and Cultural Organization, and other specialized United Nations groups. Israel fervently believes in the principle that no nation is entitled to dominate another, and has lent her support to U.N. resolutions aimed at ending colonialism and racial discrimination. The U.N., on the other hand, has not succeeded in alleviating the lot of Jewish minorities suffering persecution in various parts of the world. Despite its adherence to the Declaration of Human Rights, the Soviet government continues to withhold such rights from its Jewish citizens, and in Arab countries fierce persecution and torture of Jews, under the guise of "anti-Zionist" or "anti-Western" activity, has been openly and violently pursued by the various Arab governments. Where Jews are concerned, the U.N. at best has paid only lip-service to the principles of the charter. Several international Jewish organizations, such as the *B'nai B'rith,* the World Union for Progressive Judaism, the World Jewish Congress, and the World Union of Jewish Students, have been granted consultative status to the U.N., and they work on those aspects of U.N.'s activities which fall within the category of human rights, refugee rights, and the reduction or elimination of statelessness.

UNITED STATES: Jewish immigration, as a group, dates from 1654. In that year, the Portuguese recaptured the Brazilian town of Recife from the religiously tolerant Dutch. The Portuguese conquest meant the introduction of the dreaded Inquisition and so five thousand Jews left, some returning to Holland, others finding refuge in Dutch Guiana, and a small group of 23 families making their way northward to New Amsterdam (subsequently New York). The governor, Peter Stuyvesant, resented the presence of these "Godless rascals," and wished to expel them but the Dutch West India Company, which had business relations with a number of wealthy Amsterdam Jews, overruled him and the Jews were allowed to remain. One year later they demanded the right "to buy a burying place for their nation."

In most other cases, Jews arrived soon after the colony was established. They came mostly from England, Germany, Holland, and Poland, while a number of Marranos arrived from the Iberian peninsula. They settled in Delaware (1656), Rhode Island (1658), Connecticut (1659), the Carolinas (1665), and Georgia (1733); in the latter, James Oglethorpe rejected the protests and complaints of those who opposed Jewish entry. Only the northernmost colonies — New Hampshire, Vermont, and Maine — had no permanent Jewish settlers until the end of the 18th century. During the 18th century, Jewish immigration expanded. The first congregations were established in Newport (1658), Savannah (1734), Philadelphia (1745), and Charleston (1750). Jews participated actively in the task of pioneering new settlements, and when the ox-trains set out to settle new frontiers, they were found side by side with the Christians pursuing the course of America's inevitable expansion. Although the Jews did not enjoy full political rights, their legal position was good. While it would not be correct to say that they were granted complete equality, they nevertheless enjoyed toleration, and in most of the colonies anti-Jewish restrictions were removed prior to and during the revolution. In the Revolutionary War, Jews fought on both sides, but most opposed the British. The first American-born rabbi, Gershon Mendes Seixas, removed the scrolls and other holy appurtenances from his synagogue rather than let them fall into Tory hands. There were Jewish soldiers in the ranks as well as Jewish officers. Jewish participation in the War of Independence and in the War of 1812 lent added weight to Jewish insistence on complete equality. Slowly but surely this equality was achieved, although not without a struggle and the overcoming of local prejudice. In Virginia, Thomas Jefferson introduced a bill for the establishment of religious freedom in 1779, and it was enacted in 1785. This was

followed by Maryland in 1816, but in North Carolina civil disabilities were only removed in 1868, and in New Hampshire legal discrimination against Jews and Catholics existed until 1876. By 1825, the Jewish population in America still numbered only about 10,000 individuals. The original Sephardi majority had given way to an Ashkenazi one, although the former were still prominent socially and financially. From 1820 to 1880, the Jewish population swelled from 10,000 to 250,000 as Jews fled Europe — especially central Europe — to escape persecution and the bloody revolutions and counterrevolutions that shook the continent. Some of these Jews, mostly of German origin, settled in New York and Boston. Many of them, however, were caught up in the pioneering spirit dominating the country at the time and headed southward and westward for Louisville and New Orleans, for Cincinatti and Cleveland, for Chicago and St. Louis. They joined in the California Gold Rush of 1849, and were among the founding settlers of San Francisco. In the opening of the West, the land settled by or given to Jews was out of proportion to their numbers. In 1859, the Board of Delegates of American Israelites was formed to watch over the rights of Jews and to guard against prejudice and bigotry. The slavery issue and its consequence, the Civil War, divided Jews just as it did the rest of the country. Jews took sides on the basis of local patriotism rather than humanitarianism. There were, however, some exceptions. Rabbi Moses J. Raphall of New York published his pro-slavery views based on the Bible. Rabbi David Einhorn, however, had to resign his pulpit in Baltimore because of his anti-slavery activity. Approximately 6,000 Jews served in the Union forces, 1,000 in those of the Confederacy. The Confederacy gave the Jews their first American statesman, Judah Benjamin, who served as Secretary of State under Jefferson Davis. When the war ended, there were nine Jewish generals and hundreds of Jewish officers in the Union army. The Civil War was followed by a period of phenomenal industrial and commercial progress in which Jews played a big part. The year 1881, however, was a turning point in American-Jewish history. The intolerable situation of the Jews in czarist Russia and other eastern European countries brought about the mass immigration which was to make American Jewry what it is today — the largest Jewish center in the world. From 1881–1914 more than 2,000,000 Jews, chiefly Yiddish-speaking from eastern and central Europe, emigrated to the U.S. Most of them arrived penniless with their worldly belongings wrapped in a bundle. The great majority of them settled in the already industrialized and overcrowded cities of the Atlantic seaboard, and in particular in New York's Lower East Side. They lived in abject poverty and privation. Moreover, there was inevitable tension between the already Americanized Jews of German origin and the newcomers. This tension manifested itself socially and religiously. Some of the Americanized German Jews looked down on the strange, bearded, Orthodox Russian Jews. The latter, on the other hand, were horrified by the degree of assimilation which had overtaken American Jews. Gradually, however, the mutual tensions were cancelled out by mutual interests. American "native born" Jews were mobilized to help remedy the plight of the newcomers. The latter proved to be thrifty, learned, and, despite their initial hardships, easily assimilable. They pioneered in trade-unionism and industrial relations, and brought to the U.S. rich traditions of community and self-help organizations. They went into all forms of trade and business, and exhibited that typical Jewish trait of providing for the education of their children. The arrival of the east-European Jews strengthened the cause of Orthodox Judaism. The decades prior to their arrival had seen the importation of German Reform Judaism which, due to the organizing ability of Isaac M. Wise, was in the ascendancy. The new immigrants, mainly Orthodox or traditional, regarded America not as a temporary stopping point, but as a permanent home. They realized that in order to hold their sons and daughters within the framework of traditional Judaism, it should not be changed but adapted and interpreted within the social and economic patterns of American life. This realization gave rise to Conservative Judaism and modern Orthodoxy, also known as neo-Orthodoxy. From then on, three religious groups with their centers of learning, the Hebrew Union College (Reform), the Jewish Theological Seminary (Conservative), and the Yeshiva University (Orthodox), were to place American Jewry on its feet spiritually. They no longer had to rely on eastern or central Europe for spiritual leaders. In the social and philanthropic field, American Jewry developed its own unique frameworks and organizations. The American Zionist Organization (1897), the American Jewish Committee (1906), the American Joint Distribution Committee (1914), the American Jewish Congress (1917), and the Anti-Defamation League of *B'nai B'rith* (1913) have all played and continue to play a vital role in the communal life of American and world Jewry. During World War I the United States, for the first time in its history, closed its doors almost completely to further immigration. After the war, immigration was resumed but it soon ended as America's fears of Communism and its influence grew. Would-be immigrants from eastern Europe were regarded as potential Bolshevik agents. Between 1921 and 1924, a series of bills was passed to block the flow of immigration. The Jewish community utilized this period, however, as one of internal consolidation, and the trend of increased

Americanization gathered force. The great depression of 1929 brought suffering to Jews and non-Jews alike. It also brought the first major outbreak of anti-Semitism in American history. The anti-Semitic outbreak was accompanied by the increased activity of the anti-Catholic, anti-Negro, and anti-Jewish Ku Klux Klan. The depression, these anti-Semites said, was the fault of the Jews. With the ending of the depression, the outbreak quite naturally subsided. After 1935, the immigration laws were relaxed to permit the entry of hundreds of thousands of Jewish refugees, victims of Nazism. In World War II,

550,000 Jews served in the American armed forces. There were 23 American Jewish generals and admirals and 53,000 Jews were decorated for bravery.

One of the most significant changes resulting from World War II was the emergence of the U.S. Jewish community to its position of pre-eminence in world Jewry. The destruction of European Jewry, the enforced silence of Russian Jews, and the consolidation of the Jews in the U.S. — whose six million Jews constitute more than half the total number of Jews in the world — has laid heavy responsibilities on American Jewry. These have been

Original main building of Yeshiva University, New York

The Kennedy Memorial in the Judean Hills

impressively met with massive support for Israel in periods of danger, at the time of its establishment in 1948; in 1956; and in May-June 1967, at the time of the Six-Day War. American Jews have not only exerted their influence on behalf of Jews elsewhere, but have contributed large sums to assist distressed Jews and especially to build up the State of Israel.

Internally, recent decades have been marked by a trend to leave their smaller communities and to move to the large cities where the overwhelming majority of American Jewry is now concentrated. At the same time, there has also been a certain tendency to move westward. The 550,000 Jews of Los Angeles make it the second largest community of the U.S. (and, in fact, of the world) after the two million Jews of New York.

Jews have been prominent in all aspects of U.S. life and have made great contributions to the building up, for example, of its finance, science, and arts. Restrictions on Jews (often implicit) entering universities have been largely lifted and, as a result, there has been great Jewish participation in all levels of university life — both as teachers and students. It is estimated that over 90 percent of Jewish boys and girls have a college education (which is a much higher proportion than for the rest of the population).

Jews were prominent in the Civil Rights movement in the 1960's — both because they are traditionally liberal and believed in civil rights for everyone, and because they realized that the curbing of any group's civil rights could affect Jews negatively in the long run. Anti-Semitism was not strong in the post-war years except for a few way-out groups on the "lunatic fringe" while there was a marked drop in examples of anti-Jewish discrimination. However, the tensions of the late 1960s brought evidence that there are still anti-Semitic feelings in certain American circles, particularly among black extremists. Nevertheless, the overall picture of U.S. Jews is that they have largely adjusted and been assimilated into U.S. society. Indeed the extent of this assimilation is worrisome to many thinking Jews who see that after intermarriage, many Jews assimilate completely, losing all Jewish identity. One reason for this is that their children do not have sufficient Jewish education to appreciate Jewish values and meet the challenges to their Jewishness when they grow up. There are still many children whose Jewish education ceases at 13, and Jewish educators and organizations have begun to devise various projects to fill the need for a deepening Jewish knowledge and appreciation after 13 so that when young Jews grow up they can play an effective role in the continuing history of the world's largest Jewish community.

WARSAW, WARSAW GHETTO: The Jewish settlement in Warsaw goes back to the 15th century and its history is tied up with that of Polish Jewry in general. In 1454, the first recorded persecution took place at the incitement of the monk Capistrano and in 1483 the Jews were expelled. In the 18th century, a select group of Jewish families were permitted to reside there on payment of a bribe of 200,000 florins a year.

During the 1794 rebellion against the Russians, a Jew, Berek Joselewicz, raised a regiment which was annihilated. This demonstration of patriotism, however, did not help to ease Jewish disabilities, and it was only in 1862 that Jews were granted full rights as in the rest of Poland. The latter part of the 19th century saw the emergence of a strong Polish nationalist movement in Warsaw, with violent anti-Semitic manifestations and an economic boycott proclaimed against all Jews. The First World War brought new and heavy sufferings, and despite official guarantees to the contrary, Jewish rights were severely curtailed even after Poland had gained independence. In fact, in the two decades preceding World War II, anti-Jewish propaganda increased and determined efforts were made to hamper Jewish economic activity. By 1938, tens of thousands of Jews were unemployed. Despite this, from the beginning of the 20th century Warsaw emerged as one of the major Jewish religious and cultural centers. Rabbinical seminaries, *Yeshivot,* teachers' training colleges, a museum, a library, three Yiddish theaters, 83 Jewish newspapers and periodicals (nine of which were in Hebrew),

orphanages, children's homes, and other charitable institutions all testified to the spiritual vigor of the Warsaw Jewish community. When the Nazis occupied Warsaw in 1939, the Jewish population numbered 360,000.

By the late autumn of 1940, 400,000 Jews had been rounded up and sealed off in a ghetto approximately two and a half miles long and a mile wide. In these overcrowded conditions, without employment and deprived of the minimal food necessary for a bare subsistence, thousands died of starvation and disease — which was precisely what the Nazis intended. The pace, however, was not fast enough for the Germans and in the summer of 1942, the "resettlement" program was put into practice; "resettlement" meant transportation of the remaining Jews to the extermination camps, most of them to Treblinka, where they were gassed. Between July and September 1942, 300,000 Jews were thus "resettled." When, in January 1943, the Nazi leader Himmler visited Warsaw, he was shocked to find 60,000 Jews still alive in the ghetto. It was decided to clear out the ghetto in a "special action" lasting three days. As it turned out, it took four weeks, for word had filtered through to the remaining Jews in the ghetto of the true meaning of the "resettlement" program. On the initiative of the members of the Zionist Youth movements, it was decided to resist further "resettlement." The arsenal available to the Jewish rebels was pitiful by any standards, and in particular, against the fire power of the mighty German Army. By various devious methods, the

Jews had built a small stockpile of arms consisting of World War I rifles, a few machine guns, and a collection of Molotov cocktails and bottles of gasoline with flammable wicks for use against tanks. Moreover, the ghetto, though tiny in area, was honeycombed with sewers, vaults, and cellars which were converted into fortified points. On the morning of April 19, 1943, when the Nazi troops entered the ghetto, they were caught in a withering hail of crossfire and were forced to beat a hasty retreat. For three days the battle raged, and in the end it was the Nazis who were forced to retreat. The Germans then proceeded to bring up heavy artillery and to destroy the ghetto by setting every block on fire. Slowly but surely, the defenders were forced to leave the burning buildings for the cellars, and toward the end of the rebellion they took to the sewers. The Germans unsuccessfully attempted to flush them out by flooding the mains and by dropping smoke bombs into the sewers. The Jewish defenders, in desperation, appealed to the well-armed Polish underground for help, but the latter remained passive onlookers. The final outcome of the battle could never be in doubt. May 16th was the last day of resistance. There was no one left to resist — the few survivors were either captured or managed to make their way out of Warsaw through the sewers. The heroic and epic defense of the Warsaw ghetto wrote a proud page in the annals of Jewish heroism. 60,000 Jews lost their lives during the Warsaw ghetto uprising.

WEIZMANN, CHAIM (1874–1952): Chemist, Zionist leader, first president of the State of Israel. Born in the village of Motol near the city of Pinsk, Weizmann's roots were in the old ghetto of the Russian Pale of Settlement, where he received the usual traditional education. After completing high school, however, he was able to receive a sound scientific education in Berlin, Fribourg, and Geneva, where he was awarded his doctorate in 1900 and appointed lecturer. After moving to England in 1904, he became a member of the faculty of Manchester University, lecturing there until 1916, when he moved to London. This combination of background and education enabled him to feel at home both in the world of eastern European Jewry and in the diplomatic corridors of Great Britain. Weizmann became an early adherent of the Zionist movement and was a delegate to the second Zionist Congress in 1898. He was opposed, however, to Herzl's purely political approach and was one of the leaders of the attack on Herzl following the Uganda proposal. Weizmann believed that Zionist work should proceed on three fronts — political, cultural, and practical — at one and the same time. His policy, known as Synthetic Zionism, was accepted by the Zionist movement at the 1911 congress.

Ironically, it was Weizmann who was responsible for early Zionism's greatest political triumph, the Balfour Declaration. During World War I, Weizmann made a major contribution to the British war effort by his work on the production of acetone, a vital ingredient of naval gunpowder. He played a leading role in the complex negotiations which led to the issuance of the Balfour Declaration, and after the war he devoted himself almost entirely to the Zionist cause. Weizmann realized that Jewish-Arab understanding was an essential ingredient of the peaceful pursuit of the Zionist program, and in the presence of the famous Lawrence of Arabia, he met with Emir Feisal and came to an understanding with him about Jewish-Arab peace and cooperation. These negotiations unfortunately led to nothing, due to the speedy fall of Feisal and the rise of militant Arab nationalism.

Weizmann was one of the leaders of the delegation which appeared before the Versailles Peace Conference in order to

Weizmann taking oath of Office

present the Zionist case. He was elected president of the World Zionist Organization, an office which he retained (except for the years 1931 to 1935) until 1946.

Weizmann's faith in Great Britain and his generally moderate outlook brought him into conflict not only with his opponents but at times even with his colleagues. As the leader of the Zionist movement, he had to deal with many internal disputes, including the bitter struggle with Jabotinsky and his supporters who demanded a more active policy, both towards Great Britain and the Arab terrorists. He had to fight on two fronts, convincing the world of the justness of Zionism on the one hand, and at times forcing his supporters to swallow very bitter pills in the form of negative British policy decisions. After the Second World War, both David Ben-Gurion and the American Zionist leader Abba Hillel Silver opposed Weizmann's re-election to the presidency of the Zionist organization. Britain's failure to honor her pledges had

disillusioned the public and led to a more active policy. Weizmann retired to Reḥovot to work at the scientific institute which he had helped to develop (and which in 1949 was renamed the Weizmann Institute of Science). Nonetheless, the people whom he had served so sincerely and untiringly were not ungrateful, and, when the state was declared, Weizmann was immediately invited to become its first president, the post he occupied until his death in 1952.

He is buried in the grounds of his home in Reḥovot where a national foundation, *Yad Chaim Weizmann,* has been established in his memory. Tens of thousands visit his grave every year.

WEIZMANN INSTITUTE OF SCIENCE: Scientific institute situated at Reḥovot, Israel, and named after Israel's first President, Dr. Chaim Weizmann. The institute, which has earned a high reputation throughout the world, engages in fundamental and applied research in the exact sciences. This includes genetics, organic and physical chemistry, applied mathematics, nuclear physics, seismology, biophysics, biochemistry, experimental biology, electronics, computer research, and plastics research, to mention but a few. The institute has attracted a number of eminent foreign scientists and has acted as host for international conferences. It is financed by the Government of Israel, the Jewish Agency, research grants and private donations and has a staff of some 1,200, including over 370 full-time scientists. It is administered by a Board of Governors and an executive council while a scientific council advises on all matters of academic policy, appointments, and promotions. Among its presidents have been Abba Eban, Meyer Weisgal, and since 1969, Albert I. Sabin, discoverer of the antipolio oral vaccine.

WESTERN (OR WAILING) WALL (Kotel Ma'aravi): Remnant of the Temple compound destroyed by the Romans in 70 C.E. The lower great stones of the lower part of the wall formed part of the outer wall which encircled Herod's Temple, the middle portion dates from the Middle Ages, and the upper rows from the last century. As the most sacred and venerated site of the Jewish people, the Western Wall has been for centuries the object of pilgrimage, devout Jews undergoing long and dangerous journeys in order to reach the site, bewail the destruction of Israel's past grandeur, and pray for future redemption. Since the wall lies adjacent to Islam's sacred site, the *Haram es Sherif* (Dome of the Rock, or Mosque of Omar), it was the object of dispute between Moslems and Jews regarding their respective rights and in 1929, serious riots broke out. In May 1930, the League of Nations appointed a commission to define the rights of the disputing parties. After

Excavations at the Western Wall

Israel's 1948 War of Independence, the Jordanians who controlled the Old City failed to abide by the armistice agreements which specifically guaranteed Jewish access to the wall. The situation was remedied only in June 1967 when the Old City was captured by the Israeli army and access to the wall restored. Since then, it has been the object of pilgrimage by Jews from Israel and throughout the world. Excavations conducted since then at the site (and along the adjacent southern wall) have revealed many remains dating from Temple times.

WINGATE, CHARLES ORDE (1903–1944): British Christian soldier. While stationed in the Holy Land, he became sympathetic to the Zionist cause and during the 1936–1939 Arab riots, undertook to train special Jewish Commando Units which retaliated against the Arab attackers. His advocacy of commando tactics under cover of darkness gave these units the name of "night squads." Many of Israel's future military leaders, including Moshe Dayan, had their initial military training and experience under Wingate. Although he was subsequently transferred to the Far East where he played a major role in the Burma Campaign, Wingate remained an ardent supporter of Zionism until the end of his brilliant military career. Israel's foremost institution for physical culture is named after him.

WISE, ISAAC MAYER (1819–1900): One of the founders of Reform Judaism in the United States and the architect of its religious institutions. He immigrated to the U.S. from Bohemia in 1846 and was appointed rabbi in Albany, New York. His introduction of reforms into the service led to a split in the congregation. In 1854, he was appointed rabbi in Cincinnati, Ohio. The lack of a centralized organization for American Jewry at the time led Wise to cooperate with the leader of the traditional wing, Isaac Leeser, in an attempt at unification. He also advocated the adoption of a unified liturgy for all American Jews which he referred to as "Minhag America."

He met strong opposition on the Eastern seaboard from the Reform rabbis led by David Einhorn, who opposed his alliance with Leeser. There were, moreover, personal differences which split the Reform movement into two groups, one eastern, and the other western and southern which generally followed Wise. Wise, who at first believed that if the diverse elements in Judaism functioned co-operatively, Reform would inevitably triumph, finally had to realize that the differences between Reform and the traditional elements were virtually unreconcilable. Accordingly, he devoted himself to the strengthening of Reform Judaism and its institutions from within. After a series of conferences and tours throughout the country, he succeeded in 1873 in establishing the Union of American Hebrew Congregations and in 1875, the rabbinical seminary, the Hebrew Union College of which he was president until his death. In 1889, Wise organized Reform Judaism's Rabbinic Council, the Central Conference of American Rabbis.

WISE, STEPHEN SAMUEL (1874–1949): American Reform rabbi and Zionist leader. Wise represented a new generation of Reform rabbis who refused to be bound by the dogmatic beliefs of the founders of Reform Judaism. Accordingly, he refused an invitation from Temple Emanuel to become its rabbi in 1906, because it denied the principle of a free pulpit. In 1907, he established the Free Synagogue in New York where the pulpit was to be free of all restraints. The synagogue was supported by voluntary contributions; the pew system, with its built-in class distinctions was abolished and greater democracy was introduced into the synagogue's organization. He served as rabbi of the Free Synagogue

until his death. Wise opposed the anti-Zionist, anti-national platform of the early Reformers. He had been one of the first to support Theodor Herzl, and with a minority of his colleagues, fought against Reform Judaism's majority anti-Zionist opinions. While, at first, his views were a voice crying in the wilderness, his influence gradually made itself felt, especially after the First World War when Reform Judaism began to support the Zionist cause. Wise, himself, was one of the founders of the Zionist Organization of America and played a significant role at the time of the Balfour Declaration. He was a founder of the American Jewish Congress, and a member of its delegation to the Peace Conference. In 1922, Wise founded the Jewish Institute of Religion in New York. Its purpose was to create a school in which the various philosophies within Judaism — Orthodox, Reform, and Conservative, Zionist and non-Zionist — would be explained to students by men representing the different points of view. In a short time, the institute rose to an important position in higher academic Jewish circles but its interdenominational character did not materialize. Most of the graduates followed the path of Wise himself. In 1950, the institute merged with the Hebrew Union College.

Wise also played an active role in American political life. He was a firm supporter of Franklin Delano Roosevelt and his "New Deal" policies. A staunch Democrat, he took an active part in the struggle for social betterment, women's suffrage, child labor reform, and international peace. A powerful orator, Wise was one of the most influential American Jews of his time.

WIZO (Women's International Zionist Organization): Women's Zionist Organization, founded in London in 1920 to organize women internationally within the framework of the Zionist Movement.

Its aims were defined as the training of Jewish girls and women in Israel and the rest of the world for useful service and providing mother-and-child care in Israel. WIZO was initially centered in London, but after 1948, it established its main headquarters in Israel. It has a membership of 250,000 in fifty-two countries, excluding the United States, where the parallel women's Zionist organization is Hadassah. In Israel, it has some 85,000 members and runs numerous projects. These include baby and children's homes, day homes for infants and toddlers, youth villages, youth clubs and centers, agricultural and vocational schools, women's clubs and centers, hostels for girl students, rest homes for mothers, legal advisory bureaux, mobile libraries, training centers and sewing courses for Arab women, and a day creche for Arab children in Jerusalem. Outside Israel, apart from its fund-raising activities, WIZO has developed an active educational program.

WOLFSON, SIR ISAAC, BART. (1897–): The head of a number of chain stores and business concerns, he has been active in philanthropic and educational institutions in both Great Britain and Israel. He is president of the United Synagogue of Great Britain and largely financed the building of the *Hekhal Shelomoh* (the religious center and seat of the chief rabbinate) in Jerusalem.

WORLD JEWISH CONGRESS: International Jewish organization founded in 1936 at Geneva. Jewish communities throughout the world are affiliated to the WJC, as are Israel's political parties. The congress aims to act as a unifying umbrella organization for world Jewry; it protects Jewish rights and interests throughout the world and supports Jewish cultural activity. It is recognized by the United Nations as an advisory body. It has headquarters in New York, London, and Tel Aviv. The first president of the congress was Stephen Wise, who was succeeded by Naḥum Goldmann.

YAD VA-SHEM (Monument and Name):
The Martyrs and Heroes Remembrance
Authority, established by an act of Israel's
Knesset in 1953. Its purpose is to investigate, study, and record the martyrdom and
heroism of European Jewry during the
Nazi period. It is located in Jerusalem on
Memorial Hill, adjoining Mount Herzl, and
its shrine, monuments, and exhibitions are
a center of daily pilgrimages. Included are
an impressive hall commemorating the
heroes of the death camps and an avenue
of trees planted by non-Jews who risked
their lives in saving Jews during World
War II. *Yad Va-shem* has published a
number of important books and documents
relating to the holocaust.

Yad Va-shem, Jerusalem

YAVNEH: Town in southern Israel
between Rishon-le-Zion and Ashdod. In
the Bible, it is referred to as *Jabneel,*
while the Greeks called it *Iamnia.* Yavneh
was the center of Jewish learning and

culture immediately after the destruction
of the Second Temple in 70 C.E. According
to legend, when the sage Joḥanan Ben
Zakkai saw that the destruction of
Jerusalem was imminent, he had himself
smuggled out of the city in a coffin carried
by his disciples. He came before the Roman
commander, Vespasian, and predicted that
the latter would shortly be proclaimed
emperor. Vespasian then told him to make
a request and Joḥanan Ben Zakkai made
his famous reply: "Give me Yavneh and
its Wise Men." His request was granted
and an academy was established called
Kerem Yavneh (Vineyard of Yavneh),
because "the scholars sat on the floor in
rows, just like the vines in the vineyards."
Joḥanan Ben Zakkai re-established the
Sanhedrin there and it sat in Yavneh until
the Bar Kokhba rebellion of 132 C.E.
After that date, Yavneh gave way to
other centers, but the activities of the
Yavneh Academy were of major importance in adapting Judaism to the new
realities resulting from the destruction of
the Temple.

It was colonized once more by Jewish
immigrants in 1948. In 1941, a religious
kibbutz was established under the same
name some four miles to the south. Adjacent to the *kibbutz* is an important *yeshiva*
bearing the name *Kerem B'Yavneh.*

YIDDISH: Language spoken by a majority
of Ashkenazi Jewry from the Middle Ages
to World War II; also referred to as Judeo-
German. Yiddish originated among the
Jews of Germany in the early Middle Ages.
Although they spoke the same language
as their German neighbors, medieval

German, they wrote it in Hebrew letters and this necessarily involved a change in the pronunciation of the words. Subsequently, the isolation of ghetto Jews brought about variations of expression and usage. Finally, although Hebrew was not a spoken language, a large number of Hebrew words were used in daily conversation and parts of Hebrew words were often joined to German verbs or suffixes. Jewish immigration into Poland in the 13th and 14th centuries introduced Yiddish to Slavonic countries where it assimilated Slavic elements and spread, developing into the language of the Jews of those countries.

Like most languages, Yiddish grew by absorbing elements from other languages, but the base of the language remained medieval German. German words supplied 85 percent of the vocabulary and the basic grammatical structure. Yiddish became the common language of the vast masses of European Jewry, developing its own literature, poetry, folk songs, legends, and proverbs.

Among the earliest literary works produced in Yiddish was the *Bovo-Buch* composed by Elijah Levita in 1507. The Yiddish phrase *Bovo-Maase,* meaning "a far-fetched story," is derived from it. Especially popular even in modern times is the *Zeenah U-Reenah* composed by Rabbi Jacob ben Isaac Ashkenazi at the end of the 16th century. It consists of a paraphrase of the five books of Moses, with many stories, legends, and commentaries added. This work was the storehouse of Jewish knowledge for generations of Jewish women.

The first Yiddish writer of real importance by modern standards was *Mendele Mocher Seforim,* Mendele the bookseller, the pseudonym of Shalom Abramowitsch, considered the "grandfather" of Yiddish literature. Other great figures in Yiddish literature are the short story writer Isaac Leib Peretz, Sholem Aleichem, the greatest

Yiddish humorist, and the novelists Sholem Asch and Isaac Bashevis Singer. A rich Yiddish theater and press contributed further to the development of the language, and when Jews from eastern Europe streamed to the West, especially the United States, they took with them their Yiddish culture in all its varied forms.

With the passing of time, Yiddish became invested with a sanctity of its own in the minds of many people. It was regarded by many of the very Orthodox as the only language in which the Talmud and the codes could be properly expounded. There were those, too, who valued Yiddish not for religious reasons but as the secular language of the Jewish people. The rise of Zionism and its stress on the revival of Hebrew as a modern language led to a controversy which fortunately was shortlived. Objective factors were strongly against the supremacy of Yiddish. First, the vast majority of second- and third-generation American and western European Jews never used Yiddish in their everyday speech. Many could barely understand it. In Israel, the native-born Jew grows up in a Hebrew atmosphere with Hebrew culture and literature, not Yiddish, predominant. The *Sabra* may not even understand the Yiddish still spoken by his grandparents. The destruction of a large part of European Jewry is the most important factor in the decline of Yiddish. At the outbreak of World War II, there were some eleven million Yiddish speakers in the world, most of them in eastern Europe.

The language is still widely used by Jews in Latin America although here, too, its occurrence is diminishing. In extreme religious circles, Yiddish remains the language both of communication and instruction. In the older *Yeshivot* in Israel and the U.S., Yiddish remains the language of instruction. The ultra-Orthodox (including *Neturei Karta*) who regard Hebrew as a sacred language not to be profaned by secular use, continue to speak Yiddish in their daily lives.

YOUTH ALIYAH: Organization for the transfer of Jewish children to the land of Israel, founded in the early 1930s by

In a children's village

Recha Freyer to meet the threat of the rise of Nazism in Germany. From 1933 to 1945, it was headed by Henrietta Szold, who dedicated her life to the fulfillment of its aims. During the period of Nazi persecution in Europe, thousands of youth were rescued from Germany and other countries and by May 1948, 29,000 children had been transferred, absorbed, and educated by Youth Aliyah in *kibbutzim,* agricultural settlements, and specially-established youth villages. These youth villages provided living accommodation, educational and cultural facilities, and can boast of thousands of graduates who have grown up to play an important role as citizens of the State of Israel. During the 1950s Youth Aliyah absorbed thousands of youth from Asia, North Africa, the Balkans, and Europe, and in Israel itself, a scheme was started whereby underprivileged youth, especially in the development areas, could enter the Youth Aliyah framework. It is estimated that over 125,000 young people have received their education through Youth Aliyah. The organization is affiliated to the Jewish

Agency but is also supported by organizations such as the American Hadassah, WIZO, and other Zionist women's groups. The educational emphasis in the youth villages is on study, self-reliance, and cultural activities that include music, folk dancing, drama, and art. In recent years, some of the youth villages have undertaken projects in which youth from western countries stay in the village for periods of time ranging from a summer camp to a full year's study.

YOUTH MOVEMENTS: The idea of special organizations for young people, in which they could give expression to their feelings, ideals, and aspirations, took hold in various parts of the world at the beginning of the century. Most of these youth movements, however, did not have any durable, basic aims, with the exception of the scout movement, founded by the British General Robert Baden-Powell in 1908. The ideals of the scout movement influenced Jewish youth movements, most of which adopted a scouting framework. The real significance of the Jewish youth movements were their contributions to the Zionist movement. They saw and still see their primary task as furthering the rebirth of the Jewish people in its ancient homeland. The youth groups stimulated a pioneering spirit and a readiness for self-sacrifice among Jewish youth. Their educational programs emphasized Jewish history and culture while intensive social activity was designed to weld the members together as a close unit. As a result Jewish youth from Diaspora and Israeli youth organizations helped to establish and defend numerous settlements throughout the country.

At first strongest in eastern Europe, the movements spread throughout the Jewish world. During the tragic war years, they played a vital role in promoting "illegal" immigration and in rescue work. The Warsaw ghetto rebellion was organized and carried out by the youth movement. The war years also saw the virtual destruction of all their centers in eastern Europe and henceforth the main centers of the youth movements and their activity were in Israel, western Europe, South America, and the English-speaking countries.

Zionist youth movements are either affiliated to or sympathetic toward Israel's political parties. The ideological differences between them follow, in the main, those between their seniors. Israel's youth movements have over 200,000 members, organized approximately as follows:

1) *Hano'ar Ha'oved Vehalomed* — The association of working and student youth is Israel's largest movement, with a membership of 100,000. It has Jewish and non-Jewish members and is directly affiliated to Israel's trade union federation, the Histadrut.

2) *Tzofim* (Scouts) — Affiliated to the international scout movement but in Israel, it is co-educational and has Jewish and Arab members. It has over 20,000 members.

3) *Bnei Akiva* (Sons of Akiva)—Affiliated to the National Religious Party and the Religious Kibbutz Movement, it is a religious Zionist movement with over. 20,000 members.

4) *Hashomer Hatzair* (The Young Guard) —Socialist pioneering movement, associated with the *Mapam* party, with a membership of approximately 13,000.

5) *Hanoar Hadati Ha'oved* (Religious Working Youth)—Has a membership of 13,000 and concentrates on evening classes and vocational training.

6) *Maccabi Hatzair* (The Young Maccabee) — Affiliated to the world Maccabi movement, and as such, places emphasis on sports and athletics. Its membership totals approximately 8,000.

7) *Dror (Mahanot Ha'olim)* — Pioneer's Camps. A socialist movement with 5,000 members.

8) *Betar (Brit Trumpeldor)* — Named after Joseph Trumpeldor, *Betar* is a nationalist youth movement affiliated to Israel's opposition party, *Herut*. In Israel, it numbers some 5,000.

9) *Ezra* — A religious group with 4,000 members, affiliated to the Orthodox *Poalei Agudat Israel*.

10) *Hanoar Hatzioni* (Zionist Youth) — With about 2,500 members, it is closely associated with the Independent Liberal Party, and has a progressive but not socialist program.

Of the above mentioned groups, *Hashomer Hatzair, Bnei Akiva, Dror, Betar, Ezra,* and *Hanoar Hatzioni* all have strong branches throughout the Jewish world. In the United States, the largest Zionist Youth Movement is Young Judea which has a liberal Zionist program. In the British Commonwealth, *Habonim* (The Builders), a group with a moderate socialist program and intensive scouting activity, plays an important role in Jewish Youth activity.

Since World War II, the role played by Zionist youth groups in certain countries has declined. In the United States, the main youth movements are those affiliated with the various synagogue organizations such as the National Federation of Temple Youth (Reform), United Synagogue Youth (Conservative), and Young Israel (Orthodox).

Z

ZANGWILL, ISRAEL (1864–1926): English author and communal leader. The son of Russian immigrant parents, Zangwill achieved literary prominence during the last decade of the 19th century when, in a series of books and stories, he depicted the life of the Jewish immigrants in London's East End with humor and sympathy. His *Children of the Ghetto, Ghetto Tragedies, Ghetto Comedies, The King of the Schnorrers* and others, were outstanding successes. In addition, his translations of the Hebrew liturgy and of Ibn Gabirol's poetry were recognized as brilliant. His literary efforts on the non-Jewish scene were only moderately successful.

In 1895, Zangwill was approached by Theodor Herzl and subsequently became an ardent Zionist. However, after the rejection by the Zionist Congress of 1905 of the Uganda scheme — a scheme which he supported — he founded the Jewish Territorial Organization known as ITO whose aim was to establish an autonomous Jewish community anywhere, not necessarily in the land of Israel. After the Balfour Declaration, however, Zangwill once again established links with the Zionist organization. In addition to his Jewish activity, Zangwill was an ardent supporter of the women's suffragette campaign and a convinced pacifist, being one of the outspoken opponents and denouncers of the First World War.

ZIONISM: Belief in the return to Zion — the ideology of the Zionist movement founded by Theodor Herzl at the First Zionist Congress in Basle in 1897 *(see* HERZL, THEODOR). The Zionist movement derived its inspiration from the Jew's age-old yearning for return to the land of his fathers. Ever since the destruction of the Second Temple (70 C.E.), this hope had been kept alive, and the association with the land of Israel constantly maintained. In its customs, institutions, and prayers, the Jewish people declared its belief in the ultimate redemption of the people of Israel in the land of Israel. In times of severe oppression, yearning for the Holy Land was intensified, and from time to time many felt the urge to make a pilgrimage and even to settle there. The land of Israel was, in the mind of the Jew, intricately interwoven with the coming of the Messiah, and many a false Messiah was able to use this belief to his advantage.

The 19th century provided fertile soil for the practical realization of this ancient dream. This was the age of European expansion and nationalism, in which minority groups began to assert themselves. If so, why not the Jew, as well? The Damascus Affair of 1840, in which the Jews of that town were accused of the ritual murder of a Franciscan monk, led Moses Montefiore and Charles Netter to make the first serious attempts at colonization in the land of Israel, and rabbis such as Zvi Hirsch Kalischer and Judah Alkalay began to preach the resettlement of the Holy Land on a religious and national basis. In 1862 Moses Hess published his book, *Rome and Jerusalem,* in which he advocated the restoration of a Jewish state on national grounds. The intolerable plight of Russian Jewry was highlighted by the pogroms beginning in 1881–1882

Herzl opening Zionist Congress (1898)

Zionist Congress

which led to the founding of the *Ḥovevei Zion* (those who love Zion) movement. Groups of Russian students known as *Biluim* (from the initial letters of the Hebrew words in Isaiah for "O House of Jacob, come ye and let us walk") settled in the land of Israel from 1882 onward, and founded Rishon le-Zion and other settlements. These early settlers, most of whom had little or no agricultural experience, could hardly be expected to cope with the reclamation of a desolate land. With the new settlements on the verge of collapse, the French philanthropist Baron Edmond de Rothschild came to their assistance and for the remainder of his life made the development of Jewish agricultural settlement in the land of Israel one of his principal cares.

Events in western Europe too favored the advent of Jewish nationalism. The dream of emancipation, of the granting of equal rights to the Jews in their countries of residence, was to many an illusion. The Dreyfus trial in France, in which a Jewish officer was falsely accused of passing military secrets to the Germans, inspired Herzl to write his *Judenstaat* (The Jewish State), which without any preparation created political Zionism. If such injustice and blatant anti-Semitism could exist in France, the land of Liberty, Equality, and Fraternity, what could be expected of the rest of the world? Herzl

was convinced that the Jewish problem could not be solved by emancipation, and at the first Zionist Congress the Zionist program was defined as "the establishment for the Jewish people of a national home in Palestine guaranteed by public law." Herzl was a man of great vision, but was also impatient. To his way of thinking, the Jewish problem was immediate and demanded a speedy solution. The process of colonization in the land of Israel was far too slow, and at that rate, he remarked in his opening speech at the congress, it would take nine hundred years to bring all the Jews back to the Holy Land. Herzl's "political Zionism" insisted that only international action on a grand scale could definitely settle the Jewish question. With this aim in view, and with the help of influential friends who acted as intermediaries, he embarked on a series of negotiations with international statesmen and governments. The Turkish Sultan, the Emperor of Germany (Kaiser Wilhelm II), and the Pope all granted him interviews. Various propositions were put forward, chief among them that of the British Colonial Secretary Joseph Chamberlain, to grant the Jews territory in the then crown colony of Uganda. This latter offer, which Herzl was inclined to accept, even if, as he claimed later, only as a preparation for the eventual return to Israel, evoked violent opposition from the Russian Zionists led by Menaḥem Ussishkin, who refused to compromise with the "land of Israel" idea. At the Zionist Congress in Basle in 1905 after Herzl's premature death, the British offer of East Africa was refused.

Thus, at this early stage of its history, differences of opinion already existed among the leadership, not on matters of basic principle, but rather on the method to be used in reaching the goal. Herzl's followers continued to advocate his political Zionism while others, believing in the slow and painful process of colonization as the surest way of achieving a foothold in the land, became known as practical Zionists. Added to this was the cultural Zionism of the writer *Aḥad Ha'am* (Asher Ginzberg). He at first heaped ridicule on the Basle program and never joined the Herzlian movement. He advocated the creation of a "spiritual center" in the land of Israel which would bring about a revival of the national consciousness among the Jews of the Diaspora and would thereby lay the foundation for a more firmly based national movement in the future. Most of his disciples, however, joined the Zionist organization and, while doubting the feasibility of political Zionism at the time, did not actually oppose it. One of the early "cultural Zionists" was Chaim Weizmann, and he, more than any other leader, was destined to contribute to the realization of political Zionism.

Apart from the differences within the movement, early Zionism had to contend with strong opposition from without. This came from divergent circles. There were those who still fervently believed in the possibility of Jewish emancipation and saw in the Zionist ideology a danger to Jewish citizenship rights in their various countries of dispersal. The Reform movement believed in the "Universal Mission" of Judaism to the gentiles, and such a program could only be hampered by the restoration of Jews to a small Near

Eastern country. Time and time again, Reform spokesmen quoted the Talmudic statement, "God has bestowed a benefit upon the Jews by dispersing them among the Nations." There were some Reform leaders, however, such as Stephen Wise and Gustav Gottheil, who from the beginning were pro-Zionist. At the other extreme, opposition arose among the ultra-Orthodox. Many rabbinic and Ḥasidic leaders believed that redemption must come about in a supernatural way, and that any attempt to bring the Jews back to Israel was futile and impious.

The internal differences within the Zionist organization led to a compromise known as "synthetic Zionism." Thus, the struggle for Jewish rebirth proceeded on all fronts at one and the same time. Practical Zionism was given added impetus by the second *Aliyah* (i.e., wave of immigration to the land of Israel) of 1905–1914 which was the direct outcome of further persecution of the Jews in czarist Russia. This *Aliyah,* which brought about a revolution in the methods of Jewish colonization, was essentially socialist in nature, preached Jewish self-help and equality, which it embodied in the form of the *kibbutz,* and was to furnish many of Israel's future leaders and politicians. Jewish cultural institutions sprang up. The revival of Hebrew as a modern language was an integral part of the Zionist endeavor. At the same time, the political struggle was intensified and Weizmann's success in winning the sympathy of the British Government resulted in the Balfour Declaration of November 2, 1917.

"His Majesty's Government view with favor the establishment in Palestine of a national home for the Jewish people and will use their best endeavors to facilitate the achievement of this object, it being clearly understood that nothing shall be done which may prejudice the civil and religious rights of existing non-Jewish communities in Palestine or the rights and political status enjoyed by Jews in any other country."

The Balfour Declaration has been variously analyzed as an act of idealism, on the one hand and an act of cynical self-interest on the other. The British, it has been suggested, wished to inherit the defeated Turks' Middle Eastern Empire, which was of strategic value for the defense of India. Moreover, before the entry of the United States into the war, the final outcome was in the balance. American Jews were reputed to be influential, and hence their sympathy could well prove decisive. Winston Churchill later stated that the adoption of the declaration was the result of the "dire need of the war" and "with the object of promoting the general victory of the Allies for which they expected and received valuable and important assistance." However, there is no doubt that many of those responsible for the declaration (such as the British Prime Minister David Lloyd George and the Foreign Secretary Arthur James Balfour himself) were motivated by the concept of righting the historical wrongs suffered by the Jews throughout their centuries of exile. Whatever the motivation, the declaration was adopted and embodied in the League of Nations Mandate for Palestine granted to Britain in 1922. Parallel to all the above negotiations, however, the British had also made promises of independence to the Arabs in return for their rebelling against the Turkish authorities. The Arab problem had not been totally ignored by the Zionist leadership, as has often been suggested. The force and extent of the growing Arab nationalism was perhaps underestimated. Weizmann was most definitely aware of the problem and in an attempt to avoid possible conflict held meetings with the Arab leader King Feisal, the cordiality of which gave him reason for optimism. Feisal's change of heart — largely a result of his betrayal by the Allies —

put an end to any future contact, and, in any event, it is extremely doubtful whether the rising forces of Arab nationalism would or could have agreed to any compromise with Zionism.

The history of the British Mandate for Palestine is one of attempted tightrope walking. The Zionist leadership interpreted the Balfour Declaration as a promise of statehood and refused to be diverted from this interpretation by verbal acrobatics ("Palestine as a Jewish national home" as against "the establishment in Palestine of a national home"). The situation was further aggravated by the fact that certain British officials in "the land of Israel" were frustrated and angered by the "Europeanized" Jews, who spoke to them as equals. They felt more at home in the presence of the often menial "natives." The attempt to placate both sides inevitably resulted in alienating them further from each other and from the ruling power. The pattern of events repeated itself with almost monotonous regularity. The Arabs, increasingly obsessed with the continuing Jewish immigration, would riot; the Jews would protest; the British authorities would belatedly intervene; a commission of inquiry would be sent to the Holy Land; its report would be issued and, after the objections of both sides, nothing would be done.

Throughout this bitter political struggle, the work of practical Zionism went ahead. New settlements were established, immigration increased, and the Jewish population grew rapidly. The Zionist organization expanded both in numbers and prestige. Previous opponents joined at least in its philanthropic work, and, by the 1930s, the majority of Reform leaders adopted a pro-Zionist stand. Within traditional Jewry, there remained only a core of intransigent objectors. The vast masses of Orthodox Jewry have, however, joined in the work of rebuilding the Jewish nation. The establishment in 1929 of the enlarged Jewish Agency, consisting of both Zionists and non-Zionists, was a major step forward. The Jewish Agency, whose Jerusalem executive was, in effect, the Jewish "shadow government," had as its leaders men like Ben-Gurion, Weizmann, and Sharett; and most of the members of Israel's future early governments had their initial experience as members of the Jewish Agency Executive. Opposition to the Zionist leadership, however, had arisen on the right. This opposition was led by Vladimir Jabotinsky's "Union of Zionist Revisionists." Jabotinsky, a fiery nationalist, advocated the establishment of a Jewish state in its historical boundaries on both sides of the Jordan. The policy of acre by acre settlement was, in his eyes, far too slow. He advocated active opposition to the British Government's immigration policy and denounced the official policy of *havlagah,* or self-restraint in the face of Arab riots. The struggle with the Revisionists reached its climax in 1935 with their withdrawal from the Zionist organization and Jabotinsky's establishment of the "New Zionist Organization." The years 1936–39 were vital. As a result of the Nazi persecution of German Jewry after 1933, tens of thousands of German Jews had gone to Israel. The Arabs were concerned at the increasing number of immigrants. The ensuing riots assumed the proportions of an outright rebellion against British authority. The British reply was the infamous "White Paper" of 1939, limiting Jewish immigration to 15,000 a year for five years, after which no Jews at all were to be admitted without Arab consent. This, in the face of the tragedy of European Jewry, was considered an act of betrayal by the Jewish people as a whole. The outbreak of the Second World War prevented the situation from getting out of hand, and the official Jewish leadership decided, in the face of the greater Nazi danger, to support the British war effort.

Thousands of Palestinians served in the British armed forces and later on in the Jewish Brigade, acquitting themselves with distinction. They were to provide much needed military experience in the time of trial ahead. Meanwhile, the Zionist leadership convened during the war for an emergency meeting and declared their objective to be the establishment of a Jewish state ("Biltmore Program").

The end of World War II revealed to the world that European Jewry had almost ceased to exist. Those who had remained alive were clamoring to enter the Holy Land, but the British Labor Government kept the gates closed. Britain's policy, seemingly logical in her own eyes, caused revulsion in the eyes of humanity. The Zionist Organization was now supported in its struggle by the masses of world Jewry, and pressure was even brought to bear on Britain by the United States government. In the land of Israel itself, the process of "illegal" immigration, started already before the war years, was intensified. Fury mounted as the British deported illegal immigrants to Cyprus and, for a time, the *Haganah,* the underground fighting arm of the Jewish Agency, actually cooperated with the dissident underground groups, the *Irgun Tzevai Leumi* (ETZEL) and *Lohamei Ḥerut Yisrael* (LEḤI) in active resistance. By and large, however, the official Jewish leadership dissociated itself from indiscriminate acts of terror against British soldiers and civilians committed by the other two groups, such as the blowing up of the King David Hotel which served as British Military Headquarters. Acts of reprisal against Arab villagers were not only frowned upon, but condemned. This difference of opinion led to friction and at times extreme antagonism between the agency and the underground. In the face of impending chaos and the breakdown of law and order, the British Government announced its intention of abandoning the Mandate and evacuating the Holy Land. It put the issue into the hands of the United Nations which sent a special committee to investigate the situation. This committee recommended the establishment of an independent Jewish and an independent Arab state in the area known as Palestine. On November 29, 1947, the United Nations passed the partition plan, and on the 14th of May, 1948, David Ben-Gurion proclaimed the establishment of the State of Israel. With the establishment of the state, Zionism's task had not ended. The mobilization of world Jewry and its resources on behalf of the state, the financing of immigration, assistance in absorbing the newcomers, and the sponsorship of Zionist Jewish education — all these and many others have been and remain among the tasks of the Zionist movement. In recent years, attempts have been made to revitalize the movement, and as a result of pressure brought to bear by "young" Zionists, plans have been made for a democratization of the movement and its institutions.

In retrospect, Zionism in all its ramifications, despite its bitter internal disputes and splits, has done its task well. Practical Zionism gave rise to new settlements and cities, so that when the time came to defend what had been built, there was something to defend. Political Zionism carried on the fight on the international plane, thus ensuring much needed international support. Cultural Zionism at the same time gave the new nation a living language and living institutions of learning such as the Hebrew University in Jerusalem and the Technion in Haifa. After the 1st Zionist Congress, Herzl said that at Basle he had founded the Jewish State. "But," he continued, "should I say this aloud today, the reply would be universal laughter. In five years perhaps, but at any rate in fifty years, everybody will understand." Herzl was the prophet, and the Zionist organization the instrument for the fulfillment of the prophecy. Almost fifty years to the day after he penned his prophecy, the Jewish State was established.

INDEX

THE POPULAR
JEWISH
ENCYCLOPEDIA

Opposite: *View of Jerusalem from Mount of Olives*